PRACTICAL POSER 7

PRACTICAL POSER 7

DENISE TYLER

CHARLES RIVER MEDIA
Boston, Massachusetts

Cover Design: Tyler Creative
Cover Image: Janne Pitkänen

CHARLES RIVER MEDIA
25 Thomson Place
Boston, Massachusetts 02210
617-757-7900
617-757-7969 (FAX)
crm.info@thomson.com
www.charlesriver.com

This book is printed on acid-free paper.

Denise Tyler. *Practical Poser 7.*
ISBN: 1-58450-478-1
ISBN-13: 978-1-58450-478-8

All brand names and product names mentioned in this book are trademarks or service marks of their respective companies. Any omission or misuse (of any kind) of service marks or trademarks should not be regarded as intent to infringe on the property of others. The publisher recognizes and respects all marks used by companies, manufacturers, and developers as a means to distinguish their products.

Library of Congress Cataloging-in-Publication Data
Tyler, Denise.
 Practical Poser 7 / Denise Tyler.
    p. cm.
 Includes index.
 ISBN 1-58450-478-1 (softcover with cd : alk. paper)
 1. Poser (Computer file) 2. Computer animation. 3. Computer
graphics. 4. Human figure in art--Computer programs. I. Title.

 TR897.7.T9653 2006
 006.6'96--dc22

2006036520

Printed in the United States of America
06 7 6 5 4 3 2 First Edition

CHARLES RIVER MEDIA titles are available for site license or bulk purchase by institutions, user groups, corporations, etc. For additional information, please contact the Special Sales Department at 800-347-7707.

Requests for replacement of a defective CD-ROM must be accompanied by the original disc, your mailing address, telephone number, date of purchase and purchase price. Please state the nature of the problem, and send the information to CHARLES RIVER MEDIA, 25 Thomson Place, Boston, Massachusetts 02210. CRM's sole obligation to the purchaser is to replace the disc, based on defective materials or faulty workmanship, but not on the operation or functionality of the product.

To Mom and Dad ... you are loved and missed.

Contents

Preface

During the planning stages of the previous edition of this book, we asked the members of the online Poser community which questions were most frequently asked by members of the Poser community. The responses helped us formulate the topics that we should address in the first edition. Interestingly enough, the topics requested fell into beginning, intermediate, and advanced level skills.

With this latest edition, *Practical Poser 7*, we have moved some of the beginning material to the CD-ROM that accompanies this book. You'll find it there in HTML format. We added some additional intermediate to advanced topics in the body of the book, including information on joint parameters, animation, new morphing features, enhanced texture creation, and more.

This book assumes that you have reviewed the Poser 7 Reference Manual and Poser 7 Tutorial Manual that ship with Poser 7 before you attempt some of the tutorials in this book. We have tried to go light on theory and heavy on practical use of the most requested topics and procedures.

The book begins by getting you up to speed on intermediate-level to advanced-level skills that you need to know. You learn in a logical manner how to create and customize clothing, characters, and textures. You'll also learn how to use lights and cameras, and how to create and save your own light and camera sets to the Poser Library.

We then move to higher-level topics, mainly covering the features that you'll find in the other Poser rooms. You'll learn how to prepare photographs so that you get the best results in the Face Room. You'll also learn how to create and save custom faces in the Face Room. You'll learn how to use the Hair Room to add hair to Poser clothing or props and how to pick up hair colors from underlying textures. You'll also learn how to work with the various types of Poser clothing and the differences between conforming clothing, dynamic clothing, and hybrid conforming/dynamic clothing. Finally, you'll learn how to decipher and build materials in the advanced Material Room view.

Some of the most frequently asked questions involve creating and customizing Poser clothing. Although these are advanced-level skills that often require software other than Poser, it is a topic that is of great interest and need to Poser users, and we will address this need in the final chapters of the book. First, you'll learn how to use magnets to create morphs in Poser. You'll also learn the steps involved to export and import morphs to and from an external morphing program. Through several chapters, you'll learn the procedures involved in modeling a simple piece of clothing, how to create UV maps for common clothing articles (shirts, skirts, and pants), how to assign materials in clothing, and how to group them correctly so that your models work correctly in Poser. You'll also learn how to save different types of Poser content into the Poser libraries so that they work properly.

You'll also learn about the basics of animation and get an introduction to the new layered animation feature in Poser 7. In addition, you'll learn what makes the Poser rendering engine work and how you can enhance your Poser renders so that they look their best.

The techniques that you learn in this book will help you get up to speed very quickly with the questions that Poser users ask most. We are also open to suggestions and additional questions that can be covered in future editions of this book and will watch the various forums in the online Poser communities for questions or comments from our readers.

Acknowledgments

There are so many talented individuals that work behind the scenes to make a book happen. In the case of this book, there are so many that deserve mention. In particular, we would like to thank the following:

Thank you to our publisher, Jenifer Niles, whose unflagging support, nerves of steel, and patience of a saint were appreciated more than she'll ever know, especially during some very difficult times. Also, to Steve Yatson, Tori Porter, and Uli Klumpp for opening so many doors, and keeping them open. My most humble gratitude to dear friend Ana Winson (Arien) for allowing her to share many of her trade texturing secrets in the Materials and Texturing chapters . . . you are the best and most uber talented! To Phil Cooke for his witty, helpful, and expert technical editing, and for the great animation tutorials—it was a pleasure throughout the entire project! Thank you also to Janne and Gina Pitkanen, Ana Winson, and Niki Browning for adding a tremendous gallery of color images to the book . . . and to Janne for gracing our cover with one of his spectacular works of art.

I would like to thank Ed, my better half, for his never-ending support and friendship . . . you're my rock! To my mom, who passed away during the progress of this book—this one is for you, mama! To my brother Paul, who does so much for so many. And to the members of the Poser community, who were constant inspiration for every word written in this book.

CHAPTER

1

USING AND MAINTAINING POSER CONTENT

In This Chapter

- Where You Can Find Content
- Maintaining Your Libraries
- Tutorial 1.1 Creating Runtime Folders on Your Hard Disk
- Tutorial 1.2 Adding a New Runtime Folder to the Poser Libraries
- Tutorial 1.3 Using the Content Room Auto Install Feature
- Tutorial 1.4 Installing DAZ Poser Content
- Tutorial 1.5 Installing Poser Content from ZIP Files

Although a good part of this book teaches you how to create and customize your own Poser content, many people need to use ready-made content. The reasons to use ready-made content are varied: lack of time, lack of knowledge, or lack of interest, to name a few.

The good news for those who don't have an interest in creating their own content is that Poser has a long-standing, very large group of users who have been nurturing several online communities for quite some time. Through these various Poser communities, a substantial amount of ready-made content is available online for reasonable prices or even free. In this chapter, you'll learn about communities of Poser users, how to obtain content, and how you can organize and maintain your content in libraries.

WHERE YOU CAN FIND CONTENT

You can obtain additional Poser content in two ways. The first way is to use Content Paradise, which is built-in to the Poser application and accessed through the Content tab of the user interface. The second way to find Poser content is to subscribe to one or more Poser communities where you can keep track of the latest and greatest creations in the Poser world. You will be amazed at the vast amount of content that is available to you, either free or at a very reasonable cost.

Content Paradise

When you click the Content tab in your Poser 7 workspace, you see Content Paradise, which is shown in Figure 1.1. You can also reach Content Paradise by pointing your browser to *http://www.contentparadise.com*. Once there, you can use one central location to browse through the selections that are available from many of the most popular Poser sites.

Obviously, you'll find content from e frontier (*http://www.e-frontier.com*), the makers of Poser, Shade, and other software. Of particular interest are e frontier's male and female figures: James and Jessi (Caucasian male and female), Koji and Miki (Japanese male and female), and Kelvin and Olivia (African male and female).

Additional Poser communities and artists are linked to Content Paradise and are listed in the left navigation bar. You can search through, single-, multiple-, or all sites to locate your desired content. As you find content that you like, you can add it to your shopping cart, and in the end, make your purchase from several different sites all at once. You'll also receive an e-mail receipt from each site that you purchase content from, although your shopping cart will process your order in one transaction.

FIGURE 1.1   Content Paradise is available directly in the Poser workspace or by navigating to the Content Paradise Web site with your browser.

In addition to content created and distributed by e frontier, you'll find creations by the following vendors in the Content Paradise stores:

Aset Arts (*http://www.aset-arts.com*): Creates high-quality dynamic, conforming, and hybrid clothing for Poser figures. Aset Arts is an integral creator for content featured in Poser 7, Content Paradise, and the Passport CD Volume 1 (which is available as a bonus to those who join the Content Paradise Passport Club).

Cubed (*http://www.cubed.ie*): The makers of Baby Dylan and Baby Jenny, perhaps the most realistic baby models available for Poser. These models are expressive and irresistible. New, photorealistic versions of the Poser animals and additional content are also planned for the future.

Digital Dreams (*http://www.contentparadise.com/us/user/partner. digitaldreams*): Home of Jim Burton's sexy supermodel versions of several popular Poser figures, also features some of the most stylish clothing and shoes available for Poser figures.

Jolly (*http://www.contentparadise.com/us/user/partner.jolly*): Relatively new to the Poser scene, but its content shows exciting quality and great promise. Jolly is the creator of the Jolly Troll and was an integral member of the content creation team for Poser 6. The Jolly Troll is an amazing work of art with incredibly realistic skin and morphs.

Maptropolis: Offers a varied selection of textures for clothing and animals.

Meshbox Design (*http://www.meshbox.com*): Creators of toon figures and elegant sets for Poser.

N2-GAME (*http://www.contentparadise.com/us/user/partner. N2GAME*): Offers a selection of original lower-polygon models and clothing, suitable for Poser or for game developers.

Netherworks Studios (*http://www.netherworks-studios.com*): Offers Poser characters, Python scripts, clothing morph kits, and many useful freebies.

PhilC Designs (*http://www.philc.net*): A long-standing member of the Poser community that creates high-quality clothing, utilities, and tutorials relating to Poser.

Poserworks (*http://www.poserworks.com*): Offers a wide selection of Poser items, ranging from aliens and robots to animal, human, medical, and cartoon content, and a large variety of props and sets.

Predatron3DA (*http://www.predatron3da.co.uk*): Offers a range of 3D products, textures, and images that can be used in Poser and other 3D applications.

Rebel 3D (*htttp://www.contentparadise.com/us/user/partner.rebel3d*): Offers many characters for the most popular Poser figures.

Renderosity (*http://www.renderosity.com*): One of the earliest and largest online art communities, features thousands of Poser items available free and for purchase. The site also hosts several forums and members' galleries that focus on many of the most popular 2D and 3D graphics programs, the most active of which is its Poser forum.

Runtime DNA (*http://www.runtimedna.com*): Creators of LaRoo 2 LE and other content furnished with Poser 7, this site is home to a select group of Poser artists, many of whom were involved behind the scenes in the development of Poser 5 through Poser 7. The content developed by the Team DNA artists is always innovative and high quality, and their forums are very helpful and friendly.

Sanctum Art (*http://www.sanctumart.com*): Home for the unique and bizarre in fantasy and sci-fi Poser content, all extremely high quality.

Shader's Cafe (*http://www.shaderscafe.com*): In addition to a great variety of Poser content, Shader's Cafe offers support for e frontier's high-level modeling program *Shade*.

Sixus1 Media (*http://www.sixus1.com*): These creators of Alpha Man, Betaboy, and other figures for Poser are in the process of updating their site as this book goes to press.

The Forge (*http://www.the-forge.ie* and **Content Paradise**): The home of PoseAmation, which is a set of motion capture files that are compatible with Poser. The product line includes animation packs that allow you to add walks, runs, battles, and other actions into your Poser animations.

Vanishing Point (*http://www.vanishingpoint.biz* and Content Paradise): The creators of many vehicles, robots, environments, and props for Poser.

Zygote (*http://www.zygote.com* and Content Paradise): Makers of high-end, professional-quality 3D models for the commercial, broadcast, biomedical, multimedia, and games industries. You can find Zygote's high-quality biomedical models on its sister site, 3DSCI.com (*http://www.3dscience.com*) and at Content Paradise. These models have been featured in the broadcast and motion picture industries. Zygote's first Poser-related product is a full-featured set of male anatomy (including skin, skeleton, and internal organs) that is extremely realistic and perfect for medical and forensic illustration and animation.

Other Poser Sites

Although many Poser content creators have come together under the Content Paradise roof, many other Poser sites also sell Poser content or make it available for free download. Some feature user forums, whereas others provide a store or download section.

With the number of Poser communities continually growing and changing, it's often difficult to keep track of them all. However, the following sites are some of the hottest and most frequently mentioned as the Poser community's favorite sites to visit:

DAZ3D (*http://www.daz3d.com*): Creators of the extremely popular Millennium Figures (Victoria, Michael, Stephanie, David, Young Teens, Preschool, and baby figures). Along with its high-quality human figures, DAZ3D also features excellent clothing, props, and accessories that are created by some of the top artists in the Poser community. Forums are also featured on the site.

Digital Babes (*http://www.digitalbabes2.com*): Run by Kozaburo Yoshimura, who supplied many of the hair models that shipped with Poser 6 and earlier versions. Perhaps the most highly regarded hair creator in the Poser community, he makes his hair models available free. You can download additional hair models from his site that are made to fit the DAZ3D characters previously mentioned, as well as the Poser 7 characters.

PoserPros (*http://poserpros.daz3d.com*): Owned and operated by DAZ3D, this site features helpful forums and a store that offers high-quality Poser content created by some of the best artists in the Poser community.

PoserWorld (*http://www.poserworld.com*): Offers an endless supply of clothing and textures for Poser and DAZ3D figures for a very reasonable monthly, annual, or lifetime subscription fee. Items are also available for individual purchase. This site is widely considered to be one of the best values in the Poser community.

Poser Library File Types and Where to Find Them

When you purchase third-party content, you usually receive it in one of two ways. The most common distribution method of Poser content is in a compressed *ZIP* or *SIT* file in which the content is already arranged in folders beneath a root folder named *Runtime*. Content purchased from DAZ3D is typically furnished in an executable file that automatically extracts the content in the proper folders beneath the Poser folder that you specify.

Most Poser artists arrange their files so that the content is placed into the correct runtime library locations automatically. Once in a while, especially with very old content, you'll find an error or omission that prevents Poser from loading the files properly. In that case, you'll need to know where to place the files so that they correctly appear in the proper Poser libraries.

Figure 1.2 shows the file extensions that you typically find in Poser content; which folders the files are installed into on your hard drive; and the corresponding Poser Library associated with each folder.

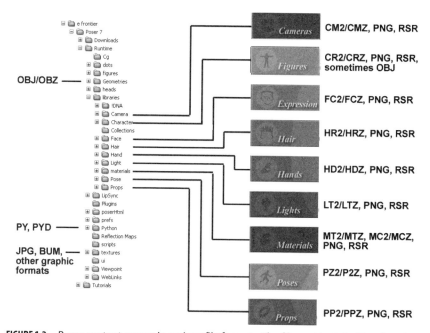

FIGURE 1.2   Poser content comes in various file formats. The files get installed in a Runtime folder structure that allows you to access the content through the Library Palette.

The following information briefly describes the types of files you are most likely to encounter when you purchase Poser content:

BUM files: Bump map files (companion textures that give some content a bumpy appearance) that are required for older versions of Poser. Beginning with Poser Pro Pack (released between Poser 4 and 5), you can use standard formats (typically JPG images) for bump maps. Bump maps are explained in more detail in Chapter 4, "Creating Materials." You'll typically find BUM files in the Runtime > Textures folders and subfolders.

CM2 (CMZ when compressed): Camera files that are installed and saved into the Runtime > Libraries > Cameras folder and found in the Cameras Library.

CR2 (CRZ when compressed): Posable or conforming figure files. The files are installed and saved into the Runtime > Libraries > Characters folder, and are found in the Figures Library.

FC2 (FCZ when compressed): Face poses, which are a special type of pose that manipulates the morphs associated with the head of a figure. The head of the figure must have the same morph targets that are controlled by the face pose to have any effect on the head mesh. These files are installed and saved into the Runtime > Libraries > Face folder, and you will find them in the Expressions Library.

HD2 (HDZ when compressed): Hand poses that are installed and saved into the Runtime > Libraries > Hand folder. You will find them in the Hands Library.

HR2 (HRZ when compressed): Hair objects that are installed and saved into the Runtime > Libraries > Hair folder. You will find them in the Hair Library.

LT2 (LTZ when compressed): Light sets that are installed and saved into the Runtime > Libraries > Light folder. You will find them in the Lights Library.

MC6 (MCZ when compressed): Material Collection files that are compatible with Poser 6 and later versions. They are installed and saved to the Runtime > Materials folder, and you will find them in the Materials Library.

MT5 (MZ5 when compressed): A single material file that is installed and saved to the Runtime > Materials folder. You will find it in the Materials Library.

MTL: Material files that are generated when you export or save an *OBJ* file. These are not Poser-compatible files, but they are sometimes required to define material assignments in other 3D programs. You will sometimes see them saved with OBJ files.

OBJ (OBZ when compressed): A Wavefront Object geometry file that is associated with a library item. Poser 4 and earlier versions generate an accompanying *RSR* file the first time the object file is used. OBJ files are most commonly found in the Runtime > Geometries folder, but you can also find them in the Figures Library in the same folder as the CR2.

PMD: External morph data files. When you save an object or project that contains morph data, Poser saves all of the morphs in a separate file, in the same directory as the saved file. Character files (such as CR2/CRZ files) make reference to these external morphs, so if you move them to a different location, you will have to edit the referencing file.

Content developers should deselect the option to save external binary morphs in the General Preferences dialog box to maintain compatibility with older Poser versions.

PP2 (PPZ when compressed): Prop files that can serve a variety of functions. Prop files can be scenery, jewelry, figure add-ons, furniture, and other content that is not posable. Dynamic clothing is also saved as a prop file. With Poser 6 and later versions, you can also find conforming clothing with this extension. Prop files are installed into the Runtime > Libraries > Props folder and can be found in the Props Library.

PY: These files are Python scripts, usable with Poser Pro Pack and later versions of Poser. They are installed to the Runtime > Python folder.

PZ2 (P2Z when compressed): Pose files that can also serve a variety of purposes. Pose files began as files that when applied, posed an object in various positions. Later, they came to be used for poses that changed the materials applied to an object (MAT poses), poses that set existing morphs to change the appearance of an object (MOR poses), or pose files that show or hide various body parts in your figures or clothing. Later, poses were used to add external morphs to a character or remove them from a character (INJ or REM poses). Pose files are installed into the Runtime > Libraries > Pose folder and can be found in the Poses Library.

RSR: You can find these files in any Poser library. They are the thumbnail files used in the Library Palette for Poser 4 and earlier versions. Poser Pro Pack and later versions use PNG graphics for thumbnails.

If you see a "shrugging man" icon in place of a proper library thumbnail, it probably means that the RSR or PNG file that corresponds to the library item is missing or named improperly. The name that precedes the library file extension must be identical to its RSR or PNG file to display correctly in the Library Palette.

MAINTAINING YOUR LIBRARIES

All physical Poser content files must reside beneath a master folder (file directory) named *Runtime* for Poser to properly display the content in the Library Palette. In earlier versions of Poser, it was mandatory for the Runtime folder to reside in the same folder as your Poser executable file. In other words, when installing Poser 4 using the Windows default installation path, the Runtime folder appeared in the C > Program Files > Curious Labs > Poser 4 folder, as did the Poser.exe file.

With Poser 5 and later versions, a *Downloads* directory also appears beneath the root installation folder. This Downloads directory has an additional Runtime folder that serves as a convenient and centrally located place for all of the content that you purchase or download. By keeping your extra content separated from the content that is furnished with Poser, it is much easier to back up and maintain your extra content.

TUTORIAL 1.1   CREATING RUNTIME FOLDERS ON YOUR HARD DISK

If you're like most Poser users, even the second folder isn't enough to manage all of your files. Eventually, you'll find that several gigabytes of content are too cumbersome to maintain in one or even two folders. In the Poser world, several gigabytes of content are not uncommon! With the Poser 7 library's Add New Runtime feature, you can create as many Runtime folders as you like. They can appear on any drive in your system, too.

You'll find it easier to locate items if you separate your several gigabytes of content into several, smaller Runtime folders. For example, you might use one Runtime folder to store hair, another to store clothing for the Poser 7 female, another to store clothing for the Poser 7 male, and yet another for props and scenery.

To create multiple Runtime folders on a secondary drive—your D drive, for example—follow these steps:

1. Using Windows Explorer or the Finder on your Mac, locate the drive onto which you want to store your extra Poser content. Let's assume your secondary hard drive is drive D.
2. Create a folder that will store your additional Runtime folders. For example, you can call the folder Poser 7 Runtimes. (It helps to indicate the version number in case you have Runtime content from previous versions of Poser.)
3. Inside the new folder, create additional subfolders as needed. For example, if you want to create a folder that stores content for each of the third-party figures you use, you could create additional folders named James, Jessi, Kelvin, Koji, Miki, Olivia, and so on for each Poser figure that you own. You might also want other folders for items that you

can use for any character, such as Hair or Scenery. Eventually, you have a folder structure that looks similar to Figure 1.3.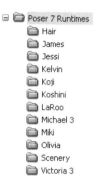

FIGURE 1.3   Create one or more folders to organize and store Poser content in categories that suit your needs.

TUTORIAL 1.2   **ADDING A NEW RUNTIME FOLDER TO THE POSER LIBRARIES**

The second step in the process of creating additional Runtime folders is to make Poser 7 aware that they exist. Here is how you add new Runtime folders into the Poser Library Palette:

1. If the Poser Library Palette is hidden, click the bar at the right side of the interface to expand it.
2. If the Library Palette opens to display the library titles and not their contents, double-click any library category name (Figures, Cameras, and so on) to display the contents within it.
3. The first folder in any library is usually a special folder, the "up folder." The arrow on the folder is an indication for you to click on this special folder to move up to the next highest folder level. You can see an example of this special folder on the left side in Figure 1.4. To move to the very top, or root, of your currently selected library folder, continue clicking the "up folder" until you see a red dot next to the folder icon. The red dot indicates your currently active Runtime folder, and it also tells you that you are at the top of your library structure, or the root. An example of the root-level library folder is shown on the right side of Figure 1.4. You can add new Runtime libraries while you are in the root folder.
4. Now that you are in the top-level folder, two icons should appear at the bottom of the Library Palette window: a check mark and a plus sign. When you hover your mouse over the plus sign icon you see the words "Add runtime." Click the plus-sign icon to open the Browse for Folder dialog box.

Top Level

Sub-level

FIGURE 1.4   To get to the top-level, or root, library folder, click on the folder with the up arrow (left) until you see a red dot near the current Runtime folder you are using (right).

5. Browse for the folder that you made earlier that contains your new Runtime folder, such as the Kelvin folder that is selected in Figure 1.5. Optionally, you can click the Make New Folder button to create a new folder to store your Runtime files.

6. Click OK to return to the Library Palette window. You should now see a new library folder, the folder you selected in Step 5.

7. Repeat Steps 4 through 6 for each additional Runtime folder that you want to add to your library.

FIGURE 1.5   Use the Browse for Folder dialog box to select the folder that will store your Runtime files in.

TUTORIAL 1.3 USING THE CONTENT ROOM AUTO INSTALL FEATURE

When you enter the Content Room, or when you point your browser to *http://www.contentparadise.com*, you can purchase third-party Poser content from some of the most popular Poser sites and content creators. After you complete an order through Content Paradise, all of your downloads appear in your Recent Purchases list.

To view your purchases, click the View My Stuff button, shown in Figure 1.6. The Recent Purchases list should then appear on your screen. At that point, you have a couple of different options in how you can install your content. You can use the Auto Install feature (available from the Content tab but not through an external browser), or you can download the installation files to your computer and install them later.

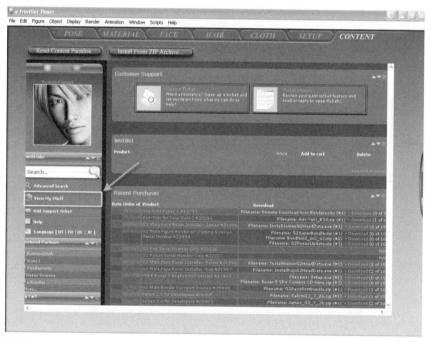

FIGURE 1.6 To view your purchases, click the View My Stuff button on the left. Your Recent Purchases then appear in a list.

To use the Auto Install feature, follow these steps:

1. Use Poser's Content Room to complete your order. The Auto Install feature is built in to Poser 7.
2. Click the View My Stuff button to view your Recent Purchases list.

3. Click the *Download* link to download the file. A progress bar will display while your purchase is downloading.
4. After your download is finished, the Install Options screen shown in Figure 1.7 appears. The steps you take next vary, depending on whether you want to automatically install your purchase or download it for later installation.

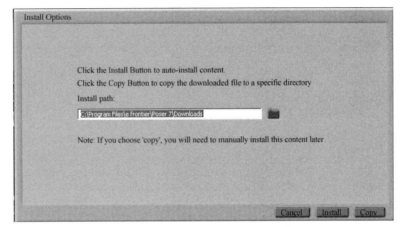

FIGURE 1.7   The Install Options screen allows you to install your content to a specific folder or download it to your hard disk for later installation.

To automatically install your file, continue from step 4 as follows:

1. In the Install Path field, enter the path of the Runtime folder that you want to install to. The installation path defaults to your Poser 7 Downloads folder.
2. You can also click the Folder icon to browse to the desired folder. When you enter the path, do not end the path with the Runtime folder, instead select the folder that should contain the Runtime folder. The installation files will install all folders and files including and beneath the Runtime folder.
3. Click the Install button. Poser installs the files to the folder that you selected.
4. After the installation is complete, Poser notifies you that the file operations are done. Click OK to exit the dialog box.
   To download for later installation, continue from step 4 as follows:
5. In the Install Path field, enter the path of the Runtime folder that you want to download to. The installation path defaults to your Poser 7 Downloads folder, but you can enter or choose any path you like.

6. Click the Copy button. Poser places a copy of the files into the folder that you selected.

7. Follow the instructions for installing content from ZIP files, which appear later in this chapter.

TUTORIAL 1.4   INSTALLING DAZ POSER CONTENT

With your custom Runtime folders in place and your purchased content in hand, you are now prepared to install your content.

Poser content is typically delivered in a ZIP or SIT compressed file format or in an executable program file, *EXE*. DAZ3D (makers of Michael, Victoria, David, Stephanie, Aiko, Hiro, and other popular Poser figures) typically distribute its content in EXE files for Windows users and in SIT files for Macintosh users. Other sites distribute content in ZIP files with the library folders properly nested within a Runtime folder.

The following is a typical sequence of events for installing DAZ3D's most recent products. Note that older versions of its installation program may vary slightly from these steps:

1. Open the EXE file that contains the product you purchased by double-clicking on it in Windows Explorer or File Manager. Newer products will ask if you want to include an uninstaller to later remove all the files that go with this installation. Answer Yes to include one or No to proceed without the uninstaller.

2. The first setup screen displays the name of the product that you are installing, along with some general notes. Click Next to continue.

3. The Software License Agreement screen appears and prompts you to accept the terms of the license agreement. Read the license agreement carefully to make sure you understand it, and then click Yes if you want to continue or No to cancel the installation. You may also print the license agreement from this screen.

4. After you agree to the license terms, a fourth screen will prompt you to choose a target application. If Poser 7 does not appear on the list of applications, choose Poser (All Files), and click Next to continue. This option installs files that are compatible with all versions of Poser, if they are included with the product.

5. The Choose Destination Location dialog box shown in Figure 1.8 appears. Click the Browse button to find and select the Runtime folder you want to install the content into. For example, if you want to install the content in the Downloads runtime folder that is created when you install Poser to the default location, choose C:\Program Files\e frontier\Poser 7\Downloads as your installation path. If you want to install the content files to your custom Runtime folders, se-

lect one of the folders you created (such as the C:\!Poser Runtimes\ Aiko folder shown in the figure). After you successfully select your desired Runtime folder and return to the setup screen, click Next to continue.

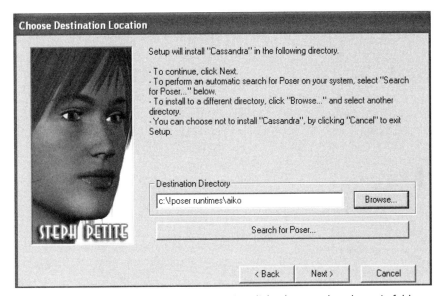

FIGURE 1.8   Use the Choose Destination Location dialog box to select the main folder that will store your new Runtime library folder.

6. Click Next again to install the content files. After installing the files, the setup program will display important notes regarding your product and where the files were installed so you can find them later on if necessary. Click Next to review the Readme file and close the setup program. Congratulations—your content has been successfully installed.

TUTORIAL 1.5   INSTALLING POSER CONTENT FROM ZIP FILES

If your product is distributed in a compressed format such as ZIP, you can use *WinZip* or a similar utility to extract the files to the desired library folder location. Before you extract the files, verify in WinZip that the installation paths begin with the Runtime folder. If they don't, the best option is to extract them to your desktop, and then manually move the contents of the Runtime subfolder into the desired location (such as D:\Poser 7 Runtimes\ Michael 3).

CONCLUSION

There are many places you can obtain ready-made content for your Poser scenes. The majority of this content is very reasonably priced and made by other Poser users. As you accumulate Poser content, you may find it useful to rearrange it into one or more additional Runtime files, which you can link into separately from within the Poser Library Palette.

2

USING CAMERAS

In This Chapter

- Camera Overview
- Tutorial 2.1 Using and Selecting Multiple Camera Views
- Using the Camera Controls
- Camera Parameters
- Camera Properties
- Tutorial 2.2 Creating and Saving Custom Head Cameras
- Tutorial 2.3 Creating Your Own Cameras
- Tutorial 2.4 Pointing and Parenting Cameras and Objects
- Tutorial 2.5 Using Depth of Field

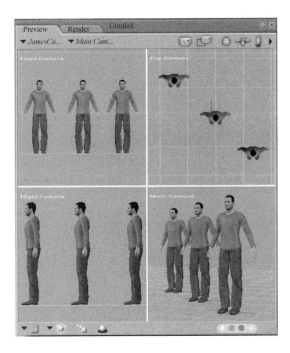

When you first create a new Poser scene, Poser displays the contents through the Main Camera. There are several other cameras in Poser, and each of them has controls that are similar to real-world cameras. You can modify the camera properties and save them in several ways. In this chapter, you'll learn how to use Poser's cameras for different applications. You'll also learn how to save your own custom cameras, and how to point cameras and objects at each other.

CAMERA OVERVIEW

Poser comes with 13 different camera presets that can help you build and render scenes. In addition, the new Object > Create Camera commands allow you to create your own custom Revolving or Dolly cameras. Cameras can help you accomplish other tasks as well. For example, you can use the *Orthogonal Cameras* (From Right, From Left, From Top, From Bottom, From Front, and From Back) to help you customize and position characters and objects, position magnets, and set up joints for character development. You can use the Left Hand Camera and Right Hand Camera to help you pose a figure's hand to get the fingers just right.

Part of the versatility and power of Poser is the ease with which you can switch between the available cameras. The two most obvious ways to change your current camera view are with the interactive Camera Controls that appear within the Poser workspace, or with the Display > Camera menu options. Both methods are shown in Figure 2.1.

FIGURE 2.1 Use the Camera Selector in the interactive camera controls (left), or the Display > Camera menu command (right) to choose a predefined camera view.

Poser's cameras are intended to help you accomplish many diverse tasks and accommodate a variety of personal work styles and needs. You can create final renders from any of the cameras in Poser.

The *Main Camera* and the *Auxiliary Camera* work in a similar manner; they rotate about the center of your scene. The focus of rotation can be changed, but by default, these cameras rotate around the center of the scene. Most people happily stick with the Main Camera to compose and render their final scene; however, other cameras are available: The Auxiliary Camera is an excellent tool to compose your scene from different viewpoints without having to change the position of your Main Camera or using up several Camera Dots.

The *Posing Camera* rotates around the center figure's hip. If the center figure does not have a hip, it rotates around the center of the body. To understand how this works, choose the Posing camera (Display > Camera View > Posing Camera). Next, open the Joint Editor window (Window > Joint Editor). Select the hip on your figure, and change the X coordinate of the Center Point to .01. You will see the viewpoint of the camera track the center of the hip. Note, however, that Poser can sometimes get confused if you try this with a scene that has one figure with a hip and one without.

The *Face Camera*, *Left Hand Camera*, and *Right Hand Camera* are specialized cameras that are specifically configured to help you develop facial expressions, style hair, or pose hands, for example. These cameras are invaluable tools that allow you to zoom around either the head of your figure or its hands and view your work from many angles, easily and quickly. These cameras are, by default, centered on the body part for which they are named. However, for the hand cameras to work properly, custom figure developers must name the right hand *rHand* and the left hand *lHand*. The head of the figure must be named *head* for the Head camera to work properly.

The *Dolly Camera* is a unique camera in that it rotates about its own center, unlike the other perspective cameras that rotate around a point or object in your scene. The Dolly Camera is extremely useful for duplicating that traditional Hollywood-style camera movement in animations.

The *Orthogonal Cameras* (Right, Left, Front, Back, Top, and Bottom) are very useful when you are setting up joint parameters, positioning magnets, placing objects on top of other objects, resting things on the floor, and other instances where a perspective view makes it difficult to determine the exact position of objects. An Orthogonal Camera uses a technique called *orthogonal projection* that shows the view without any perspective distortions. To get an idea of how this is accomplished, imagine holding a huge sheet of X-ray film in front of your camera, and then shooting parallel X-rays from the very opposite side of your scene to expose an exact "image shadow" of your objects onto the film. The key here is that the X-rays are parallel. This means that objects are displayed at their actual sizes, regardless of how distant they are from the camera. Orthogonal cameras move along two of the three spatial axes, which vary depending on the camera view.

When you work with orthogonal cameras, you will probably find that having several up at once is a great help. You can divide your Preview window into several camera views to allow you to view left, right, top, and bottom for quick and accurate placement of objects with respect to each other. Tutorial 2.1 shows you how to accomplish this.

TUTORIAL 2.1   **USING AND SELECTING MULTIPLE CAMERA VIEWS**

Poser 7 allows you to see more than one camera view at a time in your Preview window. This is handy when you are trying to position content in your scene. You can select which cameras will appear in each of the views. To configure the Preview window to display more than one camera, follow these steps:

1. From the menu, choose File > New to create a new scene in Poser. The default figure appears in your scene. Adjust the camera view, if necessary, with the Camera Controls.
2. Locate the Document Window Layout menu in the lower-left corner of the document window. The Document Window Layout menu appears circled in Figure 2.2.

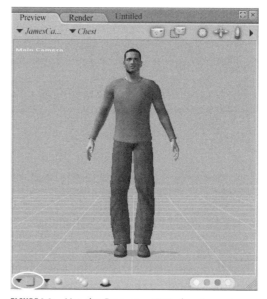

FIGURE 2.2   Use the Document Window Layout menu to choose the number of camera views to display in the Document window.

3. Click the down arrow to display the Document Window Layout menu options. The Full Port option displays one camera (the default selection). Additional options divide the document window into two-, three-, or four camera views.

4. For this tutorial, choose Four Ports. This divides the document window into four equal parts. By default, the views are Front Camera and Top Camera in the top row and Right Camera and Main Camera in the bottom row.

You can also choose the Display > Camera View > Four Cams menu command to display four camera views in the document window. To return to a single camera view document window, choose Full Port from the Document Window Layout menu in the lower-left corner of the document window.

5. If the camera names are not displayed in the ports in the Document window, choose Display > Show Camera Names to display them. To change the camera that is displayed in one of the camera ports, right-click on the camera name. Choose Camera View, and then drag right to open the menu shown in Figure 2.3. Then choose the camera that you want to display.

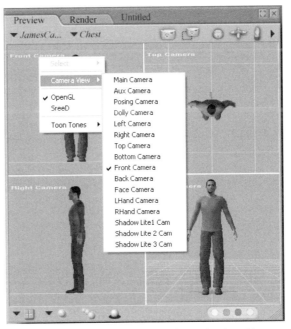

FIGURE 2.3   To change the camera that is displayed in a camera port, right-click the camera name to display the Camera View selection menu, and select a camera from the list.

USING THE CAMERA CONTROLS

The *Camera Controls*, shown in Figure 2.4, allow you to interactively select and position cameras for various purposes. By default, the Main Camera is selected.

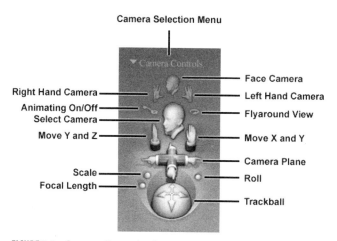

FIGURE 2.4   Camera Controls allow you to interactively select and position cameras.

The Camera Controls make the following functions available:

Camera Selection Menu: Displays a list of cameras to choose from.

Face Camera: This camera pivots around the currently selected figure's face, even as you zoom in, out, or rotate the camera view.

Right Hand and Left Hand Cameras: These cameras pivot around the designated hand while zooming in or out or rotating the camera.

Animating On/Off: Toggles the addition of camera keyframes to the animation timeline. To prevent the addition of camera keyframes while posing objects or body parts during animation, click the key icon to turn it red. This turns camera animation OFF. Click it again to resume camera animation.

Flyaround View: Click this icon to get a 360-degree flyaround view of your scene. Click again to turn the flyaround view OFF.

Select Camera: Click to cycle through the various camera views: Main, Top, Front, Left, Right, Face, Posing, Left Hand, Right Hand, Dolly, Back, Bottom, and Auxiliary.

Move Y and Z: Click and drag left or right to move the camera along the Z (forward/backward) plane. Drag up or down to move the camera along the Y (up/down) plane.

Move X and Y: Click and drag left or right to move the camera along the X (left/right) plane. Click and drag up or down to move the camera along the Y (up/down) plane.

Camera Plane: Click and drag left or right to move the camera along the X (left/right) axis, or up or down to move the camera along the Z (forward or back) axis.

Scale: This zooms into or out from the scene without affecting focal or perspective settings.

Roll: Click and drag to roll the camera clockwise or counterclockwise.

Focal Length: Click and drag toward the left to decrease the camera's focal length; click and drag toward the right to increase the focal length.

Trackball: Drag the trackball to rotate the camera around its center; drag in the direction you want the camera to rotate.

CAMERA PARAMETERS

The Parameters window contains dials that allow you to set additional camera parameters, although many of the parameters are the same as those in the interactive Camera Controls area. To view the parameters and properties of a camera as shown in Figure 2.5, select the camera from the menu at the top of the Parameters window.

FIGURE 2.5 Poser camera parameters mimic settings found in real-world cameras.

The parameters are as follows:

Focal: Sets the camera's *focal length*. The default setting of the Main Camera is 55 millimeters, which is great for landscape renders because this focal length results in a fairly wide field of view. Smaller focal lengths may produce a noticeable "fisheye" effect as more and more of the surrounding view is compressed into the camera's field of view.

Perspective: The Perspective setting is usually calculated automatically by Poser and is the same as the Focal setting. You can change the perspective of your current camera and zoom in or out without affecting the physical location of your camera. Changing this setting from the automatically calculated default can be confusing, so unless you have a reason, it's probably best to leave it at default.

Focus Distance: This setting allows you to specify the distance at which objects will be most in focus. A focus indicator moves backward or forward through the scene to indicate where focus will occur. Objects that are farther away from the focal plane will be blurred.

fStop: The fStop is a measure of the size of the lens aperture (the opening that allows light to come in to the camera during an exposure).

fStop settings determine the depth of field for your renders. The depth of field is a measure of how far in front of and how far behind your focus distance objects will remain in focus. A good rule of thumb about the relationship between fStop and depth of field is that the higher the fStop, the deeper (or longer) the field of focus. For a quick explanation with examples explaining depth of field, try the following online resources: http://www.dofmaster.com/dof_defined.html, and http://www.azuswebworks.com/photography/dof.html.

shutter_Open and shutter_Close: These two settings represent the point in an animation frame when the camera shutter opens and when the camera shutter closes. 0.0 represents the beginning of a frame, and 1.0 represents the end of a frame. The results of this setting are only visible when you activate 3D motion blur.

hither: This setting controls the location of the *clipping plane*, which is a specified distance from the camera that defines what objects are visible. Anything between the camera and the clipping plane will not appear in the Preview window. After you get past the clipping plane, you will see the objects in your scene. Figure 2.6 shows what happens if an object is too close to the hither setting. If you see the front portions of your object disappear as if being dissected along the same plane, decrease the hither setting until you can view the entire object.

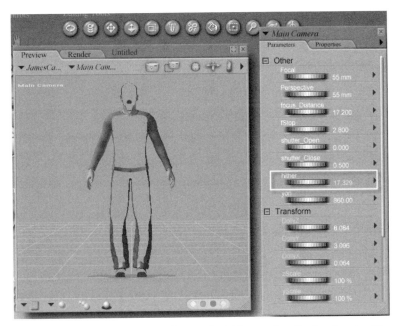

FIGURE 2.6 If your object is too close to the hither setting, the front parts of it may disappear. Decrease the hither setting if portions of an object appear to be cut away in the same plane.

yon: This setting works similar to the hither setting, except that it controls the far end of the clipping plane. Anything that lies beyond the yon setting will not appear in your Preview window. This parameter only applies with Open GL hardware rendering.

A standard all-purpose camera in the real world is the 35 millimeter (35 mm), which you recognize because most real-world, general-purpose cameras are referred to as '35 mm Cameras. In this case, however, the 35 mm refers to film size, not camera lens size. In regards to camera lenses, however, a 60 mm camera lens sees objects in the same way as the human eye. 50 mm to roughly 70 mm lenses are recommended for portraiture. In fact, a 50 mm lens is called a "portrait" lens by professional photographers and is considered a reasonably "flat perspective" lens. Finally, a 135 mm lens is the start of the telephoto, or zoom lenses. A telephoto lens will make things appear closer to the camera and focus on a tighter region. An additional effect of using a telephoto-range lens is that your objects will appear very flat or approach an orthogonal view. Poser does a great job of mimicking real-world camera physics, but you'll have to find your own comfort zones and preferences when working with various focal settings and subjects.

Camera Properties

The Properties window, shown in Figure 2.7, allows you to assign a new name to any camera in your scene. There are also some additional properties that can be useful in certain situations as you are building and animating your scene:

Visible: When you see a camera in the Document window, it is important to note that the camera will not show in the final render. However, if your scene contains a lot of props and figures, it can help clear up some of the clutter if you hide the camera. When the camera is hidden, you can still view your scene through a hidden camera or make changes to the settings of the camera in the Parameters window. However, if you want to manually reposition the camera by dragging it with your mouse using one of the editing tools, you will need to check the Visible option.

Animating: Check this option if you want to animate the camera. Uncheck this option when you want to reposition the camera without adding a keyframe that will cause the camera to animate.

Remember Changes for Undo: With the new Multiple Undo feature in Poser 7, Poser will store up to 100 undo actions in its history. If you uncheck this option, Poser will not store changes for the selected camera in the Undo/Redo history.

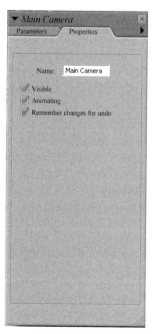

FIGURE 2.7 The Camera Properties window allows you to customize your camera name. You can also choose to hide, animate, or remember undo changes for each camera.

TUTORIAL 2.2   **CREATING AND SAVING CUSTOM HEAD CAMERAS**

Although the Face Camera allows you to focus on the face, it is also helpful to look at the face from the front-, left-, and right sides without perspective distortion, especially when you are trying to create custom morphs for facial features and expressions, or when you are trying to refine features or fix seams in photorealistic textures. In this tutorial, you'll use some of the camera's Transform parameters to position and create useful head cameras.

The Transform parameters are very similar to those you see in any other object:

DollyX, DollyY, and DollyZ: The Dolly settings move the camera left or right (X), up or down (Y), or forward and backward (Z).

xScale, yScale, and zScale: The Scale settings scale the camera's width (X), height (Y), or depth (Z). In addition, the Scale setting increases or decreases the overall size of the camera.

xOrbit, yOrbit, and zOrbit: The Orbit settings rotate the cameras forward to backward (X), around (Y), or side to side (Z).

Roll, Pitch, and Yaw: These settings apply to the Dolly, Posing, Face, and Hand cameras and how they rotate around their own axes. Positive Roll settings turn the camera to its left (scene's right); positive Pitch settings make the camera pitch upward (scene appears to go downward); and positive Yaw settings tilt the camera to the left (scene appears to tilt right).

Although the process to make these cameras is somewhat similar for all Poser figures, you'll create a set of cameras for the figure of your choice here. These cameras will allow you to view your character's head from the front, back, left, and right when you add it to a Poser document from the library. To create and save the cameras, follow these steps:

1. Choose File > New from the menu to create a new scene. The default figure appears in the scene.
2. If desired, delete the default figure and add a different character from the Figures Library. In this example, we use SimonG2, which you can find in the Poser 7 > Figures > G2 > Simon G2 Library.
3. Use the Figures > Inverse Kinematics command to turn off Inverse Kinematics on the right- and left legs. Choose Window > Joint Editor, and click the Zero Figure button in the Joint Editor to zero the position of your figure. Close the Joint Editor when you are finished.
4. From the menu, choose Display > Camera View > From Front. This switches to the Front Camera view.
5. If the Parameters window is not open, select Window > Parameter Dials from the menu to display it. Use the pull-down menu at the top of the Parameters window to display the parameters for the Front Camera as shown in Figure 2.8.

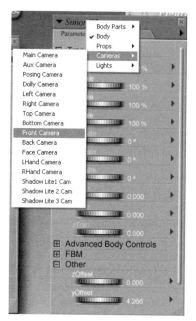

FIGURE 2.8   Use the pull-down menu in the Parameters window to select the Front camera.

6. Adjust the DollyY setting and the Scale settings until you get a close-up of your character's head. If you are also using SimonG2, you'll find that you need settings of 42.500 for the DollyY parameter (which moves the camera up or down) and about 14% for the Scale parameter to be in the right ballpark.

7. To save this camera to the library, click the icon in the upper-right corner of the Library window (circled in Figure 2.9) to expand the Library window to show the Runtime drop-down list. Select the Poser 7 Runtime folder as shown in Figure 2.9, and then select the Camera Library. At the top level of the Camera Library, you should find a folder named Camera Sets.

8. Expand the Camera Library menu as shown in Figure 2.10, and choose Add New Category. In the Library Name dialog box, name the new library. For SimonG2, we call the new library **SimonG2 Head Cameras**. Click OK to create the new library entry and folder on your hard drive.

9. Double-click the newly created library folder to open it. Then click the Add to Library button at the bottom of the Library Palette window. The New Set dialog box appears.

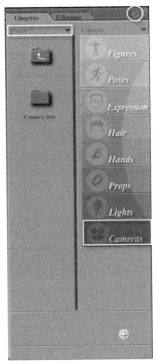

FIGURE 2.9   Choose the Poser 7 runtime folder, and open the Camera Library.

FIGURE 2.10   Expand the menu in the Camera Library to create a new category.

10. Enter **SimonG2 Head Front** (or a similar name for your character) for the camera set name. Then click the Select Subset button.

11. The Select Objects dialog box shown in Figure 2.11 displays all of the cameras you can choose from. In this case, you only need to select the Front Camera, which you used to create your current camera view. Check the Front Camera, and then choose OK to return to the New Set dialog box.

12. Choose OK again to display the Save Frames dialog box, which asks if you want to save a single-frame or multi-frame animation camera. Choose Single Frame, and click OK. The new camera appears in the library.

13. For the Left Camera, select Display > Camera View > From Left from the menu. Then from the Parameters window, select the Left Camera from the pull-down menu.

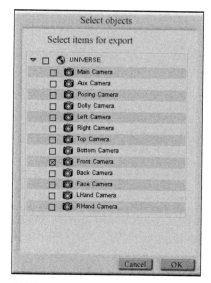

FIGURE 2.11   Use the Select Objects dialog box to select the camera that you want to save.

14. Set the DollyY parameter to the same value you used for the front camera (42.500 in our case). This will position it at the same height as the Front Camera. Then set the Scale to the same value you used for the Front camera (14% in our case).

15. Adjust the DollyX setting until the head is centered in the document window (a setting of 1.000 works well in our case).

16. Repeat Steps 7 through 10 to save the new camera as **SimonG2 Head Left** or a similar name for your character. Make sure you select the Left Camera from the Select Objects dialog box.

17. You can create Back and Right Head Cameras for your character as well. The Right Camera settings will be 42.5 for DollyY, −1.000 for DollyX, and 14% for Scale. The Back Camera settings will be 42.5 for DollyY and 14% for Scale. When you're finished, your Head Cameras Library will look like Figure 2.12. You'll have a complete set of cameras that you can use while creating head morphs or for checking out head textures for your character.

 Refer to Appendix B "Frequently Asked Questions" at the end of this book for information on how you can use Camera Dots to save cameras that you frequently use, or how to memorize and restore one camera that gets saved with your Poser project.

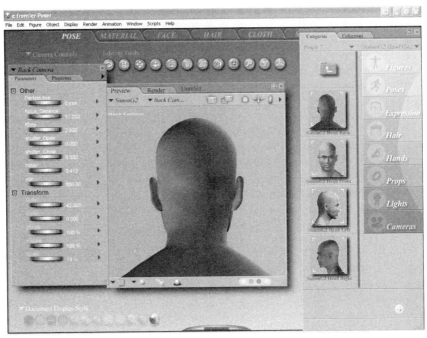

FIGURE 2.12   Four Head Cameras (Back, Front, Left, and Right) are created and saved for SimonG2.

TUTORIAL 2.3   **CREATING YOUR OWN CAMERAS**

New to Poser 7 is the ability to create your own cameras and have them appear in the camera selection menus. What this means is that you are no longer limited to using one of the 13 basic types of cameras that were found in earlier versions of Poser.

Poser allows you to create two types of cameras.

To create a new camera, follow these steps:

1. Choose Object > Create Camera, and choose either Dolly or Revolving from the expanded menu:
   - The center point of a Dolly camera is the camera itself. That is, it rotates around its own axis. The view of the camera changes as you move the camera around in the scene. When you create a Dolly camera, Poser names it *Dolly Camera*, followed by a number. Dolly cameras accept Roll, Pitch, and Yaw transformations as well as DollyX, DollyY, and DollyZ translations.

- The center point of a Revolving camera is the center of the Poser workspace. When you move a Revolving camera, you still look at the same part of the scene, but you look at it from a different angle. When you create a Revolving camera, Poser names it *Aux Camera*, followed by a number. Revolving cameras also accept Roll, Pitch, and Yaw transformations as well as DollyX, DollyY, and DollyZ translations.

2. To change the name of the camera, select the camera from the Actor list in the Properties window (it should automatically be selected right after you create the camera). Enter a new name in the Name field as shown in Figure 2.13. Press Enter to set the new name for the camera.

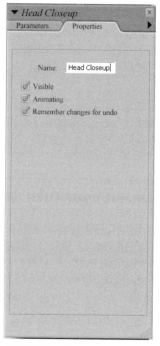

FIGURE 2.13 You can rename your custom cameras in the Properties window.

3. Adjust the settings for the camera in the Parameters window until you get the view you want in the Document window.
4. To view your project through your new camera, right-click on the camera name in the Document window, and select your custom camera from the Camera View menu shown in Figure 2.14.

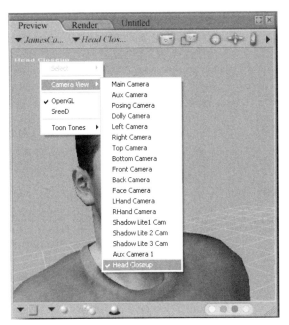

FIGURE 2.14   Select your custom camera from the Camera View list after right-clicking the camera name in the Document window.

TUTORIAL 2.4   **POINTING AND PARENTING CAMERAS AND OBJECTS**

Poser cameras can track any object in your scene; conversely, any item in your scene can follow the position of a camera. For example, let's say you create an animation in which your figure walks around the scene in a circle. You can set up the project so that the camera always points at the head of this figure. As a result, the figure remains centered in the camera view while it walks around the scene.

In a similar manner, you can also point objects toward a camera. For example, you can point the eyes of a character so that it is always looking at a camera. Posing the eyes of your figure helps to get rid of the "blank stare syndrome" that the default eye position is famous for creating in renders. Posed eyes help give your character life and personality.

As an alternative to using the Point At feature to pose eyes, you can also use the Up-Down and Side-Side parameter dials that appear for each eye.

To point eyes at a camera, follow these steps:

1. Pose your figure—get everything but the eyes exactly the way you want it. In the example that follows, we added SydneyG2 (from the Poser 7 > Figures > G2 > SydneyG2 Library) to the scene. From the Poser 7 > Hair > G2 > SydneyG2 Library, we added the SydneyStyle_2 hair and conformed it to her head. From the Poser 7 > Figures > G2 Female Clothes > Poser7 Casual Library, we dressed her in the G2 Tank and G2 Pants and conformed them to her body. Then, we applied a pose from the G2 Poses Library.

2. The next step is to choose the camera that you want to use for your final render. For this example, we moved the Main Camera closer to the figure's face for a portrait render. (The Face Camera does not feature a Point At option.)

3. Click one eye to select it. The object list beneath the Render tab displays rightEye or leftEye when either eye is selected.

4. Select Object > Point At from the menu. The Point At dialog box shown in Figure 2.15 appears. Notice that this dialog box allows you to point the eye at anything in your scene. You can point it at an object the character is holding, for example, or at another figure in the scene.

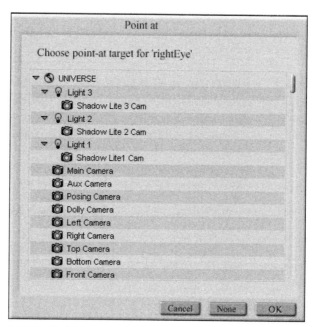

FIGURE 2.15 The Point At dialog box allows you to point an object toward any other figure, body part, object, light, or camera in your scene.

5. Choose the camera that you selected in Step 2 (in our case, the Main Camera). You can also click the None button to remove a previous Point At choice. Then click OK to apply the setting.

6. When you return to the Document window, one eye should be pointing at your camera. Select the other eye, and repeat Steps 4 and 5 to point it at the same camera. Figure 2.16 shows the eyes before and after they are posed. Notice the difference it can make to an image.

The Point At *feature will only work as shown if the end point of the eye is toward the front of the figure. Some figures have the end point of the eye above the head. Under these conditions, the eye will appear to roll up and just show the whites of the eye. If you find that this happens, select the eye again, and choose the Object > Point At command again. Select None as the object to point at. Then, you can use the Up-Down and Side-Side parameter dials to manually position the eye. Use similar settings for the other eye.*

FIGURE 2.16   Before her eyes were posed, Sydney had a blank stare (left). After her eyes are pointed at the camera, she comes to life (right).

TUTORIAL 2.5   **USING DEPTH OF FIELD**

Depth of field effects can be achieved quite easily with the FireFly render engine and with some simple settings on your camera. This process also makes use of a Python script written by Stefan Werner, who was generous enough to allow it to be included with the base installation of Poser 7.

The camera's focal length, fStop, and focus_Distance all play a part in determining the areas of your scene that will be in focus and the areas that will fade with depth. Smaller fStop values create a smaller area that is in focus.

1. Add figures or other content to your scene. In this simple example, three male figures have been added to the stage. One is in the default center stage position. A second figure is behind and to the figure's right side. A third figure is forward and to the left of the figure. Figure 2.17 shows the setup from four camera views. An 80 mm Main Camera is used for the scene.

You can use Poser 7's new Duplicate feature to create exact copies of a figure quickly and easily. Select the figure or prop that you want to duplicate, and choose Edit > Duplicate, which will list the name of the currently selected prop or figure. Poser will duplicate the selected item in the same position as the original. You can then use the Parameter dials or the Editing tools to reposition the copy in your scene.

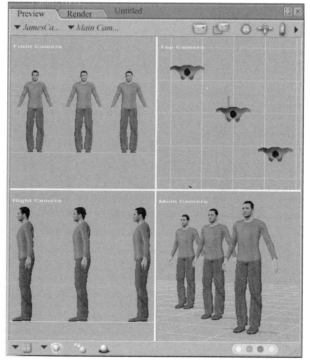

FIGURE 2.17   Three figures are added to the scene for the depth of field example.

2. Use the Edit > General Preferences command to open the General Preferences dialog box. Click the Interface tab, and verify that the Display Units setting is set to Feet.

3. Choose Window > Python Scripts to open the Python Scripts dialog box.

4. Click to select the figure that you want to be the focus of the scene. In this example, we select the middle figure.

5. From the main Python Scripts menu, click the Render/IO button. Then click the Calc DoF Focal Distance button.

6. After the script runs, you will see a pop-up window that has a number in it. The number represents the distance, in feet, from the current camera to your currently selected object.

7. Copy the number into your clipboard or write it down.

8. Use the Choose Actor menu in the Parameters window to select the current camera. In this example, we select the Main Camera as shown in Figure 2.18.

FIGURE 2.18   Choose your current camera (in this case, the Main Camera) from the Current Actor menu in the Parameters window.

9. Enter or paste the number generated by the Python script from your copy buffer into the focus_Distance field.

10. At this point, you'll need to decide how strong you want your depth of field effects. Enter a small value in the camera's fStop parameter if

you want a smaller area to stay in focus. Enter a larger value in the fStop parameter to keep a larger area in focus.

11. To see the depth of field results you have to use the FireFly renderer and configure the Render Options dialog box to use depth of field. To do so, choose Render > Render Settings to open the Render Settings dialog box.

12. In the FireFly tab of the Render Settings dialog box, first apply the Final render settings from the Auto Settings options. Then, check the Manual Settings button shown in Figure 2.19. Increase the pixel samples setting to reduce blotchiness in the Render. We will start with a value of 5 for our example.

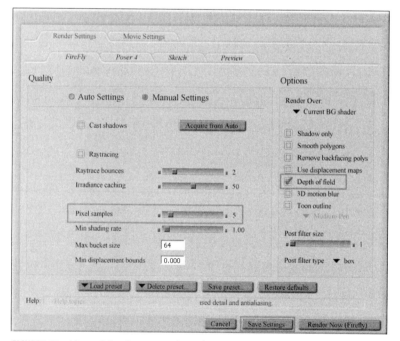

FIGURE 2.19 Manual Settings must be selected in the FireFly tab to render depth of field effects.

13. Check the Depth of field option in the Manual Settings screen.

14. Click the Save Settings button to exit the Render Settings dialog box. Then choose Render > Render to render the scene. Figure 2.20 shows an example of a render that uses depth of field.

When you use the depth of field option, your renders will take much longer!

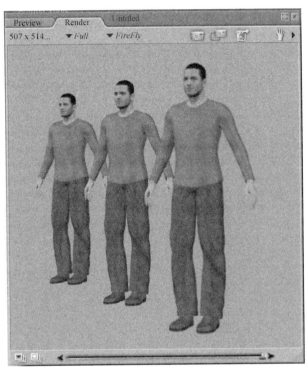

FIGURE 2.20   Interesting results can be achieved using depth
of field.

CONCLUSION

In this chapter, you were introduced to several things you can do with
the Poser cameras. The Camera Controls help you select and position
cameras interactively. The Camera Parameters allow you to adjust settings and positions for a camera, one parameter at a time. You can point
objects at the camera or point the camera at other objects.

Now that you've learned how to use cameras to improve the way
your scene looks, you'll learn how to light your scene to improve your
renders even more.

MASTERING LIGHTS AND SHADOWS

In This Chapter

An Overview of Lighting

Ask any accomplished 3D artist, and they will tell you that the *single most important thing* that can make or break a render is lighting!

Lighting adds realism and texture to a scene in ways that can't be accomplished with models or textures alone. Even detailed models and meticulously crafted textures will look mediocre if you don't pay attention to the way you light your scene. Poor lighting choices can make a render look dull and lifeless. Carefully planned lighting can make an image or scene come alive. The advanced lighting and shadow features in Poser 7 enable you to achieve lighting effects comparable to what you would expect from more expensive software.

In this chapter, you'll learn the basics of creating your own light setups. Starting from an unlit scene, you'll learn how to configure a standard three-point lighting system that will lay the groundwork for your understanding of how lights work. You'll also learn about the different types of lights and shadows and how to achieve the best results with them. You'll be able to create and modify light sets and make your renders look their best.

Poser 7 Light Types

The four types of lights in Poser 7 are Infinite Lights, Spotlights, Point Lights, and Image-Based Lights. Each of these light types shares similar properties such as color, angle, intensity, and a few other parameters. However, each type of light distributes light in a different way. Figure 3.1 shows a comparison of the four types of lights. All lights are configured to illuminate the figure's head.

- *Infinite Lights* shine light at the same angle throughout your scene. When you add an Infinite Light to your scene, all of the content is lit from the same angle and on the same side. For example, you can add a pale yellow Infinite Light to simulate sunlight or a pale blue Infinite Light to simulate moonlight in your scene. The light from an Infinite Light is parallel, resulting in orthogonal lighting.
- *Spotlights* shine light from a single point of origin and cast their light in a cone-shape. Spotlights are similar to lights used by photographers or in stage productions. You can control the angle and distance of the cone, allowing you to create lighting effects such as street lamps, candlelight, or the light from a crackling fire. Use the Angle End setting to adjust the size of the area that will be illuminated; higher values light larger areas, whereas lower values light smaller areas.
- *Point Lights*, introduced in Poser 6, are *omnidirectional* (meaning that they shine light in all directions from a central point). Point Lights are

also called *global lights*. A soft Point Light in your scene can prevent total darkness in your render and give your scene a minimum threshold of ambient light. Take care not to make point lights too bright because they can wash out your scene and make it appear flat. Because point lights cast light in all directions throughout the scene, it might take a long time to calculate Depth Map Shadows. For that reason, these lights cast Raytrace Shadows only.

• *Image-Based Lights* (*IBLs*) were introduced in Poser 6. They simulate many colors in a single light. The colors and placement of the light in your scene are derived from an image or movie that you specify. The end result makes your render appear as if your character is actually a part of the original image or movie, making it a great choice for work that requires photorealism. Image-Based Lighting is *diffuse-only*, meaning that if you want specular highlights in your scene (such as eye glints or highlights in hair), you will need additional lighting that is not Image-Based Lighting.

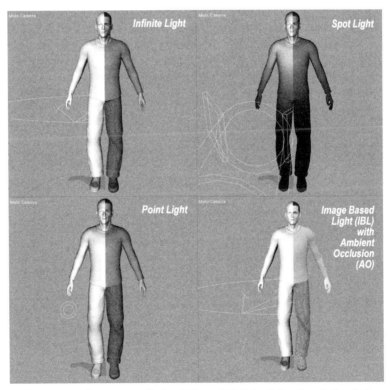

FIGURE 3.1   The four types of lights in Poser 7: Infinite lights, Spotlights, Point Lights, and Image Based Lights.

POSER 7 SHADOW TYPES

You can choose which lights cast shadows in your scene. It is common practice to cast shadows from only one light in your scene, which results in reduced rendering times.

Lights in Poser 7 can cast several different types of shadows:

Depth Map Shadows: When you use Depth Map Shadows, Poser generates a shadow map for each light that uses them. By default, the shadow map for each light is 256 by 256 pixels. You can increase the shadow map size if the shadows look pixilated. Larger sizes produce more defined and accurate shadows but also use more resources. (Remember, doubling your shadow map size will add four times the number of pixels that need to be calculated for the map.) You can also control the amount of blur on Depth Map Shadows with controls in the Properties window associated with the light. Depth Map Shadows are the best option when you want shadows with softer edges and faster render times in general.

Raytrace Shadows: Raytrace Shadows are typically very sharp and also very accurate with respect to the original shapes of the object meshes. They are calculated during the render, rather than before the render as is the case with Depth Map Shadows. Render times are significantly increased when using Raytrace Shadows. For the best results, use the FireFly render engine in Poser 7 with quality settings at least halfway, as shown in Figure 3.2. Raytrace Shadows will not render when FireFly is set to draft render mode.

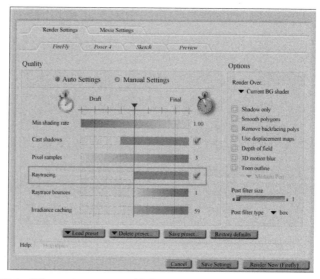

FIGURE 3.2   When using raytraced lights, set the FireFly render quality settings to at least the halfway point if you want to also calculate Raytrace Shadows.

Ambient Occlusion (AO): AO adds additional contrast to images by reducing the amount of ambient light in the shadows, making them appear darker. This option is typically used with IBL but can also be used with the other light types. Occlusion Master, a product by face_off is a utility that makes it extremely easy to produce excellent and highly realistic results with Ambient Occlusion. You can find this utility in both Mac and PC formats in face_off Renderosity store (*http://market.renderosity.com/mod/bcs/index.php?vendor=face_off*).

LIGHTING CONTROLS

The Light Controls are shown in Figure 3.3. You can show or hide the light controls in the Pose Room, Material Room, Hair Room, or Cloth Room. To toggle the display of the light controls, choose Window > Light Controls.

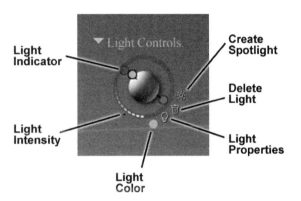

FIGURE 3.3   The Light Controls help you create, color, and position the lights in your scene.

A shadow map is basically a depth map of the scene as viewed from the light's point of view. The purpose of a shadow-depth map is to tell the render engine how far the effect of the light goes and which surfaces are in front of others, from the light's perspective. At render time, the shadow map for each light is consulted to see if the spot on the currently calculating ray/object is receiving light from the light source or if it is in the shadow of another object or another part of itself.

Ambient Occlusion is a measure of the amount of ambient light received by a point on the surface of an object surface. It simulates a huge dome light that surrounds the entire scene. If a surface point is under or behind another object (for example, a spot behind your figure's ear), that point needs to be much darker than the top-most object (such as the top of your figure's head). The occlusion map is used to darken the ambient levels at render time where appropriate. This subtle and potent lighting effect adds quite a bit of realism to renders without the addition of many diffuse lights in your scene. Although ambient occlusion calculations take up render time, they are not nearly as costly as using dozens of individually calculated light sources.

The light controls help you add, change, or remove lights from your scene as follows:

Create Light: Click to create a new light, which is configured as a Spotlight by default. New lights generally appear above and to the right of the Document window (left side facing you).

Delete Light: Deletes the currently selected light. Verify that you have selected the correct light before you delete it, as this action is not reversible.

Light Properties: Displays the properties of the currently selected light in the Properties window.

Light Colors: Click the Light Color icon to open a color picker, and select a new color for the light.

Light Intensity: Adjusts the brightness of the light from 0 to 100%. You can increase the setting to greater than 100% to create very bright lights. You can also enter negative values for interesting shadow effects.

Light Indicator: Click and drag a Light Indicator around the globe to position the light in your scene. The center of the globe represents the center of your camera view. As you rotate the camera, the positions of the lights move according to where they are with respect to your scene and the current camera view.

LIGHT PARAMETERS AND PROPERTIES

After you create a light, you can select it in several different ways. In the Light Controls area, click one of the small circles around the globe to select the light you want to edit. You can also select a light from the parts list that appears at the top of the Document window (just beneath the Render tab). You can also use the menu command, Window > Parameters, to open the Parameters window and select a light from the top pull-down menu. To view the properties for the light, click the Properties tab. The parameters and properties for lights are shown in Figure 3.4.

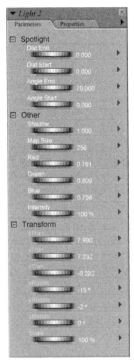

FIGURE 3.4   The Parameters and Properties of a light define the color, position, light type, shadow type, and much more.

You will find the following light settings in the Parameters window:

Shadow: Sets the strength of the shadow that is projected by the light. A value of 1 indicates 100% shadow strength. A value of 0 disables the shadow. Intermediate values make the shadow lighter or darker.

Map Size: Defines the size of the Depth Map Shadow for the associated light. The default is 256, which fits the shadow for the associated light into a 256 × 256-pixel square. Low values can result in shadows with very rough, pixilated edges; higher values create sharper shadows but also consume more system resources and rendering time.

Red, Green, and Blue: Defines the amounts of Red, Green, and Blue that are mixed to create the light color. When all three values are set to 1, the resulting "color" will be white (or a Red, Green, Blue value of 255, 255, 255). Color values are also automatically set when you choose a light color from the Light Controls color selector.

Intensity: Sets the strength of the light. The default intensity setting is 100%. Lower values create a dimmer light and higher values create a brighter light. Values above 100% and negative values can also be used.

The selections in the Properties window provide the following functions:

Visible: Check to display the Light Indicator in the Document window. Uncheck this option to hide the Light Indicator.

Animating: On by default, this option creates a keyframe when you make changes to a light in any frame but the first frame. This allows you to animate light properties such as color, position, rotation, or intensity. Uncheck this option if you want your light to remain the same throughout an entire animation.

On: When unchecked, turns the light off so that it no longer shines light.

Shadows: Check this option if you want your light to cast shadows. It takes longer to render scenes in which multiple lights cast shadows. If you choose to cast shadows, choose one of the types of shadows (Raytrace Shadows or Depth Map Shadows as introduced earlier).

TUTORIAL 3.1	DELETING LIGHTS

You may find that you have unnecessary lights in your scene. For example, when you create a new scene in Poser, you get three infinite lights by default. (Light 1 is olive green and appears at the figure's right. Light 2 is gray and is the center light in the scene. Light 3 is a shade of orange and appears at the figure's left side.) Rather than editing each light individually, it might be easier to just start over. You may want to delete these and create your own defaults. You may encounter situations when you purchase or download light sets that have so many extra lights turned OFF that it just makes sense to delete them. Or you might want to remove all of the lights in the scene and start from scratch.

There are two different ways to remove lights. In the first method, you select and delete one light at a time; in the second method, you delete all lights at once:

1. Use the menu command File > New to create a new scene for this tutorial. The default figure appears in the Document window by default, with three lights.
2. Select one of the lights using any of the following methods, as shown in Figure 3.5:
   • Click one of the light indicators that appear around the globe in the Light Controls (1).

- Choose a light from the Parts List beneath the Render tab in the Document window (2).
- Choose a light from the Parts List in the Parameters window (3).

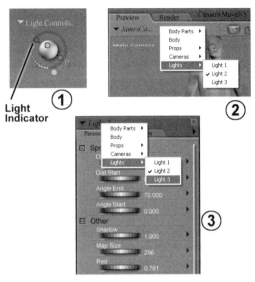

FIGURE 3.5   To select a light, click a light indicator (1), use the menu in the Document window (2), or choose a light from the Parameters window (3).

3. To delete the selected light, click the Delete (trash can) icon in the Light Controls or use the Figure > Delete Figure menu command.
4. You can use a Python script to delete all the lights in your scene. To begin, choose Scripts > Utility > Delete Lights, as shown in Figure 3.6.

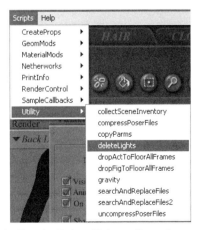

FIGURE 3.6   Use the Delete Lights utility script, available in the Scripts menu, to delete all of the lights in your scene.

5. Poser asks if you are sure that you want to delete all of the lights in your scene. Click the OK button to complete the operation.

TUTORIAL 3.2   **CREATING THREE-POINT STUDIO LIGHTING**

A versatile lighting setup for portrait or still-life photography is a *three-point lighting setup*. This lighting style typically uses three lights: a Key Light, a Fill Light, and a Back Light. In the following three-part tutorial, you'll learn more about what role each of these lights plays and how to create them in Poser. You'll also learn how to create a three-point studio lighting setup for any scene you choose.

Before we get into the lighting part of our tutorial, you'll need to set up your scene. In the following example, you'll see e frontier's Miki 2 figure, but you can use any figure, clothing, and pose that you choose.

1. Use the File > New menu command to create a new scene in Poser. The default figure appears in the scene.
2. Delete the default figure and replace with the figure of your choice. In this example, we are using one of the G2 females, Miki 2, an e frontier figure that can be purchased from Content Paradise (*http://www.contentparadise.com*). Add suitable hair and conforming clothing to your figure if necessary.

If you need help with adding hair and clothing to a figure, you can find some basic tutorials on the CD-ROM that accompanies this book. Refer to CD2-BuildingScenes. html for tutorials that help with adding, dressing, and posing your figures.

ON THE CD

3. Select or create a pose for your figure. The pose that we have selected here is from Yve Miki Poses 2, available at the Renderosity Marketplace (*http://www.renderosity.com*). We selected the Miki 058 pose from this package.
4. The next step is to set up your camera. For this tutorial, we selected the Main Camera. After setting the Main camera to 80 mm Focal and Perspective, we positioned the camera so that Miki's upper body filled a Document window size of 425 pixels wide and 500 pixels high as shown in Figure 3.7. The settings used for the camera are default settings with the exception of the following: DollyZ –4.385998; DollyY 4.656237; DollyX –0.253126; zOrbit 1 degree; and yOrbit 7 degrees.
5. Use the Delete All Lights Python Scripts option (described in Tutorial 3.1) to delete the default lights. Your scene should now appear dark.

FIGURE 3.7   Position the Main Camera as you would like your final render to appear in your portrait render.

Creating the Key Light

The *Key Light* is the main light in the scene, and the one that defines the most visible lights and shadows. It typically appears anywhere between 15 and 45 degrees to the left or right of the camera and 15 to 45 degrees higher than the camera. The lighting of a Key Light should appear similar to the lighting you want in your final scene, except that the shadows will be darker and have very harsh contrast. The most obvious choice for a Key Light is a spotlight that casts shadows.

1. When there are no lights in the scene, the Create Light icon is the only icon that appears in the Light Controls area. Click the icon to create a new light. The color of the light varies, but Poser usually places the light at about the 10 o'clock position near the Light Control globe. By default, Poser creates a spotlight, which is what we want to use for our Key Light.

2. You want to position your Key Light in front of the figure, and within 45 degrees of your camera. When you see the light indicator in the exact center of the globe, the light is directly in front of or behind the camera. To position the light appropriately for a Key Light, move the light indicator to the upper-left or upper-right area of the globe, as shown in Figure 3.8.

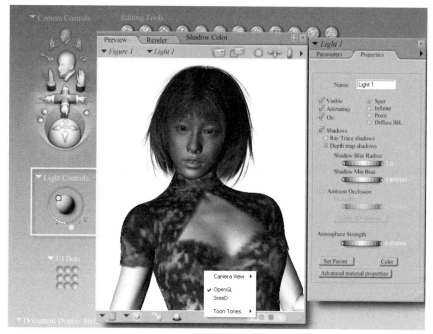

FIGURE 3.8   Position the light indicator above and to the left of the current camera position using the globe as reference.

3. With the Key Light in its proper position, the next step is to point it in the right direction. Select the light and choose Object > Point At from the menu. Then, when the Choose Actor dialog box appears, select your figure's head as the object to point at.
4. White and gray lights are neutral color lights that don't affect the colors in the materials of the objects you are rendering. When the Red, Green, and Blue values are each set to 1, the light is pure white or gray, depending on the Intensity setting. Set the Red, Green, and Blue parameters to 1, and set the Intensity of the light to 100%. After you render, your image should look similar to Figure 3.9.

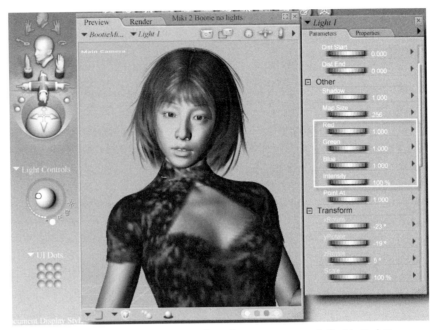

FIGURE 3.9   For pure white lighting, set the color parameters to 1; that is, Red, Green, and Blue all to a value of 1. Then set the intensity parameter to 100%.

You can also use the Set Up Light Style wacro in the Material Room to create a white light. With your light selected, enter the Material Room. Click the Set Up Light Style wacro button in the right side of the material window. When the Choose a Light Style dialog appears, select "White Only" from the drop-down list and click OK. The currently selected light will turn all white.

5. If desired, adjust the Angle End setting of the light to light more or less of the area to your taste. For the example in this book, this value was left at the default of 100, which increased the range of the light to brighten her arms a little more.

6. Go to the Parameters window, and click the Properties tab. Change the name of this light from "Light 1" to **Key Light**. Press Enter to change the name.

Creating the Fill Light

The *Fill Light* softens the contrast of the Key Light and makes more of the subject visible. The Fill Light usually comes from the opposite side of your Key Light (for example, if your Key Light is on the left, your Fill Light is on the right). Because they are typically used to add ambient color in your scene, Fill Lights are sometimes tinted to use a color that is predominant in the scene (such as blue for moonlight or yellow for sunlight). Fills are usually about one-eighth to one-half as bright as the Key Light, depending upon how much shadow contrast you want in your final image. Spotlights can be used for Fill Lights, but Point Lights are most common. Shadows are optional. In addition, Fill Lights are sometimes created as diffuse-only lights so that they do not add additional specular highlights to the scene in areas that are supposed to be shadowed.

To create the Fill Light, follow these steps:

1. Click the Create New Light icon again. A new light appears around the globe.
2. Move the Fill Light to the opposite side of the camera and toward the front. Asymmetric lighting tends to create a more dynamic and natural looking final result. Use your own judgment to place the camera so that the effect is pleasing to you. Figure 3.10 shows the new position for the Fill Light used in our portrait.

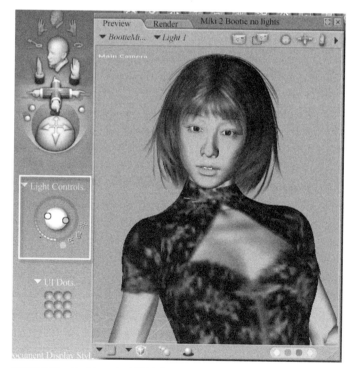

FIGURE 3.10 Position the Fill Light on the other side of the camera so that the effect is pleasing to you. Asymmetric lighting tends to create a more dynamic and natural looking final result.

3. If your scene has a backdrop or other scenery prop, observe what the most predominant color is. If you don't want to use white as a fill, try to add a tint of that predominant color for ambience. To change the color of the light, click the Light Color icon in the Light Controls and set the new light color. For example, let's say you are using a red curtain backdrop. You can select very pale shade of red (somewhat pink) for the Fill Light. In real life, light bounces off of all objects so that their colors interact with each other. If you pick up a bit of the more predominant background color, you help simulate natural radiosity-type lighting effects and inter-object reflections.

4. When the color selector appears, select a color for your Fill Light, as shown in Figure 3.11. Try to select a less intense or pastel version of a color that is predominant in your scene. If, on the other hand, you would rather keep your Fill Lighting neutral, choose white or gray.

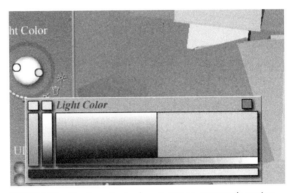

FIGURE 3.11   Try to select a less intense or pastel version of a color that is predominant in your scene for your Fill Lighting. If you would rather keep your Fill Lighting neutral, choose white or gray.

5. After you are satisfied with the color of your Fill Light, use the Intensity dial in the Parameters window to lower the intensity to somewhere between 20 and 80% (use 50% for this tutorial). Lower values will create more dramatic shadows. Higher values will create less contrast between lit and shadowed areas of your image.

6. Speaking of shadows, you might want to turn shadows off for the Fill Light. To do so, click the Properties tab (in the Parameters/Properties window). Uncheck the Shadows option. Try test renders with and without shadows to see which you prefer.

7. While you're in the Properties tab, change the name of the light to **Fill Light**. Then change the Fill Light to a Point Light as shown in Figure 3.12. This makes the Fill Light serve as ambient light that fills the scene, rather than limiting it to the cone shape of a Spotlight.

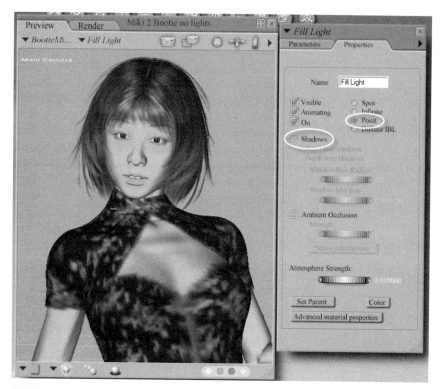

FIGURE 3.12 Optionally, turn off shadows for the Fill Light. Then change the light to a Point Light.

8. Now you can make the Fill Light diffuse-only, so that it will not add specular highlights that conflict with the main (key) light. First, click the Material tab to go into the Material Room.

9. The *Wacros* panel appears on the right-hand side of the material workspace. Click the Set Up Light Style button in the Wacros panel. (Wacros are scripts for the Poser 7 Material Room.)

10. A dialog box prompts you to choose a light style for your current light. Verify that Fill Light (or the name of your Fill Light) is selected. Then choose Diffuse Only from the list of options in the dialog box. Click OK to apply the new settings to the light.

11. Poser informs you that the light has been changed to diffuse-only. Click OK to exit the dialog box.

Creating the Back Light

The *Back Light* appears above and behind the subject and usually directly opposite the camera. The purpose of the Back Light is to separate the subject from the background by creating a rim of light around the top or side. A Spotlight or Point Light is good for a Back Light, and shadows are usually turned off because Back Lights are intended for highlights only, to pull the subject away from the background.

1. The easiest way to tell where the highlights will fall from the Back Light is to turn the other two lights off. Return to the Pose Room. Use the menu in the Properties window to select the Fill Light. Then uncheck the On check box as shown in Figure 3.13. Repeat for the Key Light.

FIGURE 3.13   Turn the Key Light and Fill Light off so that you can see the highlights from the Back Light.

2. Click the Create Light icon for the third time. A new light appears around the globe.
3. In the Parameters window, change the color of the new light to white (Red, Green, and Blue values set to 1). Set the intensity to 115%.

This will create a light that is slightly brighter than the others and will bring the highlights out when the light is behind the figure.

4. Verify that the light is still selected (if you changed the name of the other two lights, this new light should currently be named Light 1). Choose Object > Point At from the menu. Point the light at the figure's head.

5. In the Light Controls area, move the Light 1 indicator to the top and slightly behind the globe. It is easier to see the effect of the backlight if you have a dark background color. You can also adjust the Angle End and Dist End settings of the light to increase the effect of the backlight. Watch the Document window until you get a backlighting effect that you are happy with. Figure 3.14 shows an example.

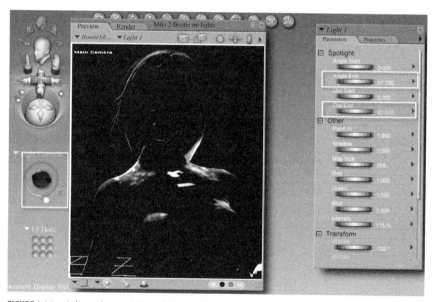

FIGURE 3.14   Adjust the position of the Back Light until you get a highlight that is acceptable.

6. Return to the Properties window, and change the name of the current light to **Back Light**. Uncheck the Shadows option.

7. While you're in the Properties window, choose the Key Light from the top menu in the Properties window. Turn it back on. Do the same for the Fill Light.

8. Render your result to check the final lighting. Make adjustments to your settings and tweak the light positions until you get the effect you want. Figure 3.15 shows the final result.

FIGURE 3.15   A final rendered portrait using the three-point lighting technique.

Saving the Light Set

To save your final light set to the library, follow these steps:

1. In the Library Palette, select the Runtime folder in which you intend to save your light (for example, you can choose your Practical Poser 7 folder). Open the Lights Library within that Runtime folder.
2. Click the Add to Library button at the bottom of the Library Panel. The New Set dialog box appears.
3. Enter a name for your new light set (such as Miki Portrait, as is the case for our example), and then click the Select Subset button. The Select Objects dialog box appears and lists all lights in your scene.
4. Check the lights you want to include in the set. For example, if you want to include all three lights, check Key Light, Fill Light, and Back Light, as shown in Figure 3.16.
5. Click OK to return to the New Set dialog box.
6. Click OK again to proceed. The Save Frames dialog box appears. By default, the light settings will be saved from a single frame (which is the frame that currently appears in the Document window). Accept

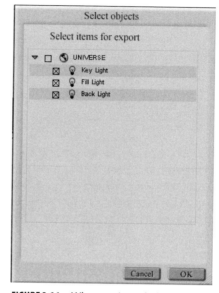

FIGURE 3.16   When saving a light set, make sure you choose the Select Subset button to check all lights in the Select Objects window.

the default, Single Frame, if you have not added keyframes to animate the lights. Then click OK to continue. The light set appears in your library, along with a thumbnail version of the scene as it was saved.

TUTORIAL 3.3   ADJUSTING LIGHTS AND SHADOWS

Each light that you create in your scene has a camera associated with it. These cameras are called *Shadow Light cameras*. They allow you to look into your scene through the light, exactly as the light "sees" it. This is a great asset when you need position lights and shadows to be accurate.

Shadows and lights are easier to position when there is more to a scene than a figure and clothes because you can view the effects of the lights and shadows on the background or floor. For example, we have added a curtain backdrop to help you visualize the positioning of the lights. This curtain set and the materials are available for free download at Runtime DNA (*http://www.runtimedna.com*).

The following steps show you how to use Shadow Light cameras to refine the lighting that you created in Tutorial 3.2.

1. Using the scene that you created in the last tutorial, right-click on the camera name that appears in the Document window. A selection menu appears.
2. Expand the Camera View submenu to display a list of cameras in your scene, as shown in Figure 3.17. At the bottom of the list, you will see three Shadow Cam Lights. The numbers are assigned in the order in which you saved your cameras. Therefore, going by the previous tutorial, the lowest numbered light will be the Key Light; the next number will be the Fill Light; and the highest number will be the Back Light.

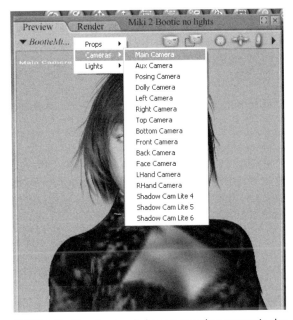

FIGURE 3.17   The shadow light cameras that appear in the Camera View menu are numbered in the order in which you created the lights.

 If you work with many lights in a scene, it can be difficult to keep track of them all, especially when you try to remember which Shadow Cam Lites go with which light. Fortunately, you can edit the names of the Shadow Cam Lites just like any other object in Poser—just open the Parameter/Properties window. The Name parameter is accessible under the Properties tab.

3. Select the lowest-numbered Shadow Light camera. This should be the camera that looks through your Key Light. The Document window should update to look through the Shadow Light camera you've currently selected.

4. Open the Parameters window, and select the Key Light from its menu at the top.

5. Because the Key Light is now the current light, it will remain in the center of the Light Control globe no matter how you adjust the position of the light. For that reason, you'll find it much easier to use the Trans dials in the Parameters window to tweak the position of the Key Light while you observe the changes through the shadow camera:

   • Adjust the xTran dial to move the light left or right.
   • Adjust the yTran dial to move the light upward or downward.
   • Adjust the zTran dial to move the light forward or backward.

 As you adjust the settings, think about where you want the shadows from the Key Light to fall. Remember that the shadows will fall in the direction from which you are viewing.

6. For Spotlights, make adjustments to the Angle Start and End settings as necessary. These settings control the starting and ending size of the light's cone, which increases or decreases the area that is covered by the light.

7. Spotlights and Point Lights also have Dist (Distance) Start and End settings. These settings control how near or far the light begins or ends from the point of origin. By default, light starts at the origin point (a setting of zero) and goes on infinitely (also a setting of 0). Adjust this setting to limit the range of your light. Figure 3.18 shows what happens after adjusting the Dist End setting of the Key Light. The left image is the default setting of 0, which shines the light infinitely. The right image shows a setting of about 18, which limits the amount that the background curtain is lit.

8. Adjust the strength of your shadow if necessary. If shadows are too dark, reduce the Shadow setting to a value below 1. A value of 0 turns the shadow off completely.

9. If you are using Depth Map Shadows instead of Raytrace Shadows, you can increase the Map Size setting in the Parameters window. The default shadow map is 256 by 256 pixels, which can create blocky shadows in a large scene. If resources allow, you can increase the shadow map size to create shadows that are cleaner and crisper. Generally, you should create shadow maps that are divisible by a power of 2 (256, 512, 1024, 2048, and so on). Remember, however, that the quantity and size of your Depth Map Shadows can increase resource usage and render times.

10. If you are using Raytrace Shadows, adjust Shadow Blur Radius and Shadow Min Bias settings in the Properties window shown in Figure 3.19. Normally, Raytrace shadows are very crisp and have hard edges. If you increase the Shadow Blur Radius setting, the shadows

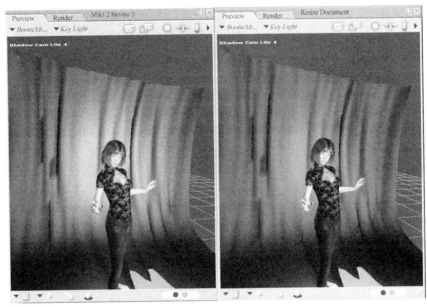

FIGURE 3.18   When you adjust the Dist End setting of a light, you control how near or far the light reaches from the point of origin.

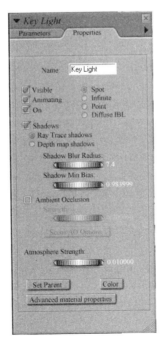

FIGURE 3.19   Adjust Shadow Blur Radius and Shadow Min Bias settings to control the appearance of Raytrace Shadows.

will have softer edges. The Shadow Min Bias helps prevent objects from casting shadows on themselves. Increase the setting to eliminate self-shadowing.

11. After your adjustments are made, choose the camera through which you want to render the image, and render your scene.

TUTORIAL 3.4   **USING PHOTOS AND IMAGE-BASED LIGHTING**

One of the most exciting features of Poser 7 is Image-Based Lighting (IBL). IBL simulates the ambient colors in a photograph or movie and lights your scene in a way that makes your Poser content appear as if it is part of the environment.

An IBL gets its light information from a *light probe*, which projects a photograph or movie onto a sphere to determine how the light will surround the content in your scene. In most cases, it makes sense to use the same image for your background and for the light probe. Figure 3.20 shows an example of a light probe.

 New to Poser 7 is the ability to use HDRI (High Dynamic Range Imaging) image formats as light probes. For a good overview of HDRI and its purpose in 3D imaging, visit the High Dynamic Range Imaging entry at Wikipedia at http://en.wikipedia. org/wiki/High_dynamic_range_imaging.

FIGURE 3.20   Light probes for IBLs use photographs or movies that are projected onto a sphere to determine the color and intensity of the light hitting the object in your scene.

Although you can use a regular photograph as an image probe, you will get more accurate results with a spherical light probe. There are a couple of utilities that can help you make more accurate light probes. One such utility is HDR Shop, which at the time of this writing is free for noncommercial use and can be obtained from the Institute of Creative Technologies at http://www.ict.usc.edu/graphics/HDRShop/. An alternative is to use Flexify, which is a reasonably priced Photoshop-compatible plug-in available for purchase from Flaming Pear Software at http://www.flamingpear.com/flexify.html.

It is important to note that IBLs are diffuse-only. That is, they don't add highlights to an image. As a result, it's good practice to use other lights in addition to an IBL—for example, you can position a second light in approximately the same position as an IBL and use it for the specular highlights.

When using a standard three-point lighting arrangement with a photographic background, it seems a natural choice to use an IBL as a Fill Light so that you capture the ambient colors from the photograph or movie. If you use an IBL for your Fill Light, you might consider using the Key Light to generate the predominant light in the scene (such as sunlight in an outdoor scene, or a streetlight or the moon in a night scene).

Poser 7 also has a feature that helps achieve more realism when using photos for a background. By default, the ground plane in Poser is set up as a *shadow catcher*. When set as a shadow catcher, the ground plane itself is invisible, but it captures the shadows as if the ground were solid. This allows you to apply realistic shadows to photographic backgrounds. If you align the default ground plane so that the perspective is the same as that in your photograph or movie, the ground plane will render a pretty decent low-cast shadow over the photographic background. It is a quick and simple solution.

 To use the default ground plane as the floor in your scene, go to the Material Room and select the ground plane from the Object menu (Props > GROUND). Near the bottom of the Poser Surface window, uncheck the Shadow_Catch_Only option. This allows you to see the ground plane. To add a texture to the ground plane, click the Diffuse_Color node button and choose the node you want to attach (such as a 2D Textures > Image Map node). You'll learn more about materials in Chapter 4, "Creating Materials."

Adding a Photo Background

In this tutorial, we'll start with a default scene and load James Casual if he isn't already there. Then, we'll add a photograph for the background image:

1. Choose File > New from the menu to create a new scene. Replace the default figure with James Casual (Poser 7 > Figures > Poser 6 > James library).

2. Choose File > Import > Background Picture from the menu. When the Open dialog box appears, open the Content > LindaWhite folder from the CD-ROM, and select the FieryGizzard.JPG photo.

3. Poser tells you that the width/height ratio of the background image is different from your Document window. Answer Yes to adjust the window to match the photograph.

4. This is a very large photo that may take up a lot of room on your screen. To reduce the size of the Document window while maintaining the aspect ratio, first move the Document window so that you can see its lower-right corner. Drag the corner upward and toward the left to resize the window to your preference.

5. If your Document window no longer displays the entire photo, select Window > Document Window Size from the menu. Then click the Match Background button, and choose OK to complete the change.

6. To display the photograph in the background, select Display > Show Background Picture from the menu. You should now see the photograph fill the Document window, as shown in Figure 3.21.

FIGURE 3.21   The background image has been loaded into the Document window.

If you go into the Material Room you will see other options that you can use as backgrounds for your Poser scenes. Choose Background from the Object menu. The Color channel of the Background Palette will be attached to a BG Picture node. Alternatively, you can use a background color of your choice (specified in the BG Color node), solid black (Black node), or a background movie (BG Movie).

Matching the Render Dimensions to the Photo

When you work on lighting changes, you'll probably find that you need a lot of test renders. The usual process is tweak, render, tweak, render, tweak, and render again until you get it right. To render the entire photo in your scene, you'll have to set up the render dimensions so that they match the dimensions of your Document window. Follow these steps:

1. Choose Render > Render Dimensions from the menu. The Render Dimensions dialog box shown in Figure 3.22 appears.

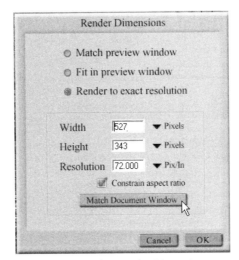

FIGURE 3.22   Use the Render Dimensions dialog box to define the size of your test and final renders.

2. Choose one of the following options:
   - If you want your test renders to remain the same size as the Preview window, choose the Match Preview Window option.
   - To render an image that is larger or smaller than the Document window, first select the Render to Exact Resolution button. Make sure that the Constrain aspect ratio check box is checked so that you maintain the required width-to-height ratio to display the photo properly. Then enter the desired width or height in either the Width or Height field. The other dimension should change accordingly to keep the photo in its proper aspect ratio.

When rendering a scene that uses a background photo, it is recommended that you set the FireFly renderer to Final quality. You'll learn more about rendering in Chapter 16, "Rendering."

Positioning the Camera

Now you'll use poses in the Poser 7 Pose Library to pose James so that it looks like he is walking over the rocks in the river. You'll also use the ground plane as a guide to get the correct perspective while you position James on the rocks.

To position James and the main camera, follow these steps:

1. In the Pose Room, open the Library Palette, and browse to the Poser 7 > Poses > Poser 6 > James Pose > Walking > Walking Library.
2. Make sure that you have selected James Casual. Then highlight the Walk 10 pose, and click the Apply Library Preset button.
3. If necessary, right-click the Camera selection menu in the upper-left corner of the Document window, and select the Main Camera (or, choose Display > Camera > Main Camera from the menu).
4. If you do not see the grid (for the default ground plane) superimposed over the photo, select Display > Guides > Ground Plane from the menu. It will also make it easier to see James' feet if you turn off the ground shadows (from the menu, choose Display > Ground Shadows to uncheck them).
5. Use the Camera Plane controls (the control with hands pointing in four directions) to move the figure back so that James appears in the horizontal and vertical center of the image.
6. Use the camera Trackball control to turn the main camera so that James is walking toward the left-hand side of your screen and so that the perspective of the ground plane matches the perspective in the photo. Figure 3.23 shows a good placement for the camera angle and position.

FIGURE 3.23   Position the camera so that James appears to be walking across the rocks and so that the perspective of the ground plane matches that of the photograph.

Creating and Placing the Image-Based Light (IBL)

Before we create the IBL, we need to delete the default light set. Then, we will add a light and use one of the wacros in the Material Room to create the IBL.

To create the IBL, follow these steps:

1. Choose Window > Python Scripts from the menu, and use the Utility Funcs > Delete All Lights script to delete the default light set from your scene.
2. Use the Create Light icon at the light controls to create a new Spotlight. Change the color of the light to white.
3. Click the Material tab to enter the Material Room. In the Wacros panel at the right, click the IBL button. The Texture Manager dialog box shown in Figure 3.24 appears.

FIGURE 3.24   The Texture Manager dialog box asks you to choose a texture for your light probe.

ON THE CD

4. The Texture Manager dialog box asks you to choose a texture for the image map. At this prompt, you will choose the image that you will use for the light probe. Click the Browse button and locate the Content > LindaWhite > FieryGizzardProbe.jpg image on the CD-ROM.
5. After you return to the Texture Manager dialog box, click OK to exit. Poser asks if you want to activate Ambient Occlusion for this light. This is a feature that prevents light from affecting recessed areas, making shadows appear darker. Choose YES to return to the Material Room.
6. Go back to the Pose Room, and render the scene. In the case of an IBL, it won't matter where you position the light indicator around your scene. The light probe image determines how the scene is lit. Figure 3.25 shows an example of what your scene might look like at this point.

FIGURE 3.25   After rendering your image with the IBL, the scene looks pretty good! But, it can use a little more fine-tuning.

7. After you render the image, you may decide that you want to add some highlights and shadows because IBLs are diffuse-only. Click the Create Light button in the Light Controls to create a second light for the scene.

8. Observe the photograph and notice the direction that the sunlight is coming from. In this case, the sun is almost directly overhead. Judging by the strong shadows at the front of the rocks, the sun is directly overhead with a slight offset behind and to the left. Because the figure is almost in the center of the scene, it won't be difficult to place the light. In the Parameters window, set the xTran, yTran, zTran, and Rotate settings for the new light to zero. This puts the Spotlight on the floor in the very center of the scene and pointing toward your right.

9. Choose Object > Point At from the menu, and point the light at James' left shoulder.

10. Set the yTran setting to around 15. This raises the light well above the figure's head.

11. To move the light back slightly and toward your right, adjust the xTran (left-to-right) and zTran (front-to-back) settings to −1.

12. Render the scene again to check the shadows and highlights. Figure 3.26 shows the final result.

FIGURE 3.26   The second light has added depth to the highlights and shadow in the image.

CONCLUSION

What you learned in this chapter is only the beginning of your adventures with Poser lights. Although it does take a fair amount of tweaking and experimentation to light a scene well, it is worth the time and effort. You should now have a good foundation that will enable you to experiment with lighting on your own. With a little experimenting, you should be able to develop lighting combinations and techniques that work best for your work style and preferences. Don't forget to read Appendix B: Frequently Asked Questions for additional tips and tricks on lighting.

CREATING MATERIALS

In This Chapter

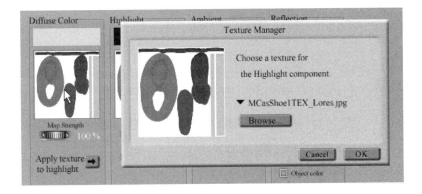

In this chapter, you'll learn to use the Poser Material Room, which has two different views that help you create materials: the Simple and Advanced views. You'll also learn about the various types of maps that are used in Poser (texture, bump, displacement, reflection, and transparency) and how to connect them in the Advanced Material Room view to create procedural shaders.

Poser's Material Room helps you to quickly and easily create and edit complex materials. Although it may initially seem complex, we'll try to show you here how to break things apart and look at them more simply. With persistence and study of the various Material Room settings and nodes, your efforts will be well rewarded.

THE MATERIAL ROOM

You can enter the Material Room in one of two ways: the first way is to click the Material tab at the top of your screen. You can also choose the Render > Materials command to enter the Material Room.

Poser's Material Room contains the following items, which are identified in Figure 4.1:

FIGURE 4.1   The main areas of the Material Room.

Editing Tools Palette (1): These are the same editing tools you find in the Pose Room, with the addition of the Eyedropper tool. The Eyedropper is found on the far right of the Editing toolbar.

Select this tool and click any object or any part of an object to load or edit the material used on the selected part.

Preview Window (2), Camera Control (3), Lighting Control (4), UI Dots (5), and the Document Display Style toolbar (6): These serve the same functions as they do in the Pose Room.

Help (7): By default, Room Help will be visible when you first enter the Material Room. To close the Help window, click on the Close icon (the "X" at the top right of the window). If you close the Help windows in one or more rooms before you save your preferences, Poser remembers your choices.

Material Room Interface Mode tabs (8): These tabs allow you to switch between the Simple and Advanced material editing view formats.

Object List menu (9): The Object List menu allows you to select an object in the current scene. You can also select the Background, Atmosphere, and Lights.

Material Group List menu (10): The Material Group List menu allows you to select any of the materials that are associated with the current object. The current object appears in the Object List menu. See Figure 4.2 for an example of what you might find on the Material Group List menu.

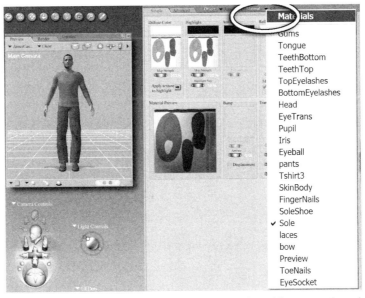

FIGURE 4.2   The Material Group List for the James Casual figure as selected in the Simple view.

Wacros Drawer (11): Wacros are Python scripts created to work specifically with materials. Several predefined wacros cover the most common Material Room tasks. You can create your own wacros scripts and make them available in the User Defined pop-up menu by placing them in the Poser 7 > Runtime > Python > poserScripts > Wacros > UserDefined folder within your Poser 7 installation. This area of your screen is a *drawer*, which means that you can "close" the drawer to hide its contents by clicking on the drawer handle. Click the handle again to toggle the drawer open.

 Python scripts should be installed in the default Poser runtime folder. If you install them in the Downloads folder or in another external runtime folder, they may generate errors.

Node Options pop-up menu (12): This menu only appears in the Advanced material view, where you can click the Node Options menu icon, or right-click anywhere within the Advanced view window, or right-click anywhere within a node. The Node Options menu allows you to cut, copy, paste, delete, apply to all, select all, and invert select nodes. Some options on the menu act upon the currently selected node. Figure 4.3 shows the Node Options pop-up menu.

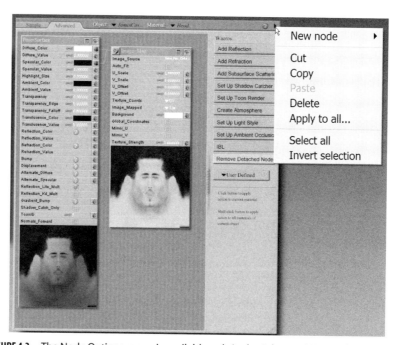

FIGURE 4.3   The Node Options menu is available only in the Advanced Material Room view.

Library Palette (13) and the Animation Drawer (14): These serve the same functions as they do in the Pose Room.

As we mentioned earlier, you can view or edit your materials using one of two views: the Simple or Advanced view. The view that you use depends on how complex your materials are. Simple materials might consist of a diffuse map that provides the color, a bump map that provides grain or bumpiness, and a transparency map that makes some parts of the clothing invisible to add additional detail. On the other hand, Poser's FireFly rendering engine supports the use of procedural shaders, which you build, control, and manage in the Advanced view of the Material Room. If you cringe in fear at the sight of the Advanced material editor, you may be surprised to discover that it isn't as difficult, or confusing, as you might at first think.

THE SIMPLE MATERIAL VIEW

The Simple material room view, shown in Figure 4.4, allows you to quickly assign colors or texture maps for the most common types of materials and material settings used in Poser. Those who are familiar with Poser Pro Pack and earlier versions of Poser will find the Simple material view to be somewhat easier to use than the Advanced view. Here, you can assign texture maps and pertinent settings to diffuse-, highlight-, ambient-, reflection-, bump-, and transparency-maps, as well as view a preview of the texture as you make your changes.

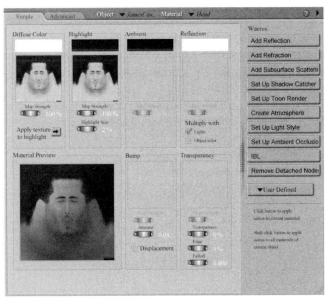

FIGURE 4.4   The Simple view of the Material room.

The Simple view includes a Material Preview pane that shows what your material looks like with the current parameter settings. A tiny yellow caution symbol serves as an alert to adjust the designated setting in the Advanced material view. Just click on the caution symbol to switch to the Advanced view.

To assign an image map to one of the channels in the Simple view, click the square texture preview area. The Texture Manager dialog box opens, as shown in Figure 4.5, and it allows you to select a new or previously used image or movie file.

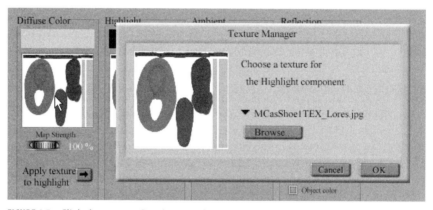

FIGURE 4.5   Click the texture Preview window to quickly access the Texture Manager dialog box.

Ana Winson (known as Arien in the Poser community) is a very talented texture artist and a master in the Poser material rooms. Ana's trademark textures make strong use of the many possibilities that the Poser 7 material room has to offer and are some of the most realistic textures you can find in the Poser community.

In the tutorials that follow, we will take a very close look at the various techniques that she uses in one of the texture variations she created for the Bootie for V3: Deluxe Edition, which are available at Content Paradise and Renderosity. This texture set consists of eight texture maps, which serve the following purposes:

Diffuse Color texture map: Applies color to the clothing (see Tutorial 4.1).
Highlight/Specular map: Determines the color of specular highlights in the clothing (see Tutorial 4.2).
Reflection map: Determines the appearance or shape of highlights in the clothing (see Tutorial 4.3).
Bump map: Adds bumpiness and texture to the clothing (see Tutorial 4.4).

Transparency map: Determines which areas of a texture are opaque and which are transparent (see Tutorial 4.5), and also prevents shininess in transparent areas (see Tutorial 4.8).

Mask map: Determines the areas that should receive stronger highlights (see Tutorial 4.6).

Displacement map: Adds additional shape to the geometry by raising areas of trim in the clothing (see Tutorial 4.9).

Mask 2 map: Determines areas that will receive additional specular highlights (see Tutorial 4.10)

The Booties for Jessi, Kate, Miki, and Terai Yuki 2 are provided on the CD-ROM that accompanies this book. You'll find the texture set discussed here, as well as additional textures by Arien, in the Aset Arts store at Content Paradise (search for Aset Arts or booties at http://www.contentparadise.com) or in her store at Renderosity (http://www.renderosity.com).

ON THE CD

TUTORIAL 4.1   **SIMPLE MATERIALS VIEW: DIFFUSE COLOR**

The Diffuse Color area of the Simple view is shown in Figure 4.6. Typically, an object's Diffuse Color is the primary color before any procedures or modifiers are added to the mix. An object's Diffuse Color can be a single, uniform color; can be based on an image that is mapped onto the surface of the object (a texture map); or can be based on a procedural calculation.

FIGURE 4.6   The Diffuse component of a
shader defines the main color of the object.

You can also have a color tint and an image texture; in which case, your entire image map will be shifted into the direction of the applied Diffuse Color tint. If you do not want to tint your image map, leave the Diffuse Color set to white. It is easy to change the Diffuse Color. Just click on the color slot and pick your desired color.

If you don't like Poser's Color Picker, click the rainbow icon at the top-right corner of Poser's Color Picker to open the system-style RGB picker. Figure 4.7 shows the Poser Color Picker on the left and the RGB Color Picker on the right.

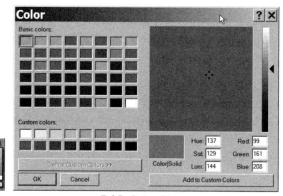

Poser Color Picker   RGB Color Picker

FIGURE 4.7   Two color pickers are available in Poser: Poser Color Picker and RGB Color Picker.

In the steps that follow, you'll learn how to apply a texture to the Diffuse component in the Basic material view. This tutorial will use Arien's diffuse texture created for the V3 Deluxe Bootie. You can use similar steps to assign textures to any clothing.

1. Click the Diffuse Color texture square. The Texture Manager prompts you to choose a texture for the Diffuse component.
2. Click the Browse button, and navigate to the folder that contains your texture map. Textures are typically located in the Runtime > Textures folder, in a subfolder that has been created by the texture artist.
3. In this case, we choose the Arien > Bootie > ba-dominara.jpg texture and click Open. You return to the Texture Manager dialog box.
4. Click OK to assign the texture. Figure 4.8 shows the results.

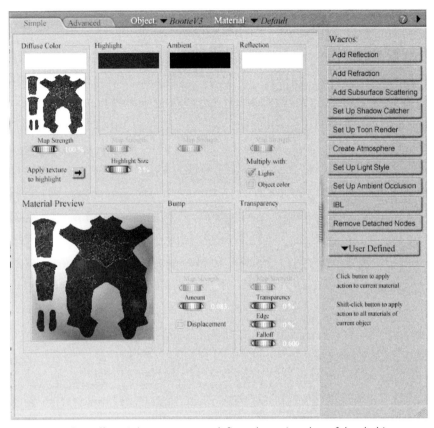

FIGURE 4.8   The Diffuse Color texture map defines the main colors of the clothing.

TUTORIAL 4.2   SIMPLE MATERIALS VIEW: HIGHLIGHTS (SPECULAR)

The most common, and the quickest, method of creating believable highlights on a material is to use the same map (or procedure) for both the base of the material (the Diffusion Color) and the highlights. The Simple view makes this super-easy with a special Apply texture to highlight button in the Diffuse Color section. When you click this button, Poser copies the texture map from the Diffuse Color component to the Highlight component and saves you from having to manually browse for the file. The Highlight component of the Simple view translates into the *Specular root node* in the Advanced view, both of which are shown in Figure 4.9.

Highlights are the areas of your material where the majority of the light's frequencies reflect straight into the camera. They are particularly important for adding realism to eyes, glass, and other shiny materials. Highlights are

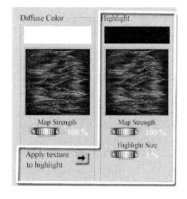

Simple View

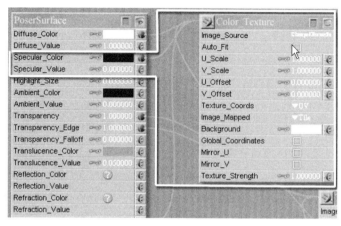

Advanced View

FIGURE 4.9   The Highlight section of the Simple view (left) translates to the Specular node in the Advanced view (right).

usually white, but you can tie them into an image map or a procedural material if you prefer to create more complicated highlight effects. You'll learn more about this in the steps that follow.

You can also vary the highlight color to create some very interesting materials. The type of highlight you create will give visual clues to your audience about the properties of your material: smooth surfaces have sharp "high-key" or white highlights, whereas rough surfaces have soft highlights that pick up some of the color of the material they reflect from. The highlight size and color can greatly affect how viewers percieve your material.

In our continued example of the Bootie texture, you see that Arien's highlight (or specular) map is a grayscale image. White areas in the highlight map will generate the most highlights, and black areas will generate no highlights. Gray areas will generate a varied amount, depending on their closeness to white or black.

To assign a Highlight image in the Basic view, follow these steps:

1. Click the Highlight texture square. The Texture Manager prompts you to choose a texture for the Highlight component.
2. Click the Browse button, and navigate to the folder that contains your texture map. Textures are typically located in the Runtime > Textures folder, in a subfolder that has been created by the texture artist.
3. In this case, we choose the Arien > Bootie > ba-dominara-spec.jpg texture and click Open. You return to the Texture Manager dialog box.
4. Click OK to assign the texture. A thumbnail of the map appears in the texture preview.

5. Click the Highlight color bar to open the Poser color picker. Choose White as the highlight color.
6. Verify that the Map Strength size is set to 100%. Adjust the Highlight Size to somewhere around 6%. Figure 4.10 shows the results.

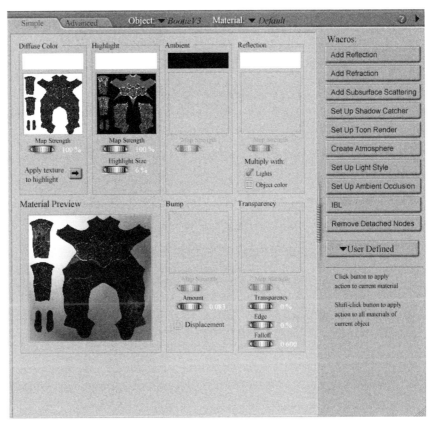

FIGURE 4.10   The highlight (or specular) texture map defines the colors of the highlights in the clothing.

SIMPLE MATERIALS VIEW: AMBIENT

The Ambient section of the Simple view is shown in Figure 4.11. Ambient color simulates the overall lighting condition in the environment. The Ambient color property is a bit different from the others because it isn't affected by the other color properties. In fact, Ambient color is essentially *emitted* from an object. Even if you delete all of the lights, an Ambient color other than black will cause an object to appear self-illuminating! On the other hand, if you set the Ambient color too bright, you will lose all the shadowed areas of the object and create an overall flattening effect on the materials applied.

FIGURE 4.11   Ambient color simulates the overall lighting condition in your environment.

TUTORIAL 4.3   **SIMPLE MATERIALS VIEW: REFLECTION**

The Reflection section of the Simple view is shown in Figure 4.12. There are two ways to configure your material's Reflection component. The Simple view allows you to use a reflection map, whereas the Advanced view allows you to use either a reflection map or raytraced reflections. A reflection map renders very quickly, whereas raytracing usually takes much longer to render.

You can change the tint of your reflection by selecting a color or image (or procedural calculation) in addition to your main reflective element. You also have an option called Multiply with Lights, which creates reflection effects that will be darker where there is no light. The Multiply with Object color option tints the reflection effect with the current Diffuse Color.

Arien's reflection looks almost like the reflection generated from a mirrored ball. There is a good deal of contrast in her reflection map, and it generates very bright reflections in the clothing.

FIGURE 4.12 Reflection maps can be assigned in Simple or Advanced views.

To assign a reflection map in the Basic material view, follow these steps:

1. Click the Reflection texture square. A dialog box prompts you to choose Spherical Map or Ray Trace Reflection. Choose Spherical Map if you want to use a texture map for a reflection source. Choose Ray Trace Reflection if you want to generate reflections from within your scene. In this case, we choose Spherical Map and click OK to continue.

2. The Texture Manager prompts you to choose a texture for the Reflection component.

3. Click the Browse button, and navigate to the folder that contains your texture map. Textures are typically located in the Runtime > Textures folder, in a subfolder that has been created by the texture artist.

4. In this case, we choose the Arien > arien-reflection4.jpg texture and click Open. You return to the Texture Manager dialog box.

5. Click OK to assign the texture. A thumbnail of the map appears in the texture preview.

6. Click the Reflection color bar to open the Poser color picker. Choose Black as the reflection color. Figure 4.13 shows the results.

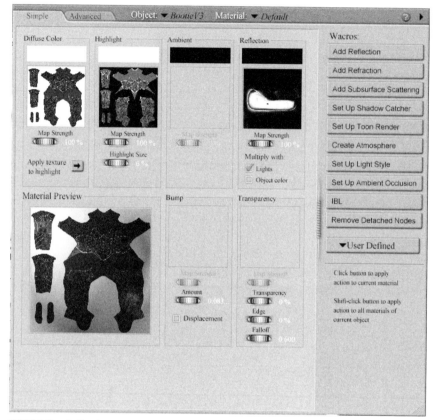

FIGURE 4.13   Reflection texture maps control the appearance of reflections in the clothing.

TUTORIAL 4.4   SIMPLE MATERIALS VIEW: BUMP

The Bump section in the Simple view is shown in Figure 4.14. You can attach an image map to the bump property of your object. The map determines how bumpy your surface appears at each point. Light areas in the map correspond with the highest bump on the surface. Bump maps do not actually modify the underlying mesh; instead, they simulate a uneven surface texture and act upon those areas that are facing the camera. This means that the outlines of your object will not be changed, regardless of how high you make your bump values.

The Displacement option in the Bump section of the Simple view allows you to use the bump map to actually alter the geometry of the surface of your object at render time. This means that your entire object will be affected by the amount of displacement that is applied by the map, including the outline. With displacement mapping,

the surface will be displaced from the original geometry by the amount defined in the Displacement parameter. If you use displacement mapping, make sure you remember to set your Min Displacement Bounds to a value high enough to accommodate the displacement of your materials.

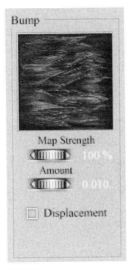

FIGURE 4.14 Bump maps add bumpiness to your object.

Although you can use colored images as bump maps, you may get more predictable results with grayscale images. Black areas produce no bump effect. White areas produce maximum bump effect. Gray areas produce varied amounts of bumpiness, depending on how close to white or black they are.

To assign a bump map in the Basic material view, follow these steps:

1. Click the Bump texture square. The Texture Manager prompts you to choose a texture for the bump.
2. Click the Browse button, and navigate to the folder that contains your texture map. Textures are typically located in the Runtime > Textures folder, in a subfolder that has been created by the texture artist.
3. In this case, we choose the Arien > Bootie > ba-dominara-bump.jpg texture and click Open. You return to the Texture Manager dialog box.
4. Click OK to assign the texture. A thumbnail of the map appears in the texture preview.
5. Reduce the bump Amount setting to .00602. Figure 4.15 shows the results.

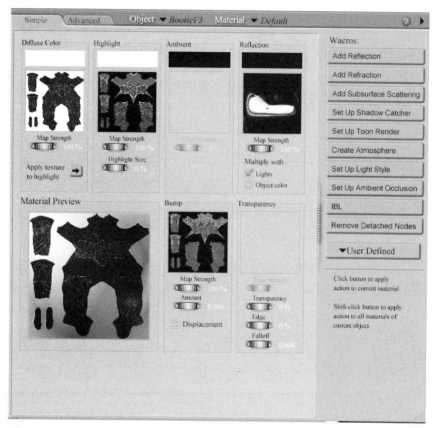

FIGURE 4.15   Bump maps add additional depth and texture to the clothing but it still looks flat when viewed perpendicular to the camera.

TUTORIAL 4.5   SIMPLE MATERIALS VIEW: TRANSPARENCY

Transparency (shown in Figure 4.16 for Simple view) can be determined by a transparency map that is usually grayscale. Each point on an object's surface is determined by the amount of lightness or darkness on the transparency map, with darker values being more transparent. The Transparency value affects the material that faces the camera, predominantly near the center of the object with respect to the camera. Higher Transparency values make the camera-facing material more transparent.

The Edge parameter dictates how transparent the edge of the object will be. As you would expect, a high Edge value makes the edges of the object more transparent. The Falloff property sets the rate at which the transparency becomes more opaque as you approach the edges of an ob-

FIGURE 4.16   The light and dark areas of a transparency map determine which areas of a material are opaque and which are transparent.

ject. A smaller value produces a sharper edge, whereas larger values create a more gradual transition and more of a cloudy-edge effect. If you set the Edge and Transparency to the same values, there will be no Falloff (because there would be no difference between the two values and therefore no transition).

To assign a transparency map in the Basic material view, follow these steps:

1. Click the Transparency texture square. The Texture Manager prompts you to choose a texture for transparency.
2. Click the Browse button, and navigate to the folder that contains your texture map. Textures are typically located in the Runtime > Textures folder, in a subfolder that has been created by the texture artist.
3. In this case, we choose the Arien > Bootie > ba-dominara-tr.jpg texture and click Open. You return to the Texture Manager dialog box.
4. Click OK to assign the texture. A thumbnail of the map appears in the texture preview.
5. Keep the Transparency setting at 100%, but set the Edge to 100% and the Falloff to 0. This will prevent ghosting around the transparent areas. Figure 4.17 shows the results.

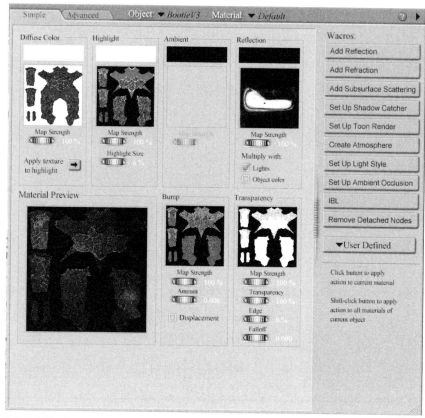

FIGURE 4.17   Transparency maps are used to vary the opacity or transparency of your textures. Black areas in the map are transparent, white areas are opaque, and gray areas are partially transparent.

THE ADVANCED MATERIAL VIEW

The Advanced view is really where you take advantage of the power of Poser's material capabilities, many of which work in conjunction with the FireFly rendering engine. When you open the Advanced view, you'll immediately notice that there are more parameters jammed into a smaller space. The left side of your Advanced view window displays the root node. Depending on what object you have selected in the Advanced view, the root node may have other nodes attached to it. For example, Figure 4.18 shows a material root node with connections to an Image Map node in the Advanced view.

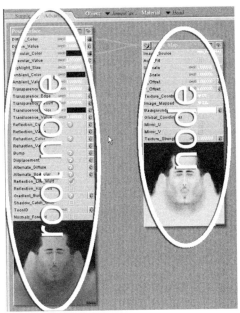

FIGURE 4.18   A material root node with connections
to an Image Map node in the Advanced view.

A node is a building block used in the creation of a material. Nodes
have specific types of inputs, internal parameters, formulas, and outputs,
depending upon what type of node they are.

The root node mixes together all of the material modifiers that are
"plugged in" to it. A material modifier can be a static value, an image, a
color, an algorithm, another node, or any combination of these things.
There are four different types of root nodes that accommodate the various types of items that can use shaders. The most common node is a Material root node, but you'll also find three additional nodes that include
specific properties for backgrounds, hair, and lights.

The Advanced view of the Material Room is like a huge collection of
pipes and control points that can be connected in an infinite number of
ways to create the material you want. Unfortunately, that's exactly what
makes the Material Room seem overwhelming at first.

Here's an analogy: think of the Advanced view as a cookie factory.
Raw ingredients (the various types of nodes) are brought into the system
and mixed via several input pipes (the inputs and outputs of the nodes).
Spices and chemicals are added to change the flavor (the parameters
within the nodes, and the operations they perform). Finally, it all comes
together to be baked in the oven (the root node, which combines everything). The final result is your wonderful-tasting cookie (the resulting
material as shown in the root node preview pane).

The various nodes, when joined together, create a material that is also known as a procedural shader (also interchangeably referred to as a material shader or more simply as a shader). All shaders start with a root node.

Nodes are versatile "black boxes" that act upon the input fed into them and output something else as a result of their unique actions. To connect a node to the root node, you click on the little "plug" icon on the right side of the root node window. From there, choose New Node and expand the menu to display the submenu shown in Figure 4.19.

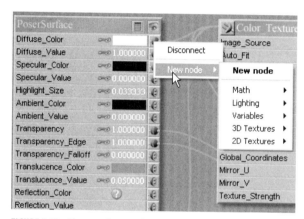

FIGURE 4.19   To attach a node, click the small "plug" icon and choose a node type from the New Node menu that appears.

There are five major types of nodes: Math, Lighting, Variables, 3D Textures, and 2D Textures. Within each major node category, there are several nodes that behave in different ways.

 Chapter 34 of the Poser 7 Reference Manual, "Material Room Nodes," goes into great detail and does a wonderful job introducing each of the nodes available in the Material Room. This is where you'll get a brief description of what each of the parameters, inputs, and outputs of all the nodes do.

Math nodes: Perform mathematical calculations and transformations based on the values of their inputs. The Math node choices are Blender, Edge Blend, Component, Math Functions, Color Math, User Defined, Simple Color, Color Ramp, and HSV.

Lighting nodes: Work with lighting properties. Each of the five categories (Specular, Diffuse, Special, Ray Trace, and Environment Map) has a submenu of additional choices. Some interesting lighting nodes gather light from environmental inputs, such as the *probe-light* (in the Diffuse subcategory) and *gather* (in the Ray Trace subcategory) nodes.

Variable nodes: Return values based on the current point on an object being rendered. These nodes have very cryptic variable names such as N, P, frame_number, u, v, Du, Dv, dPdv, dPdu, dNdv, and dNdu. Their purpose is to look at various values that are being returned at any given point in time. For example, the N node returns the value of the normal at the current point on an object, the frame_number node returns the current frame number, and the v node returns the coordinate in space of the current point on the current object.

3D Texture nodes: Math-based, (often fractal-based), and create output that is calculated for all three spatial dimensions (X, Y, and Z). Many of these nodes can be used to simulate natural materials. Nodes included in this category are fractal aum, fBm, turbulence, noise, cellular, clouds, spots, marble, granite, wood, and wave3d.

2D Texture nodes: Produce output based on 2D transformations (X and Y). You can use these nodes to create 2D patterns such as wave2d, brick, tile, and weave. Two additional 2D textures, image map and movie, allow you to choose image maps or animated AVI or MOV files as textures.

THE ANATOMY OF NODES

The variety and complexity of nodes can be overwhelming when you are trying to select the right node to develop a certain type of material, but after a little bit of practice, you'll get the hang of which groups of nodes work best for your tastes.

A node's output (which appears in the upper-left corner of the node's "black box") can be used as input for any number of other nodes. Wherever you see a "plug" icon on the right side of a root node or a regular node, that indicates that you can plug the output of another node in to affect that parameter. For example, you can feed two images into a Subtract node (a subcategory of the Math nodes) and use the resulting output image to create the Diffuse Color of your material. It is common practice to use the same output to drive several parameters and often helps make the materials and environments more believable. In real life, we often find that many properties of materials affect and are dependant upon each other.

The basic anatomy of nodes is shown in Figure 4.20, where you see the various components that can make up a node. Here you see the root node (1); Output (2); Parameter View toggle (3); Output Preview toggle (4); Input(s) (5); Output Preview pane (6); Animation toggle (7); Material Preview pane (8). Each of these items serves the following purposes:

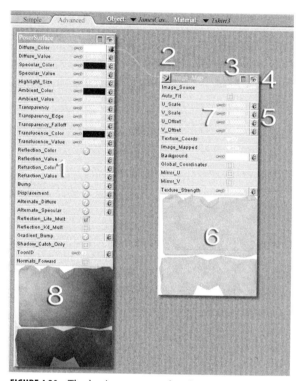

FIGURE 4.20   The basic anatomy of nodes.

Root node (1): The root node is the central gathering point for each shader. It accepts input from various components (colors, settings, and other nodes) to define and create the current material. A root node has no node outputs to connect to other nodes; instead, its "output" is the material shader itself. The root node shows a preview of the material in the Material Preview Pane (8) in real time—a handy feature when editing nodes and making changes to parameter values.

Output (2): Each node (except the root node) has at least one output connector. The output value is based on the functionality of the node, the input(s) fed into it, and the values of the parameters used in its calculations. Outputs are depicted by the male half of a two-pronged electrical plug.

Parameter View toggle (3): This toggles the display of the node's parameter value area.

Output Preview toggle (4): Toggles the display of the node's Output Preview pane (6).

Input(s) (5): All nodes have at least one input connection, although not all nodes require external inputs to function. Inputs are depicted by the female half of a two-pronged electrical plug.

Output Preview pane (6): Displays a preview of the node's current output.

Animation toggle (7): Toggles animation On and Off for the selected parameter. The animation toggle icon is a small key.

Material Preview pane (8): This pane, on the root node, shows a real-time display of the material with the current node and parameter configuration.

Using Nodes

Now that you know a bit about the anatomy of a node, let's examine how you actually handle them:

Parameter values: Nodes typically accept several parameter types. The most common are numbers, colors, image files, and outputs from other nodes. To edit parameter values, click on the number you want to edit and either type the new value in the number field or use the dial to change the current value.

When the parameter is an image file (such as in the Image Map node), click the name of the image source, and use the pull-down menu to browse your hard drive for the image file you need, or select an image that you have already used from the history list.

When the parameter is a color, click the color block to open up the Poser Color Picker. If you would rather use the RGB Color Picker, just click on the rainbow icon at the top right of the Poser Color Picker (refer to Figure 4.7, referenced earlier in this chapter, for the location of the Poser Color Picker).

Selecting Nodes: Click any blank area within the node you want to select. You can select multiple nodes by pressing and holding the Shift key while selecting, or by using the Node Options pop-up menu to Select All nodes or to Invert selection.

Arranging Nodes: The position of a node in your view window will have no effect on its operation. In fact, your material may become so complex that your nodes will "disappear" underneath your Wacros drawer. If this happens, just use the Advanced view scrollbar along the bottom to scroll to those hidden nodes. You may find that you need to rearrange the nodes to get a better idea of how they are interconnected. To move a node, select it and drag it to where you want it while holding down your left mouse button.

Creating New Nodes: To create a node, use the Options menu and progress through the submenus to find the specific type of node you want to create. Clicking on a node's input (or output) icon will also open the Options menu, except, in this case, the only available menu choice will be to make a New node. An alternate way to access the Options menu is to click a node's input (or output) icon and drag to create a wire. When you release the mouse, the Options menu will open up with the option to create a New node. These methods will only work when clicking on empty input and output icons. Just adding a new node won't do any good until you link it up to something.

Deleting Nodes: To delete a node, select and press the Del key. Alternatively you can right-click on the node and use the Options menu to Delete the node.

Linking Nodes: You can click the output icon of one node and drag it over to the input icon of the node you want to connect it to. Conversely, you can start with the input icon and drag to an output of another node to connect those two nodes. After your nodes are connected successfully, you will see "wires" going from one node to the other.

Moving Links: To move a link to another node, just grab the end you want to move with your mouse, drag it to where you want it to go, and then release it. If you want to leave that end unconnected just drop it anywhere on the Advanced view window pane.

Many to Many Links: Remember, you can connect the input and output of a node to as many other inputs and outputs of other nodes as you need! However, an output can only go into another node's input.

Deleting Links: To delete a link, just click on the end you want to disconnect and drag it to anywhere on the Advanced window pane. You can also click on the end of the link you want to delete and use the Options menu to disconnect that end of the link.

Animating Node Parameters: To toggle animation On or Off, click the Animation Toggle icon, the key, for the parameter you want to animate.

Node "Window Shades": When you start working with many nodes in your materials, you might want to minimize the nodes you are not currently focusing on. You can "roll up" a node into a smaller display in a few different ways. You can toggle the display of the Output Preview by clicking on the Output Preview Toggle icon, the "eye" in the upper right of the node. You can also toggle the display of the node Parameters by clicking on the "window" icon just to the left of the "eye" icon. Figure 4.21 shows the nodes in their various minimized and maximized configurations.

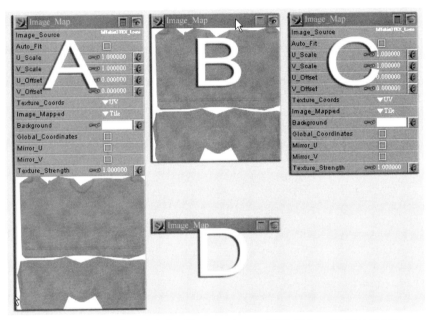

FIGURE 4.21   Nodes can be minimized in several ways: (A) Full View, (B) Parameters hidden, (C) Output Preview hidden, (D) Parameters and Output View hidden.

TUTORIAL 4.6   **ADVANCED MATERIALS VIEW: DIFFUSE ENHANCEMENTS**

The Advanced material view allows you to connect nodes to an Alternate Diffuse channel, which will provide additional enhancements to the normal Diffuse channel. (You'll also notice an Alternate Specular channel that accomplishes the same thing for the Highlight or Specular channel, as you'll learn later.) When you attach an input to the Alternate Diffuse channel, the two inputs blend, based on your settings, to result in a material with more depth.

One way to use the Alternate Diffuse channel is to make modifications to the appearance of the diffuse texture without taking it into an image editor. By making texture modifications in tbe Material Room, you open up a wider variety of results that can be achieved with one set of image maps.

We've been studying Arien's texture throughout this chapter. Now we'll take a look at how she used the Alternate Diffuse input to enhance her Bootie texture. The following example uses a mask image to limit the effects of the Alternate Diffuse channel to the metallic trim parts on the outfit. The diffuse texture is given a color boost through a Blender node that passes the brightened trim through to the Diffuse Color input of the root node.

The following steps show how this effect was accomplished:

1. Click the plug icon on the Diffuse Color input of the root node. Choose New Node > Math > Blender, as shown in Figure 4.22. The image map that was originally connected to the Diffuse Color input will disconnect from the root node.

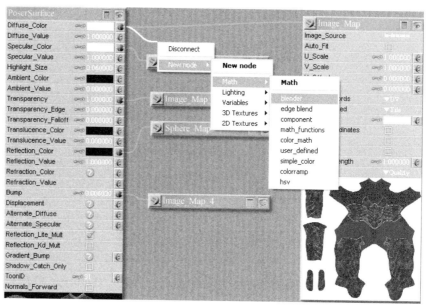

FIGURE 4.22 When you attach a new input to the root node, the old input disconnects from it.

2. Click the Input 1 plug to the new Blender node, and drag the connection link to the output of the image map that you disconnected in step 1.

3. Click the Input 1 color rectangle in the Blender node to open the color picker. Select a middle gray color (somewhere around Red 100, Green 100, Blue 100) for the input 1 color.

4. Click the Input 2 plug to the new Blender node, and drag its connection link to the output of the same image map. Leave its color set to white. Your diffuse connections should now look as shown in Figure 4.23.

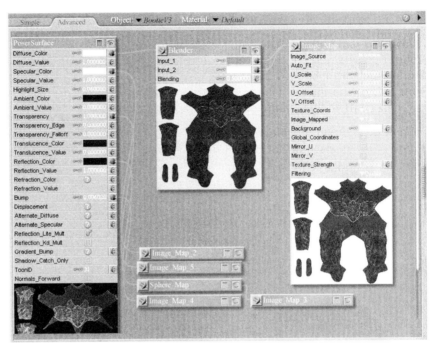

FIGURE 4.23   The Blender node requires two inputs, although they can both be from the same source.

5. By default, the Blender node mixes input 1 with input 2 equally, when you set the Blending setting at .5. However, you can also blend colors by a varying amount throughout your texture, based on the color values in an image map. When you use a grayscale image as an input to a setting, black areas equal a setting of zero. White settings equal a setting of 1. Gray areas are values between 0 and 1, depending on how light and dark they are. With this in mind, you click the Blending input plug in the Blender node, and choose New Node > 2D Textures > Image Map.

6. When the Image Map node appears, click the text in the Image Source field that reads None. The Texture Manager opens and prompts you to locate a texture for the image map source. Browse to the location where your image resides. In this case, we select the Textures > Arien > Bootie > ba-dominara-mask.jpg image as the input for the Blending setting.

7. The black areas in the mask image that you just connected will result in a numerical input of 0, and the white areas of the mask image will pass through the maximum value that is set in the Blending setting. As a result, you want to increase the Blending setting to 1 so that the

mask image has the full effect of the Blending setting. You will notice that the trim on the Blender texture preview becomes brighter, whereas the rest of the texture remains the same. Figure 4.24 shows the final result of the diffuse material enhancements.

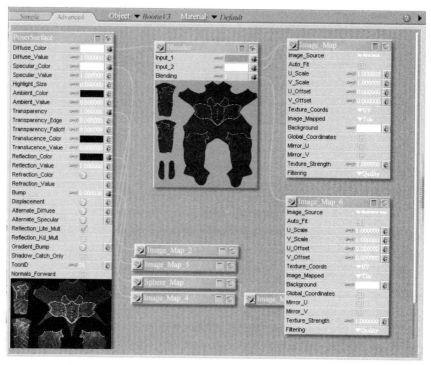

FIGURE 4.24   The enhanced diffuse color texture brightens the trim on the clothing.

TUTORIAL 4.7   ADVANCED MATERIALS VIEW: HIGHLIGHT (SPECULAR) ENHANCEMENTS

In its present form, the sizes of the highlights on the clothing are pretty uniform throughout the clothing. You can vary the size by using a grayscale image map to vary the highlight size in the garment.

You'll notice that the specular map that we assigned in the Basic material view is black and white. This makes it an ideal image to control the highlight size. White areas on the specular map will create the maximum allowable size of highlights (as set in the root node). Darker areas of the specular map will create smaller or no highlights.

To attach the specular map to the highlight size input, simply drag a connector from the output of the specular image map to the Highlight Size input on the root node. The changes will look as shown in Figure 4.25.

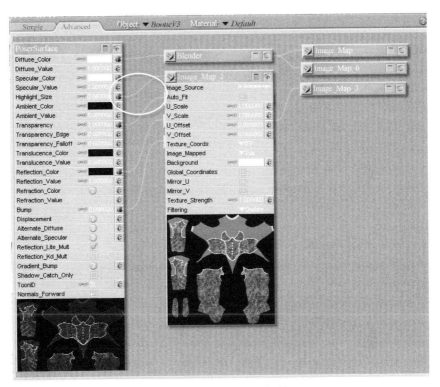

FIGURE 4.25   The size of the highlights can be controlled by a texture map.

TUTORIAL 4.8   **ADVANCED MATERIALS VIEW: REFLECTIONS AND TRANSPARENCY**

There is another issue that we can address in the Advanced material view which cannot be addressed in the Basic material view. Before the release of Poser 5, when Poser did not have advanced material shaders, it was impossible to turn off highlights in transparent areas. If you tried to add highlights to any prop or clothing item that had a transparency map, you would still see shine in the transparent areas of the clothing.

With the Advanced Material Room, it is very easy to provide a solution to this problem. To turn off the shine in transparent areas, simply attach the transparency map to the Reflection Value input of the root node as shown in Figure 4.26. The black areas in the transparency map will turn off the shine and reflection in the transparent areas of the clothing.

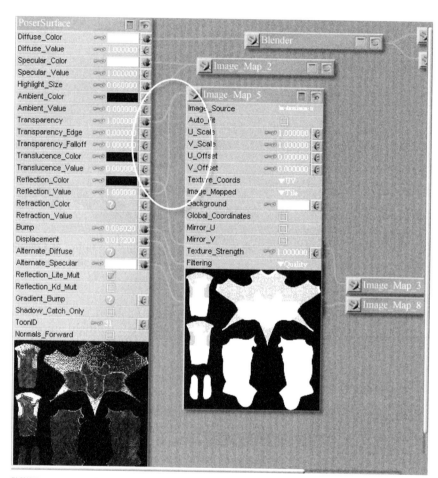

FIGURE 4.26   Attach a transparency map to the Reflection Value input to turn off reflections in transparent areas.

TUTORIAL 4.9   ADVANCED MATERIALS VIEW: ADDING DISPLACEMENT

We mentioned earlier in Tutorial 4.4 that Poser 7 allows you to work with bump maps and displacement maps, and that there was one key difference between these two types of maps. Although a bump map gives the illusion of a bumpy surface, it does not change the geometry. A displacement map, on the other hand, actually does affect the geometry and makes it look more intricate than it actually is. A displacement map can add warts to a face or wrinkles and folds to aged skin, and the geometry will look exactly as if that extra detail had been modeled into the geometry.

In Arien's texture set, she used a grayscale displacement map to vary the amount of displacement in portions of the garment. The white areas in her displacement map recieved the full Displacement setting (set in the root node). The gray areas of the displacement map receive less of an effect.

To assign a displacement map to a material, follow these steps:

1. Click the plug icon on the Displacement input of the root node. Choose New Node > 2D Textures > Image Map.
2. When the Image Map node appears, click the text in the Image Source field that reads None. The Texture Manager opens and prompts you to locate a texture for the image map source. Browse to the location where your image resides. In this case, we select the Textures > Arien > Bootie > ba-dominara-displ.jpg image as the displacement map.
3. Choose OK to exit the Texture Manager. The texture is now assigned to the displacement channel.
4. You won't see the effects of the displacement map until you render the image, and before you render the image, you have to adjust render settings so that the FireFly engine renders the displacement. To do this, choose Render > Render Settings. The Render Settings dialog box opens. If necessary, click the FireFly tab shown in Figure 4.27, and then choose the Manual settings view.

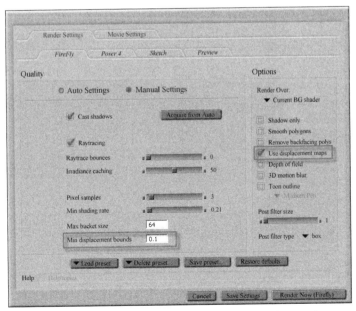

FIGURE 4.27   Choose Render > Render Settings to open the Render Settings window.

5. The Options setting area of the FireFly Render Settings dialog box contains a Use Displacement Maps option. Verify that this option is checked.

6. Near the bottom of the main area of the FireFly Render Settings dialog box, you see a setting for minimum displacement bounds. This setting represents the maximum amount of displacement you will allow throughout the render. It should be slightly higher than the highest displacement setting you use in your scene. Currently, the displacement value for your material shader is at the default setting of .08333. We will temporarily set the Minimum Displacement Bounds setting to .1 to see if we need to adjust the Displacement setting of the material (more than likely, you will have to reduce it).

7. After you set the displacement bounds, use the Area Render feature to do a test render of an area that will be affected by the displacement map. After your render is finished, you'll probably see that the displacement setting is too strong for the clothing.

8. At this point, you will need to reduce the displacement setting in your material until you find a value that is suitable for your clothing. In the case of the material we are using in our example, we reduce the Displacement value in the root node to .0172. Figure 4.28 shows the difference between the default setting (top) and the reduced setting (bottom).

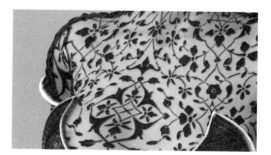

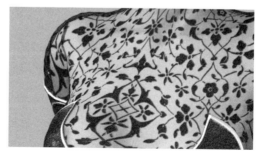

FIGURE 4.28   After reducing the default displacement setting (top) in the root node of the material, the new displacement setting (bottom) looks much better.

9. After you determine the correct setting for your displacement, adjust the Maximum Displacement Bounds setting in your Render Settings window so that it is slightly higher than the value you entered in the root node of your material. If you have more than one object in your scene that uses displacement, make sure that the setting is slightly higher than the highest setting used in the materials in your scene.

TUTORIAL 4.10 **ADVANCED MATERIALS VIEW: ALTERNATE SPECULAR HIGHLIGHTS**

The material shader that we have created so far uses a specular map to create highlights on the outfit. However, you can enhance highlights with the Alternate Specular node in the Advanced Material Room. In the final Material Room tutorial for this outfit, we'll show you how the highlights are enhanced on the lacy portions of the outfit.

1. The first thing we want to do is make the lace a bit glossier. Click the plug icon on the Alternate Specular input of the root node. Choose New Node > Lighting > Specular > Glossy.
2. If you have the texture preview in the root node expanded, you'll notice a *very* large gloss on the base texture. You'll also notice that it covers the whole texture, and we only want the gloss to affect the lacy parts of the image. To accomplish that, we need to use a mask that allows the gloss to affect only the lacy areas. We'll attach the mask to both the Roughness and Sharpness inputs of the Glossy node. First, click the Roughness input plug, and choose New Node > 2D Textures > Image Map.
3. When the Image Map node appears, click the text in the Image Source field that reads None. The Texture Manager opens and prompts you to locate a texture for the image map source. Browse to the location where your image resides. In this case, we select the Textures > Arien > Bootie > ba-dominara-mask2.jpg image as the alternate specular map. The black areas of this image will not affect the underlying texture. Only the white areas of the alternate specular map will pass the highlights on to the final material. Choose OK to exit the Texture Manager. The texture is now assigned to the displacement channel.
4. Now, draw a connection from the Sharpness input plug to the same texture map. Your alternate specular material should now look similar to Figure 4.29.
5. Increase the Roughness and Sharpness settings to .2 each. This increases the size of the reflection on the gloss.

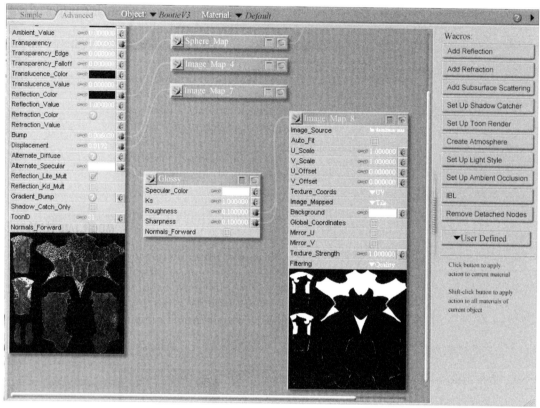

FIGURE 4.29 A mask serves as the input to the Roughness and Sharpness nodes of the Glossy node. This prevents gloss in the black areas of the mask.

6. Now we'll add some noise to the gloss, so that it isn't quite so evenly spread. From the Glossy node, click the Ks connection and choose New Node > 3D Textures > Noise. Leave all settings of the Noise node at their default values.

7. Set the Ks value in the Glossy node to .3 to reduce the effect of the noise. The final Alternate Specular settings should look as shown in Figure 4.30.

To close, we will take a look at how the changes in the Advanced material view affected the clothing. In Figure 4.31, you'll see two renders of the outfit. The render on the left is what the material looked like after all the materials were created in the Basic material view. The render on the right shows how the changes in the Advanced material view affected the

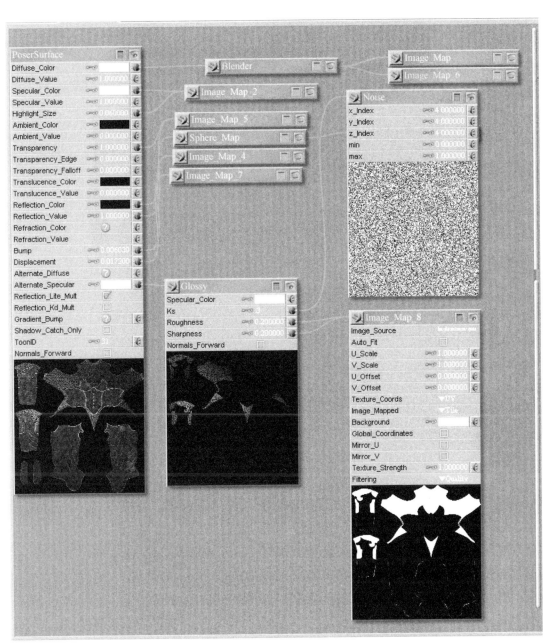

FIGURE 4.30   Alternate specular settings are added to create a varied sheen in the metallic and lacy portions of the clothing.

FIGURE 4.31   Materials created in the Basic material view (left) are made much richer with enhancements in the Advanced material view (right).

clothing. The enhancements in the Advanced Material Room make the clothing more dramatic, and the displacement maps give more depth to the metallic trim, sleeves, and boots.

CONCLUSION

Now that you have first-hand experience creating complex materials, you can see how powerful the Poser 7 material shaders are. You can tackle any material if you just study it and break it down into its components. You've learned that procedural shaders go a long way in making even low-resolution image maps look great.

With the knowledge you've acquired in this chapter, you don't ever have to be satisfied with flat and lifeless default materials again.

5

CREATING CUSTOM FACES

In This Chapter

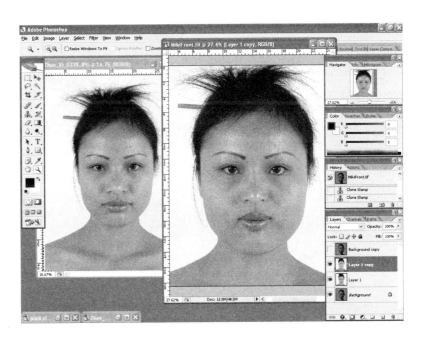

ou can create custom faces in Poser in many ways. The most obvious method is to use the Face Room, initially introduced in Poser 5 and included in all releases through the present Poser 7. This room allows you to customize the faces of the Poser 5, 6, and 7 male and female characters, along with some additional figures developed by e frontier. By importing front and side photos of a person, users can create a wide variety of characters. In fact, through the many facial morphs available in the Face Room, the range of characters that you can create is limitless.

Because a wide variety of third-party figures are also available for use in Poser, you'll learn about a handy Poser 7 feature that works for any figure that contains morphs. With the *Randomize Morphs* Python script, you can create unique faces for other Poser-compatible features.

This chapter gives a brief overview of the Face Room and the various ways that you can apply Face Room heads to your Poser 7 figures. You'll also learn how to use the Randomize Morphs script on other figures to generate new character faces quickly and easily. And, you'll learn the best way to match Face Room heads to your figure's body.

FACE ROOM OVERVIEW

The main areas of the Face Room are shown in Figure 5.1. Each of these areas serves a specific purpose and helps you achieve a wide range of

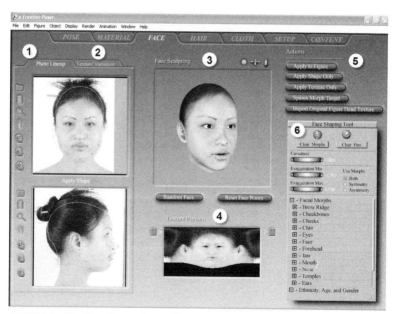

FIGURE 5.1   The Face Room Areas: Photo Lineup (1), Texture Variation (2), Face Sculpting (3), Texture Preview (4), Action Buttons (5), and Face Shaping Tool (6).

characters for your Poser scenes. The following sections give a brief overview of the Photo Lineup, Texture Variation, Face Sculpting, Texture Preview, Action Buttons, and Face Shaping Tool areas.

PHOTO LINEUP

The *Photo Lineup area*, perhaps the most challenging part of the Face Room, is shown in Figure 5.2. Use this area to import front and side photos of the same person and to create a face texture for your character. As you work with the facial outlines and feature points in the Face Room, you will get the best results in the Photo Lineup area if you take your time, save often, and make changes in baby steps.

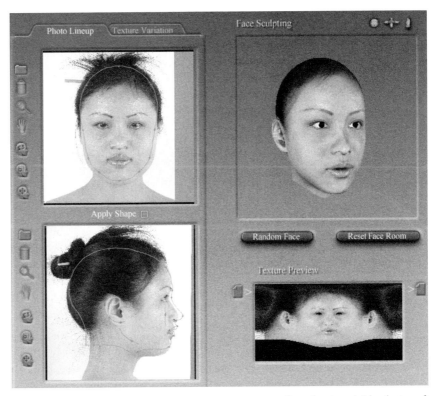

FIGURE 5.2   Use the Photo Lineup area to create a texture from front and side photos of a person.

Most people who are new to the Face Room try to use the Photo Lineup area to both morph and texture the Face Room head to look like the photos they are using. However, when you keep the Apply Shape option checked while you adjust the red outline and green feature points, you quickly end up with a severely distorted head, and you need to start all over again. The best approach is to leave the Apply Shape option unchecked, and use the Photo Lineup area strictly for texture generation.

And on that note, it's also good to prepare your figures so that you get the best results. The following tutorial shows how to prepare your photos so that you get the best results possible when you generate your own Face Room texture.

TUTORIAL 5.1   CREATING TEXTURE GUIDES

The Photo Lineup area of the Face Room allows you to move feature points to match photos. This can often be a very tricky endeavor because head shapes vary from person to person. Differences in gender, age, race, height, and weight can make the shape of the head entirely different from the default figure you are using. As a result, if you try to move the feature points to match your photographs, you can end up with areas in your texture that are stretched or distorted.

So, you can compromise by preparing the photos so that they somewhat match the shape of the head in the photos that you are using. To start that process, you create texture guides that will help you place the photos correctly.

At press time, there are a few figures that have Face Room compatibility, including the Poser 5 male and female (Don and Judy), the Poser 6 male and female (James and Jessi), and the Poser 7 male and female (Simon and Sydney). In addition, e frontier sells more characters that have Face Room support. Among them is Miki, a wonderfully expressive and popular oriental female that is used in these examples.

The following steps were used to create the head guides for Miki. Similar steps can be used to create texture guides for any figure that is compatible with the Face Room.

1. Create a new Poser document, and delete the contents of the scene.
2. From the Figures Library, add any Face Room-compatible figure to your scene. This includes the male and female figures from Poser 5, 6, or 7, along with Miki.
3. Choose Window > Document Window Size. The Preview Dimensions dialog box shown in Figure 5.3 appears. Enter equal values in the Width and Height fields to create a square document. In this example, a value of 400 is entered in both fields. Choose OK to change the document size to the desired window size.

4. Now, you need to configure the render settings so that you render an image at the same aspect ratio. Square textures are more efficient with memory than rectangular ones, and it also helps to create textures that are divisible by a power of 2. Recommended sizes for textures are 512 × 512, 1024 × 1024, and 2048 × 2048. (Poser will not go higher than 4000 × 4000.) To create a texture guide that measures 2048 × 2048 pixels, choose Render > Render Dimensions. The Render Dimensions dialog box appears.

5. You want the render to match the aspect ratio of the Document window size, and you also want to create a render that measures 2048 × 2048. To accomplish this, first select the Render to Exact Resolution option. Then make sure that the Constrain Aspect Ratio check box is checked. Next, click the Match Document Window button. The values in the Width and Height fields should change to match the dimensions of your Document window (400 × 400, in this case).

6. Now, enter **2048** in either the Width or Height fields. The other value should automatically change to match. Click OK to set the new values as shown in Figure 5.4.

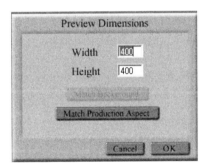

FIGURE 5.3   Create a square Document window for your project.

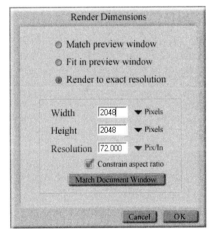

FIGURE 5.4   The Render Dimensions dialog box configures the size of the image that you will render.

7. The goal is to create texture guides from the front- and left sides, so you'll need to create a Front Camera view and a Left Camera view for your renders. You learned how to do this in Tutorial 2.2, "Creating and Saving Custom Head Cameras" in Chapter 2. For Miki's Front and Left cameras, the DollyY setting should be around 43.25, and the Scale setting should be around 12%. After you create the cameras,

save them to the Camera Library so that you can use them again in the future.

8. After you save your cameras, apply the Front camera setting to your scene. Your figure should appear in the Document window as shown in Figure 5.5.

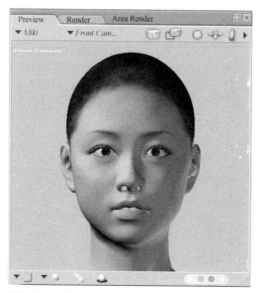

FIGURE 5.5 Start with the Front Camera setting, to create your first texture guide.

9. Because you've already set your Document window size and render settings, it should now be time to render your first texture guide. Choose Render > Render. Default render settings are fine for this purpose. Save the front image to your hard drive in TIF format.

10. Repeat Steps 8 and 9 with the Left Camera, and render the left guide. Now you can use the guides to prepare your photos.

TUTORIAL 5.2   **PREPARING YOUR PHOTOS**

In this tutorial, you'll learn how to use your Face Room guides to assist in preparing your photos for the face room. Although the instructions here use the Miki face guides that were described in Tutorial 5.1, the steps will apply to any other guides that you create yourself.

1. Open an image-editing program that allows you to work with layers (such as Photoshop, Corel Painter, or Paint Shop Pro).
2. Open the Front and Side texture guides that you created according to Tutorial 5.1.
3. Duplicate the render of your guide onto a new layer. This new layer will allow you to adjust the transparency of the guide so that you can see your texture work beneath it. Set the transparency of the layer to 40%.
4. Open the front view of the photo that you want to use in the Face Room (high-resolution photographs, such as those found at *http:// www.3d.sk, Human Photo References for 3D Artists and Game Developers,* will give best results). Paste a copy of the photo into the first image you opened, in between the base layer and the partially transparent copy.
5. Scale the photograph so that the outline of the head stays slightly inside the photo. Figure 5.6 shows an example in Photoshop CS2 up to this point.

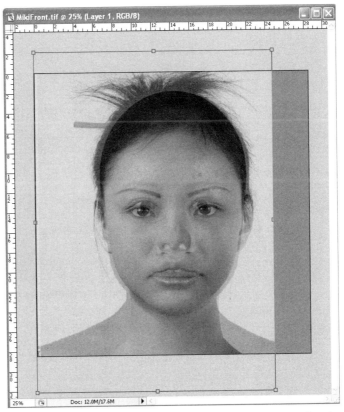

FIGURE 5.6   Load the front photo on a layer beneath the James head outline, and scale the photo so that the outline is within the facial area.

6. Set the photograph layer opacity to 100%, and duplicate the photograph layer. If necessary, move the duplicate photo layer immediately above the first photo layer. Turn the bottom-most photo layer off, so that you see the new layer above the texture guide.

7. Make a selection that surrounds the eyebrows and eyes. Make sure that you have enough area around these features so that when you make the selection smaller, you will cover the features at their original size.

8. Feather or soften the edges of the selection. In this example, we used 20-25 pixels; however, you might need to adjust this depending on how large your own photograph is.

9. Resize and rotate the facial features so that they match up as closely as possible to the texture guide. Figure 5.7 shows an example of what you are looking for.

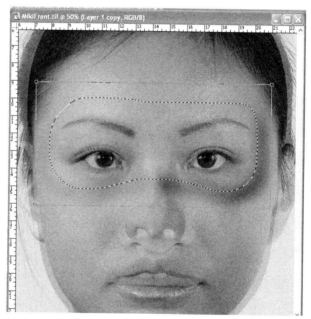

FIGURE 5.7 Scale the features on a copy of the photo layer so that they correspond with those of the Poser figure.

10. Repeat Steps 7 through 9 for the nose and finally the mouth. Now all features should be repositioned to more closely match the features of your base Poser figure.

11. Turn off the transparent guide layer to see how the repositioned features look over the original base photograph. If necessary, use the *Rubber Stamp* or *Cloning* tool to blend areas where needed. Figure 5.8

shows the original photo beside the final version of the front texture, with cloning repairs made where necessary.

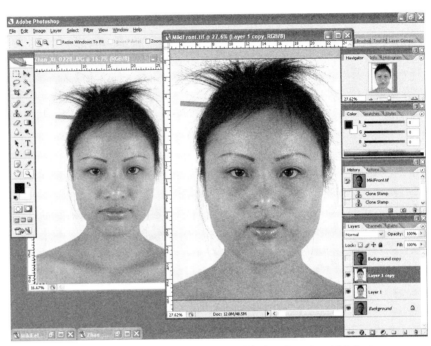

FIGURE 5.8   A comparison of the original photo with the photo in which features are adjusted.

12. Save the front image in the format of your choosing, preferably in a lossless format. The Face Room can accept images in JPG, PNG, BMP, TIF, GIF, and PCX formats. The JPG format is a lossy format, and GIF can only contain a maximum of 256 colors so you want to avoid those for this process.
13. Now for the side view. This view is probably the most critical when it comes to avoiding distortion in the final texture, most especially if the head is tilted differently from the Poser figure. You may have already noticed that if you try to tilt the head outline using the tools in the Photo Preview area, the entire face and texture gets distorted. To prevent this, to tilt the side photo before you bring it in to the Face Room. The texture guide for the side view helps you with this process. Open the left texture guide in your image editor.
14. As you did with the front photo, scale the side view photo to size. The most important step is to *rotate* the head so that it matches the angle

of the head outline. In the case of the source photos used in this example, the head was rotated and scaled very slightly, as shown in Figure 5.9.

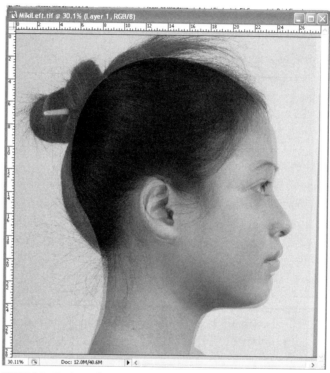

FIGURE 5.9   Scale and rotate the side view until it matches the angle of the head in the side view as closely as possible.

15. Save the side image in the format of your choosing, preferably in a loss-less format.
16. Import the revised photographs into the front- and side views in the Photo Lineup area in the Face Room. You will probably see that the altered photographs make it much easier to create your new face tex-ture with a minimal amount of resizing and moving the feature points. Only move the feature points when you need to refine the texture placement on the 3D model in the Face Sculpting window. Figure 5.10 shows an example of a finished texture after some points have been adjusted.

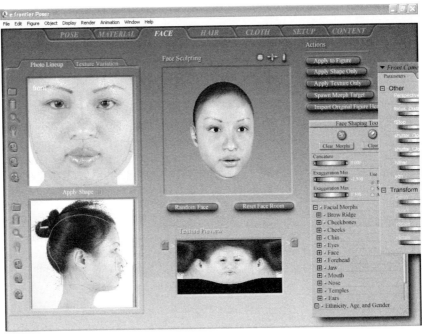

FIGURE 5.10   After you import the revised photos, you will find it easier to create your head texture. Feature points will need minimal adjustment and fine-tuning.

If you are using photographs to create a face texture, you have two options in matching the head texture to the body texture. When you save or try to apply the head texture to the figure in the Pose Room, Poser asks if you want to change the head texture to match the body texture. If you choose Yes, Poser blends your head texture to the body texture by adding a graduated alpha (transparency) edge over the image. This is a good option if you have a body texture that is close in color to the photographs you are using for your figure. If your new texture is too far off, you might have to create an original body texture, using photographs of the same person that you used in the Face Room, or bring both texture maps into your graphic-editing program and make adjustments to the color of the body texture. Even if your texture is far off in color, having Poser blend the head texture down into the body texture may be a good way to get a baseline color and texture area to use when adjusting the rest of the body texture color.

Texture Variation

The Texture Variation area is shown in Figure 5.11. Use the controls in this area to apply color and shading changes that change the ethnicity, sex, or age of the face texture. You can also darken eyebrows or darken the lower face to create a beard.

FIGURE 5.11 The Texture Variation area allows you to alter the texture for ethnicity, age, or gender differences.

To achieve consistent results between head and body textures when adding texture variation, you should start with head and body textures that match. The default Face Room texture may not be same as that used on your Face Room-compatible figure. As a result, you will need to import the head texture that matches the body texture *before* you make your texture variation modifications. The following tutorial shows you how to do this.

If you have one or more light-skinned textures that you like but want to create darker-skinned ethnic characters, there are a number of approaches you can take. One way to darken skin is to use the Material Room to adjust the procedural shaders for the skin. Try darkening the

Diffuse Color for the face texture and body texture by the same amount. Try gray or a tinted gray color to keep from introducing additional colors to the skin tone.

When using Poser 6 figures, an alternative to the manual approach is to purchase the Poser 6 Realism kit, by face_off (which is available at the MarketPlace at http://www.renderosity.com). It is not known as this book goes to press whether an updated version will be made available for the Poser 7 and G2 generation figures. The Poser 6 Realism kit allows you to lighten or darken textures while adding other realistic features such as sheen, bump, and skin imperfections.

TUTORIAL 5.3   MATCHING ETHNIC TEXTURES TO THE BODY

In this tutorial, you'll learn how to match ethnic texture adjustments to the body. This example will use James, the P6 male. After loading James into the scene, we change his appearance with the Texture Variation features in the Face Room. The next step is to apply the altered head texture and change the body texture to match.

To create an ethnic variation of a texture, follow these steps:

1. Create a new scene, and replace the default figure with a Face Room-compatible figure of your choice. In this example, we are using James, the Poser 6 Male.
2. Switch to Texture Preview mode (Display > Document Style > Texture Shaded), and view the document with the Face camera.
3. Click the Face tab to enter the Face Room.
4. We will make the changes to the textures applied to James in the Pose Room, not to the default Face Room texture. From the Actions section, click the Import Original Figure Head Texture button. The Face Room imports the head texture that James is using in the Pose Room.
5. Click the Texture Variation tab to display the options in the Texture Variation area.
6. Expand the Ethnicity, Age, and Gender options, and then expand the Ethnicity options. Set the Less/More African texture variation setting to 1.000.
7. In the Face Shaping Tool area (shown at the right side of the screen in Figure 5.12), expand the Ethnicity, Age, and Gender morph category, and then expand the Ethnicity morph category. Set the less/more African morph to 0.600. Your character should now look as shown in Figure 5.12.

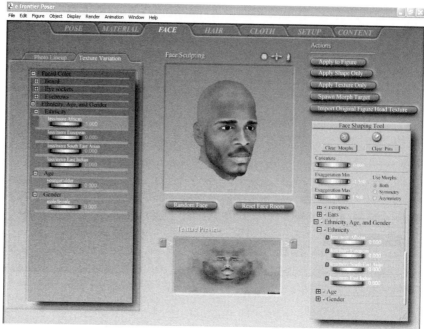

FIGURE 5.12   Changes in Texture Variation and the Face Shaping Tool sections create an African male.

8. In the Actions area, click the Apply Shape Only button to add the face morph to James. He should now have the facial features characteristic of an African male.

9 If you try to apply the head texture to James at this point, Poser automatically generates an alpha map that blends the head texture with the current body texture. Unfortunately, this won't look quite right with an ethnic texture. The way around it is to save the ethnic texture into a separate file and manually apply it to the head in the Material Room. To begin this process, click the Save icon that appears at the right of the Texture Preview area. Poser asks if you want to change the resolution of the texture. Choose Yes to save the texture at 1024 × 1024. Choose the folder to which you want to save the texture, and name it **JamesEthnicHead**. If you intend to add to or improve the texture in your image editor, save the texture to a lossless format such as TIF. If you will use this texture as the final version, you can save it as a JPG file with 100% quality.

10. Click the Material tab to enter the Material Room. Select James as the current figure and the Head as the current actor. You will see the material screen shown in Figure 5.13.

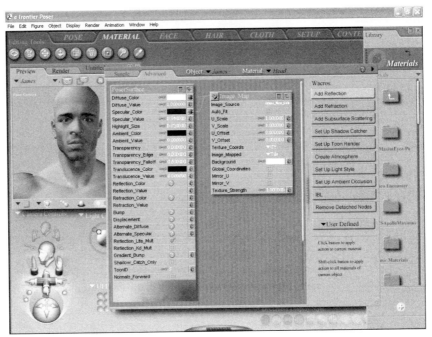

FIGURE 5.13   Change the texture map from the default James texture to the ethnic texture that you created in the Face Room.

11. Notice the Image Map node that is attached to the Diffuse Color input. Click the name of the image map that appears in the Image Source field. The Texture Manager opens and prompts you to locate an image. Locate and select the ethnic face texture that you saved in Step 9, and click OK to apply the change.
12. Now select James' Body as the current material. In the PoserSurface root node, click the white Diffuse_Color swatch (which is white by default).
13. After the Poser color selector window appears, click the tricolored square in the upper-right corner to open the RGB Color Picker. Set the RGB color values to 150, 150, and 150 to create a medium shade of gray as shown in Figure 5.14. The face and body colors should now match.

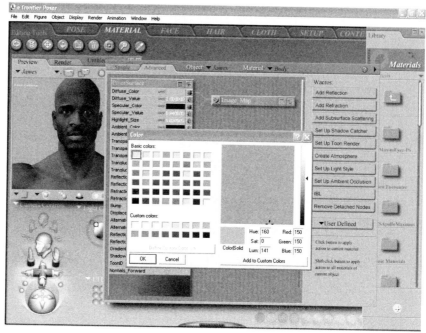

FIGURE 5.14   Change the diffuse color for the body to a medium shade of gray to match the ethnic head texture created in the Face Room.

The Face Sculpting and Face Shaping Tool Areas

Use the Face Sculpting area to view the changes in your face texture while you are moving feature points in the photo lineup area. You can use the mini camera controls in the Face Sculpting area to rotate the head around while you make changes to the texture.

The Face Sculpting area also allows you to visually sculpt, or create, morphs onto your Face Room head. Click the Morph Putty icon (1) in the Face Shaping Tool area, shown in Figure 5.15. Then click on the 3D preview in the Face Sculpting area in the area you want to morph (2). A green dot appears after you click an area that you can morph. Move the dot to reshape the morphs until you are satisfied.

Rather than sculpting the morphs by dragging with your mouse, you can dial-in a face using the many morph dials (3) available in the Face Shaping Tool. You can control the minimum and maximum range of all dials by the values you enter in the Exaggeration Min and Exaggeration Max (4) settings in the Face Shaping Tool.

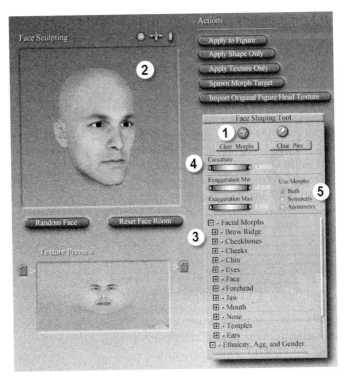

FIGURE 5.15   Preview your textures in the Face Sculpting area (2), and use the *Morph Putty* tool (1) to visually sculpt your head shape.

The Facial Morphs are arranged in the following categories. A value of zero means that the morph has no effect. Negative values morph the feature toward one end of the spectrum, whereas positive values morph the feature more toward the other end. The morphs in italic in the following list add asymmetry to the face, which can make your character look more realistic and natural. The asymmetrical morphs are removed from use when you select the Symmetry option (5) in the Face Shaping Tool.

Bridge (subcategory of Nose): Shallow/Deep, Short/Long, *Transverse Shift.*

Brow Ridge: High/Low, Inner-Up/Down, Outer-Up/Down, *Forward Axis Twist.*

Cheekbones: High/Low, Shallow/Pronounced, Thin/Wide, *Protrusion Asymmetry.*

Cheeks: Concave/Convex, Round/Gaunt.

Chin: Forward/Backward, Pronounced/Recessed, Retracted/Jutting, Shallow/Deep, Small/Large, Short/Tall, Thin/Wide, *Chin Axis Twist, Forward Axis Twist, Transverse Shift.*

Ears: Up/Down, Back/Front, Short/Long, Thin/Wide, *Vertical Shear, Forward Axis Shear.*

Eyes: Up/Down, Small/Large, Tilt Inward/Outward, Together/Apart, *Height Disparity, Transverse Shift.*

Face: Brow-Nose-Chin Ratio, Forehead-Sellion-Nose Ratio, Light/ Heavy, Round/Gaunt, Thin/Wide, *Coronal Bend, Coronal Shear, Vertical Axis Twist.*

Forehead: Small/Large, Short/Tall, Tilt Forward/Back, *Forward Axis Twist.*

Jaw: Retracted/Jutting, Wide/Thin, Jaw-Neck Slope High/Low, Concave/Convex.

Lips (subcategory of Mouth): Deflated/Inflated, Large/Small, Puckered/Retracted.

Mouth: Drawn/Pursed, Happy/Sad, High/Low, Protruding/Relaxed, Tilt Up/Down, Underbite/Overbite, Mouth-Chin Distance Short/ Long, *Corners Transverse Shift, Forward Axis Twist, Transverse Shift, Twist and Shift.*

Nose: Up/Down, Flat/Pointed, Short/Long, Tilt Up/Down, *Frontal Axis Twist, Tip Transverse Shift, Transverse Shift, Vertical Axis Twist.*

Nostrils (subcategory of Nose): Tilt Up/Down, Small/Large, Thin/ Wide, *Frontal Axis Twist, Transverse Shift.*

Sellion (subcategory of Nose): Up/Down, Shallow/Deep, Thin/ Wide, *Transverse Shift.*

Temples: Thin/Wide.

Other morphs in the Face Shaping tool vary the ethnicity, age, and gender of your figure:

Age: Younger/Older.

Ethnicity: Less/more African, less/more European, less/more South East Asian, less/more East Indian.

Gender: Male/Female.

Texture Preview

The Texture Preview area, shown in Figure 5.16, provides a two-dimensional preview of the texture you are creating. The preview is a bit misleading, however, because the Face Room generates square texture maps with one exception: when you import textures for the Poser figures that have rectangular textures and then make texture variation modifications to them, the texture is exported at the same size as the original texture.

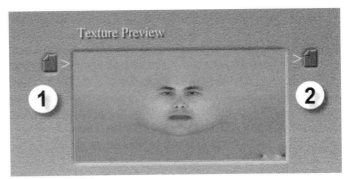

FIGURE 5.16 The Texture Preview area provides a small texture preview of the texture you are creating in the Face Room.

How to Use Third-Party Textures

You may have third-party textures that you want to use on your Face Room-compatible figures. It can be helpful to use those face textures while you create a character morph in the Face Room. To import a third-party head texture into the Face Room, click the Import icon (1) (refer to Figure 5.16) that appears at the left of the Texture Preview area. Locate the face texture that you want to use, and click Open to return to the Face Room. Your third-party head texture should now appear on the head. You are now ready to create your character morph with the Face Shaping Tool.

How to Save Face Room Textures

Because they are created "on the fly," Face Room textures aren't as perfect as those that are meticulously created by hand. They contain smudges, and may be slightly misaligned from the physical geometry of the features. For example, you might notice when you close the figure's eyes that there are unwanted smears on the eyelids. It's important to be aware that Face Room textures contain these undesirable artifacts; however, they still make a great starting point. You can always use the original photos to improve the Face Room texture in an image-editing program afterward.

By default, Poser stores the Face Room textures in PNG format in the Poser 7 > Runtime > textures > faceroom folder, shown in Figure 5.17. The filename is based on the date and time that you applied the texture to the figure. When you edit the faceroomSkin material in the Material Room, it points to the PNG file in this folder.

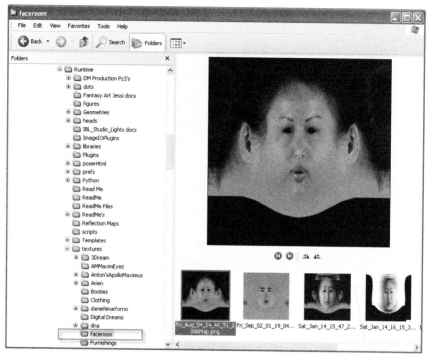

FIGURE 5.17   Poser stores the textures you create in the Face Room in the Poser 7 > Runtime > textures > faceroom folder.

If you want to save the Face Room texture to a folder and filename that you choose, click the Export (2) icon in the Texture Preview area (refer to Figure 5.16), locate the folder in which you want to save the texture, and use a filename and format of your own choosing. Use your custom texture in place of the faceroomSkin material in the Material Room (if you have already applied a Face Room texture).

Action Buttons

The Actions buttons shown in Figure 5.18 are used to apply the shape of the head, the texture, or both to the currently selected figure in the Pose Room.

 If you only have one figure in the Pose Room, the changes will apply automatically. If you have multiple figures, make sure you have the correct figure selected as the current figure before you use these buttons.

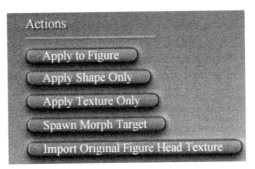

FIGURE 5.18   Actions buttons apply the head,
texture, or both to the figure in the Pose Room.

Each button in the Actions buttons area is described in the following
list:

Apply to Figure: Click this button to apply the head shape and
texture to the currently selected figure. This option replaces the
default James head with the head you created in the Face Room.
If the new texture has sufficient resolution to be larger than 512
× 512, Poser asks if you want to change the texture resolution.
Click No to keep the texture at 512 × 512, or click Yes to create a
larger texture of the dimensions stated in the dialog box. After
Poser generates the texture, you may be informed that the face
color is different from the figure color. Click No to apply the face
texture exactly as you see it in the Face Room (this will probably
require that you create or alter the body texture yourself). If you
click Yes, Poser will create a blend between the Face Room texture and the body texture through the use of an alpha mask. Figure 5.19 shows a blended result.

Apply Shape Only: Applies the shape, but not the texture, to the
figure that is currently selected in the Pose Room.

Apply Texture Only: Applies the texture, but not the face, to the
figure that is currently selected in the Pose Room.

Spawn Morph Target: Adds morph dials for the head, left eye, and
right eye to the figure that is currently selected in the Pose Room.
When set to 1, the morph dials duplicate the face you created in
the Face Room.

Import Original Figure Head Texture: Applies the head texture
from the figure that is currently selected in the Pose Room onto
the head in the Face Sculpting area.

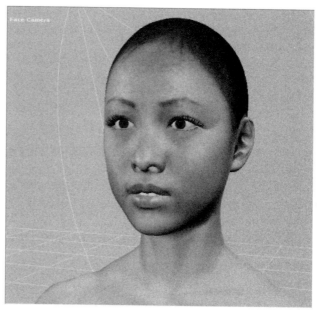

FIGURE 5.19   If desired, Poser can blend the Face Room texture to the existing body texture to create a smooth transition.

TUTORIAL 5.4   **SAVING MULTIPLE FACES IN ONE FIGURE**

Many Poser users like to save one single figure that contains all of their characters. You can use the Face Room to generate a head morph and then apply it to your figure as a morph. Then save the figure to the library after you add the morph. When it's time to create another morph, start with this custom character.

To illustrate this process, we will generate some custom faces with the Random Face button that appears beneath the Face Sculpting area. Choose your favorite Face Room figure for the following steps:

1. Create a new scene, and replace the default figure with your favorite Face Room-compatible figure.
2. Turn off Inverse Kinematics, zero the figure, and turn on Texture Shaded mode. Complete steps for these procedures are found on the CD-ROM that accompanies this book, in the "Building Scenes" file.

ON THE CD

3. Change to the Face Camera so that you can see your figure's face as you create the new characters. Brighten the default lighting, if necessary, so that you can see the facial features more clearly.
4. Click the Face tab to enter the Face Room.

5. From the Actions buttons area, click the Import Original Figure Head Texture button. The default face texture for your figure appears on your Face Room head.
6. It will help create more realistic faces if you set the Caricature value in the Face Shaping Tool to a negative number. For purposes of this tutorial, set the Caricature setting at –1.750. This will help create faces that are more realistic than those created with the setting at its default of 0. Leave the Exaggeration Min and Exaggeration Max settings at their defaults of –1.5 and 1.5, respectively.
7. Click the Random Face button until you get a face that you like. Figure 5.20 shows an example of a nice morph created in this manner.

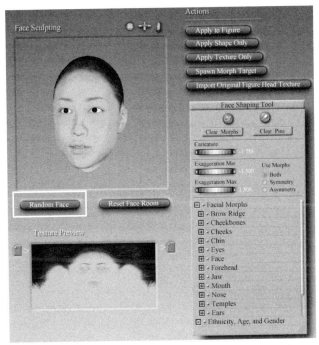

FIGURE 5.20   Click the Random Face button until you get a face that you like.

8. To transfer the face to the figure in the Pose Room, click the Spawn Morph Target button in the Actions area of the Face Room.
9. Go to the Pose Room. Initially, it may not appear as though anything happened. Select your character's head, and open the Parameters Palette if necessary.
10. Scroll down to the bottom of the Parameters Palette, and you should see a new morph category named *Morph*, along with a new morph

named *head*, as shown in Figure 5.21. This is the head that you created in the Face Room. Click the arrow that appears at the right of the morph, and choose Settings to rename the dial to a character name that you recognize as your own.

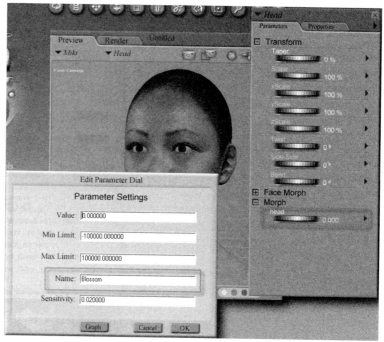

FIGURE 5.21   Your Face Room morph appears in the head as a morph named *head*. Rename it to something that is more descriptive.

11. The eyes also have a Face Room morph associated with them. Click the right eye to select it. In its Parameter window, you'll notice a new morph named *rightEye*. This is the eye morph that is associated with your first Face Room morph. Rename this dial the same as you did the head. Repeat this step for the left eye.

 If you dial the face, left eye, and right eye morphs to 1, the face should appear as it did in the Face Room. Don't forget to dial them back to 0 when you want to use another morph, or you may get unexpected results from the combination of the two morphs.

12. Repeat Steps 7 through 11 for additional characters, if desired.

13. When your morphs are all created and renamed, locate the Figures Library to which you want to save your custom figures. Click the Add to Library icon (the + sign) at the bottom of the Library Palette. The New Set dialog box appears.

14. Enter a name for your multicharacter figure, and click OK. A thumbnail appears in the library. Every time you want to add custom morphs, load this figure into the library, and resave it after you are finished.

TUTORIAL 5.5   RANDOMIZING FACES FOR THIRD-PARTY FIGURES

All is well for the adult figures that are furnished with Poser, including Poser 5 and 6 adult figures. But not all third-party figures work in the Face Room because their geometry isn't compatible.

Although Poser 6 doesn't offer a way to create textures from photos on third-party figures, it does offer a way to create random faces based on the morphs included in a figure's face. You can access the *Randomize Morphs Python script* from the scripts menu. To use the Randomize Morphs script, follow these steps:

1. Create a new Poser document, and add the figure that you want to morph. In the example in this tutorial, we are using Victoria 3, a figure that is available from DAZ3D (*http://www.daz3d.com*) whose morphs work well with this feature.

2. The Randomize Morphs script randomizes all morphs that are present on the selected body part. So if you want to morph only specific regions, you'll have to delete morphs from figures that have them all built in, or inject specific morphs for figures that initially contain no morphs. For example, if you want to create some different noses, keep or add only the nose morphs. If you want to create some different mouths, keep or add only the mouth morphs. If you want to create different facial expressions, keep or add only the morphs that convey emotion.

Chapter 8, "Creating Custom Morphs," goes into more detail about morph creation and management.

3. Select the head of the figure whose face you want to change. Verify in the Parameters window that it contains all of the morphs you want to randomize.

4. Choose Scripts > GeomMods > Randomize Morphs as shown in Figure 5.22.

5. Repeat Step 4 until you find a face you like.

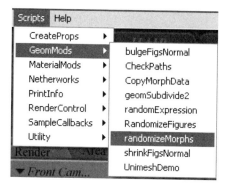

FIGURE 5.22   The Randomize Morphs Python script allows you to randomize morphs on any selected body part of any selected figure.

6. To save the face, choose or create an Expressions Library in which to save the face pose. Then click the Add to Library icon (the + sign) at the bottom of the Library window. The New Set dialog box appears. Click the Select Subset button to open the Select Objects window.

7. The Select Objects window lists all morphs in the face, and they are all automatically selected. If you keep all of the morph settings checked, your face pose will always override the existing expression when you apply it. If you check only some of the dials (for example, those pertaining to the mouth), the library pose will apply the mouth settings and leave the remaining areas untouched. After you make your selections, click OK to return to the New Set dialog box.

8. Click OK again to save the face expression to the library. The Save Frames dialog box appears.

9. If this is a single-frame pose—that is, if you are not animating anything—leave the default selection as Single Frame. If you have created an animated facial pose, click the Multi Frame Animation option, and designate the starting and ending frames to save.

10. Click OK to finalize the save operation. Your pose is added to the Expressions Library.

CONCLUSION

Poser allows you to customize your Poser figures in a number of ways. Through the Face Room, you can create several different characters of varying ethnicities that are based on the Poser 7 male and female (Simon and Sydney), the Poser 6 male and female (James and Jessi) or on the

Poser 5 male and female (Judy and Don). If you have other third-party figures, Poser provides a way to create random expressions for them by using the Randomize Morphs Python script. You can also use built-in morphs on any character and manually dial in morphs that are built-in to your figures.

In the following chapter, you'll learn how to use the Hair Room to add dynamic hair that moves while you animate your figures or add wind effects to your project. This exciting feature adds to the realism of your Poser renders and animations.

WORKING WITH POSER HAIR

In This Chapter

- Types of Poser Hair
- Tutorial 6.1 Using Prop Hair
- Tutorial 6.2 Using Conforming Hair
- Styling Prop and Conforming Hair
- Dynamic Hair
- Tutorial 6.3 Creating a Fur Coat
- Tutorial 6.4 Creating a Feathered Quill Pen

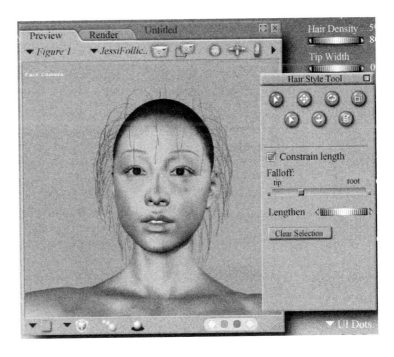

Poser uses three different types of hair: *prop hair, conforming hair,* and *dynamic hair.* In this chapter, you'll learn how to identify each of these hair types, the advantages of each type, and where to find them in your Poser libraries. You'll also learn how to use the Poser Hair Room to create dynamic hair and fur in Poser.

TYPES OF POSER HAIR

Over the years, Poser users have seen increasing realism in the hair objects that have been created for Poser figures. Today we have hair models that look real, along with strand-based dynamic hair that moves quite realistically when animated.

An example of each of the three hair types is shown, left to right, in Figure 6.1. Each of these hair types has strengths and weaknesses, and the following information will help you determine how to tell the differences among them, when to use them, and how to use them.

Prop
Hair

Conforming
Hair

Dynamic (Strand)
Hair

FIGURE 6.1 Poser 6 allows you to use three types of hair: prop hair, conforming hair, and strand-based dynamic hair.

TUTORIAL 6.1   USING PROP HAIR

Hair props were first introduced in Poser 3, where they were found in the Hair Library that we still see in Poser 7. Prop hair uses the HR2 or HRZ extension when saved into the Hair Library. Because Poser 7 can include all three types of hair in the Hair Library, it can be difficult to tell at a glance from the library thumbnails which hair is prop hair and which is conforming hair. Even after you have used the hair in your scene, you may not be able to visually distinguish between prop and conforming hair. To determine whether you are using prop hair, use the pull-down menus in the Document window to display the contents in your scene. Prop hair appears beneath the Props submenu, as shown in Figure 6.2.

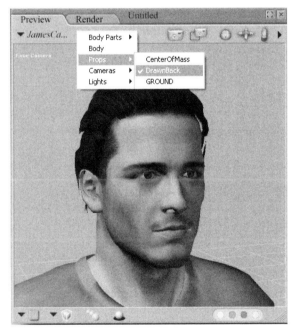

FIGURE 6.2   The menus in the document Preview window list prop hair in the Props submenu.

Of all hair types, prop hair is, perhaps, the easiest to use. Most prop hair models find and attach themselves to a figure's head, although some third-party hair props do not. In addition, prop hair is relatively easy to fit to figures other than those for which they are designed. Simply use the xTrans, yTrans, and zTrans dials to position the hair on the head, and use the xScale, yScale, and zScale dials to scale the hair to fit the alternate figure. It's easiest to do this while your figure is in the "zero pose," before you make any changes to the pose of your figure; otherwise, it can be quite time consuming to match the angles of the head to the hair.

After you reposition your prop hair, select it as the current object, and use the Object > Lock Actor command to lock the hair. Otherwise, the first pose you apply will reposition the hair and you will have to reposition it again.

In this tutorial, you'll add James to the scene, and add prop hair to his head. Follow these steps:

1. Choose File > New to create a new Poser scene. Poser loads the default figure into the scene. Use the Display > Document Style > Texture Shaded command to change the display mode to Textured.
2. Click the default figure to make him the current figure. Then, press the Delete key or choose Figure > Delete Figure to delete him from the scene.
3. Locate the Poser 7 > Figures > Poser 6 > James Library. Highlight James or JamesHiRes, and click the Create New Figure icon (the double checkmark) at the bottom of the Library window to add the James figure.
4. Use the Camera controls, or choose Display > Camera View > Face Camera to get a closer view of James' head.
5. Open the Poser 7 > Hair > Poser 6 > James Hair Library. Highlight the Parted Side hair thumbnail. Note that the thumbnail shows this hair as "trans map" hair but does not identify whether it is prop hair or conforming hair. The term *trans mapped* hair refers to the fact that a transparency map is used to give the prop a realistic look when rendered.
6. Click the Apply Library Preset button (the single check mark) at the bottom of the Library window. The hair should appear in your scene.
7. If your figure has been posed, the hair should appear on the figure's head as shown in Figure 6.3. This happens because the hair is a "smart prop," and it will find the head of the selected figure automatically, whether or not the figure has been posed.

Some older prop hair created by third-party vendors may not automatically attach itself to the figure's head. After you add a prop hair model that you have never tried before, move the head slightly to determine that the hair moves with it. If the hair does not move with the head, reselect the hair as the current object. Then choose Object > Change Parent. When the Choose Parent window appears, select the figure's head as the parent. Choose OK to close the dialog box. Your hair should now follow the figure's head.

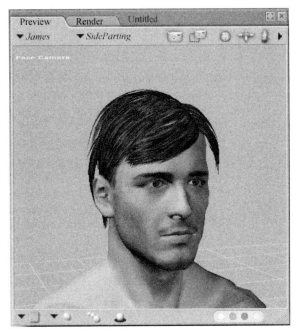

FIGURE 6.3 Prop hair should automatically find and attach itself to the figure's head.

TUTORIAL 6.2   USING CONFORMING HAIR

Conforming hair is slightly different from the prop hair discussed in Tutorial 6.1. Conforming hair was first introduced in Poser 4, with the Conforming Curls hair model.

Sometime after the release of Poser 4, hair props began to look more realistic, thanks to the pioneering efforts of Kozaburo, a prominent member of the Japanese Poser community. He created hair textures for the hair props that were furnished with Poser 4 and made them look much more realistic. Poser enthusiasts really took notice, however, when he added transparency maps and morphs to his own hair models. Transparency-mapped hair had realistic and irregular edges instead of straight, blunt edges. The included morphs allowed the hair props to be styled, lengthened, or shortened.

You will find hair models made by Kozaburo in the Poser 7 > Hair > Poser 6 > Kozaburo Hair Library. These hair sets are preconfigured to fit the Poser figures. Additional hair models are made to fit other popular Poser figures and are available for free download from his Web site at *http:// digitalbabes2.com/*.

Conforming hair contains body part groups in the same manner that conforming clothing does. The body part groups are named identically to those contained in the figure for which the conforming hair was made. For example, long hair that reaches to halfway down a figure's waist will probably contain groups named head, neck, chest, lCollar, and rCollar. You attach conforming hair to your figure with the Figure > Conform To command. When the figure bends or turns its head and neck, the hair automatically bends or turns with the head.

As mentioned earlier, Poser 7 allows you to store conforming hair in the Hair Library. However, most Poser content creators prefer to maintain compatibility with earlier versions of Poser. As a result, you'll most often find conforming hair in the Figures Library, where library items have a CR2 or CRZ extension. When you load conforming hair from the Poser 7 libraries, it appears in the Figures list in the Document Preview window, as shown in Figure 6.4.

FIGURE 6.4   Conforming hair, most often found in the Figures Library, is listed in the Figures list in the Document window.

One limitation of conforming hair is that it will not automatically work on figures other than those for which it was created. For example, a conforming hair object that is created for the Poser 7 female will not work on DAZ's Victoria 4 figure right out of the box. The height, positioning, and scaling will be off.

To make conforming hair conform to a different figure, you'll need to resize and reposition the hair object, and create a new CR2 file that loads the proper joint configurations onto the repositioned hair object. Chapter 12, "From Modeler to Poser Library," discusses the process of creating conforming clothing and hair.

In this tutorial, you'll add Jessi (the Poser 6 female) to the scene, apply a pose, and add conforming hair to her head. Follow these steps:

1. Choose File > New to create a new Poser scene. Poser loads the default figure into the scene. Use the Display > Document Style > Texture Shaded command to change the display mode to Textured.

2. Click the default figure to make him the current figure. Press the Delete key, or use the Figure > Delete Figure command to delete him from the scene.

3. Locate the Poser 7 > Figures > Poser 6 > Jessi > Jessi Library. Highlight Jessi or JessiHiRes, and click the Create New Figure icon (the double checkmark) at the bottom of the Library window to add the Jessi figure to the scene.

4. To pose Jessi, choose the Poser 7 > Pose > Poser 6 > Jessi Pose > Conversation > Happy library. Highlight the Happy Talk 03 pose. Make sure that Jessi is selected as the current object, and click the Apply Library Preset button at the bottom of the Library window.

5. Now, zoom in to Jessi's head with the Face Camera. Use the FaceCam icon in the Camera Controls, or choose Display > Camera View > Face Camera to get a closer view of Jessi's head. Your scene should now look as shown in Figure 6.5.

6. Now select some conforming hair for Jessi. Open the Poser 7 > Hair > Poser 6 > Kozaburo > Jessi Library. Highlight the Long Hair Evo Jessi thumbnail, which is labeled as conforming hair.

7. Click the Apply Library Preset button at the bottom of the Library window. The hair should appear in your scene, but there is something strange going on! Where did Jessi go? Jessi disappeared because you are using the Face Camera, which will focus on the head of the current figure. Because the hair is now the current figure and has a part named "Head," the camera shifts focus on the head part of the hair. Jessi is still in the scene, but because she is sitting down she is lower than the camera can see. If your figure has been posed or is not in the default position, the hair may not appear on the head correctly because the hair loads in the default center position in the scene.

8. Conforming hair "snaps" to the figure after you conform it. To attach the hair to Jessi, verify that the hair object is currently selected. Then choose Figure > Conform To. The Conform To dialog box shown in Figure 6.6 appears.

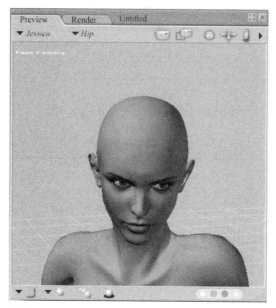

FIGURE 6.5 Jessi is added to the scene and posed. Use the Face Camera to zoom in closer to her head.

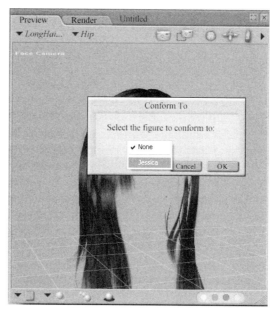

FIGURE 6.6 The Conform To dialog box allows you to select the figure that wears the conforming hair.

9. Choose Jessica as the figure to conform the hair to, and choose OK. The hair then attaches itself to Jessi's head and poses correctly for the pose she is in. The final result as shown through the Face Camera is shown in Figure 6.7.

FIGURE 6.7 With the conforming hair conformed to Jessi's head, the face camera now centers on Jessi's head and hair.

STYLING PROP AND CONFORMING HAIR

Many Poser hair artists add morphs that will lengthen, shorten, or style the hair object. Without morphs, you cannot easily modify the appearance of prop hair or conforming hair.

 You'll learn more about morphs, including how to create your own, in Chapter 8, "Creating Custom Morphs."

When hair props have morphs, the morphs appear in the Parameters window when you select the hair prop. For example, Figure 6.8 shows KiriTe hair (a prop hair set by FK Designs, a vendor at 3D Commune [*http://www.3dcommune.com*]). Although this hair prop was not originally

FIGURE 6.8 Many hair props contain styling morphs that let you easily change the appearance of the hair.

created for Jessi, it only took a simple adjustment to place it on her head. After loading the V3 version of this hair prop, the KiriTe hair is selected as the current object. Then, the yTran value in the Parameters window was set at –.146, and zTran value set at .034. By changing some of the styling morph values above the 0 setting, you can make the hair longer or wavier than the default style.

Although you simply click prop hair to find its morphs in the Parameters Palette, it's not always easy to find styling morphs on conforming hair. The most obvious place to look is on the *head* body part of the conforming hair because most would consider the head group to be the main part of the hair. Sometimes, however, you may find all of the morphs under the *body* part. In addition, extra parts may appear in the hair. An example of extra parts is found in the Aiko 3 Ponytail (available at *http://www.daz3d.com*) shown in Figure 6.9. Here, there are posing controls in the part named *Tail01* that control the bending, shaping, and twisting of the entire ponytail. When styling conforming hair, it is always good to check the Readme document that comes with the hair object. If there isn't one, check through all parts of the hair to see what the morphs do in each body part.

FIGURE 6.9   Conforming hair can contain extra body parts that have their own styling morphs.

Dynamic Hair

Dynamic hair, the third type of Poser hair, was introduced in Poser 5. Unlike the other two types of hair, which are based on polygons and geometry, dynamic hair is strand-based. What this means is that dynamic hair is actually made up of hair strands that "grow" from the prop called *skullcaps* or *follicle sets*. Although you can grow hair directly on a figure's head, skullcaps or follicle sets are necessary to create hair that you can use more than once or to create hair that you can share with or distribute to others.

Dynamic hair has advantages and disadvantages over the geometry-based hair that you have already become familiar with. The key advantage is that dynamic hair can respond to changes in position, movement, and wind forces. Instead of creating morphs that make the hair move, you use controls in the Hair Room to calculate how the hair responds to those forces. You can also "style" (bend and shape) individual guide hairs to create complex hairstyles for your figure without ever having to adjust polygons in a 3D-modeling application.

As an alternative to dynamic hair, you can also take some prop hair models into the Cloth Room and clothify them. Clothified prop hair will respond to changes in position, movement, and wind. Although dynamic hair might behave more realistically, clothified prop hair will calculate faster and be easier on system resources.

The main disadvantage of dynamic hair is that all of the calculations and rendering consume a lot of resources. If your computer is barely above minimum recommended system specs, you may prefer prop or conforming hair because it requires fewer resources.

You'll find very detailed Hair Room tutorials in Chapter 12 of the Poser 7 Tutorial Manual, including information on how to create and group skullcaps. You can access this manual through Poser 7 by choosing Help > Poser Tutorial Manual, or by opening the Poser 7 Tutorial Manual.pdf file located in your Poser 7 > Tutorials folder on your hard drive.

Basic Steps for Dynamic Hair

In this chapter, we'll give only a brief explanation of the Hair Room so that we can move on to some hands-on tutorials that go a bit beyond the examples in the tutorial manual that comes with Poser 7.

To create dynamic hair, you place a skullcap or follicle surface on the figure's head. This gives you a base from which you can grow hair. The skull cap can contain one or more hair growth groups, depending on the style of hair you want to create.

Skull caps are also called follicle sets in Poser 6 and 7. Before the release of Poser 6, most skull caps were positioned exactly where the head geometry lies, which sometimes caused issues when rendered. The follicle sets for Poser 6 were created to sit just below the surface of the figure's head. There are some skull caps for James and Jessi, as well as for the Poser 5 figures, in the Poser 7 > Hair > Poser 6 > SkullCaps Library. You can find follicle surfaces for all of the Poser 6 figures (Ben, James, Jessi, and Kate) in the Poser 7 > Hair > Poser 6 > Follicle Sets folder. You apply them to your figure in the same way that you apply a hair prop.

After you load a skull cap (or follicle set) onto your figure, click the Hair tab at the top of the Poser interface to enter the Hair Room, shown in Figure 6.10. This room contains four main areas: Hair Growth Groups, Growth Controls, Styling Controls, and Dynamics Controls.

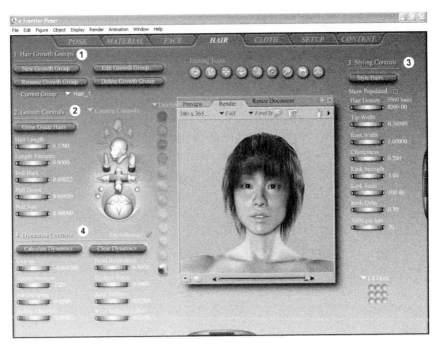

FIGURE 6.10   The four main areas of the Hair Room.

In brief, each of the areas in the Hair Room allows you to perform the functions explained in the following sections (described in more detail in Chapter 12 of the *Poser Tutorial Manual*).

Area 1: Hair Growth Groups

Before you can grow hair on an object, you have to create *hair growth groups* that define which polygons in the object will grow hair. A hair object can contain several growth groups, and each group can be a different length or have different properties such as curliness or how it responds to gravity. Make sure you have selected the correct object on which to grow hair. Click the New Growth Group button and assign a growth group name for the area you want to affect. To specify the polygons in the group, click the Edit Growth Group button, and use the Group Editor to select the polygons. Continue in this manner until you have finished creating one or more growth groups.

Area 2: Growth Controls

Select the group that you want to grow hair on from the Current Group menu in section 1. Then click the Grow Guide Hairs button to grow a starting group of hair. Use the dials or number settings in the Growth Controls area to specify the length and length variance (or "shagginess") of the hair. The Pull Back, Pull Down, and Pull Side controls are not intended for styling. Instead, they define the "base properties" of the hair. For example, hair on the sides of a male head normally pulls back. A buzz cut doesn't pull down at all; it goes straight up, so the Pull Down setting is a negative value. Long hair has more weight in real life, so it should be set to pull down.

Area 3: Styling Controls

The Styling Controls offer tools that help you select, deselect, move, twist, and curl hair. This is where the real styling takes place. Click the Style Hairs button to open the Hair Style Tool window, shown in Figure 6.11. Use the Select Hairs tool to select a group of hairs for styling. After

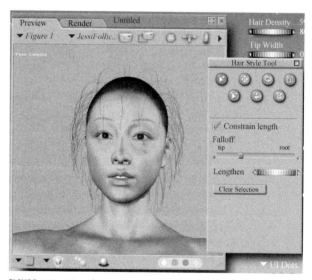

FIGURE 6.11 Use the controls in the Hair Style Tool to translate, curl, scale, or twist hairs.

the hairs are selected, the other tools are activated. You can translate, curl, scale, or twist hairs. Deselect some or all hairs with the Deselect Hairs tool, or click the Clear Selection button to deselect them all. Take note that after you style your hair, you should not adjust the dials in the Growth Controls area, as it will regrow all of the hair, and you'll lose your styling.

When you uncheck the Constrain Length option, hairs will lengthen when you drag them; otherwise, use the Lengthen dial to lengthen or shorten the selected strands. The Falloff slider controls the amount of length in each strand that is affected by your changes. To affect only the ends of the hair, move the slider more toward "tip." To affect the entire strand of hair, move the slider more toward "root."

Area 4: Dynamics Controls

The Dynamics Controls, shown in Figure 6.12, contain settings that define how hair moves during animation, when objects collide against it, or when affected by wind forces. These settings are most important when you are using dynamic hair in an animation. However, they are also useful when you want to render a still image of hair while it is in motion, such as when a long-haired woman turns her head quickly.

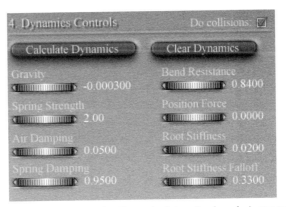

FIGURE 6.12 Dynamics Controls determine how hair moves and responds to motion and wind.

There are eight dynamics controls:

- *Gravity* controls how much or how little the hair is affected by gravity. Higher values weigh hair down more, and negative values cause hair to "float" (which is great for underwater or space scenes).
- *Spring Strength* defines how much hair bounces when in motion (higher values are more bouncy).

- *Air Damping* defines how much or how little the hair reacts to wind (higher values blow more easily).
- *Spring Damping* defines how stretchy it is (lower values allow the hair to bounce longer).
- *Bend Resistance* controls how much or how little the hair is allowed to fold or bend.
- *Position Force* controls how much or how little the hair reacts to dynamic forces. (Higher values cause the hair to remain stiffer and more resistant to movement, collision, and wind.)
- *Root Stiffness* controls the stiffness of the root of the hair (the hair closest to the head).
- *Root Stiffness Falloff* controls how near or far from the head the stiffness range extends.

The Dynamic Controls area also includes a Do collisions check box. When this option is checked, dynamic calculations will take longer, but they will also prevent the hair from intersecting with body parts or other objects that have collision detection enabled. To enable collision detection on a body part or object, select the part or object you want the hair to collide with. Then check the Collision detection checkbox in the Properties window, as shown in Figure 6.13.

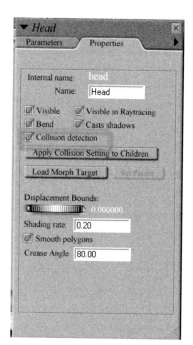

FIGURE 6.13 To prevent hair from disappearing inside a body part or object, select the body part and check the Collision detection option in the Properties window.

TUTORIAL 6.3   CREATING A FUR COAT

Although the obvious use for the Hair Room is to create human hair, it can also serve many other purposes. For example, you can also use the Hair Room to create fur on animals or clothing.

When you create hair for Poser figures, you usually grow the hair on one body part: the head. When you add hair to conforming clothing, each body part (such as the hip, abdomen, or chest) will require its own hair group. As you select each body part, the Group Editor allows you to choose which polygons in that body part should grow hair.

You can grow hair directly on a figure's head, or on an animal, piece of clothing, or other object. However, when you save the hair object to the library, it includes references to the original vertices of the object. Because this referenced geometry is copyrighted information and contained within your hair object, you can only use the object and hair for your own personal use. To distribute a hair product (either free or for sale), the geometry on which it is based must be your own original creation or based on geometry that you specifically have distribution rights to.

Creating the Hair Groups

In the following tutorial, you'll generate the hair groups for each body part in the coat. There are eight body parts in all, each of which will have its own hair group that includes all of the polygons in the body part.

To create the fur coat, follow these steps:

Locate the Tutorials > Chap06 folder on the CD-ROM that accompanies this book. Copy the Runtime files to the Downloads folder beneath your Poser 7 installation (or, to the Runtime library of your choice). This Runtime file contains the content and materials that you will use for the remaining tutorials in this chapter.

1. Choose File > New to create a new Poser scene. Delete the default figure so that the scene is empty. Switch to Texture Shaded display mode (Display > Document Style > Texture Shaded).
2. Select the default Poser 7 > Props > Poser 6 > Jessi Clothing Library, and add *Coat Long* to the scene. This is a conforming coat for Jessi. It appears in the Select Figure pull-down menu as FOverCoat.
3. Click the Material tab to open the Material Room. Open the library that contains the Practical Poser 7 materials mentioned just before this tutorial. You'll find the materials in a folder named Chap06.

4. Make sure that FOverCoat is selected as the current object in the Object menu in the Material Room, as shown in Figure 6.14. Then highlight the *coat* material, and click the Apply Library Preset button at the bottom of the Library window. Poser changes the material to the fur coat texture.

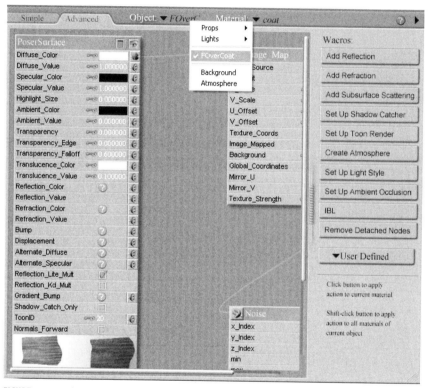

FIGURE 6.14   Select the FOverCoat from the Object menu in the Material Room, and then select coat from the Material menu.

5. Click the Hair tab to open the Hair Room. The coat appears in the Document window with the texture you just applied.

6. Click the bottom section of the coat to select the *Hip* part on the coat. Then click the New Growth Group button in section 1 of the Hair Room. When prompted for a name for the new hair group, name the group **Coat-Hip**. Click OK to continue.

7. Repeat Step 6 for the remaining parts of the coat (abdomen, chest, lCollar, lShldr, lForeArm, rCollar, rShldr, and rForeArm). Name the appropriate sections **Coat-Abdomen**, **Coat-Chest**, **Coat-rCollar**,

Coat-rShldr, **Coat-rForeArm**, **Coat-lCollar**, **Coat-lShldr**, and **Coat-lForeArm**. When you are finished, all of the new hair groups should be listed as props in the current actor pull-down menu, as shown in Figure 6.15.

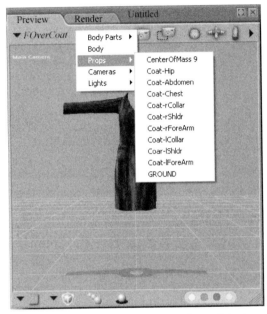

FIGURE 6.15 Create a new hair group for each body part in the coat. The hair groups appear as props in the Current Actor pull-down menu.

8. After you create all of the hair groups, click the hip of the coat. Verify that the Current Group list in section 1 of the Hair Room reads "Coat-Hip."
9. Click the Edit Growth Group button. The Group Editor opens.
10. To assign all of the polygons in the hip, click the Add All button in the Group Editor. All of the polygons in the hip turn red.
11. Continue through all body parts in the coat in a similar manner. As you click each body part in the Document window, its associated hair growth group becomes active in the Group Editor. Click a body part in the Document window, and then click the Add All button in the Group Editor. Continue in this manner until you work through each body-part group and add all of the polygons. Close the Group Editor after all polygons have been assigned.

Adding the Hair

After you create all of the hair growth groups and assign the polygons, you can grow the hair on each part. Start again with the hip, and work your way up as you add hair to each section until they are all complete. Proceed as follows:

1. Click the hip of the coat, and verify that Coat-Hip is the currently selected hair growth group.
2. In the Growth Controls section, click the Grow Guide Hairs button. Hair appears on the hip section of the coat. Initially, it is rather long and sticks almost straight out.
3. Set the Hair Length to 0.2500 and the Pull Down at 0.00300. This decreases the length of the default hair strands and pulls them downward.
4. In the Styling Controls section, set the Hair Density to 2500 (17149 hairs) to make the hair on the coat more full. These numbers will vary, depending on your geometry. Then reduce the Verts per Hair setting from the default of 20 down to 4. This will consume fewer resources and make the hair render more quickly. Also, to make the hair a little thicker than the default, increase the Tip Width setting to 0.60000 and the Root Width setting to 1.50000. Your coat should look similar to Figure 6.16.

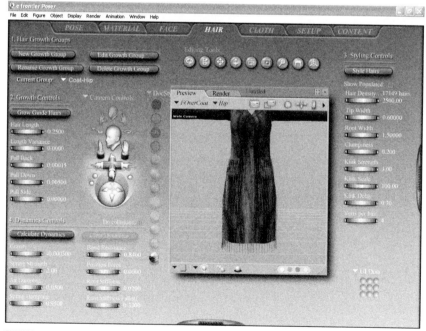

FIGURE 6.16 Fur is added to the hip section first.

5. Repeat Steps 2 through 4 for the abdomen, chest, right collar, and left collar (settings for the sleeves follow next).

6. Click the right shoulder to select it in the Document window. Set hair length to .2500 (the same length as all of the others). But instead of setting Pull Down to .0005, set Pull Side to .0005.

7. In the Styling Controls section, set the Hair Density to 2500, reduce the Verts per Hair setting to 4, increase the Tip Width setting to 0.60000, and set the Root Width setting to 1.50000.

8. Repeat the settings listed in Steps 6 and 7 for the right forearm.

9. Click the left shoulder to select it in the Document window. Again, set hair length to .2500. Set the Pull Side to -.0005 (note the negative number).

10. In the Styling Controls section, set the Hair Density to 2500, reduce the Verts per Hair setting to 4, increase the Tip Width setting to 0.60000, and set the Root Width setting to 1.50000.

11. Repeat the settings listed in Steps 9 and 10 for the left forearm. When you are finished, your coat should look as shown in Figure 6.17.

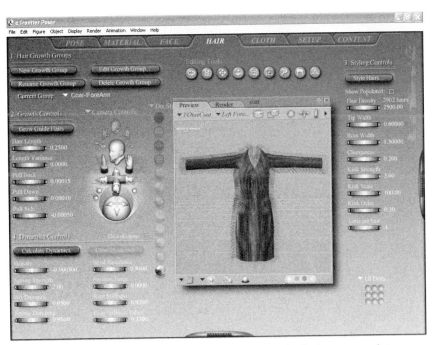

FIGURE 6.17   Using similar settings in all parts of the coat, the fur is now complete.

Changing the Hair Material

If you try to render the fur coat at this point, you'll notice that all of the fur uses the default light-blonde hair color. The Practical Poser 7 materials that you added to your Runtime contains a hair material that picks up the colors from the underlying texture that you applied at the beginning of this tutorial. To add this material to your hair sections, follow these steps:

1. Click the Material tab to open the Material Room.
2. Navigate to the Runtime Library that contains the Practical Poser 7 materials that you installed for this tutorial.
3. Locate the Materials > Practical Poser 7 > Chap06 Library. You will find two materials for the fur coat. Highlight the material named *Fur-CoatHair*.
4. From the Object menu in the Material Room, select Props > Coat-Hip, as shown in Figure 6.18.

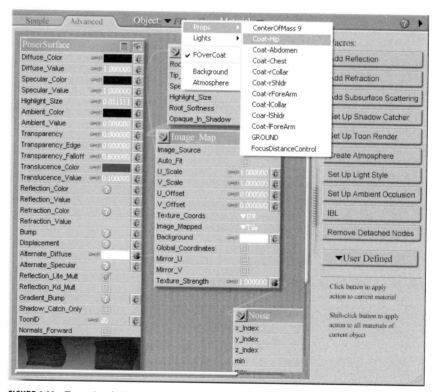

FIGURE 6.18   To assign hair materials to the coat, select the hair growth groups from the Props list.

5. Double-click the FurCoatHair material in the library to change the Coat-Hip material. The material will change to a hair node that uses the fur coat texture map to determine the coloring in the fur.

6. Select each hair growth group (shown earlier in Figure 6.19) one at a time, and change the hair materials until they are all complete.

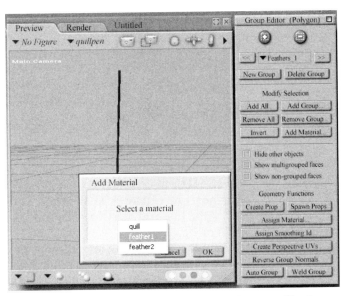

FIGURE 6.19　Select the feather1 material for the first row of feathers.

7. Conforming clothing should be saved in the Figures Library. Choose or create a Figures Library folder in which to save the fur coat. Click the Add to Library button to save the conforming fur coat to the library. The New Set dialog box prompts you for a name. Enter **Fur Coat**, and click OK. The coat is saved to the library.

TUTORIAL 6.4　CREATING A FEATHERED QUILL PEN

You don't have to limit the Hair Room to creating hair and fur—in fact, it's a great solution for grass, plants, and other natural objects such as feathers. In this tutorial, you will use the Hair Room to complete the feather of a quill pen.

To create the quill pen, follow these steps:

1. Create a new scene in Poser, and delete the contents so that the stage is empty.
2. Choose File > Import > Wavefront OBJ. The Import Options dialog box appears.
3. Uncheck all options so that you import the quill pen at its original size and in its original position. Click OK to continue. The Import: Wavefront OBJ dialog box appears.

4. Locate the folder that contains the library files that you installed from the Practical Poser 7 CD-ROM. Open the Runtime > Geometries folder, and highlight quillpen.obj. Click Open to import it into the empty scene.
5. Click the Hair tab to open the Hair Room. A Help screen opens in HTML format. If you haven't already read it, you'll find some useful tips and instructions in the file. Close the file when you're finished.
6. Use the Camera Controls to move in closer to the quill.
7. Verify that the quill pen is selected as the current object. Then click the New Growth Group button in section 1 of the Hair Room. Name the new growth group **Feathers 1**. Click OK to assign the name.
8. Click the Edit Growth Group button. The Group Editor opens in Polygon mode.
9. It is much easier to assign polygons by predefined materials than to select polygons in the Group Editor. The quill pen contains three material zones named *quill*, *feather1*, and *feather2*. The quill material is for the part of the pen that will not have hair. The feather1 material is for the feathers that will grow out in one direction, and feather2 will grow hair in the other direction. To pick one of the feather materials, click the Add Material button in the Group Editor. Then select feather1 from the dialog box shown in Figure 6.19.
10. To create the second feather growth group, click the New Growth Group button in section 1 again. Name the new group **Feathers 2**. Feathers 2 automatically becomes the current growth group in the Group Editor.
11. Click the Add Material button, and choose feather2 from the Add Material dialog box.
12. Close the Group Editor after you create the second growth group.
13. Select Feathers_1 as the current growth group from the menu in section 1, as shown in Figure 6.20.
14. Click the Grow Guide Hairs button in section 2 of the Hair Room. Guide hairs grow out from the top and right side of the pen.
15. In the Growth Controls section, change the Hair Length to .3. Set the Pull Down setting to –.0005 so that the hairs bend upward a little bit.

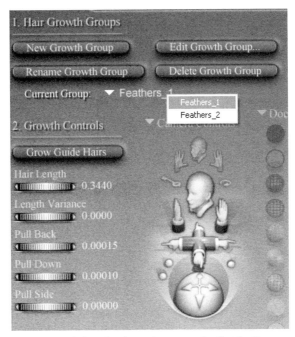

FIGURE 6.20   Select Feathers_1 to grow the first feather section.

16. Now, to create the feathers on the quill. In the Styling Controls section, set the hair density to 7500. To make the hairs a little thicker, increase Tip Width to 1 and Root Width to 2. Set the Kink Delay to .5 so that the feather starts to curve a bit farther from the root. Finally, reduce the Verts per Hair setting to 6. Render to see the results. Your feather should look similar to Figure 6.21.

17. Select Feathers_2 as the current growth group from the menu in section 1.

18. Click the Grow Guide Hairs button in section 2 of the Hair Room. Guide hairs grow out from the top and right side of the pen.

19. In the Growth Controls section, change the Hair Length to .3. Set the Pull Down setting to −.0005 so that the hairs grow upward a little bit.

20. In the Styling Controls section, set the hair density for the second feather group to 7500. Increase Tip Width to 1 and Root Width to 2. Set the Kink Delay to .5, and reduce the Verts per Hair setting to 6. Render to see the results. Your feather should now look similar to Figure 6.22.

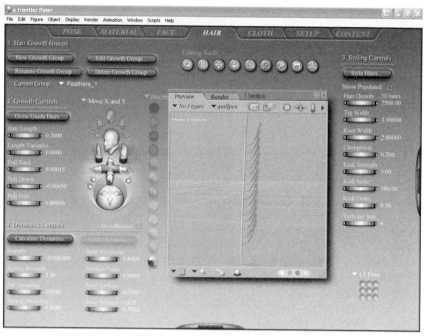

FIGURE 6.21 The first side of the feathers have been added.

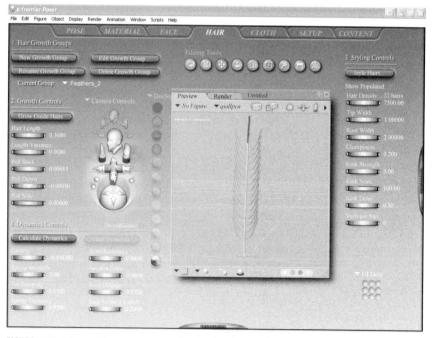

FIGURE 6.22 The quill pen now contains feathering on the right- and left sides.

21. Click the Style Hairs button in the Styling Controls section to refine the feathering if desired. For example, the ends of the feathering branch out into two rows of vertices. You can select both rows of vertices, and use the Scale Hairs tool to bring the ends closer together. You can curl or twist the feathers to make the pen fancier, or you can shorten or lengthen specific hairs as desired.

22. When you are done with the quill pen, go back to the Practical Poser 7 Props Library. Click the Add to Library button (the + sign) at the bottom of the Library window. Poser informs you that you should save the hair along with its parent prop. Click OK to continue.

23. In the New Set dialog box, enter **Feathered Pen** for a name. Click the Select Subset button to open the Select Objects dialog box shown in Figure 6.23.

FIGURE 6.23   Hair groups (Feathers_1 and Feathers_2) should be saved to the library with the underlying prop (quillpen).

24. Check quillpen, Feathers_1, and Feathers_2 in the Select Objects dialog box. Then click OK to return to the New Set dialog box. Click OK again to save the pen to the library.

CONCLUSION

The Hair Room not only helps you create hair and fur for humans and animals, but with some creative thinking, you can use it for other natural elements such as grass, sea anemones, flowers, pine trees, and feathers. In this chapter, you learned some creative uses for the Hair Room and how to save your furry conforming clothing and props to the libraries. With imagination and patience, you can continue to use the Hair Room for more than hair and fur—the rest is up to you!

7

WORKING WITH POSER CLOTHING

In This Chapter

- Types of Poser Clothing
- Common Clothing Problems
- Cloth Room Overview
- Creating and Saving Dynamic Clothing
- Tutorial 7.1 Loading the Content
- Tutorial 7.2 Creating Multiple Simulations
- Tutorial 7.3 Calculating Multiple Simulations

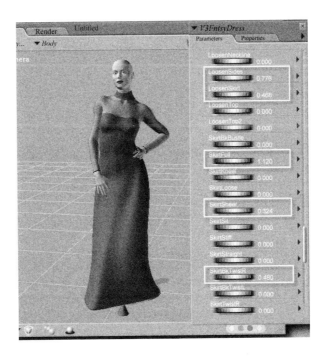

TYPES OF POSER CLOTHING

Poser 7 allows you to work with several types of clothing and props. *Conforming clothing*, which automatically poses with the figure that wears it, is only one type of clothing that Poser figures can wear. You can also use *dynamic clothing* in Poser's Cloth Room. The Cloth Room allows you to turn clothing props into garments that respond to movement and wind in animation and drape over the figure in a more realistic manner. You'll also learn about other ways that you can use props for clothing.

Conforming Clothing

Conforming clothing typically appears in the Figures Library, where it uses a CR2 or CRZ extension. Poser 7 also allows conforming clothing in the Props Library with a PP2 or PPZ extension. When it appears in the Poser 7 Props Library, the library thumbnail designates it as conforming clothing.

It's very easy to apply conforming clothing to a figure. After you add your character to the scene, browse through the Figures Library until you find clothing that was created specifically for the figure you are using. Then, click the double checkmark to add the clothing to your scene (the single checkmark will replace the currently selected figure). To "attach" the clothing to your figure, make sure that the clothing item is still selected. Then choose the Figure > Conform To command to place the conforming clothing onto your figure. After that point, the clothing automatically poses along with the figure.

ON THE CD

For a more detailed tutorial on adding conforming clothing to a figure, refer to the tutorials that are included on the CD-ROM that accompanies this book. You'll find a complete tutorial in the pracposer7/CD2-BuildingScenes.html page.

When you add conforming clothing to your scene, it appears in the Select Figure menu, just under the Preview tab in the Document window. If it does not have a unique name assigned to it, it appears in the list as "Figure n," where "n" is the lowest available number when you added the figure to your scene. To rename the clothing to something more recognizable, select the clothing object, choose its body part as the current actor, and rename it in the Properties window as shown in Figure 7.1.

Conforming clothing presents some challenges, especially when it comes to posing skirts and dresses. The main issue is that conforming clothing will only fit the figure that it was specifically made for. We'll discuss some of these issues later in this chapter, in the section titled "Common Clothing Problems." You can also obtain utilities that will help convert clothing from one figure to another. One such utility is Wardrobe Wizard by Phil Cooke (PhilC), which you can purchase from his web site at *http://www.philc.net*.

FIGURE 7.1   Conforming clothing appears in the Select Figure menu. Select the body and rename the clothing in the Properties window.

Dynamic Clothing

Dynamic clothing, in Poser terms, is a prop. You will always find it in the Props Library, where it will have a PP2 or PPZ extension. You attach dynamic clothing to a figure with the Figure > Set Figure Parent or Object > Change Parent commands. Figure 7.2 shows an example of a dynamic dress, which is being worn by DAZ3D Stephanie Petite.

Aside from some construction guidelines, there isn't really a lot of *technical* difference between dynamic clothing and the other types of accessories and props that you can use in Poser—that is, until you want to use it in the Cloth Room. Unlike conforming clothing, you need to *clothify* the prop (turn it into "cloth") and perform dynamic calculations that make the clothing move with the figure in a very realistic manner.

There is one thing about dynamic clothing that might initially seem confusing. Even if you intend to create a still image, you need to create an animation that makes the clothing fall into place. The animation allows Poser to calculate how the clothing will drape and fall on the figure over a series of frames.

FIGURE 7.2   Dynamic clothing makes use of the Cloth Room to create realistic draping and folding.

Basically, the simplest way to perform calculations is to start with your figure in the default pose in the first frame of your animation. Pose the figure in the final pose in frame 15 or later. By allowing a minimum of 15 frames for the simulation calculations, your figure will change from the default pose toward the final pose in small steps. The clothing will softly drape over the figure appropriately until it reaches the final pose. Then the remaining frames in the simulation will allow the clothing to drape naturally for the pose. The cloth will drape and fold to follow the natural contours of the figure. For a more thorough explanation of the process, refer to Chapter 11 of the *Poser 7 Tutorial Manual* (Help > Poser Tutorial Manual) before completing the dynamic clothing tutorials in this chapter.

Props and Smart Props

You will, on occasion, find accessories that don't fit into either of the previously mentioned categories and are considered props. Accessories such as hats, glasses, and jewelry are most often found in the Props Library and have a PP2 or PPZ extension.

Props can behave differently, depending on whether they are standard props or smart props. The difference between them isn't readily obvious, until you know what to look for. Standard props and smart props both appear in the Props Library, and both appear as Props in the Current Actor menu of the Document window.

Where you do notice the difference is after you add them to your scene.

Standard Props

Standard props initially appear in your scene in their default "as modeled" position. Generally, this is in the exact center of the stage. If you already have other content located in the center of the stage, there is a chance that you won't be able to see that the prop was properly loaded into your scene.

It is much easier to attach a prop to a figure when the figure is in its zero (or default) pose. It takes more time to place a prop on a figure that is already posed because you have to translate and rotate it precisely to position it correctly. You'll have to manually position a standard prop with the editing tools or with the Trans and Rotate dials in the Parameters window. After that, you'll need to parent the prop to the figure by selecting the prop and choosing Object > Change Parent. Make sure you attach the prop to the appropriate body part (such as the head for a hat or earrings, or the hand for a ring or a sword). Afterward, whenever you move the parent body part, the prop should move as well.

Refer to the pracposer7/CD2-BuildingScenes.html tutorial, included on the CD-ROM that accompanies this book, for more information on how to put a figure in its "zero pose."

ON THE CD

Smart Props

Smart props already know what they are supposed to be attached, or *parented,* to. Basically, a smart prop is a standard prop that was saved to the library *after* it was attached to the appropriate body part. When you load a smart hat, for example, it finds the head and positions itself at or near the correct position and at the same angle of the figure's head. Figure 7.3 shows some examples of smart props that are included in the Jessi Clothing Props Library. The hat, glasses, and earrings all find their way to the correct places when you add them to Jessi. If the hat is made for a different figure, however, you may need to adjust the scale or position with the Parameter dials.

To "unattach" a prop from a figure, choose Object > Change Parent, and select Universe as the new parent of the prop.

FIGURE 7.3 Smart props appear in the Current Actor menu and automatically find and attach themselves to the proper body part.

COMMON CLOTHING PROBLEMS

Let's say you've added clothing to your figures, and something doesn't seem right. Body parts stick out. The clothing doesn't pose correctly, or it doesn't pose at all. Sometimes you add items from the library and you don't see clothing at all! What's going on, and how do you fix it? The following sections anticipate some of the more common problems that Poser users face and explain how to prevent them from occurring.

Clothing Doesn't Conform Correctly

Basically, for conforming clothing to work properly, you have to use clothing that was built for the figure that wears it. The main reason for this is because each figure has its own body shape, along with unique *joint parameters* that tell Poser how to bend and blend the body parts when you pose them.

If clothing is made for a different figure from the one you're working with, it may not be enough to rescale the clothing so that it fits around the figure correctly. To work properly, conforming clothing must also use joint parameters that are extremely close, if not identical, to the figure that wears it.

It isn't always easy to determine if you have the right clothing, especially because several Poser figures have been released in multiple versions.

For example, DAZ3D Victoria 1 and 2 share the same basic body shape and joint parameters, but Victoria 3 is built a bit differently. As a result, clothing made for Victoria 3 will not fit properly when placed on Victoria 1. Figure 7.4 shows an example of this. Because the joints on the two figures are different, *poke-through* is most evident in extreme poses.

FIGURE 7.4   Clothing for Victoria 3 is applied to Victoria 1 (left) and Victoria 3 (right). The differences in joints are most evident in extreme poses.

If your clothing doesn't seem to conform properly, here are some things that you can check:

Use clothing that is made for the figures you are using: Pay attention to the figures that you are using, and select clothing made for those figures. At the same time, be aware that there may be other "generations" of a figure that use different clothing parameters.

You accidentally posed the clothing and not the figure: You're not alone with this mistake. When you work with conforming clothing, it's all too easy to apply a pose to clothing instead of to the original figure. If you catch it right away, you can undo the operation with the Edit > Undo command. You can also reconform the clothing to the character with the Figure > Conform To command. A third option is to open the Joint Editor (Window > Joint Editor), select the clothing that is not posed correctly, and click the Zero Figure button in the Joint Editor to get the clothing back to its default state. Then apply the pose to the human figure.

The arms and legs bend when conformed: You're certain you are using the right clothing, but when you conform it to the figure, the arms and legs bend. This is a common symptom when clothing is saved in a nonzero pose. Select the clothing and zero the pose with the Joint Editor as mentioned in the previous paragraph. Then choose Edit > Memorize > Figure. Resave the new memorized version to your Figures Library under a new name, and use your fixed version in place of the original.

Fixing Poke-Throughs

Even when you put the right clothing on the right character, there will be times when you see skin poking through the clothing. In fact, you probably noticed it earlier in Figure 7.4, when you compared Victoria 1 and Victoria 3 posed in a tight-fitting catsuit.

If you frequent the Poser communities, you'll probably notice that tight-fitting clothing is quite common. Although it's obvious that one of the reasons is because people like to create images of beautiful women in sexy clothing (a *mild* understatement in Poserdom), another reason is because tight-fitting clothing is easier to create and use than looser-fitting clothing, which requires adjustments in the joint parameters (not an easy task!).

One solution is to fix problem areas after you render, using an image editor to blend or clone surrounding areas over the skin that shows through the clothing. However, you can address them before you render your scene. Here are some ways that you can fix poke-throughs in Poser before you render:

- Select the body part that is poking through the clothing. Open the Properties panel, and uncheck the Visible check box to hide the offending body part, as shown in Figure 7.5. Repeat this for each body part that is poking through the clothing.
- Sometimes a body part is only partially covered by clothing, so you won't have the option of hiding it. In cases like these, select one of the problem sections in the clothing or the body of the clothing. Check the Parameters window for morphs that loosen the clothing in the offending body part, and use them to adjust the clothing.
- Another option to address partially covered body parts is to do two renders, one with the body part visible and another with the body part invisible, and then composite the two images in your favorite graphics editor. If you decide to use this method, you can also take advantage of Poser 7's Area Render feature and only re-render that small section of your scene as needed.

FIGURE 7.5   Select a part and uncheck the Visible check box in the Properties window to hide a body part that pokes through clothing.

- For clothing that does not have sizing or adjusting morphs, use the x-Scale, yScale, or zScale dials in the Parameters window to scale the body part down, scale the clothing part up, or do a combination of both.
- Use magnets or Poer 7's new morphing tools to alter the shape of the clothing so that it fits better. These tools shape and morph any object in Poser. You'll learn more about them in Chapter 8, "Creating Custom Morphs."

When Body Shapes are Different

Many Poser figures offer morphs that change the overall body shape. Busty, buxom women and muscular, heroic men pervade the Poser art galleries, but when you try to create and dress one of your own, the figure bursts out of his or her clothing like the Incredible Hulk going through his metamorphosis. The morphed figure of James shown in Figure 7.6 shows you an example of this.

Having the ability to create your own characters is part of the fun of Poser. But what fun is it if they don't fit into their clothing? Certainly there must be a solution. Actually, there are several:

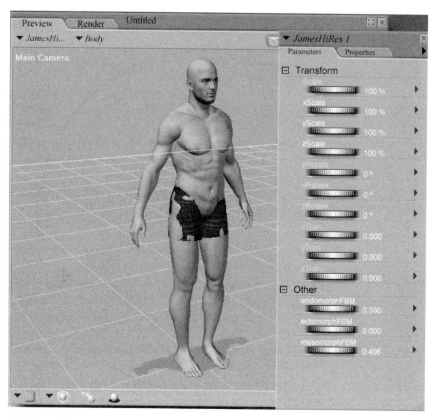

FIGURE 7.6 When you morph figures into custom characters, you also have to morph clothing to fit.

- If you are using DAZ3Dfigures (Michael, Victoria, Stephanie Petite, David, Aiko, and others), many DAZ original conforming clothing products include most, if not all, of the morphs that the figures include. Other merchants that make clothing for DAZ3D figures include morphs that are compatible with only the most popular body morphs. When body morphs are included, a complete morph list usually appears on the DAZ3D product information pages. Use the same morph settings in the clothing as you did when you created your character.
- When conforming clothing does not contain body-shaping morphs, you can use utilities such as The Tailor (available at *http://www.daz3d. com*) or Wardrobe Wizard (available at *http://www.philc.net*) to help create them. The Tailor allows you to alter clothing made for a particular figure so that it fits a morphed version of the same figure. Wardrobe Wizard is a Python script that converts clothing from one Poser figure to fit another. This utility supports clothing conversion

between many of the popular Poser figures and boasts excellent support and frequent updates.

At the time of this writing, The Tailor requires the use of CR2s that are manually edited to remove all references to the Center of Mass props used for Auto Balancing in Poser 7. These extra parts result in errors when you try to open CR2 files that have been saved in Poser 7 libraries. The Tailor version 1.6 (or later) resolves this incompatibility.

- If you're a do-it-yourself type of person, you can use Poser's magnets or an external 3D modeling program to morph conforming clothing so that it fits your custom figure.
- Use dynamic clothing, and the power of the Cloth Room, to morph the clothing for you. Dynamic clothing is very easy to morph so that it fits custom figures. A full explanation of the process is included in Chapter 11 of the *Poser Tutorial Manual.*

Posing Skirts

Before dynamic clothing was introduced in Poser 5, one of the "holy grails" of Poser was the development of skirts and long robes that moved and posed realistically. Although dynamic clothing fills that void quite admirably, the quest for the ultimate conforming skirts still exists. In fact, of all the types of conforming clothing that you can use in Poser, the most difficult to develop and use are dresses, skirts, and robes.

The reasons for their difficulties are due, in part, to the technicalities involved in making Poser objects. When dividing the human character into body part groups, the right and left legs are separated by the hip. To pose automatically with a figure, the clothing must be divided in the same manner. That means that skirts, dresses, and other long robe-like garments have to be divided that way as well.

For dresses and similar clothing, you will often find right- and left thighs serving as the legs of the skirt, and a full-length hip section separates the two sides. Because of this, the skirt has no shins, so it doesn't bend at the knees. Additionally, the center hip section remains fairly rigid and serves as the blending zone between the two legs. As Figure 7.7 shows, this design makes it difficult to achieve sitting poses in all but very short skirts. The middle hip section of the dress has a tendency to stretch and distort the texture when legs are moved sideways, forward, or backward.

As a result of these limitations, long dresses and skirts usually look their best with standing poses, and even then, mostly in poses where legs are not spread too far from their original, straight position. To remedy some of these problems, *body handles* began to appear in Poser clothing and accessories.

FIGURE 7.7   Long conforming skirts present problems in sitting positions.

Using Body Handles

As early as 2000, even before the release of Poser 5 and dynamic clothing, there was discussion in the Poser community about different ways to approach the morphing and posing of figures and clothing. Developers on the Poser technical boards began discussing the possibility of using *phantom* or *ghost body parts* (parts that are not actually visible on the body or clothing but exist in the underlying hierarchy structure) to pose and otherwise manipulate clothing and figures. The challenge was developing them in such a way that the "average Joe" would be able to use them without too much difficulty.

As a result of the discussion regarding ghost parts, body handles as we know them today were introduced during the first quarter of 2002. This ingenious method of posing figures adds extra ghost parts to the figure's standard hierarchy. For example, in addition to the upper body parts, the abdomen, and the hip, a dress might have another extra part named "skirt." To pose the skirt, you drag a little piece of geometry called a body handle, which is typically shaped like a cone or a sphere. These body handles allow the user the freedom to work with clothing that poses in part with the character and in part by manual interaction.

Although body handles can be used in long hair, beards, and extra clothing parts, you see them used most often in long dresses, robes, and other flowing clothing. The solution for dresses is to make the skirt as one group—the hip, or a different group named skirt (or something similar). The body handle appears centered beneath the figure, generally below ground level.

Figure 7.8 shows the DAZ Morphing Fantasy Dress for Victoria 3. Notice the cone-shaped body handle beneath the clothing. When you pose the figure, you can drag the body handle to position the skirt appropriately for the figure's pose.

FIGURE 7.8 Drag the body handle, shown here as a cone, to position the clothing appropriately for the pose.

After you pose the clothing with the body handles, you will typically find morphs that will improve the flow of the clothing. For example, in the DAZ3D Morphing Fantasy Dress, several morphs appear in the Body that widen, loosen, flare, twist, and otherwise style the pose of the dress. Figure 7.9 shows an example of some of the morphs in use.

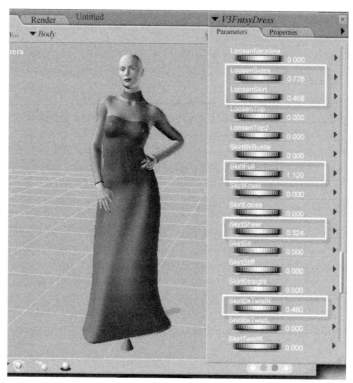

FIGURE 7.9 Clothing with body handles typically includes additional styling morphs that adjust the fit of the clothing.

Posing Shoes

Shoes come in all shapes and sizes, ranging from sandals to thigh-high boots. For the most part, shoes conform to the feet in much the same way as other conforming clothing. As long as shoes are relatively flat, there isn't a lot of extra work involved to pose them.

The exception to this is shoes that have high heels. Because clothing is typically modeled around figures that are in their default pose, high heels look extremely strange when you first put them on your figure. The position of the shoes on the feet makes it look like your character has just stepped on a banana peel and is about to slip and fall. The heels are usually below ground level and appear to be poking through the floor. Figure 7.10 shows an example of high-heeled shoes that are added to a foot that is in its default pose.

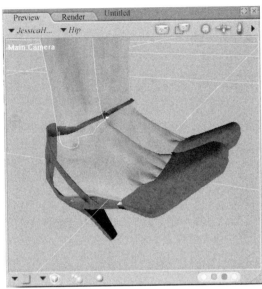

FIGURE 7.10 High-heeled shoes look unnatural when they are added to feet that are posed in their default positions.

The solution to the posing of the feet is pretty obvious. You'll need to angle the front of the foot downward and possibly (but not all the time) angle the toes upward. While doing so, you also have to make sure that the shoes are landing properly on your floor or on the ground.

ON THE CD

Let's use Jessi's Shoe Heel R and Shoe Heel L as examples. If you've followed the basic tutorials on the CD-ROM, these are the same shoes that you added in the *CD-2-Building Scenes.html* tutorial. For these shoes to land properly on the floor, you have to bend each foot 35 degrees. After that, you'll need to raise or lower Jessi's hip or body so that the feet rest properly on your floor. The easiest way to do that is to use an Orthogonal Camera (Left, Right, Front, or Back) to view your scene without perspective. Zoom in on one of the feet, and make sure you see the plane of the floor or surface as well. Select the hip or body of the figure, and move the yTrans dial up or down as necessary to place the foot on the surface as shown in Figure 7.11.

Clothing Doesn't Load from the Library

There may be times when you add conforming or dynamic clothing to your scene and don't see it appear on your figure. If this happens, verify that you have selected your clothing from the Figures or Props Library, instead of the Poses Library, as shown in Figure 7.12.

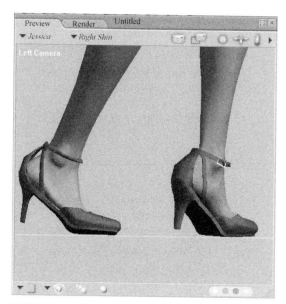

FIGURE 7.11 Make sure that your feet touch the ground after you reposition the foot.

FIGURE 7.12 Load figures, characters, or clothing from the Figures (left) or Props (center) Libraries. The Poses Library (right) contains pose files that change the materials on the clothing in your scene.

The Poses Library often contains library items that show clothing in the thumbnails, so it *is* very easy to get confused by them. The clothing thumbnails that you see in the Poses Library apply textures or material settings to clothing that you have already added to your scene. These poses are more commonly known in the Poser community as MAT poses (*MAT* being an abbreviation for *material*). Their sole purpose is to make it easier for users to apply different textures to their clothing.

MAT Poses Don't Load Textures Properly

As long as we're on the subject of MAT poses, we should probably mention one more problem that can occur when you use them. MAT poses only work properly on the figures or clothing for which the textures were created. Although objects can have materials that are named the same, the texture maps that are used from those materials must also be the same. For example, the Poser 5 female (Judy) and the Poser 6 female (Jessi) both have materials named Head, Body, Gums, and so on. However, the two figures have different UV map configurations, so any image-based textures are very different. To see an illustration of this point, look at Figure 7.13, which shows a comparison between the body texture for Judy and the body texture for Jessi.

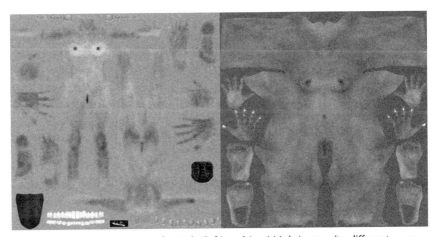

FIGURE 7.13   The body textures for Judy (left) and Jessi (right) are quite different, even though many of the materials in each figure have the same names.

Because the texture maps for Judy and Jessi are arranged differently, the body texture for Judy won't line up properly if you apply it to Jessi. Figure 7.14 shows the result when Judy's body texture is applied to Jessi. As you can see, portions of the teeth and tongue texture appear on Jessi's legs and feet.

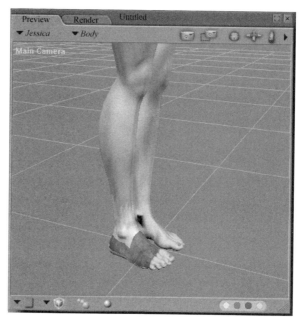

FIGURE 7.14 Textures do not line up properly when they are used on the wrong object.

Before you apply a MAT pose from the Poses Library, make sure that you have selected the correct object in your scene first. Then apply the MAT pose, and you should see the object change color or texture.

CLOTH ROOM OVERVIEW

Now that we've covered some of the common problems that can occur when using conforming clothing, you'll learn a bit more about dynamic clothing and the Cloth Room. Dynamic clothing works a bit differently from conforming clothing. The main differences between conforming clothing and dynamic clothing appear in Table 7.1.

Table 7.1 Conforming Clothing versus Dynamic Clothing

CONFORMING CLOTHING	DYNAMIC CLOTHING
Able to handle complex geometry, such as multilayered clothing or overlapping faces more easily than dynamic clothing. underneath clothing.	More particular about clothing construction. Avoid overlapping or self-intersecting geometry, or hems that fold.

CONFORMING CLOTHING	DYNAMIC CLOTHING
Clothing geometry is divided into body part groups that are named the same as the figure for which they are created. The body part groups should match those of the underlying figure as closely as possible.	If clothing geometry contains more than one group, the boundaries between the groups must be welded. You can also use the Group Editor in the Cloth Room to create cloth groups that give areas of the clothing different dynamic properties that simulate different types of cloth.
To attach the clothing to the figure, select the clothing item and choose Figure > Conform To. Select the name of the character as the object to conform to.	To attach the clothing to the figure, select the clothing item and choose Object > Change Parent. Generally, you select the character's hip or body as the parent, but items such as scarves or hats are better parented to the head.
After conforming the object, the clothing poses automatically when you pose the character.	After assigning the parent, you must create a simulation in the Cloth Room to pose the clothing.
Morphs may be necessary to make the clothing move more realistically in an animation.	Cloth simulations make the clothing move realistically in an animation.

The Cloth Room is shown in Figure 7.15. This is where you change static clothing props into clothing that can move and animate with more realism than conforming clothing. You accomplish this by working through the four main areas of the Cloth Room: the Cloth Simulation area (1), the Cloth area (2), the Cloth Groups area (3), and the Dynamics Controls area (4).

Each area of the Cloth Room serves specific purposes. For example, in the Cloth Simulation area, you assign a name and additional parameters for your cloth simulation. You specify parameters such as the frame numbers through which the simulation takes place, whether or not you want to drape the cloth before calculations start, and additional cloth collision options.

Use the Cloth Area to choose the item to turn into cloth and to specify the objects that will cause the clothing to react when the cloth collides against them. You can choose any body parts on your figure, other cloth objects, or other props in your scene. Remember, however, that you should keep the number of collision objects as low as possible to conserve resources. The more items you select, the longer calculations will take, and the more resources will be used.

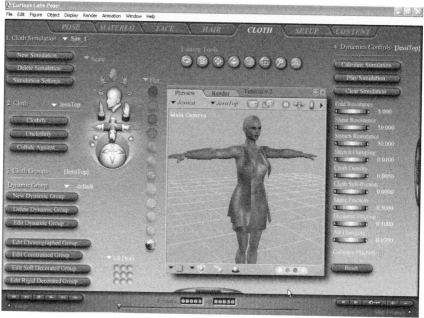

FIGURE 7.15 The Cloth Room contains features that help you create clothing that moves and animates realistically.

The Cloth Groups area contains several buttons that help you divide your clothing object into several types of cloth groups:

- *Dynamic Groups* give you the ability to create more than one type of clothing in your object. By default, all polygons in your clothing are assigned to one cloth group, and they all behave the same. If you create additional dynamic groups, you can assign different properties to the vertices that are included in the new dynamic group.
- *Choreographed Groups* can respond to keyframed animation.
- *Constrained Groups* help keep vertices in place in relation to your figure (for example, they will keep the strap of a dress in place if your figure drops her shoulder).
- *Soft Decorated Groups* are used for items such as pockets or other flexible decorations that are not attached to the main clothing article. This prevents the pockets from falling off the clothing.
- *Rigid Decorated Groups* are used for items such as buttons, cuff links, jewelry, or other rigid objects that are a part of the clothing but not attached to the geometry.

Finally, the Dynamics Controls area contains several parameters that help you define the behavior of the cloth.

Chapter 11 of the Poser 7 Tutorial Manual covers each area of the Cloth Room in great detail. Chapter 19 of the Poser 7 Reference Manual explains the Cloth Room controls and cloth simulations. We recommend that you review and become familiar with the material in both manuals before you proceed with the tutorials in this chapter.

CREATING AND SAVING DYNAMIC CLOTHING

Although the Cloth Room is relatively easy to use, it is very resource-intensive. Chances are, you might need to use more than one article of dynamic clothing in a scene. If resources are scarce, make sure you pay attention to the polygon counts in your dynamic clothing, especially if you are going to use more than one piece of dynamic clothing in each scene. Remember that each piece of clothing will require a separate simulation. You can either calculate all simulations at the same time or calculate each simulation individually.

It is also easier to use clothing that was designed to work together. For example, if you have a shirt, pants, vest, and coat that were purchased in the same set, chances are very good that they were designed in layers. In other words, if you put the shirt on, it tucks under the pants, the vest goes over the pants and shirt, and the coat goes over all other clothing without the previous layers poking through.

If you randomly pick clothing that was not designed to work together, you may need to adjust the scale of each layer of clothing or use magnets to reshape the clothing so that the underlying layers do not poke through the layer or layers that are above them.

If you do not address the poke-through issues in your dynamic clothing before you calculate the simulations, you may get error messages that the simulations have failed. This is because Poser expects the cloth to remain outside of the figure, so when clothing intersects the geometry of the figure, calculations can go out of bounds.

TUTORIAL 7.1   **LOADING THE CONTENT**

The clothing that you'll use in this tutorial was designed to work together. You'll add a top, skirt, and jacket to Jessi before you create the simulations. You'll begin this tutorial by importing each clothing article:

ON THE CD

1. Before you open Poser, locate the JessiTop.obj, JessiSkirt.obj, and JessiJacket.obj files in the Tutorials > Chap07 folder on the CD-ROM that accompanies this book. Create a folder named PracticalPoser7

beneath the Poser 7 > Downloads > Runtime > Geometries folder, and copy the objects to that location.

2. Locate the JessiTop.jpg, JessiSkirt.jpg, and JessiJacket.jpg files in the Tutorials > Chap07 folder on the CD-ROM. Create a folder named PracticalPoser7 beneath the Poser 7 > Downloads > Runtime > Textures folder, and copy the images to that location.

3. Load Jessi or Jessi Hi Res into a blank Poser scene.

4. Use the Figure > Use Inverse Kinematics command to turn IK off on each leg, and use the Joint Editor to zero the pose of Jessi. The Zero Pose button will not zero the XTrans, YTrans, or ZTrans dials in the Parameters window, so you may need to adjust those settings manually. Then choose Display > Document Style > Texture Shaded to view Jessi in Texture Shaded mode.

5. Click the Cloth tab to enter the Cloth Room. Read the HTML Room Help page, if needed, and then close it so that you have room to view the contents of the room.

6. Choose File > Import > Wavefront OBJ. The Import Options dialog box shown in Figure 7.16 appears. Uncheck all of the options to import the OBJ file at the scale and position at which it was created. Click OK to continue.

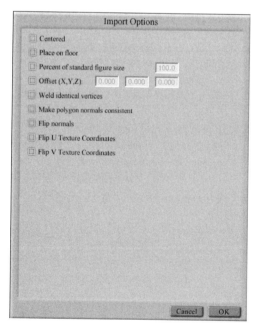

FIGURE 7.16 The Import Options dialog box appears when you import a 3D object into Poser.

7. When the Import: Wavefront OBJ dialog box appears, navigate to the Downloads > Runtime > Geometries > PracticalPoser7 folder, and select JessiTop.obj. Click Open to import the object.
8. With the top selected, choose Object > Change Parent. The Object Parent dialog box appears.
9. Select Jessi's hip as the parent for the top, as shown in Figure 7.17. Choose OK to continue.

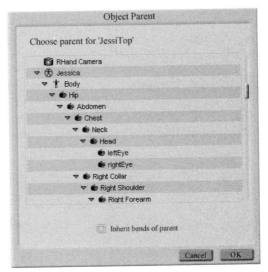

FIGURE 7.17   Select Jessi's hip as the parent to the clothing item.

10. Repeat Steps 6 through 10 to import JessiSkirt.obj from the same location as the top. Again select Jessi's hip as the parent to the skirt.
11. Repeat Steps 6 through 10 to import JessiJacket.obj from the same location as the top. Once more, Jessi's hip will be the parent to the jacket.

TUTORIAL 7.2   **CREATING MULTIPLE SIMULATIONS**

When you have more than one layer of dynamic clothing on a figure, you should always create the simulations for the underlying layers first, and follow with each subsequent layer until you reach the top-most layers. Think of the way that you dress and the order in which you put on your clothing. You put your shirt on before your pants or your skirt, and you put the jacket on over both.

The same is true of dynamic clothing in Poser. In the case of the clothing that we now have on Jessi, we will create the simulation for the top first and set it to collide with Jessi's torso. Then, we will create the simulation for the skirt and set it to collide with Jessi's lower body and the shirt. Finally, we will set up the simulation for the jacket and have it collide with some of Jessi's body parts as well as the top and the skirt. If you don't choose the previous layers of clothing as collision objects, the layers above them will act as if the underlying layers aren't even there, and chances are, will end up intersecting the layers below.

Starting first with the top, create the simulations as follows:

1. Click the Cloth tab to enter the Cloth Room if necessary.
2. Create animation keyframes for your figure, or place your figure in its final pose in a frame other than the first frame. These procedures are outlined in Chapter 11 of the *Poser Tutorial Manual*.
3. Click the New Simulation button in area 1 of the Cloth Room. The Simulation Settings dialog box shown in Figure 7.18 appears.

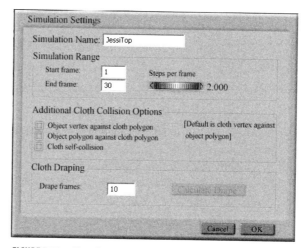

FIGURE 7.18   Simulation settings create a new simulation for a dynamic clothing prop.

4. Enter **JessiTop** in the Simulation Name field.
5. The default settings create a simulation that starts at frame 1 and ends at frame 30 (the default length of a Poser animation). Leave these settings at their default.
6. Set the Cloth Draping value to 10 frames. This allows the top to settle on the figure's body before the dynamic control calculations begin. Then click OK to exit the Simulation Settings dialog.

7. Next, click the Clothify button in section 2 of the Cloth Room. The Clothify dialog box shown in Figure 7.19 appears.

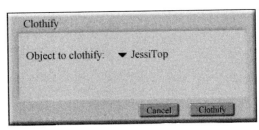

FIGURE 7.19   You must Clothify a dynamic clothing prop to turn it into dynamic cloth.

8. If necessary, select JessiTop from the Object to Clothify drop-down list, and then click the Clothify button. After you turn the object into cloth, the buttons in section 3 are enabled. These buttons are explained in detail in Chapter 11 of the *Poser Tutorial Manual*.

9. Before you leave the Cloth section, you have to tell Poser which objects the top is supposed to collide against. If you do not choose any collision objects, the clothing will fall to the ground. Generally, you want the clothing to collide with the smallest number of body parts possible, because it will save on system resources by reducing the number of calculations that have to take place. Click the Collide Against button to open the Cloth Collision Objects dialog box shown in Figure 7.20.

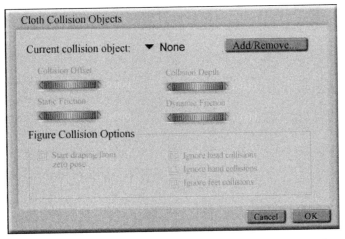

FIGURE 7.20   Dynamic clothing must collide against your character's body, other clothing articles, or other objects that might come into contact with the clothing.

10. To select collision objects, click the Add/Remove button in the Cloth Collision Objects dialog box. The Select Objects dialog box opens.

11. Select any body parts, clothing, or other objects that you expect will come into contact with Jessi's top. Select the hip, abdomen, chest, neck, right collar, and left collar. Figure 7.21 shows a portion of the selected parts.

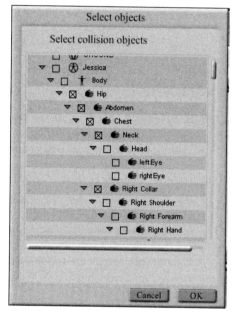

FIGURE 7.21   Select the body parts that will come in contact with the top.

12. Click OK to return to the Cloth Collision Objects dialog box, and click OK again to assign the collision objects and return to the Cloth Room.

13. The next layer above the top is the skirt. This piece of clothing must be set to collide against some of Jessi's body parts but must also collide with the top. To begin, click the New Simulation button in section 1 of the Cloth Room. Name the simulation **JessiSkirt**, and set the Drape Frames to 10, as shown in Figure 7.22. Click OK to create the simulation.

14. Click the Clothify button in section 2 of the Cloth Room. Select JessiSkirt as the object to clothify, and then click the Clothify button.

15. Click the Collide Against button in section 2 of the Cloth Room. When the Cloth Collision Objects dialog box opens, click the Add/Remove button to open the Select Objects dialog box.

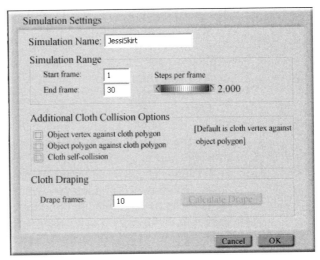

FIGURE 7.22   Create a new simulation for the skirt.

16. Select Jessi's hip, abdomen, right thigh, right shin, left thigh, and left shin. Then scroll down to the bottom of the Select Collision Objects list and check JessiTop, as shown in Figure 7.23. Click OK to return to the Cloth Collision objects dialog box, and click OK again to return to the Cloth Room.

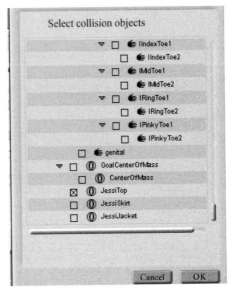

FIGURE 7.23   The skirt should collide against Jessi's top (listed as JessiTop) in addition to some of her body parts.

17. The final layer is the jacket, which must be set to collide against Jessi's arms, along with the top and the skirt. Once again, click the New Simulation button in section 1 of the Cloth Room. Name the simulation **JessiJacket**, and set the Drape Frames to 10. Click OK to create the simulation.

18. Click the Clothify button in section 2 of the Cloth Room. Select Jessi-Jacket as the object to clothify, and then click the Clothify button.

19. Click the Collide Against button in section 2 of the Cloth Room. When the Cloth Collision Objects dialog box opens, click the Add/Re-move button to open the Select Objects dialog box.

20. Select Jessi's chest, neck, right collar, right shoulder, right forearm, left collar, left shoulder, and left forearm. Then, scroll down to the bottom of the Select Objects dialog box and check JessiTop and JessiSkirt as shown in Figure 7.24. Click OK to return to the Cloth Collision objects dialog box, and click OK again to return to the Cloth Room.

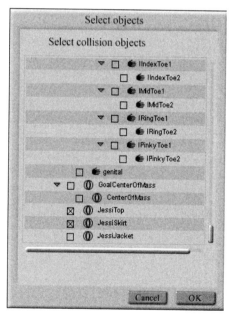

FIGURE 7.24   The jacket should collide against Jessi's top and skirt in addition to some of her body parts.

TUTORIAL 7.3   CALCULATING MULTIPLE SIMULATIONS

The next step is to configure the dynamic properties of each item of clothing, and then calculate the simulations. Dynamic properties are explained in Chapter 11 of the *Poser Tutorial Manual* and will not be addressed here.

The main purpose for this tutorial is to show you how to perform dynamic calculations when there are multiple simulations in one scene.

There are three different ways that you can approach multiple simulations. You can calculate all cloth simulations, all hair simulations, or all cloth and hair simulations.

The following tutorials assume that all simulations have been set up properly for still images or animations (as described in the preceding tutorials or in the Poser Tutorial Manual), and all dynamic properties have been set to the required settings for your simulations.

To calculate each simulation individually, follow these steps:

1. Select the cloth simulation that you want to calculate from the drop-down menu in the Cloth Simulation area, as shown in Figure 7.25. The simulations are listed in the order in which you created them.

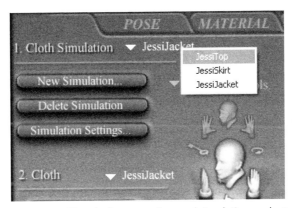

FIGURE 7.25   To calculate one of several simulations, select the simulation you want to calculate.

2. Click the Calculate Simulation button shown in Figure 7.26. The calculations are completed for the current simulation.
3. Repeat Steps 1 and 2 for additional simulations as required. If you created the clothing simulations in the correct order (as described in Tutorial 7.2), complete the calculations in the same order.

If you make changes to your poses, or you add or delete keyframes in your animation, you will have to recalculate all simulations in your project. To calculate all cloth simulations in the order in which you created them, choose Animation > Recalculate Dynamics, and select one of the options shown in Figure 7.27, as follows:

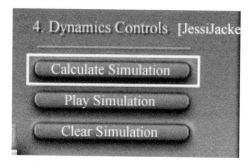

FIGURE 7.26   Click the Calculate Simulation button to calculate the dynamics for the currently selected cloth simulation.

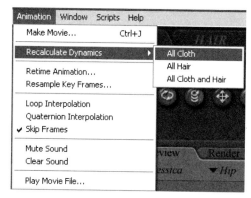

FIGURE 7.27   The Animation > Recalculate Dynamics commands allow you to calculate all cloth and/or hair simulations with one click.

- Choose *All Cloth* to calculate all cloth simulations in the order in which they were created.
- Choose *All Hair* to calculate all dynamic hair simulations in the order in which they were created.
- Choose *All Cloth and Hair* to calculate all dynamic cloth and hair simulations in the order in which they were created. Cloth simulations are calculated before hair simulations.

CONCLUSION

In this chapter, you've learned about some of the most common issues that you'll have to think about when you work with Poser clothing. You've learned about some of the solutions that you can implement when clothing doesn't conform or fit correctly, how to use body handles for long skirts, and how to pose high-heeled shoes. You've also learned to pay attention to the libraries from which you load clothing, so that you don't accidentally use pose files that are meant to change the textures of an item that is already in your scene. You also got a brief overview of the Cloth Room and learned how to set up and configure multiple cloth simulations in your scene.

In the next chapter, you'll learn how to create morphs that help you customize your figures and clothing. You'll work with Poser's magnets, as well as the great new and enhanced morphing features found in Poser 7.

CHAPTER

8

CREATING CUSTOM MORPHS

In This Chapter

- What Are Morphs?
- The Anatomy of a Morph
- Creating Morphs in Poser
- Tutorial 8.1 Creating Morphs with Poser Magnets
- Tutorial 8.2 Saving a Magnet
- Tutorial 8.3 Mirroring a Magnet
- Tutorial 8.4 Spawning a Single Morph Target
- Tutorial 8.5 One Magnet Affects Multiple Body Parts
- Tutorial 8.6 Creating Full Body Morphs
- New Poser 7 Morphing Tools
- Tutorial 8.7 Creating Face Morphs with the Morphing Tool
- Tutorial 8.8 Fixing Poke-Throughs with the Morphing Tool
- Distributing Morphs
- Magnets and the "Next Generation" Poser Figures
- Avoiding Problems

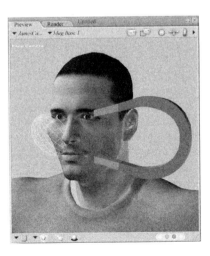

ON THE CD

Y ou've heard morphs mentioned in various places throughout this book and in the tutorials on the included CD-ROM. In this chapter, you'll learn what morphs are, how to create them, and how to manage the morphs you have. You'll also learn about *external binary morphs,* which save morphs in an external compressed file, separate from the character file. We begin with an explanation of what morphs are and what they do.

WHAT ARE MORPHS?

Morphs are used in Poser to alter the shape of a Poser object. For example, if you want to open a character's mouth, close the character's eyes, or change the character's shape, you turn a dial to make that happen. For example, if you purchase DAZ3D's Victoria 3 along with her face and body morph packs, you get a wealth of morph targets that change her appearance and body shape. Figure 8.1 shows a portion of the face morphs that are available for Victoria 3.

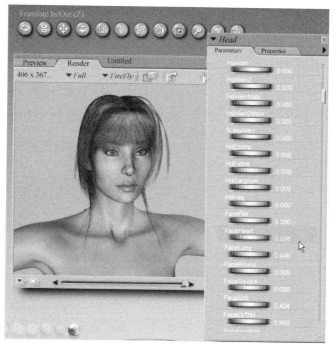

FIGURE 8.1   DAZ3D figures such as Victoria 3 come with accessory morph packs that help you change their faces and body shapes.

When you move a body part with a bone, it always bends, twists, or turns around the same center point. The basic shape of the body part doesn't change much, except around that center point. Morphs, on the other hand, can affect one or all of the vertices in an object. For example, if you want to make your figure smile, puff up his or her cheeks, raise his or her eyebrows, or even gain or lose weight, you use one or more morphs to do it.

To make a morph work, you adjust the dials in the Parameters window or in the Face Shaping Tool in the Face Room. Simply adjust the dial to the left to decrease the value or to the right to increase the value of the morph. You can also enter values in the number fields.

THE ANATOMY OF A MORPH

When you create a morph in Poser, or import a morph target that was created in an external program, Poser compares the starting shape (or the source shape) to the ending shape (or the target shape). When you save the morphed character to the library, the library file includes the *delta information* for each morph. That is, the library file stores information that describes how far each vertex in the morph moved, and from where and to where it moved.

Let's say, for example, that you see a dial that changes the size of the eyeballs on a character. When you increase the setting on the morph dial, the entire eye gets larger, as shown on the left eye in Figure 8.2. When you decrease the setting on the morph dial, the entire eye gets smaller. If each eye contains 200 vertices, the morph information adds 200 extra lines of information to your library file for each eye because you are changing the position of every vertex in the eyeball.

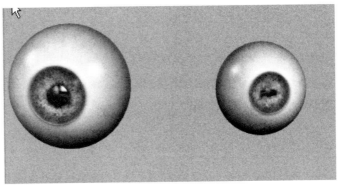

FIGURE 8.2 Morphs can affect all vertices in an object (left) or some of the vertices, such as only those for the pupil of an eye (right).

On the other hand, let's say that there is another dial that only affects the vertices in the pupil of the eye. In this case, let's say that the dial only moves 20 of those 200 vertices. Poser doesn't store the morph information for all 200 vertices for that morph. Instead, it only stores the information for the 20 vertices that change the size of the pupil.

CREATING MORPHS IN POSER

If the figure or clothing doesn't have a morph that will accomplish what you want your Poser content to do, you have to create the morph yourself. There are several programs that you can use to create morphs for Poser content. One method is to use Poser magnets, which help you deform the polygons in an object by pushing, pulling, twisting, moving, translating, or rotating them.

After you wrap your head around the three basic parts of a magnet, it's not too difficult to create morphs with them. In fact, some very popular Poser morph artists create their morphs strictly with Poser magnets! One such artist is Capsces, whose character morph packs enhance many popular third-party Poser figures with entirely new levels of caricature and realism.

A magnet has three parts: the magnet base, the magnet zone, and the magnet. These parts are shown in Figure 8.3.

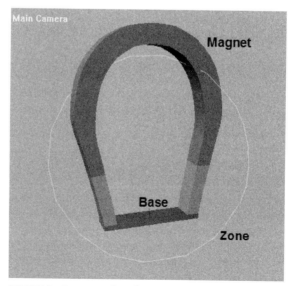

FIGURE 8.3   A magnet has three parts: the magnet base, the magnet zone, and the magnet.

- The *magnet base* is the bar-shaped rectangle that appears at the base of the magnet. The center of the magnet base defines the operating point of the magnet. Dials in the Parameters window allow you to scale the base, which changes the overall size of the magnet prop without affecting the geometry. If the magnet is too large or too small to work with, you can change the scale of the base to change the size of the magnet. Parameter dials also allow you to rotate and translate the position of the magnet base. The magnet base can actually be positioned at some distance from the object being deformed, and then you can translate the magnet. If you then move the base, you won't see any change in the deformation the magnet produces.
- The *magnet zone* is the spherical outline that indicates the area where the magnet will affect the object. The magnet will have the most effect in the center of the falloff zone (which initially appears as the outline of a sphere). The effect of the magnet gradually falls off as it reaches the outer edge of the zone. You adjust the shape of the magnet zone by increasing or decreasing the xScale, yScale, or zScale values of the magnet zone. You can also change the shape of the magnet zone using the Magnet Zone Falloff graph. Select the magnet zone, open the Properties window, and click the Edit Falloff Graph to open the Graph Editor. You can adjust the curve to have more or less effect in different areas of the magnet zone. When you enlarge the size of the magnet zone, you affect more polygons in the object you want to morph. Reduce the size of the magnet zone to affect fewer polygons. You can also translate or rotate the magnet zone on the x- (left/right), y- (up/down) or z (forward/backward) axis to position the magnet base away from the center point of the magnet zone.
- The *magnet* is the element that actually moves the polygons in the object. The polygons that move are determined by the area defined by the magnet zone. You translate, rotate, or scale the magnet to move the polygons in the object. After you move the magnet, you can make changes to the placement of the magnet zone or magnet base until you achieve the desired shape of your morph.

TUTORIAL 8.1   **CREATING MORPHS WITH POSER MAGNETS**

You will better understand the function of each magnet part if you use them yourself. In this tutorial, you'll create a morph for James Casual's face. The morph will change the shape of his cheeks. Actually, you'll use two magnets to create the morph: one on each side of the face.

To create the face morph for James Casual, follow these steps:

1. Create a new Poser scene, and load James Casual if necessary. Turn off Inverse Kinematics, and use the Joint Editor or the Zero All Python script to zero his pose.
2. Select the Face Camera, using the icon in the Camera Controls or by choosing Display > Cameras > Camera View > Face Camera. Change the display to Texture Shaded mode.
3. Click James Casual's head to select it as the current actor. Then choose Object > Create Magnet. Your scene should look similar to Figure 8.4.

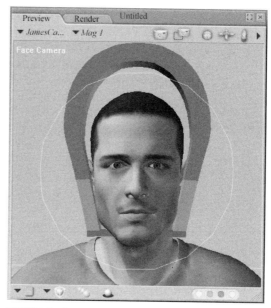

FIGURE 8.4 A magnet is created for James Casual's head.

4. The first thing you notice is that the magnet zone automatically encloses and is centered around the selected body part, and the magnet base appears near the base of the head. We want to affect one of the cheeks with this magnet, so let's start by moving the magnet base right and upward toward the right cheek. Click the yellow magnet base to make it the current object. Adjust the xTran dial in the Parameters window to -0.141, the yTran dial to 5.856, and the zTran dial to .351.
5. Because part of the magnet is buried inside his head, we can also rotate the magnet base so that you can see the magnet better. We'll also make the magnet a little smaller. Scale the magnet base to 7%, and adjust the zRotate value to 90 degrees. Your magnet should now look as shown in Figure 8.5.

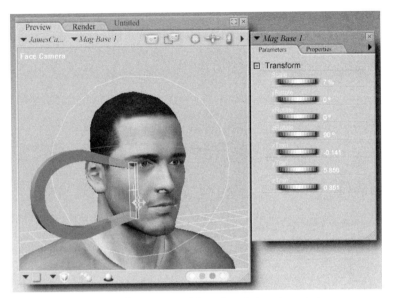

FIGURE 8.5   The magnet base is repositioned, scaled, and rotated.

Notice in Step 5 that instead of scaling and rotating the magnet (which would move the polygons in James Casual's face), we scaled and rotated the magnet base to change the size and rotation of the magnet. Always change the magnet base when you need to reposition or scale the magnets without affecting the geometry.

6. If you move the magnet at this point to morph the cheeks, the magnet will change the polygons in the entire head. This is because the magnet zone currently *surrounds* the entire head. We need to move the magnet zone forward, toward the front of the face, and decrease its size so that it only affects the right cheek. To begin, click the magnet zone (the white outline around the head) to make it the current object. The Parameters window will show Mag Zone 1 as the current object.

7. Some Poser users find it easier to work with magnet zones when they can view them in three dimensions. You can change the display of the magnet zone to wireframe to help you visualize the area that it affects. With the magnet zone selected, choose Display > Element > Wireframe. The magnet zone turns into a wireframe ellipsoid.

8. Adjust the camera so that you see James Casual's head toward the side (or use the Head cameras that you created in Chapter 2, "Using Cameras.")

9. We're going to change all scale settings; zRotation values; and x, y, and zTran values for the magnet zone. We want to create an elliptical

magnet zone that will enhance and raise James' right cheekbone. To modify the magnet zone, use the following settings:

Scale: **3%**

yScale: **47%**

xScale: **67%**

zScale: **81%**

zRotate: **–40** degrees

xTran: **–0.162**

yTran: **5.881**

zTran: **0.370**

10. Now that you have changed the shape of the magnet zone, you can move the magnet to examine how it affects the right cheek. We will scale the cheekbone so that it is a little bit larger, and also pull the faces forward (zTran) and to the right (xTran). After you set the Magnet values in the Parameters window as follows, your cheek magnet should look as shown in Figure 8.6.

Scale: **107%**

xTran: **–0.378**

zTran: **0.636**

FIGURE 8.6 The new magnet makes the right cheekbone more pronounced.

TUTORIAL 8.2   SAVING A MAGNET

You have two options to create the magnet for the other side. The first option is to start from scratch with a new magnet. The second option is to save the first magnet to the library, and then mirror some of the settings to flip the magnet to the other side of the face. This tutorial will show you the latter approach.

1. You'll need to create a library category in the Props Library of your choice so that you can save your new magnet. Navigate to the Props Library in the Runtime of your choosing. Click the down arrow at the top of the Props Library and choose Add New Category from the menu shown in Figure 8.7.

FIGURE 8.7   Add a new Props Library category for the magnets.

2. The Library Name dialog box prompts you for a new library name. Assign a name to the new Props Library, such as **James Magnets**. Click OK to continue.
3. Double-click your new library folder to select it as the current library.
4. Click the Magnet in your Preview window, and then click the Add to Library icon at the bottom of the library window. The New Set dialog box appears.
5. Click the Select Subset button to open the Hierarchy Selection dialog box. Check Mag Base 1, Mag 1, and Mag Zone 1 as shown in Figure 8.8.

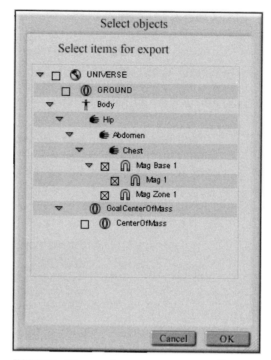

FIGURE 8.8   When saving a magnet to your library, remember to select all three magnet components.

6. Click OK to return to the New Set dialog box. Assign a name to the magnet, such as "**JamesRightCheek**." Click OK to save the magnet to the library.

TUTORIAL 8.3   MIRRORING A MAGNET

Now that you've created the magnet for one cheek, you need to create a magnet that does exactly the same thing on the other cheek. It's actually pretty easy to accomplish. Because you've saved the right cheek magnet to the library, you can modify the magnet that is already in your scene. You'll only have to make some minor adjustments to the settings that are already there.

To modify the existing magnet, follow these steps:

1. Save the existing magnet as described in Tutorial 8.2 if you have not already done so.
2. Click the magnet base. Change the xTran setting from –0.141 to 0.141 (in other words, change it from a negative number to the equal

positive number). This places the base on the opposite side, in the same relative position.

3. Adjust the zRotate value from 90 degrees to –90 degrees. This flips the magnet in the other direction. Your magnet should now look as shown in Figure 8.9.

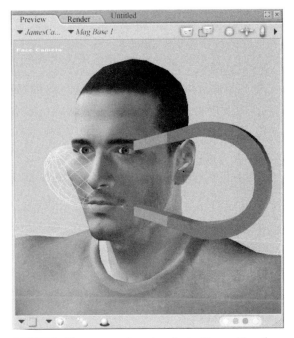

FIGURE 8.9   The magnet base is adjusted to position the magnet on the opposite cheek.

4. Now we have to change the magnet zone so that it flips the other way. Click the magnet zone to select it as the current object.
5. To rotate the magnet in the opposite direction, and change the zRotate value from –40 to 40 degrees (change the negative value to a positive value). The ellipse rotates in the opposite direction.
6. Change the xTran value from –0.162 to .162 (changing the negative number to a positive number).
7. Now click the magnet. Change the xTran value from –.378 to .378 (changing the negative value to a positive value). Your magnet should now be a mirror opposite of the one you created for the right cheek.
8. Using the steps as described in Tutorial 8.2, save the magnet to the library as **JamesLeftCheek**.

TUTORIAL 8.4   SPAWNING A SINGLE MORPH TARGET

After you change the shape of a body part with a magnet, you have to "spawn" a morph target. Basically, *spawning* is a process that takes the shape of the magnetized part and turns it into a morph dial. Afterward, you can delete the magnet or magnets, and set the morph dial to 1 to achieve the same shape as created by the magnets. Make sure to save the magnets to the library before you delete them, so that you don't have to re-create them later.

Before we create the face morph, we'll add the right cheek magnet from the library so that both cheeks are symmetrical. Then we'll create a facial morph that moves both cheeks at the same time. Follow these steps:

1. Double-click the JamesRightCheek magnet in the library to add it back into the scene. Both cheeks should now be symmetrical.
2. Click James' head to select it as the current object. Both magnets appear next to the face.
3. Choose Object > Spawn Morph Target. The Morph Name dialog box appears.
4. Enter a name for the morph dial (such as **CheekHeight**). Click OK to save the morph to the Parameters window. You should see the morph dial in the Morph section of your Parameters window as shown in Figure 8.10.

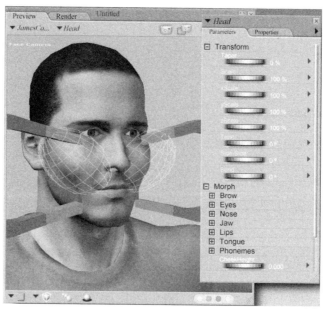

FIGURE 8.10   After you spawn the morph, you will see a morph dial in the Parameters window.

5. Click one of the magnets, and press the Delete key to delete it. Answer OK to confirm that you want to delete the magnet.

6. Click the head to make the second magnet visible, and then click the second magnet to select it. Press the Delete key, and then choose OK to confirm that you want to delete the magnet.

7. Click the head to select it as the current object. Then set the dial for your new morph target to 1. You should see the head morph as shown in Figure 8.11. You have now used magnets to create your first morph!

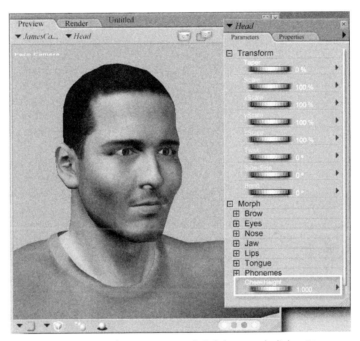

FIGURE 8.11 Remove the magnets, and dial the morph dial to 1 to create the same effect as the magnets.

TUTORIAL 8.5 ONE MAGNET AFFECTS MULTIPLE BODY PARTS

You've learned how to affect one body part with more than one magnet, and now you'll learn the reverse—how to affect multiple body parts with one magnet. For this exercise, we'll continue with the scene that you have been working with in this chapter. This time, we'll add a magnet that will give James Casual a "pot belly." You will start by creating a magnet for the abdomen, and then add the additional body parts to the list that the magnet will affect.

To create a magnet that affects more than one body part, follow these steps:

1. Choose Display > Camera View > Main Camera to switch to the main camera view if necessary.
2. Click James Casual's abdomen to select it as the current actor.
3. Choose Object > Create Magnet. Note that the magnet initially appears inside James Casual, so that you cannot see it. You should, however, see Mag 1 displayed in the Parameters window, and you'll also see a small magnet zone that surrounds the abdomen, as shown in Figure 8.12.

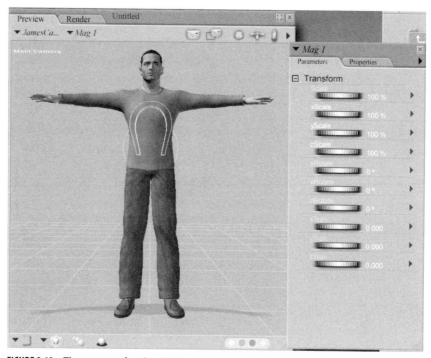

FIGURE 8.12   The magnet for the abdomen is placed inside James Casual's body.

4. Click the magnet base to select it, or choose Mag Base 1 from the menu in the Parameters window. Adjust the zTran value to .6 to bring the magnet outside of the abdomen.
5. Set the xRotate value for the magnet base to 90 degrees to rotate the magnet. Note that this step is not necessary. We are only rotating the magnet base to make the stomach area a bit more visible. Rotating the magnet base also affects the orientation of the X-, Y-, and Z axes,

so it can be confusing if you rotate the magnets often. We'll explain later when you move the magnet how the base rotation affects the orientation.

6. Right now, the magnet will only affect James Casual's abdomen. To add a second part, click the magnet to select it as the current object. Then click the Properties window, and click the Add Element to Deform button. The Choose Actor window shown in Figure 8.13 appears.

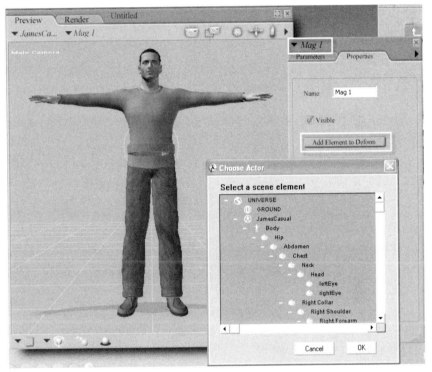

FIGURE 8.13   The Choose Actor window allows you to control more than one body part with a single magnet.

7. Select the hip from the Choose Actor window and click OK. You return to the Poser document.

8. Repeat Steps 6 and 7 to add the right thigh, left thigh, and chest to the magnet. Your magnet will now control five body parts.

9. Click the Parameters window, and make the following changes to the magnet zone. These changes will make the magnet zone narrower and move it forward on the z axis, so that it only affects James' front area:
   Scale: **14%**
   zScale: **60%**

yTran: **3.983**
zTran: **0.568**

10. Now, click the Magnet to select it. We will now see how it affects James Casual's belly. Change xScale to 115%, and change yTran to 2.915 to make his belly wider and make it stick out more. Also, remember when you rotated the magnet base earlier? Because of this, the yTran parameter moves the magnet forward and backward, instead of up and down as it normally would. When you're done, James should have a big belly as shown in Figure 8.14.

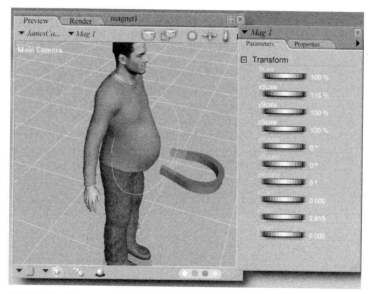

FIGURE 8.14   The magnet affects multiple body parts and creates a big belly on James.

11. Before you delete the magnet, you have to spawn morphs for each of the body parts affected by the magnet. For each of the affected body parts (chest, abdomen, hip, right thigh, or left thigh), select one of them. Choose Object > Spawn Morph Target. Name the morph target for each of the body parts as **PBMBigBelly** as shown in Figure 8.15. The prefix PBM reminds you that it is one of several *partial body morphs (PBMs)* that are to be combined into a final shape.

12. Save your magnet to the library, if desired, as described in Tutorial 8.2. Then delete the magnet. Your morphs are complete.

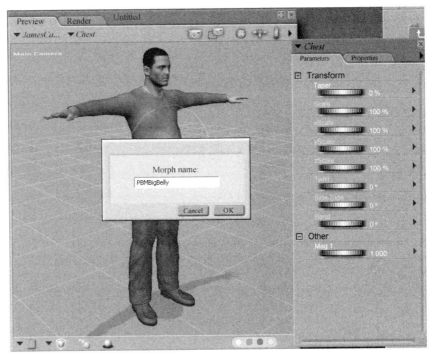

FIGURE 8.15   Spawn a morph target for each of the affected body parts, naming them all **PBMBigBelly**.

TUTORIAL 8.6   **CREATING FULL BODY MORPHS**

As you learned in the previous tutorial, you have to spawn each body part individually if a magnet affects more than one body part. You also learned that it is common to precede the name of each individual body part morph with "PBM." This gives you an indication that this morph dial should only be used in combination with other morphs of the same name.

So now, we have several PBM morphs that, when combined, create a pot belly on James Casual. To make them all work together, you set all of the PBMBigBelly dials to 1 to achieve your pot-bellied James figure. Then you create a Full Body Morph so that you can make your figure look pregnant with one dial, instead of seven individual ones.

To create the full body morph, follow these steps:

1. Continuing from the previous tutorials, click James Casual's chest, and set the PBMBigBelly morph dial setting to 1.

2. Repeat Step 1 for the abdomen, hip, left thigh, and right thigh. James should now look as shown in Figure 8.16. All of the partial body morphs that make up the big belly morph have been dialed to 1.

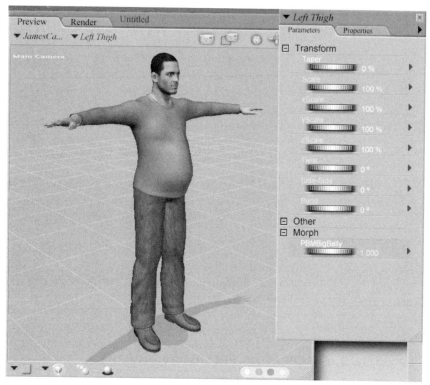

FIGURE 8.16   With all PBMBigBelly morphs dialed to 1, James Casual has a big belly.

3. Before you create your full body morph, make sure that there are *no other morphs* that are dialed in anywhere else on your figure, other than the ones you want to include in the full body morph. For example, if you are creating a full body morph to make a big belly and *only* a big belly, make sure that you don't have any extra muscles dialed in anywhere else on the chest, arms, or legs. Otherwise, every time you use your big belly morph, you'll also get muscles thrown in to the mix.
4. Choose Figure > Create Full Body Morph. The Morph Name dialog box appears.
5. Enter **BigBelly** for the morph name, and choose OK.

6. Now, go through each of the individual body parts to set all five PBMBigBelly morphs to zero (0). James Casual should return to his default shape.
7. Now, with James Casual selected, choose Body from the Current Actor selection menu in the Parameters window, as shown in Figure 8.17.

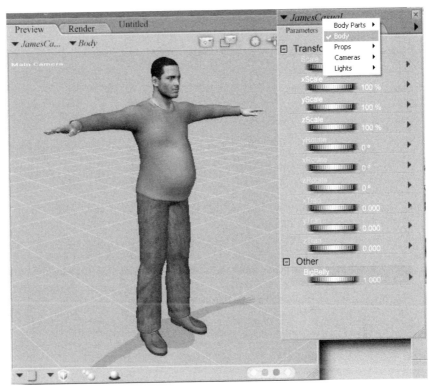

FIGURE 8.17   With James Casual selected, choose Body from the current actor menu.

8. You should see your BigBelly full body morph in the section named Other. When you dial this morph to 1, you'll see all of the individual body parts morph together at the same time to create your big belly, as shown in Figure 8.18. Your full body morph is now complete.
9. Locate the Figures Library into which you want to save your morphed figure. Click the Add to Library button to add your new morphed character to the library, assigning a name of your choosing.

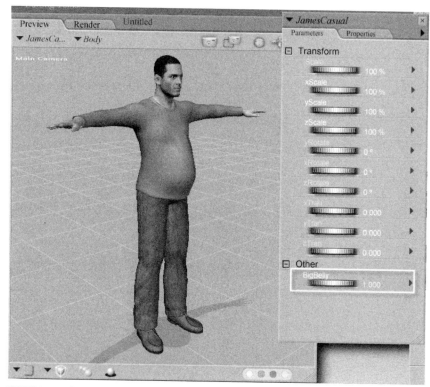

FIGURE 8.18 The Full Body Morph dial appears in the Body section of James Casual and moves all affected body parts at once.

NEW POSER 7 MORPHING TOOLS

Some of the most exciting new features in Poser 7 are the enhanced morphing tools. You open the new morphing tools by clicking the Morphing Tool icon in the Editing Tools, shown in Figure 8.19.

FIGURE 8.19 Click the Morphing Tool icon in the Editing Tools to open the new morphing tools in Poser 7.

You'll see two tabs in the Morphing Tool window: the Create tab and the Combine tab. The Create tab, shown in Figure 8.20, contains tools that allow you to push, pool, smooth, or restore vertices to their original positions. In other words, you can create your own custom morphs by moving vertices and polygons around with a tool that is similar to a paintbrush.

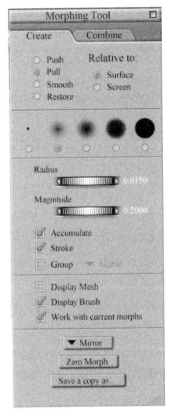

FIGURE 8.20   The Create tab in the Morphing Tool allows you to create custom morphs by moving vertices and polygons around with a tool that is similar to a paintbrush.

There are five sections in the Create tab. The controls in these sections serve the following functions:

> **Push, Pull, Smooth, and Restore:** Select one of these options to determine how the Morphing Tool will affect your geometry. *Push* moves the vertices inward (like a dimple) toward the direction

that you push the tool. *Pull* moves the vertices outward (like a bump) toward the direction that you pull. *Smooth* evens out the irregularities in the morph, creating softer transitions between high and low areas. *Restore* gradually removes the morph in the areas that you use the tool.

Relative to: Select one of these options to determine the point of reference that relates to the changes in the morph. Choose *Surface* (the default) to create changes based on the direction at which the surface normals of the polygons are facing. Choose *Screen* to move the vertices toward the current view relative to the screen.

Brush styles: The five brush shape icons shown in Figure 8.21 display how the Morphing Tool will affect the area that you morph. Choose the first option button to move one vertex at a time. The remaining options affect the area that you define by the radius setting, but each option has a different falloff rate. The second brush shape affects the vertices in the middle of the brush but gradually falls off to having no effect in the outer areas. Each successive brush falls off more rapidly until the last brush shape, which has no falloff at all, and will affect all vertices equally.

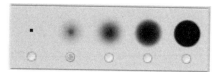

FIGURE 8.21 The brush styles provide several options that affect the areas under control of the Morphing Tool and how quickly the effect of the Morphing Tool falls off from the center point.

Radius: The radius setting defines the area that will be affected by the Morphing Tool. If you have the Display Brush feature enabled (as described later), you can see the effect of the radius setting and how large the affected area will be. Decrease the setting to affect a smaller area, and increase the setting to affect a larger area.

Magnitude: This setting determines the strength of the Morphing Tool. Reduce this setting to obtain finer control over the response of the brush. Higher settings will create results that are more dramatic but not as easy to control.

Accumulate: Check this option to make changes to the mesh for as often as a single brushstroke passes over the same polygons. Uncheck this option to make changes to the mesh when the brush passes over polygons only once.

Stroke: Check this option to allow mouse movements to adjust the degree of the morph in the area on which you first clicked the brush. Uncheck this option to allow the brush to affect areas outside the initial area you clicked upon. This latter option allows you to paint morphs on your geometry very freely.

Display Mesh: Check this option to display the wireframe mesh as a guide while you create your morphs.

Display Brush: By default, Poser displays the area that the Morphing Tool will affect as a multicolored circular area, with the red part of the circle having the most effect and the green area of the circle having the least effect. An example of this display is shown in Figure 8.22. If you find the display distracting, check this option to hide the multicolored display while you work on your morphs.

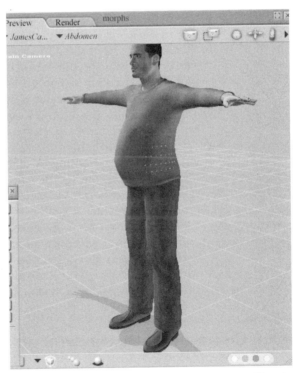

FIGURE 8.22 The area affected by the Morphing Tool brush is displayed in multicolored dots. To turn off this display, deselect the Display Brush option.

Work with current morphs: If you want to create a morph that works in combination with other morph settings, check this option. Set the existing morphs as desired, and then use the Morphing Tool to customize the morphs further. When you set the previous morphs back to zero, you will then see *only* the custom morph that you created yourself. If you want to create a totally original morph, leave this option unchecked and use a combination of magnets and the Morphing Tool to create your morphs.

Group: Check this option to specify the groups the Morphing Tool will affect. Enable this option to display a list of all polygon groups that exist for the current actor, and select a group to work on.

Mirror: Select an option from the Mirror menu to mirror the effects of a morph on one side of a group to the opposite side. Note that this option does not affect multiple groups at this time; the affects of the morph are only mirrored in the current group that you are working on. The *+x to –x* option mirrors morphs on the left side to the right side. The *–x to +x* option mirrors morphs on the right side to the left side. The *+y to –y* option mirrors morphs on the top side to the bottom side. The *–y to +y* option mirrors morphs on the bottom side to the top side. The *+z to –z* option mirrors morphs on the front side to the back side. The *–z to +z* option mirrors morphs on the back side to the front side.

Zero Morph: Click this button to remove all changes made by the Morphing Tool in the current group.

Save a copy as: Click this button to save a copy of the morph under a name of your choosing. A dialog box prompts you to enter a name for the morph. The new morph dial appears in the Parameters window when you select the body part from which the morph was created. Note that if you created the morph with the Work with current morphs check box selected, the morph saved with this option will only include the changes that you made with the Morphing Tool. If you want to combine morphs made with magnets along with morphs made with the Morphing Tool, choose Object > Spawn Morph Target instead.

TUTORIAL 8.7   CREATING FACE MORPHS WITH THE MORPHING TOOL

One of the first things that you can do with the new Morphing Tool is enhance or create new face morphs to create totally original characters. The morph brush helps you push or pull vertices around to reshape the features of your character. In this tutorial, you'll learn how you can create a few facial morphs and add new morph dials for the face.

This example will use James G2, which you can find in the Poser 7 > Figures > G2 > James G2 Figures Library. Of course, you can use any figure you choose. After you load your figure, follow these steps:

1. Choose Display > Cameras > Face Camera to switch to the Face Camera.
2. Click the Morphing Tool icon in the Editing Tools (shown in Figure 8.23) to open the Morphing Tool Palette.

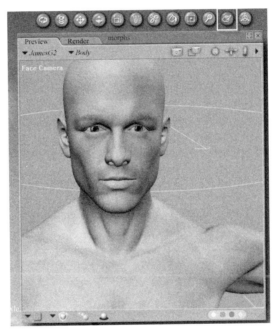

FIGURE 8.23   Click the Morphing Tool icon in the Editing Tools.

3. In the Morphing Tool Palette, choose Pull, relative to Surface, and select the second brush shape option (these should all be default settings).
4. Verify that the Display Brush option is selected, and adjust the Radius of the brush until you get a brush size that is appropriate to morph James' cheek. We are using a setting of .0140 in our example.
5. Adjust the Magnitude setting until the brush responds to your liking. Too high of a setting makes the morph brush work too easily. Lower settings give you finer control of the brush effect. Test the setting by making adjustments to the face with the Morphing Tool, and click the Zero Morph button to restore the face to its original shape before you continue finding a setting you like. In our example, we used a setting of .14.

6. Uncheck the Accumulate setting, and check the Stroke setting. This allows you to work anywhere on the face with the Morphing brush.

7. Make some changes to the left side of James' face. In our example, we have removed the indentation in his left cheek to make his cheeks puffier. You may need to use a combination of Push, Pull, Smooth, and Restore to get the shape you want. An example of our changes is shown in Figure 8.24.

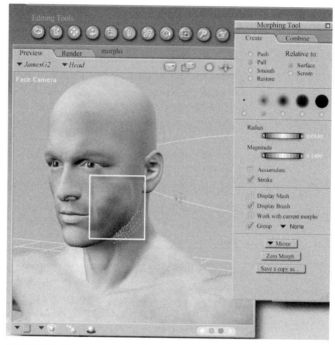

FIGURE 8.24   Changes are made to one side of James' face.

8. Fortunately, there is an easy way to make the morph symmetrical on the other side of the face. You can use the Mirror feature to create an identical morph on the right side of James' face. To do so, click the Mirror button in the lower section of the Morphing Tool. Because you want to mirror the left side (+x) to the right side (–x), choose the +x to –x option as shown in Figure 8.25.

Note that to mirror a morph, the left and right sides of the morph must be contained in the same group that you are currently working on. You can mirror a morph on the right side of the face to the left side of the face. However, if you create a morph for the left collar and want to mirror it to the right collar, you'll have to first use the

Group Editor to create a group that includes both of those parts. Morph one side of the group, and then mirror the morph to the other side.

Another option for mirroring morphs is to purchase Poser Tool Box from http://www.philc.net. This reasonably-priced, very ingenious set of Python scripts includes many utilities that enhance the use of Poser. Among them is a Mirror Morph script that will mirror morphs from one side of a figure to another.

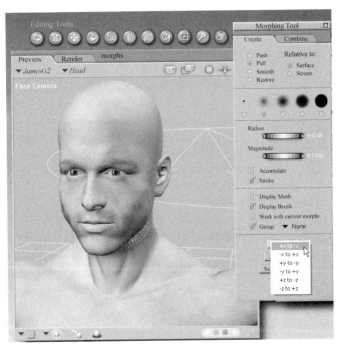

FIGURE 8.25   The Mirror feature allows you to mirror the morph onto the other side of the face.

9. Finally, after you complete your original morph, click the Save a copy as button at the bottom of the Morphing Tool. Poser will prompt you to add a name for your new morph as shown in Figure 8.26. Your morph will then appear in the Combine tab as a new morph for the head.

10. If you want to continue making unique morphs, click the Zero Morph button in the Morphing Tool to start from an unmorphed head. You can continue making as many morphs as you like in this manner.

11. After you complete your morphing session, don't forget to save your new character to the Figures Library. Simply navigate to the library of your choice, and click the Add to Library button at the bottom of

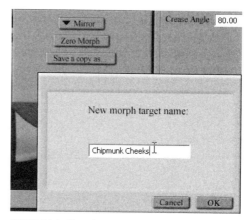

FIGURE 8.26 Use the Save a copy as command to save the morph to the face.

the Library Palette. Poser will prompt you to enter a name for your new figure, and then you should see a thumbnail appear in the Figures Library.

TUTORIAL 8.8 FIXING POKE-THROUGHS WITH THE MORPHING TOOL

Another very handy use for the new morphing features is to help eliminate poke-throughs in clothing when you pose your figure. Figure 8.27 shows an arm muscle that is poking through a sleeve. The Morphing Tool is much easier and quicker to use than magnets for fixing these types of problems. You'll also find the tool to be a very effective solution to fitting clothing to body shapes that are different from the default body shape.

The following steps work really well when you are trying to adjust poke-through in clothing:

1. Add your figure and clothing to your scene, and conform the clothing to the figure.
2. Morph and pose your figure as you would like it to appear in your final image.
3. Examine the figure for poke-through issues. In the example shown in Figure 8.27, we see the arm poking through the bottom of the left sleeve.

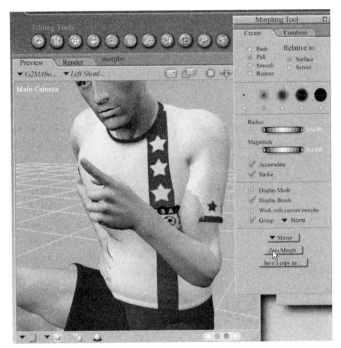

FIGURE 8.27   The Morphing Tool is also a great solution for fixing poke-through problems in clothing.

4. Before you open the Morphing Tool, click the offending body part that is poking through the clothing. For example, in our case, we click James' left shoulder.

5. Choose Figure > Lock Figure. This prevents accidental morphing of James' body while you work on the clothing morph.

6. Now, click the Morphing Tool icon to open the Morphing Tool.

7. Make sure that you have Pull selected as the morphing mode. Select the type of brush you want to use, and adjust the Radius and Magnitude of the tool to get the results you desire.

8. Check Accumulate and Stroke so that you can build up on the morph as you are working. Start the stroke on a section on the shirt where the arm is not poking through the sleeve, and then work your way in toward the area that is poking through. You will eventually "brush away" the poke-through of the arm as you pull the sleeve out over the arm. Figure 8.28 shows this procedure in progress.

FIGURE 8.28   Before morphing (left), the arm pokes through the sleeve quite a bit. To fix the issue, start in an area where the body is not poking through the clothing (middle), and work inward until the poke-through is covered with your new morph (right).

DISTRIBUTING MORPHS

Morphs can be distributed in a number of different ways, and the method you use depends on the user's license of the figure that you created the morphs for. Before you distribute any of your own custom morphs, be sure to verify which of the following methods is the correct way to distribute morphs for your figure:

- By default, Poser saves morph data for objects as external binary morph files. These files have a PMD extension and are saved in the same library as the original character file. The only drawback to this option is that PMD files are compatible only with Poser 6 and 7. If you want to create morphs that are compatible with earlier versions of Poser, you should disable this feature so that Poser saves the morph data within the CR2 file. To do so, choose Edit > General Preferences, and click the Misc. tab. Uncheck the Use external binary morph targets check box as shown in Figure 8.29.
- If you want to distribute morphs with your own original clothing, you can save the morph data within the CR2 library file. To do this, make sure you have the Use external binary morph targets check box unchecked and also that you do not use file compression when saving your files to the library. Your morphs will be saved along with the clothing, in an editable CR2 file when saved in this manner.

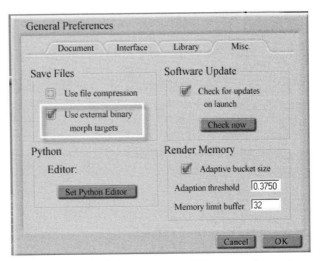

FIGURE 8.29   Uncheck the Use external binary morph targets check box to create morphs for earlier Poser versions.

- Many characters (most notably the DAZ3D Unimesh figures such as Victoria 3, Michael 3, David 3, and Stephanie Petite) are furnished with separate face and body morphs. The base character file has morph channels within it that are ready to accept "injected" morphs. The morph data is furnished separately, and library files are included in the Pose Library to inject or remove the morph data from the model. Utilities such as Injection Magic and Injection Pose Builder are available at DAZ3D to help you prepare injection morphs such as these. There are also some tutorials available at DAZ3D's Tutorial Arcana (*http://www.daz3d.com/support/tutorial/index.php?cat=6*) regarding creating Injection morphs by hand or with the previously mentioned utilities.

MAGNETS AND THE "NEXT GENERATION" POSER FIGURES

As this book goes to press, we are beginning to see the next generation in Poser figures. For the e frontier figures, these characters are known as the G2 Males and Females (G2 meaning *Generation 2*). For DAZ3D, the first figure that will arrive in the new generation is Victoria 4, the fourth generation of their popular female figure.

These new figures make extensive use of magnets that aid in posing and morphing figures. With magnets, the added advantage over regular morphs is that you will be able to apply the same effects to clothing. Here's how it works . . .

Although you can't immediately see them, these new generation figures have many magnets included in them. These magnets are added to the base figure, and are preprogrammed to move joints in specific ways when you pose a figure. They are, in effect, *joint-controlled magnets*.

These magnets are not readily visible in your scene until you click a body part. You'll then notice the magnet and magnet zone on the body part, as you'll see later in Figure 8.31. Remember the bulging muscle that we covered over with the Morphing Tool in Tutorial 8.8? Had this been an earlier generation figure, you would need to create a morph to fix the poke-through issues on the muscle, as we explained in the previous tutorial. However, now you'll learn how easy it is to fix the issue with James G2 and clothing made for him.

The new generation of Poser figures comes with a CR2 (figure file) that is especially prepared for clothing content creators to use as the source CR2 for their clothing. This developer's rig contains all of the information that defines the magnets used to shape and contour the body of James G2 when you pose him. In effect, by using the developer's rig as the starting point for making their clothing posable, they put the same magnets in the clothing that are used in James G2. By using the same magnets in the clothing, the clothing responds in exactly the same way as the figure when you pose it. Figure 8.30 shows the developer's CR2 for James G2, which you'll find in the same library as the character. The file name is JamesG2_DEV.

FIGURE 8.30 Clothing developers use a special development rig for the G2 Poser figures. This CR2 contains all of the information for the joint-controlled magnets.

On the developer's side of things, he or she ensures that the rig puts all of the magnet information in place in the clothing. On the user's end, there is one extra step in making the clothing work. The reason for this additional step is that the information that "links" the magnets to the clothing and the figure is not automatically saved to the library. Instead, the end user has to apply the magnets to the clothing with a pose. In the case of James G2, you'll find the pose in the Poser 7 > Poses > G2 Male folder. The pose is named AddDeformers, as shown in Figure 8.31.

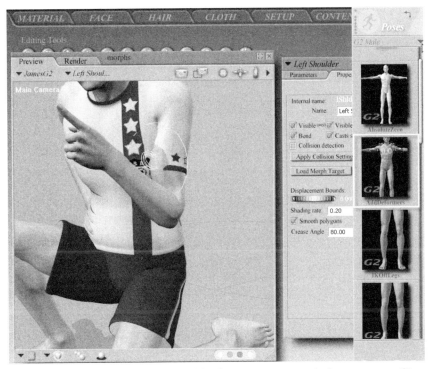

FIGURE 8.31   The end user applies an AddDeformers pose to apply the magnets to G2 generation clothing.

The basic steps are the following:

1. You load your G2 figure: James G2, Jessi G2, Koji G2, Miki G2, Kelvin G2, or Olivia G2.
2. You apply a piece of conforming clothing that was created for one of these figures.
3. You conform the clothing to the figure in the normal manner.

4. You make sure that the conformed clothing is selected when click the AddDeformers pose in the applicable Pose Library. After that, you should see the poke-throughs disappear, as shown in Figure 8.32.

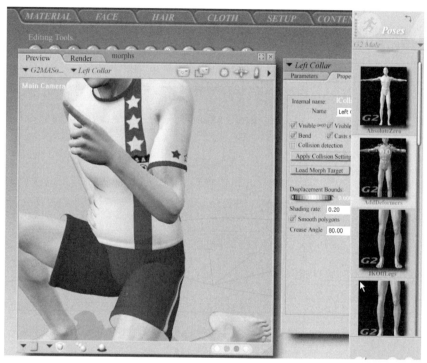

FIGURE 8.32 After applying the AddDeformers pose, the clothing responds exactly the same way as the figure.

AVOIDING PROBLEMS

Many things can go wrong when you create morphs. For example, the software that you use to create the morphs might place the vertices in a different order when you save the geometry. Or, you can accidentally move the geometry, and when you apply it to your figure, the geometry might fly off in a different direction than you intended. To avoid these problems, here are a few things to keep in mind:

- Don't move the position of the figure after you import the figure into your modeling program. For example, if the figure comes into your modeling program with its feet above or below ground level, don't translate the position. It will affect the ending position of your morphs.

- Many modeling programs cannot handle the extremely small scale used in Poser, so you'll need utilities to scale the figures up for morphing and then scale the figure back down by the equivalent amount for importing into Poser. Because procedures vary from 3D program to 3D program, it's a good idea to touch base with others who use the same modeling software that you use. Chances are, they have figured out the best approaches for your software and can help you through the process.

- When using an external program for morphing, don't make any changes to the *construction* of the geometry. That is, don't weld vertices, don't add or remove vertices, don't subdivide any vertices. Doing so will make your morphs incompatible with the original figure.

- When you try to import a morph target into Poser, you might get a message that says "Target geometry has wrong number of vertices." Check first to make sure that you have selected the right body part to add the morph to. Then check to make sure that the morph target you are importing was created for that body part. If the body parts are the same, you may have inadvertently added or removed vertices during the process of creating the morph. One way to verify this is to open the morphed version in UV Mapper Professional and compare the number of vertices in the original and in the morphed part.

- Sometimes the morph target appears to apply itself correctly. But when you dial the morph in, the body part looks all wrinkled and jumbled. This is because your morphing software reordered the vertices. If this happens, delete the morph from the Parameters window. Then when you reimport the morph, check the Attempt Vertex Order Correction check box in the Load Morph Target dialog box. This may resolve the problem. If it doesn't, UV Mapper Professional also has the capability to reorder vertices, and you may be able to fix the morph that way.

CONCLUSION

Morphs and magnets help a character or clothing become more versatile. You can also use morphs or magnets to help fit clothing to a character more easily. Whether you decide to create morphs with Poser magnets or with a third-party modeling program, you can add value to your own creations by providing a good selection of morphs that alter the appearance or function of your original creations. With the knowledge you've gained in this chapter, you'll be able to add versatility and functionality to your original Poser objects.

CHAPTER

9

UV MAPPING

In This Chapter

- Why You Need UV Maps
- Types of UV Maps
- Using UV Mapper Professional
- Tutorial 9.1 UV Mapping a Skirt
- Tutorial 9.2 UV Mapping Pants
- Tutorial 9.3 UV Mapping a Shirt
- UV Mapping with Body Paint 2.5
- Tutorial 9.4 Importing an OBJ File into Body Paint
- Tutorial 9.5 UV Mapping a Shirt with Body Paint
- Tutorial 9.6 Exporting the Body Paint OBJ File for Poser
- Making Templates

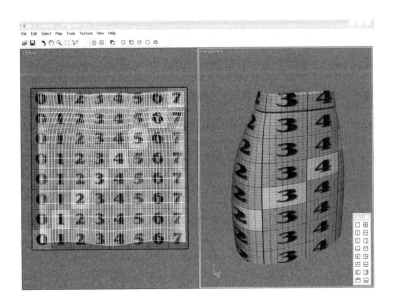

When you create an object in a 3D-modeling program, you need a way to tell the software how the surface of the object looks at each point. The material properties—color, specularity, bumpiness, and so on—need to be assigned to each portion of the surface. In the 3D world, this information is contained a *UV map*. A UV map is, more or less, a flattened representation of the surface of a 3D object. Without some way of mapping textures and other properties on the surface of an object, the entire surface of the object could only be one color or one material.

If poorly mapped, the UV map can make textures appear distorted. In this chapter, you'll learn about various types of UV maps that you can generate and how to break an object down into its basic shapes so that distortion and stretching are minimized when you map textures onto it.

WHY YOU NEED UV MAPS

Basically, a UV map "flattens" the surface of a 3D object so that you can create a texture for it in a 2D paint program, such as Photoshop. To explain UV maps in simple terms, imagine peeling an orange and then smashing the peel flat onto the surface of the table. The peel of the orange would need to be cut in several places to accommodate being flattened out. The important thing is that, if we wanted to, we could pin the peel back onto the surface of the orange and all the seams would line up perfectly—we could wrap our orange back up in its peel. Another way to think of it is to imagine taking a map of the world and wrapping it around a sphere. If you have a map that is flat and rectangular, the poles appear to be as wide as the equator. But the Earth is truly a sphere, and the equator is wider than the poles, so to wrap a flat world map around a sphere, you would have to reduce the width of the texture toward the top and bottom of each side to make it fit without wrinkling.

UV maps work on the same principle. When you create a UV map, you are "unfolding" your 3D object onto a flat plane. Along with telling the software what shape your object is, you are also determining which axis to orient the texture map to—in other words, whether you are looking at the object from the top, side, or front.

That is what a UV map does. It basically tells your 3D software that the pixels in one portion of a flat 2D texture are applied to one or more specific polygons in the 3D model. So, to wrap the Earth texture around the sphere properly, you have to create a UV map that says, "Wrap a rectangular texture around this object in a spherical fashion, and place the top-left corner of the image at this point of the 3D model."

Carnivale, © 2006, Ana Winson (Arien)

Lithium Flower, © 2006, Ana Winson (Arien)

Coyness, © 2006, Denise Tyler (Deecey)

Black Agnes, © Gina Pitkänen (Ravnheart)

Fairy Magic, © Gina Pitkänen (Ravnheart)

Fallen One, © Gina Pitkänen (Ravnheart)

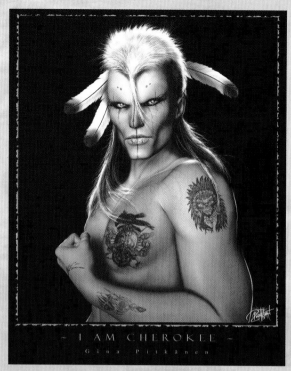

I Am Cherokee, © Gina Pitkänen (Ravnheart)

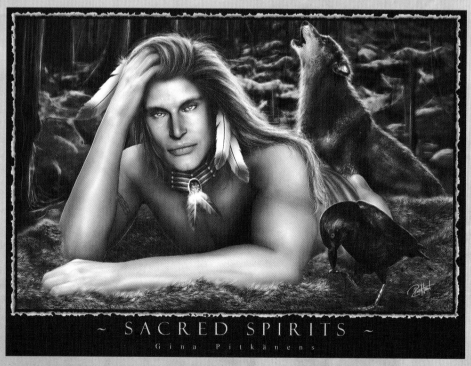

Sacred Spirits, © Gina Pitkänen (Ravnheart)

The Guardian, © Gina Pitkänen (Ravnheart)

The Forest Lake, © 2002, Janne Pitkänen (ToxicAngel)

I Rule, © 2006, Janne Pitkänen (ToxicAngel)

Little Dragon, © 2004, Janne Pitkänen (ToxicAngel)

My Freedom, © 2003, Janne Pitkänen (ToxicAngel)

River of Skulls, © 2002, Janne Pitkänen (ToxicAngel)

Revenge of the Horseclans, © 2006, Niki Browning (SkyeWolf)

Don't Even Think About It. © 2006, Denise Tyler (Deecey)

TYPES OF UV MAPS

Most modeling or UV-mapping software allows you to create at least four common types of UV maps:

Spherical: Best for globes and other objects that are shaped like a sphere.

Planar: Best for flat objects, such as a door, a tabletop, or a mirror. A playing card is also a good example of planar mapping. If you flipped the card over, you'd see a mirror image of the map that is projected on the front.

Box: A natural for box-shaped objects that require a different texture or orientation on each side.

Cylindrical: Good for cans, sleeves, and many types of clothing. Cylindrical mapping can also include mapping for solid ends (also known as *end caps*) when needed.

If you take the time to use the right type of mapping on each object or each portion of an object, you can avoid stretching and distortion. Sometimes the right mapping isn't obvious, especially with organic shapes, so you have to experiment with what works best. With careful study, you can break any object into one or more of these different shapes.

Before we get on with the tutorials, it will help you to see how the different types of mapping look on different shapes. It is important to note that the results of the various types of mapping also vary depending on which axis you orient the mapping to. With that in mind, the examples shown in Figures 9.1 through 9.3 show objects oriented as they would normally appear: top up, bottom down, and with front facing toward the viewer at a slight angle.

Figure 9.1 shows how a sphere looks when mapped with each of the different mapping types. In this example, both spherical (top left) and cylindrical (bottom right) mapping do an adequate job of mapping the sphere with minimal distortion. On the other hand, planar mapping (top right) creates distortion on the sides, and box mapping (bottom left) creates too many seams.

In Figure 9.2, you see a cube that is mapped with the various mapping types. The most natural choice for a cube is box mapping, shown at the bottom left. Spherical mapping (top left) distorts the map on all sides, and cylindrical mapping (bottom right) distorts the top and bottom. Planar mapping would map opposite sides perfectly, although the back side would be mirrored when it faced the camera, and the remaining four sides would be distorted. You *can* map each individual side of a box with planar mapping, but you would have to change the orientation of the planar map for each side. Box mapping does this for you automatically.

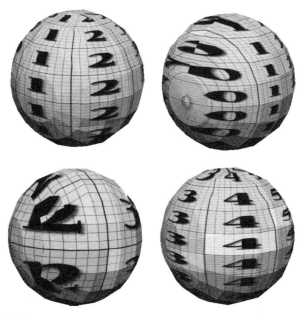

FIGURE 9.1   A sphere is usually mapped with spherical UVs (top left); remaining shots show planar (top right), box (bottom left), and cylindrical mapping (bottom right) on the sphere.

FIGURE 9.2   A box is usually mapped with six-sided box UVs (bottom left); remaining shots show the effects of spherical (top left), planar (top right), and cylindrical mapping (bottom right).

Figure 9.3 shows how the various types of mapping affect something that is cylindrical in shape. The natural choice is cylindrical (bottom right) if the object is open at either end. If closed at both ends, as a can of soup would be before you opened it, some UV-mapping programs give you the option to include the end caps in the UV map. In that case, the end caps would be mapped in flat, or planar, mode.

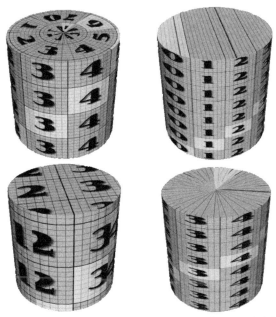

FIGURE 9.3   Although cylindrical mapping (bottom right) is a logical choice for objects that are cylindrically shaped, spherical mapping (top left) also works very well.

Continuing with our cylinder examples, note that spherical mapping (top left in Figure 9.3) can also be used to successfully map a cylinder. The tops and bottoms of the cylinder will be mapped so that the texture meets in the center of the flat plane. Planar mapping (top right) will cause distortion at the sides and top, and box mapping (bottom left) will create unwanted seams.

With the basics out of the way, let's take a look at how you can actually apply this information. You'll use UV Mapper Professional (*http://www.uvmapper.com*), a demo of which is included in the Demos > UV Mapper folder on the CD-ROM that accompanies this book. Note that you won't be able to save your models with the demo version, so we've included a mapped version of the models on the CD-ROM to show you the final results.

ON THE CD

USING UV MAPPER PROFESSIONAL

UV Mapper Professional, written by Steve Cox, is a utility that Poser enthusiasts use frequently to create UV maps and texture templates for their 3D models. UV Mapper Professional contains many features that are found in more advanced mapping utilities, yet the price is very reasonable. A free version, UV Mapper Classic, is also available. You can use the free version of UV Mapper Classic to create UV maps or templates, but you won't have the advanced selection modes or relaxing features that are available in the Pro version.

We'll start with something simple and basic: a skirt.

TUTORIAL 9.1 | **UV-MAPPING A SKIRT**

Think about the main types of mapping that you have: spherical, planar, box, and cylindrical. (UV Mapper also creates *polar mapping*, but the needs for this type of mapping aren't as common as the others). Of these types of shapes, a skirt most closely resembles a cylinder.

To map a skirt with UV Mapper, follow these steps:

ON THE CD

1. Open UV Mapper Professional. Choose File > Open Model, and locate the Tutorials > Chap09 folder on the CD-ROM that accompanies this book. Choose skirt.obj, and click Open.
2. UV Mapper displays the statistics of the object. Click OK to continue. A 3D version of the skirt appears in the Perspective view on the right side of the screen. Initially, the left side is blank, indicating that the object does not have any UV information.
3. Choose Texture > Checker > Color. This puts a checkered pattern with numbers in the left Texture display. This helps you position objects so that seams match and also helps you determine whether the texture map is facing in the right direction.
4. Because the skirt most resembles a cylinder in shape, choose Map > Cylindrical. The Cylindrical Mapping dialog box shown in Figure 9.4 appears.
5. In the case of the skirt, we want the UV mapping to map the skirt along the Y (up/down) axis, which is selected by default. Also note the Seam Rotation setting. When set at 0, the seam appears in the back of the garment, which is what you want. Accept the remaining default settings, and click OK.
6. Observe the left and right sides of the UV map. You may notice that the seam didn't break evenly along the same line of polygons. One way that you can fix this is to select polygons from one side and move them to the other. You'll find it easier to perform this task if you turn

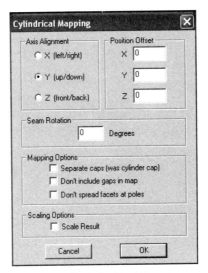

FIGURE 9.4   The Cylindrical Mapping
dialog box contains settings to help map
objects that are cylindrical in shape.

the checkered texture off, so choose Texture > Clear. Answer Yes
when UV Mapper asks if you really want to clear the background.

7. Use the Magnifier tool and the Hand tool to move in closer to the left
side of the texture area.

8. With the Selection tool, select the polygons that you want to move to
the other side of the skirt. Figure 9.5 shows the polygons selected.

9. Pick the Hand tool, and pan the Texture view down to see the remaining polygons if you couldn't get them all in the first round. Shift-click
to add the additional polygons to the selection if necessary. You can
also Alt-click to remove polygons from the selection.

10. Use the magnifier to zoom out until you can see the entire texture
again. Or, use the View > Reset View command.

11. Press the Shift key while you use the right arrow key to move the selected polygons to the right side. When the polygons get close to where
you want them, use the right-arrow or left arrow keys (without pressing the Shift key) to nudge them in place 1 pixel at a time. If necessary,
zoom in closer with the Magnifier tool to position them immediately
next to the existing polygons. Figure 9.6 shows proper placement.

12. To stitch the moved polygons back into the skirt, you need to switch
to Vertex Selection mode. To do so, choose Select > Select Method >
By Vertex.

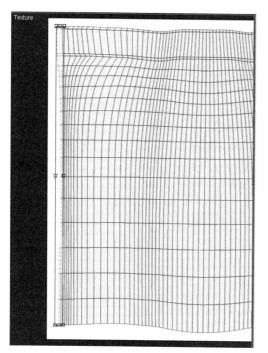

FIGURE 9.5 A portion of the polygons are selected. These polygons will move to the other side of the skirt.

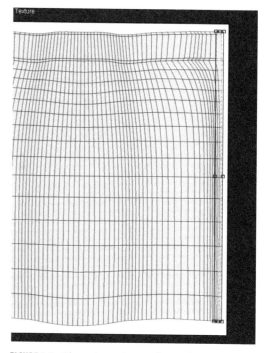

FIGURE 9.6 Place the polygons immediately adjacent to those on the other side.

13. Zoom out until you see the entire right side of the skirt. Use the Rectangular Selection tool to draw a selection around the polygons on the right side, making sure that you enclose all of the polygons you moved plus some additional for good measure. The selected vertices turn red.

14. To stitch them together, choose Tools > UVs > Stitch. When UV Mapper asks if you really want to stitch the vertices together, choose YES.

15. If desired, choose Texture > Checker > Color to view the final result before you save the new skirt. (Note that you cannot save with the demo version of UV Mapper Professional.)

16. If you have the full version of UV Mapper Professional, choose File > Save Model. Leave all options unchecked, and choose OK to save the model with its UV information. A mapped version of the skirt appears on the CD-ROM in Tutorials > Chapter 09 as skirt-mapped.obj. Figure 9.7 shows the final result of the UV maps.

ON THE CD

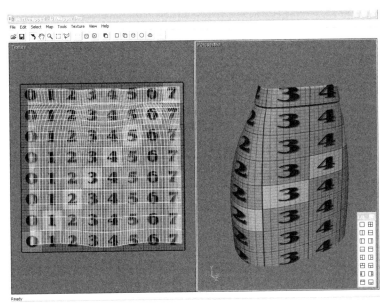

FIGURE 9.7   The final map for the skirt.

TUTORIAL 9.2   UV-MAPPING PANTS

Pants are a little more complicated to map than a skirt, but the process will teach you how to look at an object and break it into separate elements to map it properly.

When you look at a pair of pants, you basically see two separate cylinders that are joined together at the top, in the center. That is also the best way to approach the mapping. First, you divide it in half, with one cylinder in each half. Then you unfold each of the cylinders to flatten them. Finally, you stitch the two cylinders back together again.

To create UV maps for pants in UV Mapper Professional, follow these steps:

ON THE CD

1. Open UV Mapper Professional. Choose File > Open Model, and locate the Tutorials > Chap09 folder on the CD-ROM that accompanies this book. Choose pants.obj, and click Open.
2. UV Mapper displays the statistics of the object. Click OK to continue. A 3D version of the pants appears in the Perspective view on the right side of the screen. Initially, the left side is blank, indicating that the object does not have any UV information.

3. Turn off the display of the background texture. It will help you see things more easily until you get to the final stage. To do so, choose Texture > Clear.

4. The best way to start with pants is to first map them in planar mode without separating the front and back. To do so, choose Map > Planar. The Planar Mapping dialog box appears.

5. By default, UV Mapper Professional does planar mapping on the Z Axis and By Orientation. These two options, together, split the clothing article between the front- and back sides. We don't want to split the clothing right now, so choose Don't Split, as shown in Figure 9.8. Click OK to continue.

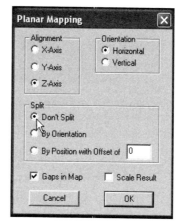

FIGURE 9.8 Don't split the pants when you begin to map them.

6. If you are continuing from the previous tutorial, you'll need to return to Facet Selection mode. To do so, choose Select > Select Method > By Facet.

7. With the Rectangular Selection tool, select the entire left side of the pants to the center seam. Make sure that you select all of the polygons on the inside of the leg. The easiest way to do this is to start with the selection on the left side of the pants and drag to the center until the selection box is exactly over the center line of the pants.

8. With the selection still active, choose Map > Cylindrical. The Cylindrical Mapping dialog box appears. Accept the default for Y (up/down) Axis Alignment, and continue with the next step.

9. By default, cylindrical mapping places the seam toward the back when you are mapping to the Y axis. We want the seam to fall on the inside of the leg. To do this, enter **90 degrees** in the Seam Rotation

field. Then click OK to exit the dialog box. UV Mapper Professional maps the pants leg in a cylindrical fashion.

10. You'll notice that some of the facets in the bottom of the leg are flipped around the wrong way and create a tear in the leg. To fix that, use the Polygonal Selection tool to select the lower half of the pants, making sure that you start the selection above where the distortion begins. An example is shown in Figure 9.9.

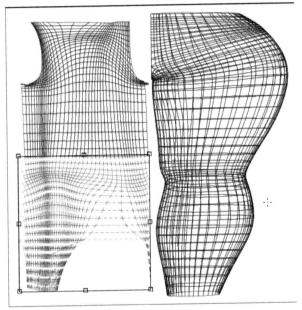

FIGURE 9.9   Select the lower portion of the pants to fix the distortions.

11. With the selection of the lower half of the pants leg in its original position, choose Map > Cylindrical again. The settings should remain from the previous time you used it. Click OK to exit the dialog box.

12. Now, choose Vertex Selection mode (Select > Select Method > By Vertex). Make a selection that includes the area where you broke the connection between the upper and lower portions of the pants, as shown in Figure 9.10. Then stitch them together (Tools > UVs > Stitch). Select the other half, and stitch them together as well.

If you select the entire width of the leg to stitch the vertices together, UV Mapper will stitch them together at the seam. This makes the UV map hard to read. Selecting half at a time prevents this from occurring.

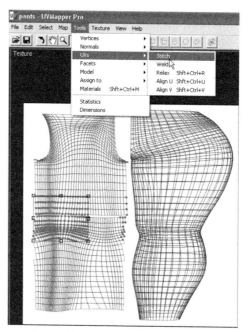

FIGURE 9.10   After remapping the lower portion, stitch the upper- and lower leg back together, one half at a time.

13. Now, return to Facet Selection mode (Select > Select Method > By Facet). Select the other leg, and choose Map > Cylindrical again. This time, enter **270 degrees** in the Seam Rotation field so that the seam appears on the inside of this leg. Then choose OK.

14. Remap and stitch the lower portion as you did in Steps 10 through 12. If the width of the lower section is different from that of the upper section after you remap it, drag the selection from any side to resize them to match the upper section. Then stitch them together, one half at a time, in Vertex Selection mode. The final result should look similar to Figure 9.11.

15. The final problem that we have to tackle is cleaning up the seams so that the break falls along the same column of polygons. First, switch back to Facet Selection mode (Select > Select Method > By Facet).

16. Let's add a little more space between the two sections of pants. Select the left half, and hold the Shift key while pressing the left arrow key once or twice to move the section toward the left edge of the work area.

17. Use the Polygon Selection tool to click just above the first two rows of polygons on the left side of the pants. As you work your way down, remain in the same column of polygons while you follow it down to the bottom of the pants. Then click outside of the selection to work

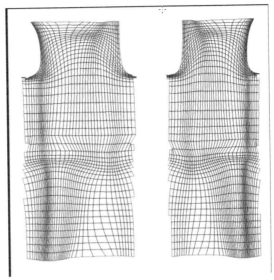

FIGURE 9.11   Both sides of the pants are mapped in cylindrical fashion.

your way back up to the top, as shown in Figure 9.12. Double-click the Polygon tool to end the selection.

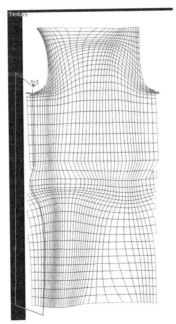

FIGURE 9.12   Select the polygons that you want to move to the other side of the pants leg.

18. Press the Shift key while you use the right arrow to move the selected polygons to the other side of the pants leg. When you get close to the target spot, release the Shift key, and use only the arrow key to nudge the selection into place. Position them as close as you can without overlapping any of the polygons (note that some may not match up exactly, but this is okay).

19. Switch to Vertex Selection mode (Select > Select Method > By Vertex). Use the Selection tool to make a selection large enough to enclose the polygons you moved and the polygons you want to attach them to.

20. Choose Tools > UVs > Stitch. Answer YES to the confirmation dialog box.

21. Repeat Steps 15 through 20 for the other leg, except that you will move polygons from the right side of the leg to the left side. When you are finished, both legs should look as shown in Figure 9.13.

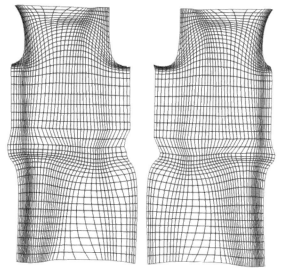

FIGURE 9.13 Both legs are now cleaned up and stitched.

If your legs are different sizes, select one of the legs with the Rectangular Selection tool, and drag the left or right side to change the width accordingly.

22. Choose Texture > Checker > Color to check the final result in the mapping. A final version appears on the CD-ROM in Tutorials > Ch09 as pants-mapped.obj if you are unable to save your model with the demo version.

If desired, you can use UV Mapper Professional's Relax feature to even out the spacing between the polygons. To do so, first choose Edge Selection mode (Select > Select Method > By Edge). Select both sections of pants, and the edge vertices should turn blue. Then choose Tools > UVs > Relax. Leave the settings at their defaults, and click the Apply button one or more times until you are satisfied with the results. Watch the checkerboard texture on the 3D Preview while you relax the vertices.

TUTORIAL 9.3   UV-MAPPING A SHIRT

Shirts present a little bit of a challenge to those who are new to UV mapping, so it helps to know the right technique. Basically, the best way to UV-map a shirt is with a combination of planar and cylindrical mapping.

When you UV-map more complex objects, it makes the most sense to split the clothing object up into parts where seams would occur in a real garment. In other words, you should separate the sleeves from the torso of the shirt; and you should also separate the front from the back. This helps flatten the shirt more easily.

To UV-map a shirt in UV Mapper Professional, follow these steps:

1. Open UV Mapper Professional. Choose File > Open Model, and locate the Tutorials > Chap09 folder on the CD-ROM that accompanies this book. Choose tshirt.obj and click Open.
2. UV Mapper displays the statistics of the object. Click OK to continue. A 3D version of the shirt appears in the Perspective view on the right side of the screen. Initially, the left side is blank, indicating that the object does not have any UV information.
3. If necessary, remove the checkerboard background from the Texture view (Texture > Clear). Also verify that you are in Facet Selection mode (Select > Select Method > By Facet).
4. To begin, we will planar-map the shirt so that we can remove the sleeves and map them separately. Choose Map > Planar. When the Planar Mapping dialog box appears, choose Z-Axis (which divides the shirt into front and back), and By Orientation (which splits the sides, so that front appears on the left and back appears on the right). Then click OK to create the map.
5. Now use the Rectangular Selection tool to select the first row of polygons for each sleeve in both views, and use Shift-click to add additional selections to the set. Your selection should look as shown in Figure 9.14.
6. Press the zero (0) key on your keyboard. This expands the selection by one row of polygons. Press nine additional times until you have selected all of the vertices in the sleeves.

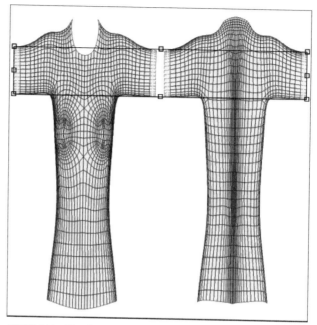

FIGURE 9.14   The first row of vertices is selected in all sleeves.

7. Position the cursor inside the selection area, so that the selection tool changes into an arrow. Drag the sleeve polygons above the work area temporarily.

8. Now, select both sections of the shirt, and choose Map > Cylindrical. Accept the default of Y (up/down). All other options are not checked or set to zero. Click OK to map the shirt.

9. You can easily leave the shirt this way except for one reason that will become obvious if you turn on the Color texture checker (Texture > Checker > Color). The polygons distort the mapping at the top of the shoulders because they are too close together. However, it's a lot easier to select the front of the shirt while the shirt is in cylindrical mode. Use the Polygonal Selection tool to select the front portion of the shirt, dividing it along the center of each armhole. Figure 9.15 shows an example of the selection.

If necessary, you can also select polygons in the 3D-Perspective view. Use the Rectangular Selection tool, and Shift-click to add polygons to the existing selection. You only need to include a small portion of the polygon to add it to the selection. If you mistakenly add polygons to the selection that you do not want, Alt-click to remove them from the selection.

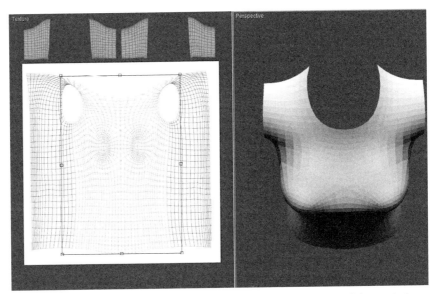

FIGURE 9.15   Select the front of the shirt, dividing the top and bottom of the armhole at the halfway point.

10. With the front of the shirt selected, choose Map > Planar. Choose Don't Split to prevent UV Mapper Professional from separating the side polygons into the back section of the shirt.

11. Press the forward slash (/) key on your number pad to halve the size of the front of the shirt, so that you have more room to work on the other two sections.

12. Select one of the back sections, and choose Map > Planar. Accept the previous settings, and choose OK. Divide it in half with the / key on the number pad. Then select the entire section, and choose Select > Rotate > Flip Horizontal so that the side with the sleeve opening faces the front sleeve opening.

13. Repeat Step 12 for the other back section.

14. Select one section at a time, and move them in closer together if necessary. Space and size the three sections similar to those shown in Figure 9.16. You can also move the sleeves back on to the work area now.

15. Change to Vertex Selection mode (Select > Select Method > By Vertex). Use the Rectangular Selection tool to enclose the vertices between the left side and the front of the shirt, starting from the underarm and continuing to the bottom. Then choose Tools > UVs > Stitch to join them.

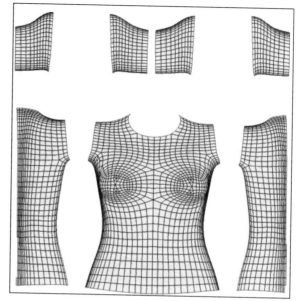

FIGURE 9.16   Scale and position the three sections of the shirt at the bottom of the UV map area.

16. Similarly, enclose the vertices between the right side and the front of the shirt. Then choose Tools > UVs > Stitch to join them. The result should look as shown in Figure 9.17.

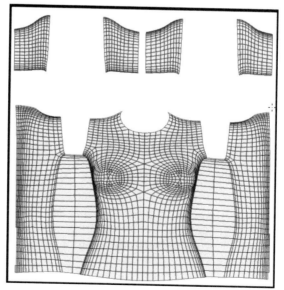

FIGURE 9.17   Stitch the front and sides together at the seams.

17. If you turn on the Color texture checker at this point (Texture > Checker > Color), you'll see that the sides look very distorted. This will result in stretching with any texture you apply to the shirt. UV Mapper Professional allows you to relax vertices to eliminate stretching. But first, we have to hide the parts that we don't want to relax. After you return to Facet Selection mode (Select > Select Method > By Facet), select the sleeves. Then press the left square bracket ([ ) key to hide them.

18. Choose the Edge Selection mode (Select > Select Method > By Edge). Draw a selection around all three shirt sections. The outer vertices will turn blue, indicating that they are selected.

19. Choose Tools > UVs > Relax. When the Relax UVs dialog box appears, accept the default choices. Click the Apply button one or more times, while watching the texture change in the perspective window. Choose OK to apply the changes when you are satisfied with the mapping on the sides of the shirt. Figure 9.18 shows the result.

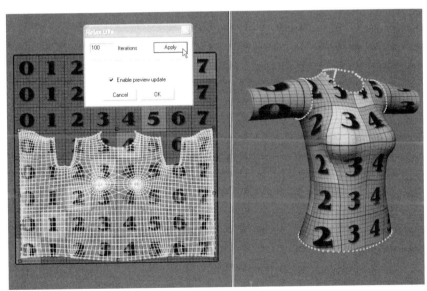

FIGURE 9.18   Relax the UV mapping until you are satisfied with the appearance of the sides of the shirt.

20. Return to Facet Selection mode (Select > Select Method > By Facet). Press the right square bracket key ( ]) to unhide the sleeves. We need to join them at the top. First, select the two sleeves at the left of the screen (the front sleeves). Choose Select > Rotate > 180 degrees to rotate them so that they match up properly with the appropriate sleeve back. Then position the sleeve fronts above the sleeve backs.

21. Switch to Vertex Selection mode (Select > Select Method > By Vertex), and draw a selection that encloses the vertices you want to join on the sleeves. Then choose Tools > UVs > Stitch to connect them. Figure 9.19 shows the result.

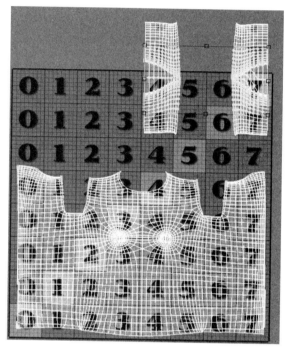

FIGURE 9.19   The sleeves are joined at the top.

22. The final step is to relax the sleeves, and position them in their final place on the map. Make sure you hide the front of the shirt first to prevent it from relaxing further. First, return to Facet Selection mode (Select > Select Method > By Facet). Select the front and back of the shirt, and hide it with the [key.
23. Return to Edge Selection mode (Select > Select Method > By Edge). Select both sleeves. Then use the Relax feature (Tools > UVs > Relax), clicking the Apply button one or more times until the top edges are blended better.
24. Press] to unhide the remainder of the shirt. Return to Facet Selection mode, then rotate and position the sleeves with the Select > Rotate command, and position them as shown in Figure 9.20.

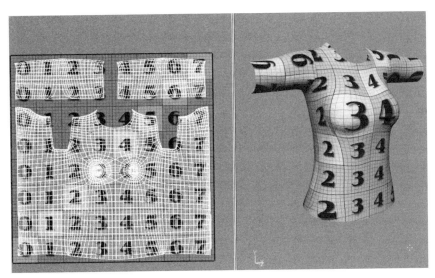

FIGURE 9.20   The finished shirt.

UV Mapping with Body Paint 2.5

Maxon's Body Paint 2.5 is a program that allows you to UV-map and paint directly on a 3D model. It is rapidly gaining popularity in the Poser community. Although it may be considered costly by some, many others consider an application such as this essential to create quality mapping and textures.

If you are going to invest in Body Paint 2.5 (or Body Paint 3 which is pending release as this book goes to press), a couple of additional plug-ins will make interaction with Poser much easier. Both are developed by Keith Young, who is more commonly known as Spanki in the Poser community. More information about these plug-ins can be obtained on his Web site at *http://www.skinprops.com*. The plug-ins are described in the following list:

- Riptide is a free plug-in that provides import and export of OBJ files to and from Poser and Cinema 4D or Body Paint. Although Body Paint does import and export in OBJ format, the Riptide plug-in offers additional capabilities that will help you retain the proper scaling between programs.
- Undertow is a reasonably-priced plug-in that provides additional UV mapping features that are not found in the present release of Body Paint 2.5. This plug-in will also add UV-mapping capability to Cinema 4D.

The UV-mapping features in Body Paint 2.5 are similar to those found in UV Mapper Pro. One major difference, however, is that you can load multiple OBJ files in and map them at the same time. Another difference is that its Relax UV feature creates mapping that is more uniform in appearance.

With that in mind, we'll show you a very simple example of how you bring an OBJ file into Body Paint, how to UV map it, and how to export it out of Body Paint so that it is ready for Poser.

TUTORIAL 9.4   **IMPORTING AN OBJ FILE INTO BODY PAINT**

This tutorial assumes that you have downloaded the Riptide plug-in and installed it into your Body Paint plug-ins folder as directed in the readme files that are included with the product. Riptide will open an object that has been scaled to Poser's very small scaling and automatically scale it up so that it is suitable to work with in Body Paint 2.5. After the UV mapping is done, Riptide then exports it back to Poser's scale.

To import the OBJ file, follow these steps:

1. Open Body Paint 2.5.
2. Assuming that the Riptide plug-in is installed properly in Body Paint, choose Plugins > Riptide > OBJ Importer. The Import OBJ dialog box appears.
3. Locate the file you want to import. For this example, we are using the JessiTShirt.obj file found in the Chapter 09 folder on the CD-ROM that accompanies this book.

ON THE CD

4. After you select the file, the OBJ File Import screen shown in Figure 9.21 appears. This screen has several options:
   - Enter a scale factor of 1000 if it is not already entered.
   - In the General section, make sure that Import Ngons, Import Groups, Import Materials, and Import UV Coords are checked.
   - In the Mesh Splitting area, choose Split By Material if your object already has materials assigned. This will make it easier to select your materials from within Body Paint.
   - In the Document Options section, check Create New Document if you want to include the OBJ file in a UV-mapping project of its own. Choose Merge Into Current Document if you want to work on more than one file at a time in a single document.
5. Press OK to import the OBJ file into Body Paint. You may get a message that there is a Matlib Open Error. This error occurs if you do not have a corresponding MTL file in the same folder as the OBJ file. Don't worry, you can check OK to continue if this message appears. Your object should then appear in Perspective view, though you may

FIGURE 9.21   Riptide's OBJ File Import dialog box provides several options that are handy for UV-mapping Poser objects.

need to use the controls in the upper-right corner of the Perspective view to move the object into view.

TUTORIAL 9.5   **UV-MAPPING A SHIRT WITH BODY PAINT**

After you import your OBJ file into Body Paint, you can begin the UV-mapping process. Just as we mentioned in Tutorial 9.3, the best way to map a shirt is to break it into parts that create seams where they would occur in a real shirt. So we will again separate the sleeves from the torso of the shirt, and we will also separate the front from the back.

To map the T-shirt, follow these steps:

1. From Body Paint 2.5, choose Tools > UV Tools > UV Polygons. If the object already has UV coordinates, they will appear in the right pane in wireframe display mode. Although you can easily start with existing UV mapping and refine it, we'll start over again for purposes of this tutorial.
2. Choose Select Polygon > Select All. All selected polygons turn red.
3. In the lower-right corner of the interface, click the UV Mapping tab. Then, from the list of commands, click the UV Commands button

shown in Figure 9.22. Then click the Start Interactive Mapping button. You will immediately see the mapping of the T-shirt change. Body Paint initially puts a Flat projection on the T-shirt and superimposes the front over the back side.

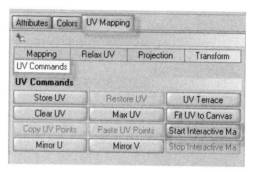

FIGURE 9.22   Body Paint's Interactive Mapping feature is accessed from the UV Commands menu.

4. What we want to do is separate the sleeves from the remainder of the shirt. Use the Zoom icon (the triangular icon in the upper-right corner of the UV layout view) to zoom out so that you can see the entire T-shirt.

5. To select the sleeve polygons, we have to exit Interactive mode. To do so, click the Stop Interactive Mapping button in the UV Mapping tools area shown in Figure 9.23.

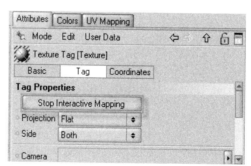

FIGURE 9.23   Click the Stop Interactive Mapping button before selecting polygons.

6. Right-click in the UV Map view, and choose Select Polygon > Deselect All from the context menu. The polygons turn blue.

7. From the toolbar at the left side of your screen, choose the Live Selection tool shown in Figure 9.24. Alternatively, you can choose Tools > UV Tools > Live Selection.

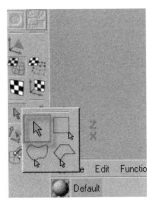

FIGURE 9.24   Use the Live Selection tool to select the sleeves.

8. With the Live Selection tool, paint to select 11 rows of the left sleeve.
9. Press the Shift key while painting 11 rows on the right sleeve to add them to the selection. When you are finished, your selection should look as shown in Figure 9.25.

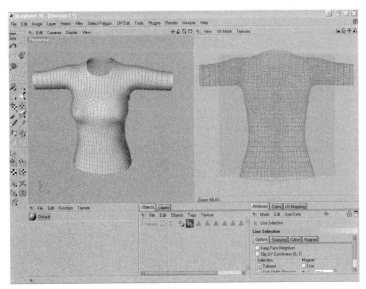

FIGURE 9.25   Both sleeves are selected with the Live Selection tool.

10. Use the Move tool (immediately to the right of the Live Selection tool in the toolbar) to move the sleeves off of the canvas. Now you should be left with the main part of the shirt.

11. Choose the Rectangle Selection tool from the toolbar, or use the Tools > UV Tools > Rectangle Selection command. Draw a selection around the body of the shirt.

12. Again, click the UV Mapping tab, and choose Start Interactive Mapping as you did earlier.

13. In the Attributes tab (shown undocked in Figure 9.26), choose Cylindrical for Projection. The seam (the green line on the cylinder in Perspective view) initially appears at the side of the shirt. This is acceptable because we will be separating the front from the back.

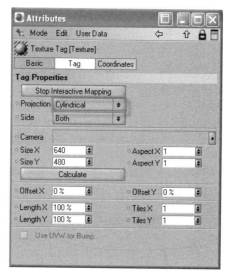

FIGURE 9.26   Choose Cylindrical Mapping from the Attributes tab.

14. Choose Stop Interactive Mapping, and then select the Polygon Selection tool. Separate the front part of the shirt from the back part. When you select the polygons, keep in mind that half of the sleeve hole should be in the front, and half should be in the back.

15. If necessary, use the Live Selection tool to refine the selection in the Perspective view. Use the Shift key with the tool to add polygons to the selection, or the Control key with the tool to remove polygons. An example of the completed front selection is shown in Figure 9.27.

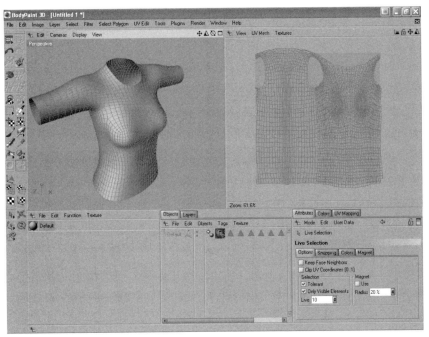

FIGURE 9.27   The front polygons are selected with the Polygon Selection tool in the UV map view and with the Live Selection tool in the Perspective view.

16. Use the Move tool to move the selected polygons off of the canvas.
17. Select the polygons for the back of the shirt (the polygons that remain in the UV-mapping area) with the Rectangle Selection tool.
18. Click the UV Mapping tab, click Projection, and then click the Flat button as shown in Figure 9.28. The polygons for the back of the shirt will flatten and fill the UV-mapping area. Move them off of the canvas.
19. Select the polygons for the front of the shirt with the Rectangle Selection tool. Again, use Flat Projection on these polygons, and move them off the canvas.
20. Select the sleeve that appears on the left side in UV Mapping view. Choose Start Interactive Mapping from the UV Mapping tab.
21. In the Attributes tab, click the Coordinates button, and then enter **90** degrees in the B field. This rotates the cylinder so that the seam is on the bottom of the sleeve. You should see the sleeve flatten out perfectly, as shown in Figure 9.29.
22. Choose Stop Interactive Mapping from the UV Mapping tab, and move the sleeve off the canvas with the Move tool.

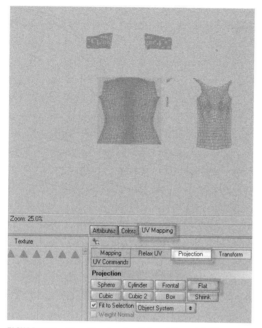

FIGURE 9.28   Map the back of the shirt with Flat Projection.

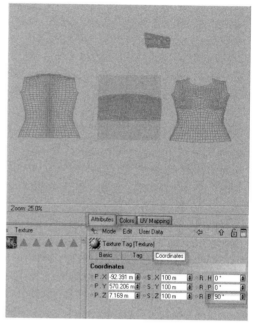

FIGURE 9.29   The first sleeve is mapped in a Cylinder projection that is rotated 90 degrees.

23. Select the other sleeve with the Rectangle Selection tool. Again, choose Start Interactive Mapping. The second sleeve should automatically use the same properties as the other sleeve.

24. So that both sleeves have the cuffs on the bottom in the texture map, you'll need to rotate the present sleeve by 180 degrees. Enter **180** degrees in the H field, as shown in Figure 9.30. Now both sleeves are facing the same direction on the map.

25. Choose Stop Interactive Mapping, and move the second sleeve next to the first one off the canvas.

26. Now we need to relax the front and back of the shirt so that the textures don't stretch. Select the back of the shirt with the Rectangle Selection tool.

27. Click the UV Mapping tab, and then select Relax UV. Uncheck Fix Border and Keep Neighbors. Then click the Apply button three times.

28. Repeat Step 26 for the front of the shirt. Your mapping should now look similar to Figure 9.31.

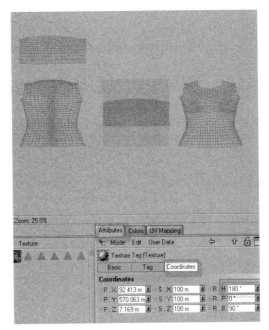

FIGURE 9.30   The second sleeve is rotated 180 degrees to face the same direction as the first sleeve.

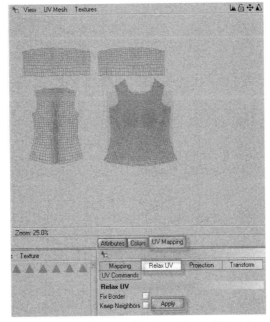

FIGURE 9.31   The front and back sections of the shirt are relaxed with the Relax UV commands.

29. Finally, use the Scale tool and the Move tool in the toolbar to position and size the various parts so that they are arranged neatly. Select all of the polygons with the Rectangular Selection tool. Then choose UV Commands > Fit UV to Canvas from the UV Mapping tab. Your final mapping should look similar to Figure 9.32.

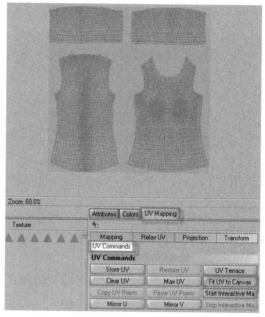

FIGURE 9.32   After arranging the pieces more neatly, use the Fit UV to Canvas command to complete the mapping.

30. At this point, choose File > Save. The Save File dialog box will prompt you for a location and file name. Note that this file will be saved in Cinema 4D format, which is not compatible with Poser. However, it is a good idea to save the Body Paint project file in case you have to make revisions in the future. Click Save after you select a folder and enter a file name.

TUTORIAL 9.6   **EXPORTING THE BODY PAINT OBJ FILE FOR POSER**

You just learned that Body Paint saves objects to the Cinema 4D format by default. To save the file in a format that Poser recognizes, you have to export it back out in OBJ format.

When we imported the object into Body Paint, we used the free Riptide plug-in to scale the object up by a factor of 1000 times. Now, we have to use the Riptide plug-in to scale it back down to Poser scale.

To export the object with Riptide, follow these steps:

1. From Body Paint 2.5, choose Plugins > Riptide > OBJ Exporter. The Export OBJ File dialog box appears.
2. Locate the folder into which you want to save the file. Enter a file name, and click Save.
3. The OBJ File Export dialog box shown in Figure 9.33 appears. Check the following options:
   - In the General section, check Export NGons, Export Faces, Export UV Coords, Export Materials, and Export Groups.
   - In the Face Sorting area, select Sort By Material.
   - In the Group Options area, check Mesh Names, and select the As UV Mapper Regions, and check Group Tag Names. These are the default options.

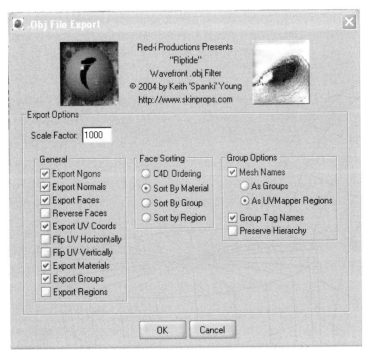

FIGURE 9.33 Select exporting options in the OBJ File Export dialog box provided with the Riptide plug-in.

4. Click OK to export your OBJ file to Poser scale.

MAKING TEMPLATES

After you get your models UV-mapped and saved, it makes sense to make a *texture template* for it. You can use these texture templates as a guide to create textures for your models.

UV Mapper Professional colors the template based on the way it is displayed in the Texture preview. By default, the template is black and white (white background with black lines). You can also color the templates based on how they are assigned by Material, Group, or Region. For example, if your object is made of different materials, and you want to represent the materials with different colors in your template, choose Map > Color > By Material. You can also color the map by Group (such as the body part groups that you use in Poser) or by Region (for example, if you want to save the items on the head as one region and the remainder of the body as another region). You'll learn more about assigning groups and materials in Chapter 14, "Assigning Groups and Materials."

It's fairly easy to save a template. After you save your model, just choose File > Save Template in UV Mapper Professional. The BMP Export Options dialog box shown in Figure 9.34 appears.

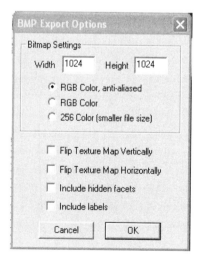

FIGURE 9.34 The options in the BMP Export Options dialog box allow you to save a bitmap template of your UV map.

The options in the BMP Export dialog box are as follows:

Width and Height: Enter the desired width and height for the template. Although the dimensions do not have to be square, many programs (including Poser) use resources more efficiently when textures are 512, 1024, 2048, or 4096 pixels in width and height.

RGB Color, antialiased: Choose this option if you want your template to be recognized as a high-color or true-color image, with antialiased edges to smooth jagged edges on diagonal lines.

RGB Color: Choose this for full-color templates that are not antialiased.

256 Color: Choose this option to create a 256-color image that creates a smaller file size. Even though you can create high-color or 256-color images for your templates, you'll find that the template only contains 16 colors. The color selections determine how your image editor sees the template.

Flip Texture Map Vertically: Check this option to flip the texture vertically (up and down).

Flip Texture Map Horizontally: Check this option to flip the texture map horizontally (right to left).

Include Hidden Facets: When checked, also includes any facets that might be hidden from view by using the [key. This is handy when you need to create templates for models that require two or more texture maps.

Include Labels: If your texture map is colored by group, material, or region, you can include labels on the texture map that show the names of the groups, materials, or regions by their color.

After you make your selections, click OK to create the texture map. You can then open the map in an image editor, such as Photoshop, to paint a texture using the map as a guide.

CONCLUSION

UV mapping is a very important process in creating a good 3D model. When care is taken in UV mapping, you can eliminate stretching and distortion that might occur in areas of a model. By breaking objects down into their basic shapes (spheres, planes, boxes, or cylinders), you can map complex objects with care and precision. In the next chapter, you will learn how to assign groups and materials to your objects to prepare them for importing into Poser.

GROUPS AND MATERIALS FOR MODELS

In This Chapter

- About Group Names
- Decompressing an OBZ File
- Tutorial 10.1 Grouping with Auto Group Editor
- Tutorial 10.2 Groups and Materials in UV Mapper Professional
- Tutorial 10.3 Using Poser's Group Editor
- Tutorial 10.4 Exporting an OBJ File from Poser

As you learned in Chapter 9, "UV Mapping", to make a model capable of having textures applied to it, you must create a UV map for the object. The UV map determines how the colors on a flat image are applied onto a 3D model.

After you create the UV map, you can assign one or more different materials to the model. For example, let's say you created a floor-length skirt for one of the female Poser figures. You can select polygons from the waist to mini-skirt level and assign them to a material named "Mini." Select the polygons that start from the bottom of the Mini material and that fall to knee-length. Call the new material "Knee." Continuing on, you select polygons from knee level to midcalf length, and call the new material "Midi." Finally, take the last set of polygons from Midi to the floor, and call the new material "Full." By dividing the skirt into several materials, you can make one or more layers invisible to vary the length of the skirt.

In addition, when you model clothing, you'll need to know ahead of time whether you want the clothing to be dynamic clothing (for the Cloth Room) or conforming clothing that poses automatically with your figure. If you decide to make conforming clothing, you will need to divide your clothing model into body part groups that coincide with the groups in your human figure. This chapter shows you how to use three different programs to assign groups and materials.

Most 3D-modeling programs allow you to assign materials and groups to 3D objects during the modeling process, and it is generally easiest to perform these tasks at that time. If you have obtained models that need groups or materials assigned, or if you prefer to use other methods to accomplish these tasks, this chapter will introduce you to other alternatives.

ABOUT GROUP NAMES

If you are creating dynamic clothing, you do not need to create predefined polygon groups. Instead, you use the Group Editor in the Cloth Room to assign vertices to one or more cloth groups. This process is explained in detail in Chapter 11 of the *Poser Tutorial Manual*.

Conforming clothing, on the other hand, works much differently. For conforming clothing to conform to a human figure, you have to divide the clothing model into body part groups that coincide with those on the model that they cover. For example, if you are creating a shirt, you'll probably need to create groups such as chest, abdomen, lCollar, rCollar, lShldr, and rShldr (the latter four being the required names for left and right collars and shoulders). The polygons in the clothing groups should be named the same and match the area of the corresponding polygons in the figure's groups as closely as possible. The reason for the "l" and "r" nomenclature is to allow Poser to perform its Figure > Symmetry commands. Although you could start right and left group names with a letter other than *r* or *l* and pose the figure, the Symmetry commands would not work.

The group names that you normally see for human figures in Poser menus and lists have names such as Left Forearm, Right Collar, and Left Shoulder. However, there are also shorter *internal* group names that Poser references in its CR2 Character Library files. Internal group names can contain capital letters, but they must *always* begin with a small letter to work properly. You can see a group's internal name when you click a body part and view the associated properties in the Properties panel. For example, you see James' Right Collar in Figure 10.1, where it has an internal name of *rCollar*.

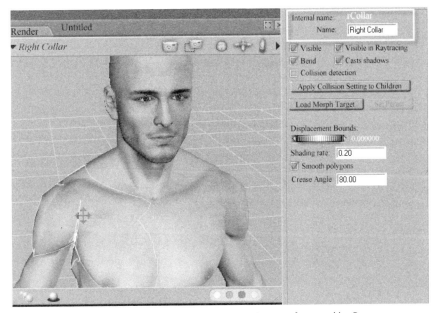

FIGURE 10.1   Each body part has an internal name that is referenced by Poser.

For conforming clothing to automatically pose the same as the figure that wears it, you have to create groups in the clothing that are named exactly the same as those in the figure. For the most part, all Poser figures use similar group names. There are minor exceptions, which will be mentioned when applicable.

It is important to understand how the polygons in a standard Poser figure are grouped. Just as the center of gravity of your own body is found at hip-level, the same is true of a Poser human figure. The hip is the central part of the figure and the point at which all of the hierarchical chains begin. The hip is the first *parent* in the hierarchy.

As you work your way from the hip to the feet, each subsequent level is a *child* of the body part that preceded it. For example, the hip is the parent of the thigh, which in turn is the parent of the shin, which is in turn the parent of the foot. Working your way backward up the chain, the left foot is a child of the left shin, which is in turn a child of the left thigh, which is in turn a child of the hip.

Figure 10.2 shows internal group names for Jessi. Many Poser figures use the same grouping that Jessi uses. Starting with the hierarchical chain that runs from the hip to the head and eyes, the internal group names are hip, abdomen, chest, neck, and head. The rightEye and leftEye parts are both children of the head. Other figures may have a second neck part, named upperNeck, which falls between the neck and head. There are sometimes differences in the way that the chest and collar sections are grouped. In Jessi, the chest group contains the breasts. In other figures, you may see the breasts as part of the right- and left collar sections.

The right- and left collar and arm sections connect from the chest. Each arm has parts with similar internal names, except that the internal names for the right arm parts begin with a lowercase "r," and the left arm parts begin with a lowercase "l". Starting from the chest and working downward, the right arm group names are rCollar, rShldr, rForeArm, and rHand. Left arm parts are named the same, with the exception of the "l" prefix.

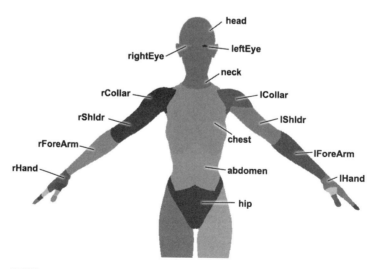

FIGURE 10.2   Group names for head, torso, and arms.

Finally, we reach the fingers, which are shown in Figure 10.3. Each hand branches out into five fingers, each of which is divided into three sections. The section closest to the base of the hand is number 1, the middle section is number 2, and the last section (with the fingernail) is number 3. As for the names of the fingers, the right hand finger groups are named rThumb1, rThumb2, rThumb3, rIndex1, rIndex2, rIndex3, rMid1, rMid2, rMid3, rRing1, rRing2, rRing3, rPinky1, rPinky2, and rPinky3. The fingers on the left hand are named the same, with the exception that "l" is the first letter instead of "r."

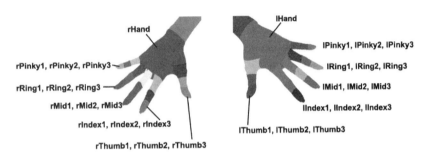

FIGURE 10.3 Left- and right hand and finger group names.

The groups for the legs and feet of Jessi are shown in Figure 10.4. Starting from the hip, the right leg is divided into rThigh, rShin, and rFoot. Other figures may also have a rButtock section that appears between the hip and the rThigh. Likewise, the parts on the left are similarly named.

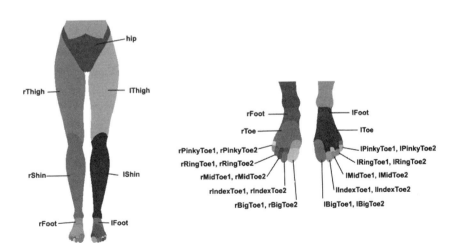

FIGURE 10.4 Leg, foot, and toe group names.

Next, we come to the toes, where there are also differences between figures. Jessi has articulated toes, meaning that each toe can be posed individually, just like the fingers in the hands. You will not find this feature in all Poser figures. When toes are not articulated, you will see groups in the right foot named rFoot and rToe and groups in the left foot named lFoot and lToe. The toe sections move all five toes at the same time.

In the case of articulated toes, the rToe and lToe sections serve as common first joints for all five toes, respectively—in other words, the rToe and lToe sections are equivalent to the balls of the human feet. From that point, each toe branches out into two joints apiece. For the right foot, these sections are named rBigToe1, rBigToe2, rIndexToe1, rIndex-Toe2, rMidToe1, rMidToe2, rRingToe1, rRingToe2, rPinkyToe1, and rPinkyToe2. As with the fingers, the toe closest to the common section is part number 1, and the part with the toenail is the highest numbered part (2, in this case). Left foot sections are similarly named.

DECOMPRESSING AN OBZ FILE

To create groups in your clothing, it helps to view the model underneath your clothing at the same time. For example, if you know where the polygons for the *abdomen* fall on the human figure, you can select the polygons in your clothing that overlap that area and assign those polygons to the *abdomen* group in the clothing. This allows you to create the clothing groups more accurately. Because Poser 7 furnishes its figures in OBZ format (a compressed version of the OBJ file), you will need to decompress it before you import the model into any utility that imports OBJ files.

There are two ways to decompress an OBZ file into an OBJ file:

- Open the OBZ file in a utility that opens ZIP files, such as WinZip for the PC or its Mac equivalent. Then extract the OBJ file to a directory of your choice. Use this default model whenever you create or set up clothing or create morphs.
- Use the Python script furnished with Poser to decompress all compressed files in a specified folder. Choose Scripts > Utility > uncompress Poser Files. A dialog box prompts you to select the directory under which to decompress the files. Make sure you check the option to Uncompress geometry files (obj). Also, if you check the Delete Original Files After Uncompressing option, you avoid having duplicate versions of the thumbnails in your library. After you select your path and options, click OK. Your OBJ file will be located in the same folder as the original OBZ file.

You can turn off automatic saving of compressed files in the General Preferences dialog box. Choose Edit > General Preferences, and click the Misc tab. Uncheck the Use File Compression option. Whenever you save library files or export geometry files, Poser will not use the compressed formats and instead will save them to the uncompressed, and editable, versions of the files.

TUTORIAL 10.1   **GROUPING WITH AUTO GROUP EDITOR**

Auto Group Editor (written by markdc and available for purchase through Content Paradise by clicking the Content tab in Poser 7, or through Renderosity) is a third-party utility that makes it much easier to add body part groups to your clothing models. The main reason for covering this utility first is because Auto Group Editor displays each body part group in a different color. This makes it very easy to determine where each group starts and ends, and helps you understand the process much more quickly.

Auto Group Editor allows you to import a human figure as a CR2 (Poser Figure Library character) or an OBJ (Wavefront 3D model) file. Each group on the original figure appears in a different color so that you can easily see where you need to create the corresponding groups on your clothing. When you import your clothing model, you can display it in Wireframe mode while you use the colored groups of the underlying figure to create equivalent groups in the clothing.

A nice feature of Auto Group Editor is that it allows you to create symmetrical selections and then assign the right- and left sections individually. This extremely handy feature is not available in the other two methods that we discuss later in this chapter.

Although Auto Group Editor does make it easy to create and assign polygons to groups for conforming clothing, it cannot assign materials. You will need to assign materials with another utility or in your modeling program.

To create clothing groups in Auto Group Editor, proceed as follows:

1. From Auto Group Editor, choose File > Load Source Figure. Use the Open dialog box to locate the uncompressed OBJ file for your character. In this example, after uncompressing the OBZ file for Jessi, you can find the OBJ file in the same folder (Runtime > Libraries > Character > Jessi folder). Select the OBJ file, and click Open to import the figure.

2. Choose File > Load Clothing Object. Locate the clothing object that you want to assign groups to. For this example, locate the tshirt-mapped.obj file in the Tutorials > Chap10 folder on the CD-ROM that accompanies this book. Click Open to import the clothing object. Your project should look as shown in Figure 10.5.

ON THE CD

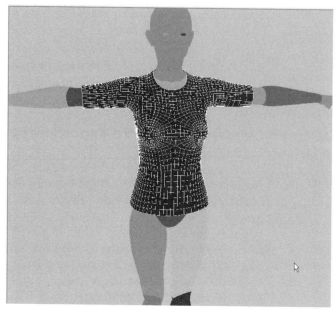

FIGURE 10.5   Import the geometry for the figure and for the clothing that you want to group.

3. Now we need to transfer some group names to the shirt. Notice that the bottom section of the Group Controls panel (in the left section of your screen) displays the name of all groups in the figure. Beneath the group list are several buttons. First, click the None button to deselect all of the group names in the figure. This will hide all of the figure groups.

4. Now, click the Upper button to select all of the groups in the upper torso and arms. In addition to those groups, check the neck and hip groups to add them to the selection.

5. To transfer the selected groups to the upper window, which will be the groups for the T-shirt, click the Transfer Groups button at the bottom of the Group Controls panel. The group names should now appear in the top pane of the Group Controls panel.

6. It is easier to assign groups to your geometry when the clothing is in Wireframe display mode. This allows you to view the groups in the original model. To display the clothing in wireframe, click the Transparent option beneath the upper section of the Group Controls window. Your project should now look as shown in Figure 10.6.

7. Groups should always be symmetrical, providing that the mesh itself is symmetrical; that is, the right side and left side always contain the same number of polygons. To create symmetrical selections in Auto

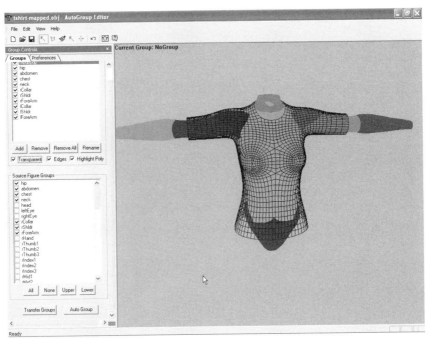

FIGURE 10.6   Transfer the appropriate group names from the figure to the clothing object.

Group Editor, first click the Symmetrical Selection icon. As you select polygons, Auto Group Editor automatically creates symmetrical selections if this option is activated.

Auto Group Editor makes use of a three-button mouse to perform some features. If you need to pan, move, or rotate the model while you are selecting polygons, use the following options:

- *Select polygons with the left mouse button.*
- *Shift-click the left mouse button to deselect polygons.*
- *Click and drag the middle mouse button or wheel to rotate the view.*
- *Shift-click and drag the middle mouse button to pan the view up, down, right, or left.*
- *Ctrl-click and drag the middle mouse button to zoom in and out.*

8. Select polygons in the chest group until your selection looks similar to that shown in Figure 10.7. Use the selection tools as follows:

- The Normal Selection tool allows you to select all polygons in a rectangular area.
- The Polygon Selection tool allows you to select all polygons in an irregularly shaped area.
- The Paint Selection tool allows you to select polygons by "painting" over them.

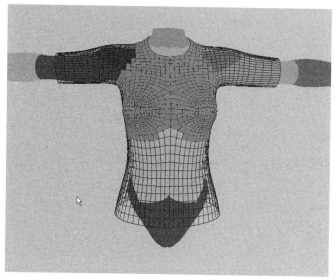

FIGURE 10.7   A symmetrical selection of polygons for the chest group is ready to be assigned.

9. With the selection made, verify that the chest is highlighted in the top section of the Group Controls panel. Then right-click over the selected polygons in the graphic view, and choose Assign Left Select to Group. This assigns the left side of the selection to the chest group in the T-shirt. Right-click again, and choose Assign Right Select to Group.
10. Uncheck the chest group in the upper section of the Group Controls panel. This hides the polygons that you just assigned to the chest and protects them from being selected further.
11. Use the selection tools to select the polygons for the left- or right collar. For Jessi, these are the polygons that separate the chest from the upper arm. As you select the polygons for one side, the polygons for the other side are automatically selected to create symmetrical groups.
12. To assign the right section of polygons to the right collar, verify that the rCollar group is selected in the top section of the Group Controls

panel. Then, right-click over the selected polygons, and choose Assign Right Select to Group. Uncheck the rCollar group in the upper section of the Group Controls panel.

13. In a similar manner, highlight the lCollar group in the Group Controls panel. Right-click over the remaining selection of polygons, and choose Assign Left Select to Group. Uncheck the lCollar group in the upper section of the Group Controls panel.

14. Repeat Steps 12 and 13 to assign polygons for the right- and left shoulder sections (named rShldr and lShldr).

15. Select polygons for the abdomen, and assign right- and left selections to the abdomen group.

16. All remaining polygons at the bottom of the T-shirt should be added to the *hip* group.

17. After you assign all polygons in the T-shirt to appropriate groups, you can save your model. Choose File > Save Clothing Object, as shown in Figure 10.8, to save over the previous version of the clothing, or choose File > Save Clothing Object As to save the grouped model to a location that you specify.

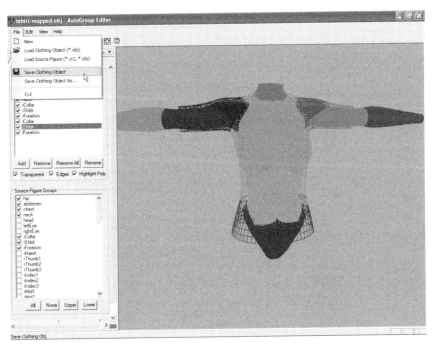

FIGURE 10.8   After you assign all polygons, use the Save Clothing Object or Save Clothing Object As command to save the grouped clothing object.

Although you can save OBJ files to the same folder in which your library files are located, you most often find OBJ geometry files in the Runtime > Geometries folders. A suitable location and filename for this T-shirt, for example, might be Runtime > Geometries > CustomFolder > Jessi > t-shirt.obj, where CustomFolder is an optional name for a folder that you assign to clothing objects that you create yourself.

TUTORIAL 10.2   **GROUPS AND MATERIALS IN UV MAPPER PROFESSIONAL**

ON THE CD

If you followed the tutorials in Chapter 9, you are already familiar with the UV-mapping capabilities of UV Mapper Professional, a demo of which is in the Demos > UV Mapper folder on the CD-ROM that accompanies this book. In addition to UV mapping, this utility also allows you to assign groups and materials to a Wavefront OBJ file.

Unlike Auto Group Editor, you cannot use the human figure as a guide while you select polygons for your groups. Secondly, UV Mapper doesn't have an option to create symmetrical selections, so you have to keep track of the groups visually. The easiest way to do this is to hide faces as you assign them to groups. The following tutorial gives you some ideas for how you can overcome these situations.

For this tutorial, you will need UV Mapper Professional. You will assign groups and materials to the pants. Follow these steps:

ON THE CD

1. From UV Mapper Professional, choose File > Open Model. Locate the pants-mapped.obj file in the Tutorials > Chap10 folder on the CD-ROM that accompanies this book. Click Open to import the pants.
2. Use the Rectangular Selection tool to select the first row of each pants section. Make sure that all polygons in the top row are selected. Then press the zero (0) key on your keyboard to increase the selection by two rows. Your selection should look similar to that shown in Figure 10.9.
3. Choose Tools > Assign To > Group. When the Assign Selection Group dialog box appears, enter **abdomen** and click OK. Answer Yes when UV Mapper Professional asks if you want to create the new group.
4. With the abdomen polygons still selected, choose Select > Display > Hide, or use the shortcut key [to hide the selected polygons.
5. Select the bottom row of polygons on the left leg facing you (this is actually the right leg of the pants). Press the zero (0) key on your keyboard 14 more times to make a total of 15 rows selected.
6. Choose Tools > Assign To > Group. Enter **rShin** to assign these polygons to the right shin of the pants. Then hide the selected faces with the [keyboard shortcut or the Select > Display > Hide command.
7. Repeat Steps 5 and 6 for the same rows on the opposite leg. Assign these polygons to the lShin group and hide them from view.

8. If you look at the way Jessi's body is actually grouped, you'll see that the front of her shins are about three polygons higher than the back of her shins. To reproduce that in the pants, use the Polygon Selection tool to select three rows of polygons on the leg on your right (the left leg of the pants), and extend the selection inward by 20 columns. Your selection should look similar to that shown in Figure 10.10. Use the Tools > Assign To > Group command to assign this selection to the lShin group

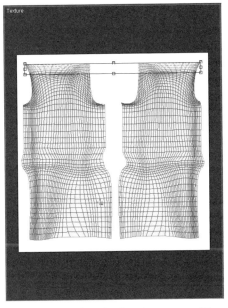 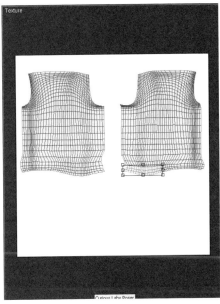

FIGURE 10.9 Assign the first three rows of the pants to the abdomen group.

FIGURE 10.10 Select three rows and 20 columns of polygons to add to the shin groups.

9. Repeat Step 8 to assign three rows by 20 columns of polygons on the opposite leg to the rShin group.
10. Deselect all polygons (Select > Deselect), and then use the] shortcut or choose Select > Display > Show to unhide all of the previously hidden polygons.
11. Use the Rectangular Selection tool to select the top row of polygons on each side of the pants. Then extend the selection by pressing the zero (0) key 14 more times. The selection should look as shown in Figure 10.11.

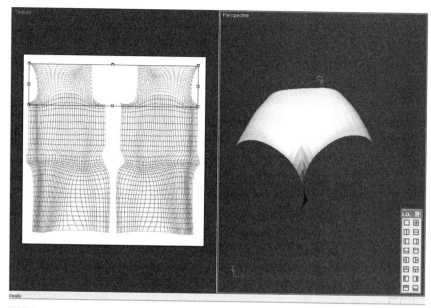

FIGURE 10.11 Make sure that the hip group includes polygons that separate the right- and left legs.

12. Choose Select > Display > Hide Unselected. This hides the polygons in the remainder of the pants.
13. Now, choose Select > Select By > Group. When the Select By Group dialog box appears, highlight abdomen, and then choose OK.
14. Hide the abdomen polygons with the Select > Display > Hide command or by using the [shortcut.
15. Use the Rectangular Selection tool to select the polygons that remain in the Texture view. Then choose Tools > Assign To > Group. Assign these polygons to a new group named hip.
16. With all polygons deselected, choose Select > Display > Show or use the] shortcut to unhide all faces. Now we need to unhide all of the polygons that have already been assigned.
17. Choose Select > Select By > Group. When the Select By Group dialog box appears, highlight abdomen, hip, lShin, and rShin. Choose OK to select the polygons, and then hide them with the [shortcut.
18. Use the Rectangular Selection tool to select the polygons on the left side of the texture view (the right side of the pants). Then choose Tools > Assign To > Group. Assign these polygons to a new group named rThigh.
19. Now, use the Rectangular Selection tool to select the polygons on the right side of the texture view (the left side of the pants). Then choose

Tools > Assign To > Group. Assign these polygons to a new group named lThigh. All of the polygons in the pants should now be assigned to groups.

20. It's actually a very similar process to assign materials in UV Mapper Professional. After you select the polygons you want to assign, you use the Tools > Assign To > Material command to create a material for the clothing. For purposes of this tutorial, we will assign all polygons to a material named Pants (material names can begin with capital letters, if desired, and do not have strict conventions like group names do). If you desire, you can optionally create more than one material zone in the pants. For example, you can select the upper portion of the pants and create a material named Shorts, and then add the remaining polygons to a material named Pants.

21. With all groups and materials assigned, it's time to save the OBJ file. Choose File > Save Model. When the OBJ Export Option dialog box appears, leave only one option checked: Don't Export Normals, as shown in Figure 10.12. This is extra information that Poser doesn't use, and it adds unnecessary file size to the object. Click OK to save the object to the folder that you will use as the final destination for your Poser clothing. For example, you can save the object to the Runtime > Geometries > *YourFolderName* > Jessi folder, and name the file object pants.obj. Further information about file locations will be covered in Chapter 12, "From Modeler to Poser Library."

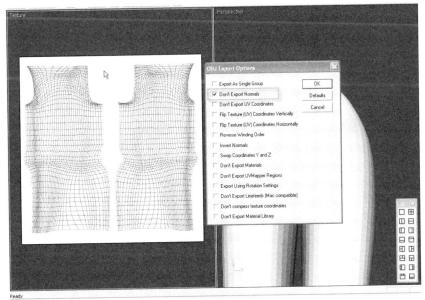

FIGURE 10.12 When you save the OBJ file, do not include Normals information.

TUTORIAL 10.3   **USING POSER'S GROUP EDITOR**

Poser's Group Editor serves a variety of purposes and operates in two modes—Polygon mode and Vertex mode. While in Polygon mode, the Group Editor allows you to select polygons in an object and assign them to a material or to body part groups for conforming clothing. Polygon mode also allows you to add polygons to hair growth groups in the Hair Room. Alternately, the Group Editor switches to Vertex Selection mode to enable you to assign selected vertices to cloth groups while you are in the Cloth Room.

When you use the Group Editor to assign groups and materials to an object, you work in Polygon mode, as shown in Figure 10.13.

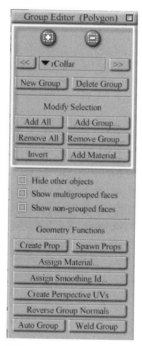

FIGURE 10.13   The Group Editor contains several buttons that help you assign groups and materials in an object.

When you select and assign polygons to groups, you will mainly use the following buttons:

- *To create a group in the clothing, click the New Group button. The New Group-Name dialog box prompts you to enter a name for the new group. Click OK to add the group. Use the Delete Group button to delete the currently selected group from your object.*
- *Previous and Next buttons allow you to move through the list of groups in your current object. Click the down arrow in between the Previous and Next buttons to select a group from the menu.*
- *When the Select button is enabled, you add polygons or vertices to the currently selected group. When the Deselect button is enabled, you remove polygons or vertices from the currently selected group.*
- *Several buttons help you add or remove polygons from the currently selected group. The Add All button adds all polygons in an object to the current group.*

The Group Editor also offers an Auto Group feature that you can use in conjunction with the Setup Room to add clothing groups. This method will be discussed in more detail in Chapter 12, "From Modeler to Poser Library."

To use Poser's Group Editor to assign groups and materials, follow these steps:

1. Starting with an empty scene in Poser, add Jessi or JessiHiRes from the Poser 6 > Figures > Poser 6 > Jessi Library. Turn Inverse Kinematics off, and zero the pose of the figure.
2. Choose File > Import > Wavefront OBJ. The Wavefront OBJ box dialog appears.
3. Locate the OBJ file you want to open. In this case, choose skirt-mapped.OBJ in the Tutorials > Chap10 folder on the CD-ROM.

ON THE CD

4. The Prop Import Options dialog box shown in Figure 10.14 appears. For this example, you don't need to check any of the options because the geometry will import in the correct scale and in the correct location. These options will be discussed in more detail in Chapter 12, "From Modeler to Poser Library." After you uncheck the options, choose OK to continue. The skirt appears in the scene.
5. The skirt will consist of two groups: abdomen and hip. To select polygons for the abdomen of the skirt, you will have to do two things: display the skirt in Wireframe mode and hide the abdomen of the human figure. To display the skirt in Wireframe mode, make sure that skirt-mapped.obj is selected as the current actor. Then choose Display > Element Style > Wireframe. The skirt changes to Wireframe display mode.

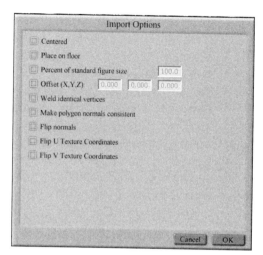

FIGURE 10.14   Uncheck all options in the Prop Import Options dialog box.

6. To hide Jessi's abdomen, first click her abdomen to make it the current object. Then open the Properties panel. Uncheck the Visible option as shown in Figure 10.15. Now you'll be able to select the proper polygons on the dress to correspond with Jessi's abdomen.

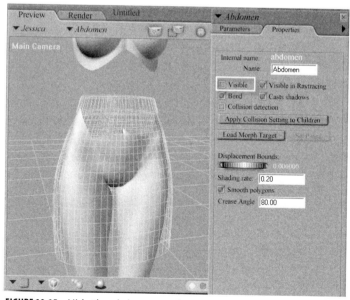

FIGURE 10.15   Hide the abdomen so that you can see where to select polygons for the skirt.

7. From the Editing Tools, click the Grouping Tool icon to open the Group Editor.

8. The skirt has two groups that you will need to remove before you create the abdomen group. The groups are named *Figure* and *1*. These groups were inadvertently added when saving the figure from an external modeling program and are not necessary to keep. Click the Delete Group button in the upper section of the Group Editor to delete each of these groups.

9. Now you'll create the new group for the abdomen. Click the New Group button in the upper section of the Group Editor. When the New GroupName dialog box appears, enter **abdomen** (in lowercase letters) for the group name. Click OK to create the new group.

10. Select polygons in the skirt that overlap Jessi's hidden abdomen. View the skirt from different camera angles to make sure that you include all polygons in the abdominal area. To select polygons, you can:
    - Left-click to select a single polygon to add to the current group, or Ctrl/Option+Left click to remove a single polygon.
    - Draw a rectangular selection area to select multiple polygons to add to the group, or press the Ctrl/Option key combination while you draw a rectangular selection area around the polygons you want to remove.

11. After you select the polygons that cover the abdomen, choose Display > Element Style > Use Figure Style to turn the skirt solid again. This displays the selected polygons in red so that you can see them more clearly. Add or remove polygons from the selection to make the abdomen symmetrical. Figure 10.16 shows an example of the faces that are selected for the abdomen.

12. The remaining polygons will be assigned to the hip. To begin this process, click the New Group button. When the New GroupName dialog box appears, enter **hip** (in lowercase letters) for the group name. Click OK to create the new group.

13. Verify that the hip is selected as the current group. Then click the Add All button to add all of the skirt polygons to the hip group. All of the polygons in the skirt turn red.

14. At this point, the polygons in the upper part of the skirt have been assigned to two groups: the abdomen and the hip. Polygons can only be assigned to one group, so you must remove the abdomen polygons from the hip group. To do so, click the Remove Group button in the Group Editor. Select abdomen from the drop-down list in the Remove Group dialog box, and choose OK to remove the abdomen polygons from the hip group. Your skirt should look similar to Figure 10.17.

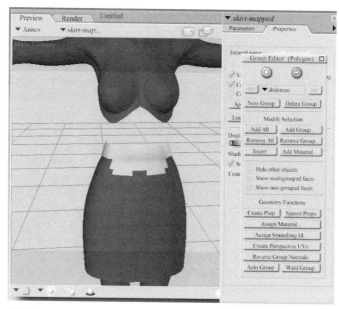

FIGURE 10.16   Switch from Wireframe display mode to Use Figure Style display mode to adjust the selection if necessary.

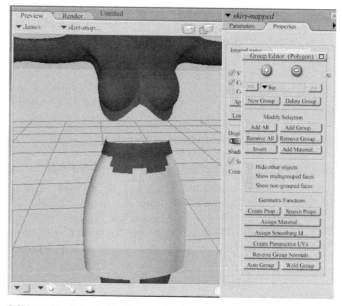

FIGURE 10.17   Select all polygons for the hip, and then remove the polygons that are assigned to the abdomen.

15. The Group Editor also allows you to assign polygons to materials on a group-by-group basis. To assign the currently selected group (which should still be the hip section) to a material named *Skirt*, click the Assign Material button that appears in the Geometry Functions section in the bottom portion of the Group Editor. The Assign Material dialog box opens.

16. Enter **Skirt** for a material name, and click OK.

17. Return to the Group Editor, and select the abdomen group. Click the Assign Material button again. When the Assign Material dialog box appears, click the Materials button, and choose Skirt from the drop-down menu. Then click OK to assign the abdomen polygons to the Skirt material. Your groups and materials are now complete for the object.

18. Before you export your object, verify that all polygons are correctly assigned to their groups. Then, use the Weld Group button in the Group Editor to weld each group. This prevents your geometry from splitting apart at the group seams when imported into other 3D software such as UV Mapper Pro or ZBrush.

19. Save the object, as described in the following tutorial.

TUTORIAL 10.4   **EXPORTING AN OBJ FILE FROM POSER**

After you assign groups and materials, in Poser you'll need to save the OBJ file with its new information. The most logical place to save the file is in the final location that will be referenced in the Poser library file. Because most Poser users are accustomed to finding the original OBJ files in the Geometries folders, it is particularly important to locate the OBJ files in a folder beneath the Poser 6 > Runtime > Geometries folder if you intend to distribute your models.

To export an OBJ file from Poser, follow these steps:

1. From Poser 7, choose File > Export > Wavefront OBJ. The Export Range dialog box appears.

2. Poser prompts you to select a range of frames for export. The only reason you choose Multi Frame Export is if you have morphed or animated the OBJ file, which is not true in this case. Keep the default selection (Single Frame), and choose OK to continue.

3. The Select Objects dialog box appears. Initially, all objects are checked. To uncheck all items, click the UNIVERSE item that appears at the top of the list. This should clear all of the other selections in the dialog box. After all items are unchecked, scroll to the bottom of the list and check the clothing object that you want to export, as shown in Figure 10.18.

FIGURE 10.18   Deselect all objects in the Hierarchy Editor except for the clothing object.

4. Click OK to continue. The Export Options dialog box shown in Figure 10.19 appears.
5. Because you are exporting an object that will be used for conforming clothing, you need to check two options: Include Body Part Names in Polygon Groups, and Weld Body Part Seams. Click OK to continue with the exporting process.
6. The Export as Wavefront OBJ dialog box appears. Create or navigate to the folder that will store your final object. For purposes of this tutorial, use a path called Poser 7 > Runtime > Geometries > PP7Projects, and name the object **JessiSkirt.obj**. Click Save to complete the process.

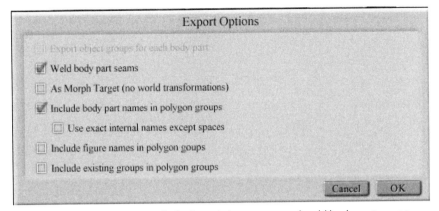

FIGURE 10.19   Make sure you include the existing groups and weld body part seams when you export the object from Poser.

When you export geometry from Poser, the options you select vary depending on the purpose of the object. For this example, check the options as follows:

- Always leave Include Body Part Names in Polygon Groups, Use Exact Internal Names Except Spaces, and Include Figure Names in Polygon Groups unchecked. These options affect the names of the groups or can remove the grouping information from your model.
- Check the Include Existing Groups in Polygon Groups option when the OBJ contains groups for conforming hair or clothing. If left unchecked, the object will export with only one group. You do not need to check this option if you are exporting geometry for dynamic clothing or props because they typically do not contain more than one group.
- Check the Weld Body Part Seams option only if you are converting conforming clothing (which contains groups) into dynamic clothing (which does not necessarily have to contain groups). If you don't weld the groups at their seams, the dynamic clothing will split apart at the group seams during dynamic calculations.
- Check As Morph Target (No World Transformations) when it is important to reference the original position, scaling, and rotation of the geometry that you are exporting. This is particularly important when you are exporting an object for the purpose of creating morphs.

After you save the OBJ file under its final name and location, it's always a good idea to perform a final check in UV Mapper Professional. Select each group, one at a time, and hide its faces to make sure that the group looks symmetrical and that it doesn't contain any stray faces or holes. Also, check the group list and the material list to make sure that there are no unwanted or erroneous groups and materials in the object that can create confusion later on.

CONCLUSION

When an object contains multiple materials, you can use different textures or transparency settings on the different parts of the object. To make an object posable, as in the case of conforming clothing, the object should contain groups that define the posable parts of the object.

You still aren't quite done with the process of creating Poser content. You still need to learn the proper way to add your model to the Poser libraries—and this process varies depending on the type of content you are creating. In Chapter 12, "From Modeler to Poser Library," you'll learn how you let Poser know the difference between props, smart props, dynamic clothing, and conforming clothing.

11

CREATING YOUR OWN TEXTURES

In This Chapter

- Textures and Copyrights
- Creating Clothing Textures

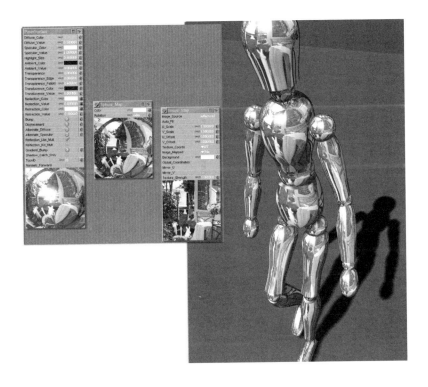

In Chapter 4, "Creating Materials," you learned how to use the Basic and Advanced Material Room views to combine several types of image maps into rich and elegant materials. By creating your own textures, you expand the versatility of your content and expand your content inventory infinitely.

In this chapter, you'll learn more about what it takes to make your own textures. You'll learn how to build your textures in layers and how to use those various layers to your advantage while creating the various types of maps used in Poser: diffuse, bump, displacement, transparency, and other types of maps. You'll also get a chance to study how textures are created by a master texture artist.

You've already learned that to create textures for your Poser content, the objects must have UV coordinates assigned to them. The UV coordinates flatten your 3D models into a 2D grid-like pattern. Each point on the grid corresponds to a point on the 3D model.

After you generate the UV coordinates for your object, you can create a *template*. This template serves as a guide while you create your texture maps. Templates show where each polygon of your object will fall on your texture maps so you can create your textures accordingly.

Figure 11.1 shows an example of a texture template generated from the UV coordinates of an object. Beside the template is the corresponding image texture map. Notice that the features on the painted texture are created in the same locations as those on the template.

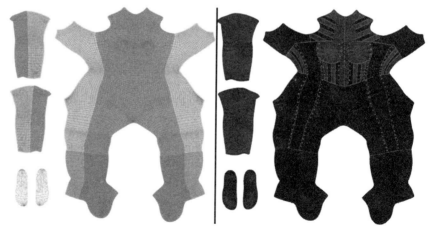

FIGURE 11.1   The texture template (left), generated from the UV coordinates of an object, serves as a guide to create an image texture map (right).

TEXTURES AND COPYRIGHTS

Because Poser content is distributed digitally, it is all too easy to reuse elements created by others in your own projects. If you purchase the content, you have the right to modify it *for your own use*. For example, if you purchase a clothing texture but want to change the color or add some extra detail to it yourself, you can use your customized version for your own renders. When you distribute all or part of it (either for free or for sale), you are entering the danger zone. Several scandals have been brought to the attention of the online Poser community. In some cases, the scandals could have been avoided with a better understanding of copyright laws and ethical standards. Ignorance of these laws does not serve as an excuse.

Copyrights are, literally, the right to copy something. The original creator of the object or the material is usually the holder of the copyright, unless ownership was transferred legally by contract or other written permission. Basically, if you don't own the copyright for something, you can't use or redistribute it, in whole or in part, unless you obtain permission from the person or persons that hold the copyright.

The safest and best rule of thumb is *if you didn't make it yourself, don't use it without permission from the original copyright holder*. If there is any reason to question whom the original copyright holder is, the rule of thumb is *when in doubt, leave it out*. This means that you cannot copy the hand of one model onto another, edit the underlying mesh or geometry of a model, or take someone's texture map file and change some colors on it, and then redistribute any of it without explicit permission from each of the original copyright holders.

For further study regarding copyrights, we recommend the following Web resources:

- *http://www.copyright.gov/*
- *http://www.chillingeffects.org/*
- *http://darkwing.uoregon.edu/~csundt/copyweb/#Useful*

In addition, the Copyright Laws and Ethical Standards forum at Renderosity addresses specific questions that Poser content creators have in regards to copyright and ethical issues. Free membership is required to access the forums. Once there, point your browser to *http://www.renderosity.com/mod/forumpro/showforum.php?forum_id=12395*.

CREATING CLOTHING TEXTURES

As you develop clothing textures, you will probably find it beneficial and practical to build your textures one layer at a time. It's also a good idea to save the layered file before you create your final, flattened versions of the textures. By approaching texture creation in this manner, you can make revisions or additions much more easily. You can also use layered elements to your advantage when you create the accompanying maps (bump, displacement, transparency, and so on.) The layered file also serves as evidence of how you created the textures yourself in the event that there are copyright disputes later on. It's a smart way of working all the way around.

In the sections that follow, you'll get a detailed overview of how Ana Winson (Arien) created all of the various image maps for The Bootie for Victoria 3. Before we begin, I would like to thank this very talented and up-and-coming texture artist for allowing me to reveal some of her deepest secrets in this book!

You will see in Figures 11.2 and 11.3 show how each type of texture map affects the appearance of the clothing. The various types of maps are presented in the order in which they appear in the root node of the Advanced Material Room view. In Figure 11.2, you see the untextured model in the upper-left section. The diffuse color texture, which provides the main colors in the model, is shown in the upper-right section. Next, highlights are added to the color texture to provide a soft sheen to the outfit as shown in the lower-left section. Finally, in the lower-right section, a transparency map allows skin to show through in the legs and in the lace sections of the top.

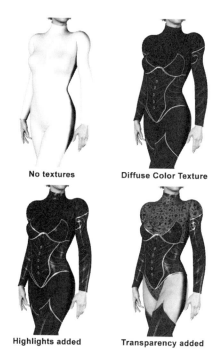

FIGURE 11.2   Before texturing, the clothing model looks very plain. By adding diffuse color maps, highlights, and transparency maps, the clothing looks more realistic.

Continuing on through the various other types of texture maps you can use, a reflection map can be used to enhance and brighten reflective areas, as shown in the upper-left section of Figure 11.3. Bump maps (upper-right) add additional texture by raising and lowering areas that are perpendicular to the camera. Displacement maps (lower-left) displace the geometry at render time to give more detail. Alternate specular maps (lower-right) enhance the highlights in the lace of the garment to complete the material shader.

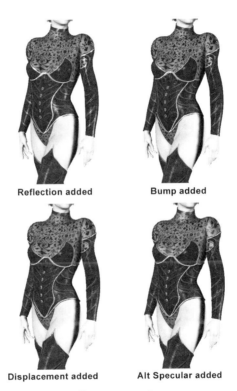

Reflection added   **Bump added**

Displacement added   **Alt Specular added**

FIGURE 11.3   Reflection maps, bump maps, displacement maps, and alternate specular maps are used to add further realism in the material shader.

Now, we'll turn to the textures created by Ana Winson, whose materials we discussed in Chapter 4, "Creating Materials." You'll learn how she used layers to her advantage when she created her texture maps for The Bootie for Victoria 3. We'll start by describing how she made her texture (or diffuse color) maps.

Diffuse Color (Texture) Maps

As you learned in Chapter 4, "Creating Materials," a diffuse color map de-fines the color of an object. If clothing objects are UV mapped so that the seams of the model occur where they would naturally occur in a real article of clothing, it is fairly easy to create textures.

Most fabrics consist of repeated seamless patterns, whether printed fabrics or solid fabrics such as wool or denim. However, you will find that your textures will appear much more realistic when you go the extra mile and provide details such as stitching, buttons, worn areas, or other details that add realism to your clothing.

On the other hand, it is generally best to keep highlights and shadows out of a texture map because they can conflict with the lighting in your scene. Add highlights and shadows in areas that they might occur regard-less of the direction that light is coming from. For example, where but-tons appear on a garment, a slight shadow will help give them dimension and pull them away from the surface of the material. On the other hand, if you use a displacement map to bring the buttons forward, you won't need to add the "fake" shadows.

There are other considerations when making clothing textures. For example, when you are using printed fabrics such as plaids, flowers, or stripes, you should watch the scaling of the fabric on your garment. If the patterns are scaled too large, the clothing will look less realistic. You should also pay attention to how patterns match at the seams or how the scaling of the patterns on seams and pockets match the scal-ing of the patterns on the base clothing.

First, Ana created a template for The Bootie, measuring 2500 by 2500 pixels. Higher resolution templates allow you to create detailed textures that can later be downsized if necessary.

A layer of white fill is placed above the template layer and turned off while developing the textures. After the textures are done, the white fill layer can be turned on to cover the template and provide the background for the texture.

Next, a new layer is created, in which all areas of the clothing are filled with a dark gray solid color with a slight bit of noise. This serves as a base for the clothing texture. The solid color extends slightly beyond the borders of the clothing to avoid the possibility of seams showing up at render time. After scanning some lace and cleaning up transparent areas, a layer of black lace is placed above the gray fill. The lace layer is then du-plicated and a slight bevel is added to give the lace some extra highlights and dimension.

Four layers of dark gray seams are added above the lace to place seams around the collar, panties, and arm lace. Finally, another layer adds a lighter, varied shade of gray leather over portions of the arms. Figure 11.4 shows the progress so far.

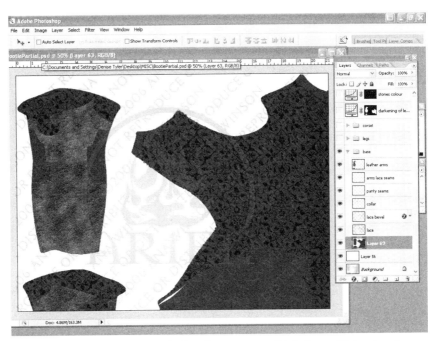

FIGURE 11.4   Several layers start The Bootie texture: a solid dark gray fill; two lace layers; seams for the collar, panties, and arms; and leather areas on the sleeve.

Similar details are added to the corset and legs. First, two layers add leather to the corset area and bust, allowing the bust covers to be shown or hidden depending on the look desired for the outfit. A central plate is added in a new layer over the center of the corset. Above that, layers of dark gray leather are added for a *busk* (the area of the corset that contains the clasps) and busk shadow. Graceful curves are added over the leather to provide detailed cutouts. Finally, a layer of gems and gem insets are added to give further detail to the busk at the center of the corset. Figure 11.5 shows these new layers on the corset.

Finally, additional trim and details are added to the clothing in several layers. First, a couple of adjustment layers darken the color of the leather areas on the sleeves, legs, and corset to give them a richer appearance. Additional cutouts are added to the leather on the legs and sleeves, and a beveled duplicate of the cutouts adds additional dimension. Curved lines are added to form a metallic border around the leather corset, sleeves, and legs, and then beveled to add dimension to the trim. Figure 11.6 shows these additions.

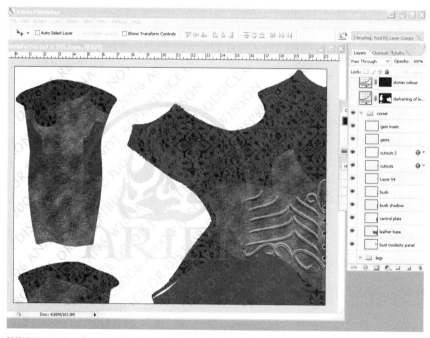

FIGURE 11.5   Leather and intricate detailing is added to the corset using several layers.

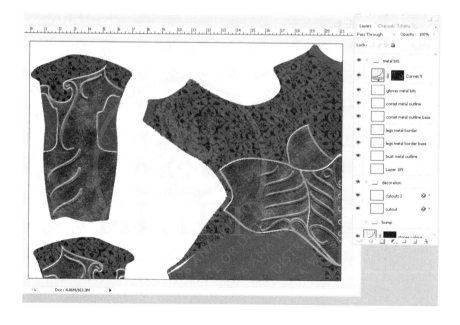

FIGURE 11.6   Metallic trim and additional details are added to the corset, sleeves, and legs.

To finish the detailing on the corset, several layers are used to build up eyelets and lacing on the back of the corset. Care is taken to line up the lacing across the back seam so that the laces match up perfectly ... a process that is well worth the effort. Figure 11.7 shows the detail on the lacing and eyelets.

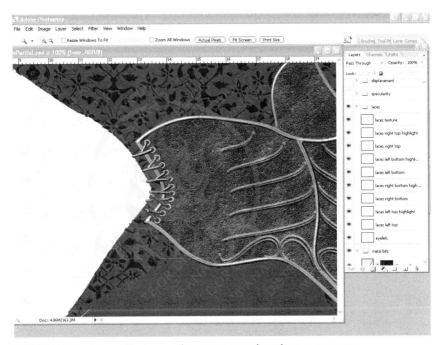

FIGURE 11.7   Eyelets and lacing on the corset complete the texture map.

Specular (Highlight) Maps

Specular maps control the color and amount of highlights in a material shader. Images that define specular color can be color or grayscale. Darker values will produce softer highlights, and lighter values will produce brighter highlights. If you are using colored specular maps, desaturated colors will produce milder highlights, whereas saturated colors create very hot highlights.

When you develop your diffuse texture in layers, you can reuse some of the layers to create additional maps for your material shader. Such is the case with the specular map that Ana created for The Bootie. Here's how she approached the specular map.

Ana starts with a black background, which represents areas that do not receive specular highlights. Next, she creates a new layer and fills all areas in the clothing that will not be transparent with solid white. By reducing the opacity of this layer to 30 percent, she is able to determine an appropriate base level for the highlights in the clothing. A new layer is created, and the leather areas on the corset, legs, and sleeves are selected and filled with a grayscale cloud pattern. Noise is added to the cloud pattern to give it a bumpy feel. Progress thus far is shown in Figure 11.8.

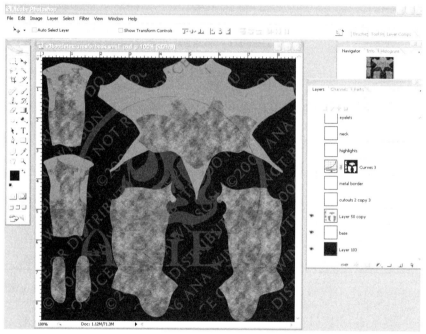

FIGURE 11.8   Dark areas in a specular map receive no highlights. Areas that are to receive highlights are selected and filled with varied shades of gray.

Next, Ana duplicates the cutouts on the arms, corset, and legs, and moves them to a new layer above the previous specular layers. She then adds bright white borders around the leather on these areas, so that the metallic trim on the leather receives the most specular highlights. An adjustment layer then brightens the underlying layers a bit. Figure 11.9 shows the progress to this point.

A new layer is added, and white highlights are hand painted in areas of the corset, arm, and leg leather. A band of light gray is added around the neck so that it receives more highlights than the lace. Finally, to complete the specular map, the eyelets are lightened to receive more highlights, and the laces are darkened to receive little to no highlights. The finished specular map is shown in Figure 11.10.

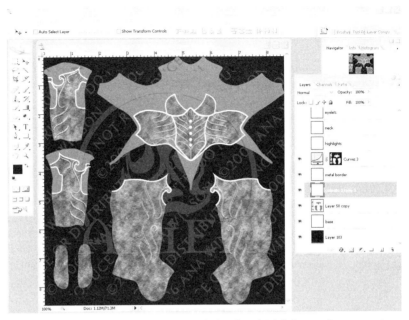

FIGURE 11.9   Lighter shades of gray provide brighter highlights on the cutouts in the arms, corset, and legs, and the brightest highlights on the metallic trim.

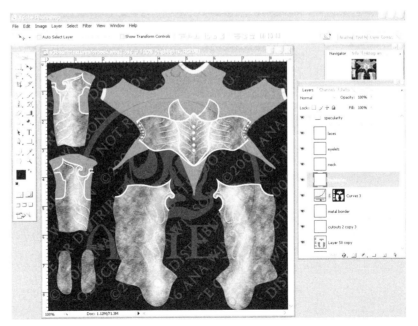

FIGURE 11.10   Highlights are painted on the leather areas, and neck and eyelets are lightened. Laces have darker areas to receive fewer highlights.

Transparency Maps

Transparency maps determine which portions of an object's surface are transparent and which are opaque. Because transparency maps only use the brightness values of an image and ignore the color data, they are usually grayscale images.

Transparency maps typically start against a pure black (Red 0, Green 0, Blue 0) background. Where black appears in the transparency map, the clothing will be invisible. All white areas in the transparency map will be fully opaque. Darker shades of gray will be more transparent, and lighter shades of gray will be more opaque.

To create the transparency map shown in Figure 11.11, Ana starts with a pure black layer. She then duplicates the lace layer and fills it with white, making portions of the lace opaque. The leather areas on the sleeves, corset, and legs are duplicated and filled with white to make them opaque. White areas are added to create seams in the panties, bodice, and sleeves. Finally, a border of white is added to make the neckband opaque, as is a layer of white that makes the lacing opaque.

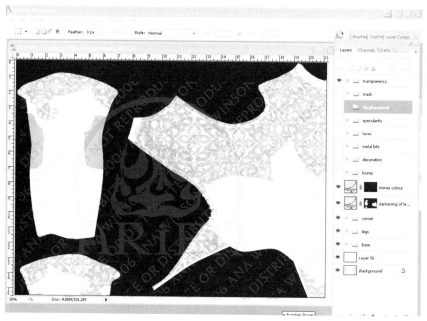

FIGURE 11.11   The transparency map makes part of the legs invisible and creates lace that is partially transparent in some areas and fully opaque in others.

Raytraced Reflections and Reflection Maps

When reflections appear in objects, they typically reflect their surrounding environment. To that end, Poser allows two different ways to incorporate reflections in your Poser scene: raytraced reflections and reflection maps.

Raytraced reflections simulate how the elements of your scene might appear if projected onto an imaginary hemisphere that surrounds your scene. The reflections are then bounced back onto your Poser content during render time. You create raytraced reflections in the Advanced Material Room view. An excellent overview of the various properties of reflections can be found at the Web site of Microbion Graphics. The first page of this excellent and detailed to tutorial can be found at *http://www.microbion. co.uk/graphics/poser/reflect1.htm.*

Raytraced reflections do take some time to render, so the option of using reflection maps can sometimes decrease your rendering time considerably. *Reflection maps* can create believable reflections where you don't have to reflect elements in your scene. Typically, a reflection map is a photograph of some "real world" elements that is spherized. To create the reflection map for The Bootie, Ana took a photograph from inside a window looking outward. She then increased the contrast to increase the difference between the light and dark areas. Finally, she ran the image through a spherize filter, giving the reflection map the appearance of looking at something through a metallic ball. Figure 11.12 shows a similar type of reflection map and the results it achieves on the Poser mannequin.

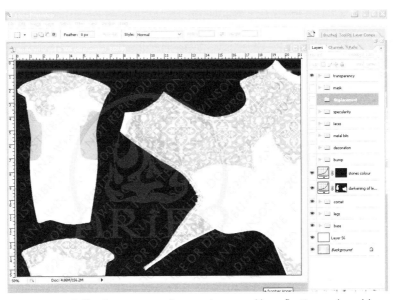

FIGURE 11.12　Reflection maps are frequently created by reflecting real-world environments onto a reflective sphere.

Bump Map

Bump maps add the *illusion* of 3D details to an otherwise smooth mesh object. During rendering, lights and shadows that correspond with the varying brightness of the bump map create the impression of an irregular surface.

Bump maps are *usually* grayscale images. Light (white) values create areas that appear more bumped out from the original surface of the mesh, and dark (black) areas appear more indented or recessed from the surface. This effect is most apparent where the surface of the object is perpendicular to the camera and falls off as you get to the edges of the object. For this reason, bump maps are great for objects that are farther away or for objects whose edges are not prominent or are hidden behind other objects. Figure 11.13 shows an example of a sphere without a bump map applied (left) and with a bump map applied. Notice that the edges of the sphere remain smooth in both cases even though the center area of the right-most sphere appears to have irregularities in its surface.

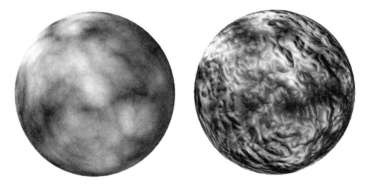

FIGURE 11.13   An object without a bump map (left) and with a bump map (right).

For the bump map, Ana starts with a black background. On a new layer, she selects all nontransparent areas in the clothing and fills the selection with a middle gray that has some noise added to it for texture. The noise adds to the bumpiness of the base bump map. Over the base noise layer, she selects the leather areas on the corset, sleeves, and legs, and fills them with a varied gray base with a slight leather appearance. The areas of the lacing and eyelets are made lighter to raise them from the leather area of the corset. Figure 11.14 shows the initial progress.

Next, Ana duplicates the beveled lace from the diffuse map and places it above the previous layers. She uses an adjustment curve to lighten the lace so that it brings the details forward in the bump map. Next, the leather areas are again superimposed over the lace and lightened so that they do not recede into the texture as much. These additional steps are shown in Figure 11.15.

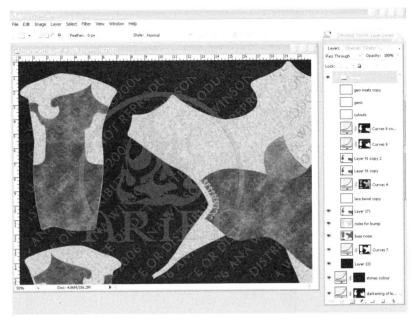

FIGURE 11.14   Starting with a black background, a layer of noise is added to all nontransparent areas. Then, the leather areas of the corset, arms, and legs are filled with a deep gray leathery texture.

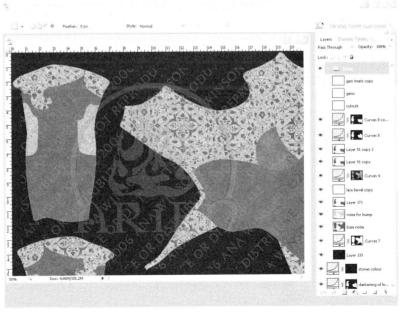

FIGURE 11.15   Lace details are added and then covered with the leather areas in the corset, sleeves, and legs.

To complete the bump map, all of the intricate details are added in the lightest colors so that they are raised higher to add more detail. The cutouts on the corset, arms, and legs are added, as are some lighter areas that raise the gems and gem insets. The metallic trim areas around the lacing eyelets, corset, sleeves, and legs are the brightest areas of the bump map, causing these areas to be raised the farthest. Figure 11.16 shows the finished bump map.

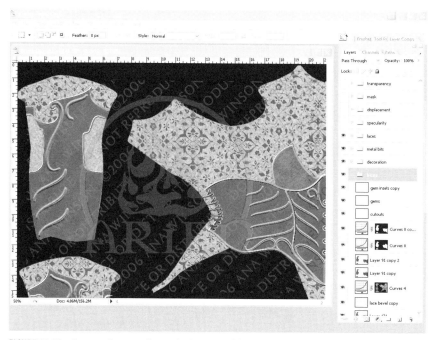

FIGURE 11.16   Decorations and metal trim are added as the brightest layers in the bump map, causing them to be raised more than the previous layers.

Displacement Map

Displacement maps are similar to bump maps in that they are used to add irregularities to the surface of your object. The amount of displacement varies based on the brightness values of the map. Light (white) values result in more displacement, whereas dark (black) values result in less or no displacement.

Unlike bump maps, displacement maps do affect the edges of your object with respect to the perspective of your camera, making them appear rough and uneven at render time. Because displacement maps work without actually changing the underlying mesh, they are an excellent way to create objects that look very complicated, even though the mesh geometry is smooth.

Figure 11.17 illustrates how bump maps and displacement maps affect the material of an object. The left-most sphere uses no bump or displacement. The middle sphere shows a bump map applied to the sphere. The right-most sphere uses both bump and displacement channels. Only the sphere on the right, with displacement, shows the geometry is affected around its edges.

FIGURE 11.17   Three spheres with diffuse only (left), diffuse and bump (middle), and diffuse, bump, and displacement maps (right).

As you learned in Chapter 4, "Creating Materials," there are a few settings in the FireFly renderer that must be enabled for displacement maps to work: The Min Displacement Bounds setting (in Manual Settings) has to be at least as high as the displacement value that you enter in the Displacement setting in the root node. Also, make sure you enable (check) the Use Displacement Maps option.

To create her displacement map, Ana once again begins with a solid black layer. Next, she duplicates a copy of the lace layer and places it above the black base. A third layer adds deep shadows at the seams of the garment. Next, lighter gray seams are added around the panties, and the leather on the corset, arms, and legs is filled with a solid gray value that is similar to the lightest color in the lace. Figure 11.18 shows the progress thus far.

A slightly lighter shade of gray is added around the center of the corset to raise its level slightly. Next, the cutouts on the arms, legs, and corset are duplicated and brightened to raise the detail outward from the base leather on the sleeves. Figure 11.19 shows this next level of displacement, which really adds a lot of detail and dimension to the leather areas.

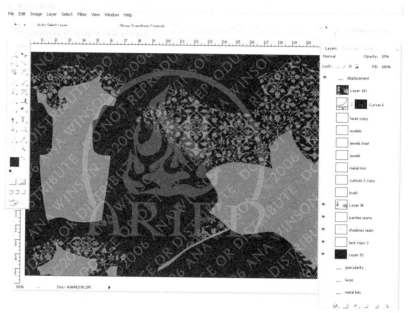

FIGURE 11.18 Starting with a black background, deep gray areas provide the least amount of displacement for the lace and leather areas in the corset.

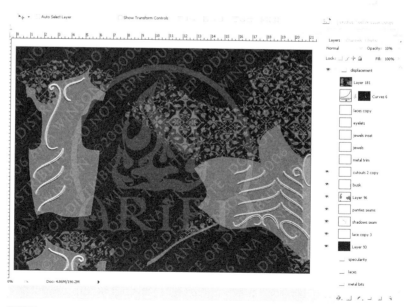

FIGURE 11.19 A greater level of displacement is added for the detailed cutouts on the leather portions of the clothing.

To complete the displacement details, Ana adds a light gray border around the edges of the leather, where the metallic trim appears in the texture map. Light gray areas are also added to raise the jewels, jewel insets, eyelets, and laces on the corset.

The last step is very important for displacement. When there are stark transitions between light and dark, the displacement will leave very sharp edges instead of soft transitions. Ana adds an adjustment curve that blurs and softens the edges of all the displacement layers so that the displacement effects transition smoothly from one level of displacement to another. A portion of the final displacement map is shown in Figure 11.20.

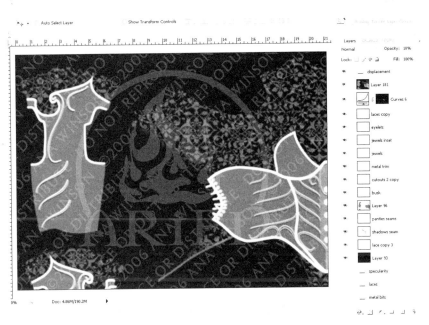

FIGURE 11.20   The highest levels of displacement are added to metallic trim, eyelets, and laces. Then, the displacement layers are softened with an adjustment layer to create smooth transitions.

CONCLUSION

In this chapter, you've been introduced to some of the techniques you can use as you create your own clothing textures. You've seen how you can make it easier to build textures if you start with the UV template and use layers, if you can. The tips you learned in this chapter should give you an idea of how to build your own texture maps for the various channels of your root node. You are now well on your way toward making your own textures!

FROM MODELER TO POSER LIBRARY

In This Chapter

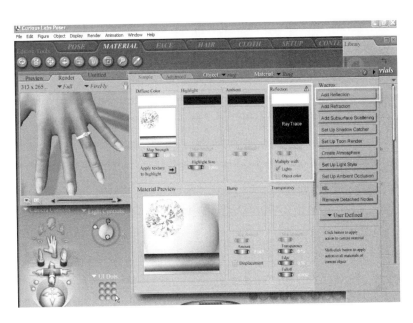

Objects modeled in a 3D program can serve many purposes in Poser, and you'll hear these 3D objects referred to by many content names. The objects that you model can be saved to the library as props, smart props, articulated props, dynamic clothing, conforming clothing, dynamic hair, conforming hair, and figures. The differences among these types of content are based upon the steps you complete before and during the time that you save them to the library.

In this chapter, you'll learn what distinguishes one type of content from another, how you prepare them for Poser, where to locate your content files, and how you save them to the library. This chapter will also address some of the edits that you must make to the files before you share them with others.

The procedures covered in this chapter are typical for creating objects that are compatible with Poser 7 only. If you want to create content that is compatible with previous versions of Poser, there are many other factors and procedures to consider. For example, Poser 4 uses proprietary file formats for bump maps and library thumbnails. Poser 5, 6, and 7 have the capability to use procedural shaders, dynamic clothing, and dynamic hair that cannot be used in earlier versions.

There are also supplementary files that users of older versions of Poser expect as a convenience, such as pose files that automatically apply material or morph changes to an object (MAT or MOR poses, respectively). Poser 7 provides solutions that help make it easier for users to share morphs or apply materials to their items.

Most of the issues that deal with creating content for older Poser versions are topics that go beyond the scope of this book. Further information about these procedures can be found at the various Poser community Web sites, forums, and tutorial archives.

In the past few chapters, you have covered quite a bit of ground, and you should understand that with practice comes perfection. Although we've tried to show you the basics, we also understand that you will approach it with your own methods and innovations from this point on, as well as through learning from additional sources. Nevertheless, we have set the groundwork from modeling to UV mapping to group and material assignment, so that you now have the basic knowledge that you need to create content for Poser.

Here's a brief overview of what should be done before you complete the tasks covered in this chapter:

- Model your object in a 3D program. Most of the objects that are made for Poser are built with rectangular (four-sided) polygons and a minimal number of triangular (three-sided) polygons.
- Create UV maps for your geometry using your modeling program or a third-party utility such as UV Mapper Professional. This is a process

that prepares your model so that it can accept textures. It also "flattens" your 3D object onto a 2D plane so that you can create realistic textures for your models using an image-editing program.

- Assign the polygons in your object to one or more materials using your modeling software, Poser's Group Editor, or a third-party utility.
- If you are creating an original posable character, conforming clothing, conforming hair, or posable props that require groups and bones, use Poser's Group Editor, UV Mapper Professional, Auto Group Editor, or any other similar method to create the necessary groups in your model. You'll learn later in this chapter how to associate those groups with bones that cause the object to become posable.

After completing all of the preceding tasks, you can bring your content into Poser, apply the materials, and save your content to the library. The tutorials in this chapter will take you the rest of the way!

IMPORTING OBJ FILES

To bring your Wavefront OBJ file into Poser, choose the File > Import > Wavefront OBJ command. When you import geometry into Poser, you are presented with several import options. The Import Options dialog box is shown in Figure 12.1. This dialog box contains options that help you size and position your prop, as well as other options that can help resolve geometry problems.

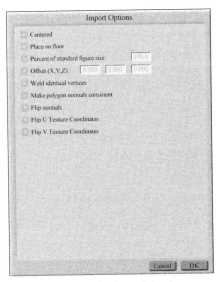

FIGURE 12.1 The Prop Import Options dialog box presents options that help you size and position your prop when you import it.

The options in the Prop Import Options dialog box serve the following purposes:

Centered: Places the object in the exact center of the scene (where the X coordinate is 0, the Y coordinate is 0, and the Z coordinate is 0). This is a good option to choose if you are not sure where the object will appear in the scene.

Place on Floor: Drops the lowest point of the object to ground level (where the Y coordinate is 0).

Percent of Standard Figure Size: Poser uses scaling units that are very small in comparison to other 3D software programs. If you model content in another 3D software program that uses different scaling, your objects may import much larger than expected. When you check this option, your object will be sized in relation to the standard height of a human figure. Enter a numerical value to rescale your object in relation to Poser's standard figure height (which is around six feet, give or take a few inches). Therefore, if you want your object to be approximately three feet high, check this option and enter a value of 50%.

In most cases, content that is created specifically for Poser is scaled correctly for use in Poser. On occasion, you'll find some wonderful content created in other 3D software. After you import the content into Poser, you quickly see that the content is substantially larger than the content you use in Poser. In fact, you may not be able to see it because it is too large, or it appears above or below the view of the camera.

One way to resolve this issue is to check the first three options in the Prop Import Options dialog box so that your object appears in the center of the stage, on the floor, and approximately 100% of figure size. You can then use the Scale dials in the Parameters window to scale the model appropriately. After the object appears to be the correct size, choose Figure > Drop to Floor so that the object rests on the floor.

Next, export it from Poser, checking only the Include Groups in Polygon Groups option if your object has body part groups. Otherwise, you do not need to check any options.

When you reimport this new object into Poser, it should appear in the center of the stage, at the correct scale, and on the floor just as you exported it. You can then complete the process of saving the object to the library.

Offset (X, Y, Z): Choose this option to offset your object from its default position or from the center position when used in conjunction with the Centered option. Enter a positive or negative number (in Poser units) for the amount of offset from the zero coordinate for the X (left/right), Y (up/down) or Z (forward/backward) axis that you want to offset.

Weld Identical Vertices: Choose this option if your geometry is split apart into separate groups or contains many common vertices in the same location. This option welds the like vertices back together.

 Objects that are made of right angles, such as boxes, may give better results if their common vertices are left unwelded. This is because Poser can smooth polygons at render time. If you weld the sides of a box together, you may end up with a bloated balloon-like box if you try to smooth polygons. To prevent this from happening, you will need to add a tiny row of polygons at each edge so that if polygon smoothing is selected, only the tiny polygons will be affected and the large portions of each side remain flat. When converting conforming clothing to dynamic clothing it is recommended that you select this option when you reimport the OBJ file.

Make Polygon Normals Consistent: 3D objects are made of faces that can be one-sided (where one side is visible and the other is invisible when facing the camera) or two-sided (where either side is visible when facing the camera). The direction of the "normals" defines which side of a one-sided face is visible and which is not. If your object appears with "holes" in it, the cause may be that some polygons face away from the camera. If you reimport the object with this option checked, it *may* alleviate the problem.

Flip Normals: Check this option if your object imports with all faces "inside out," so that the front of the object is invisible but the back of object is visible.

Reimport with Flip U Texture Coordinates if textures appear to be mirrored horizontally when you render. Reimport with Flip V Texture Coordinates if textures appear to be mirrored vertically when you render, as shown in Figure 12.2. See Table 12.1 for prop information at a glance.

TABLE 12.1   Prop Information at a Glance

CONTENT TYPE	PROPS
File Extensions	PP2 (not compressed); PPZ (compressed)
Path to Geometry Files	:Runtime Geometries : (custom folder name)
Path to Texture Files	:Runtime : Texture : (custom folder name)
Path to Library Files	:Runtime : Libraries : Props : (custom folder name)

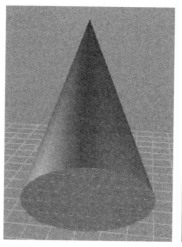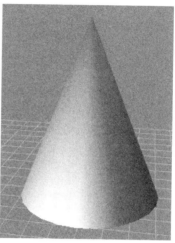

FIGURE 12.2   If an object appears "inside out" after you import it (left), reimport the object with the Flip normals option checked (right).

TUTORIAL 12.1   SAVING PROPS TO THE LIBRARY

Most people who become interested in creating Poser content start with props because they are probably the easiest type of content to create. After you model your object and prepare it with UV maps and material assignments, you simply import the object into Poser, add morphs (if desired), and save the prop to the library.

In this tutorial, you'll import a garden bench into Poser, assign a stone texture map as the diffuse and bump channels for its material, and save the prop to the library. Follow these steps:

1. Locate the Poser 7 > Downloads > Runtime > Geometries folder on your hard drive. Beneath that folder, create a new subfolder named PracticalPoser7.

ON THE CD

2. Locate the Tutorials > Chap12 folder on the CD-ROM that accompanies this book. Copy the bench.obj file into the Poser 7 > Downloads > Runtime > Geometries > PracticalPoser 7 folder that you created in Step 1.

3. Locate the Poser 7 > Downloads > Runtime > Textures folder on your hard drive. Beneath that folder, create a new subfolder named PracticalPoser7.

4. From the PracticalPoser7 > Tutorials > Chap12 folder, copy the bench.jpg texture map into the Poser 7 > Downloads > Runtime > Textures folder you created in Step 3.

5. From an empty Poser scene, choose File > Import > Wavefront OBJ. The Import Options dialog box shown in Figure 12.3 appears.

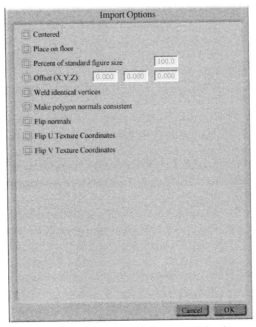

FIGURE 12.3   The Prop Import Options dialog box appears when you import 3D content into Poser.

6. The bench is sized properly for Poser, and it will also load into the center of the scene by default. Because of this, you do not need to check any of the options in the Prop Import dialog box. Click OK to continue.

7. The Import: Wavefront OBJ dialog box appears. Locate the bench.obj file that you saved in Step 2. Highlight the file, and click Open. The bench appears in your scene.

8. Choose Display > Document Style > Texture Shaded. You won't see the bench change because it doesn't have a texture applied to it yet. To add one, click the Material tab to enter the Material Room.

9. If necessary, click the Simple tab to display the simple material editor shown in Figure 12.4.

10. The Diffuse Color settings control the main color or texture of the object. To assign a bitmap texture, click the empty square that appears directly beneath the white Diffuse Color rectangle. The Texture Manager dialog box shown in Figure 12.5 appears.

11. Click the Browse button to locate the bench.jpg texture that you saved in Step 4. After you return to the Texture Manager dialog box, you'll see a preview of the texture in the Preview window. Click OK to return to the Simple material editor. The bench in the Preview window should update to show the texture applied to the bench.

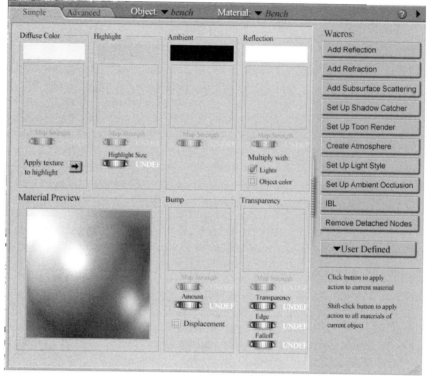

FIGURE 12.4 You will use the Simple material view to add a texture map to the diffuse and bump channels of the bench material.

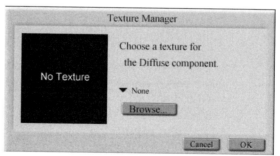

FIGURE 12.5 The Texture Manager dialog box prompts you to browse for a texture for your object.

12. We will use the same rock texture to add some "bumpiness" to the bench. To do so, click the square beneath the Bump heading in the Simple material view (the square beneath the cursor in Figure 12.6).

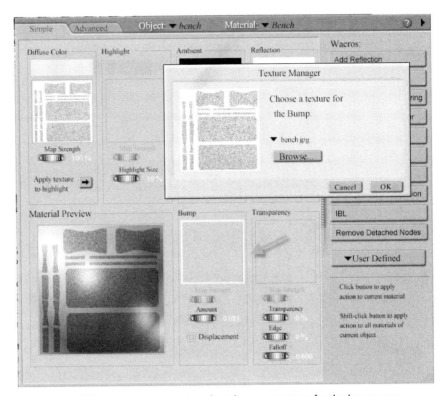

FIGURE 12.6   Click the Bump square to select the same texture for the bump map.

13. Click the Browse button to select the same texture (bench.jpg) for the bump map. After you return to the Texture Manager, click OK to assign the bump map.

14. You might be able to tell from the Material Preview that the bump map is a little strong. To reduce the setting, click the numbers beside the Amount slider, and set the value to .02 as shown in Figure 12.7.

15. If possible, choose Render > Render to do a test render of your bench to make sure that you are satisfied with the bump map setting. You will see the render appear in the small Document window in the Material Room. Increase or decrease the Amount slider until you are satisfied with the result.

16. Now you're ready to save the bench to the Prop Library. Before doing so, verify that you have deselected the option in General Preferences to use compressed files. To disable this option, choose Edit > General Preferences. Click the Misc tab in the General Preferences dialog box. Uncheck the *Use file compression* option in the Save Files section as

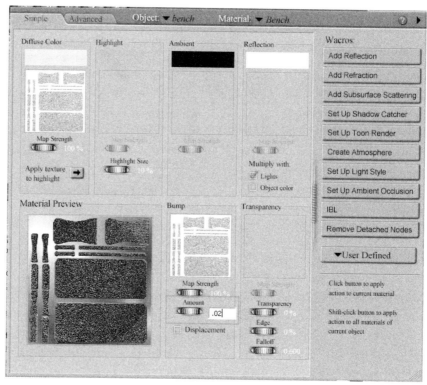

FIGURE 12.7 Reduce the Bump Map setting to .02.

shown in Figure 12.8. The reason for this is because you will have to make some changes to the file after you save it, and compressed files are not directly editable.

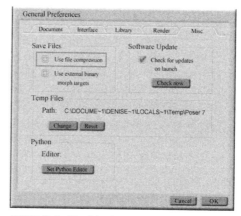

FIGURE 12.8 Disable the option to use file compression before you save your prop to the library.

17. Expand the Library view to show the Runtime list. From the Run-time drop-down list, choose the Downloads runtime folder. Then, choose the Props Library as the current library.
18. We are going to create a new category for your new prop. To do so, click the down arrow at the top of the Library window, and choose Add New Category from the menu, as shown in Figure 12.9.

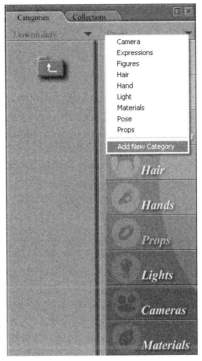

FIGURE 12.9   Click the Add New Category menu item to create a new library folder for your prop.

19. The Library Name dialog box prompts you to enter a name for your new library. For purposes of this tutorial, enter **PracticalPoser7**, and click OK to continue.
20. Scroll down if necessary to find the new PracticalPoser7 folder in your Props Library. Double-click the folder to select it as the current library.
21. Return to the Pose Room. Click the bench in the Document window to select it as the current item. The Add to Library icon (with a plus sign) should appear at the bottom of the Library window.

22. Click the Add to Library icon. The New Set dialog box shown in Figure 12.10 appears. Enter **Bench** for the Set Name. Then click the Select Subset button.

23. The Select Objects dialog box prompts you to select the items that should be included with the prop. Check bench, as shown in Figure 12.11. Then, click OK to continue.

FIGURE 12.10 Enter the name of the prop in the Set Name field of the New Set dialog box.

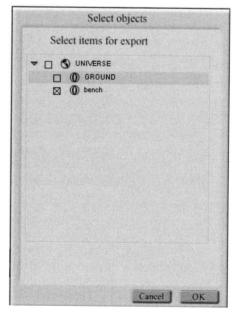

FIGURE 12.11 Select the bench in the scene to save it to the library.

24. Return to the New Set dialog box, and click OK. Your bench should now appear in the library.

You may notice that shadows appear in the thumbnail when you add your prop to the library. To prevent shadows in thumbnails, choose Display > Ground Shadows to turn off the shadow option. Then repeat Steps 20 through 24 to overwrite the previous version of your prop to remove the shadows from the thumbnail. When Poser asks if you want to replace the existing item, select OK.

TUTORIAL 12.2   REMOVING EMBEDDED GEOMETRY FROM PROPS

When you first save your prop to the library, Poser embeds the geometry information into the library file. This may seem to be advantageous because you would only have to keep track of one library file, rather than a library file and a geometry file. However, if you embed the geometry in the prop file, you won't be able to make new UV maps or regroup the object without destroying the prop file.

As a result, most content creators strip the geometry information out of the prop file and add some lines in the prop file that reference an external OBJ file in the Runtime > Geometries folder. This means you will have to open the prop file in a text editor and make the changes manually. If you follow the next set of procedures, the change should be relatively painless.

Hacking library files is not for the faint of heart. Always make a backup copy of the file you are editing before you make any changes. Keep the backup copy in a safe place in the event that you ever need the original file again!

To remove the embedded geometry from a prop file and reference an external OBJ file, follow these steps:

1. Create a backup copy of your prop file. For this example, copy the bench.pp2 file that you created in the previous task, and save it as benchBAK.pp2.
2. Open bench.pp2 in a text editor that can save ASCII-compatible text files (such as Microsoft Word, WordPad, or an equivalent Mac program).
3. At the beginning of the prop file, you will notice several lines that appear similar to those shown in Figure 12.12. These lines are to remain untouched.
4. The custom geometry section begins with a line that reads `geomCustom`. Following that will be a few lines that tell the number of vertices for several different categories. Finally, there will be many lines that begin with the letters `v`, `vt`, and `f`. All of these lines should be removed. Figure 12.13 shows the beginning and the ending sections of

```
{
version
    {
    number 7
    }
prop bench
    {
```

FIGURE 12.12 The first few lines of your prop file should remain untouched.

the custom geometry. Make sure you also remove *only one* ending bracket that follows the lines that begin with f.

```
geomCustom
{
        numbVerts 1008
        numbTVerts 984
        numbTSets 4008
        numbElems 1002
        numbSets 4008
        v -0.396000 0.193000 0.100000
        v 0.396000 0.193000 0.100000
        v 0.396000 0.193000 -0.100000
        v -0.396000 0.193000 -0.100000
        v -0.396000 0.213000 0.100000
        v 0.396000 0.213000 0.100000
```

> **This section will include many lines that begin with the letters v, vt, and f, until you see the end of these lines as shown below ...**

```
        f 1008/979 845/980 841/981 1006/977
        f 992/963 1004/972 1007/983 998/982
        f 1004/972 1003/970 1008/979 1007/983
        f 1003/970 840/984 845/980 1008/979
}
```

FIGURE 12.13 Remove the custom geometry section that begins with geomCustom and ends with several lines that begin with f. Also remove one single closing bracket that immediately follows the last line that begins with the letter f.

5. After you delete the custom geometry as outlined in Step 4, the lines that remain at the top of the prop file should look as shown in Figure 12.14. The dotted line in the figure shows where the custom geometry existed and where you need to add a couple of lines of code.
6. In the area designated by the dotted line in Figure 12.14, add the following lines of code, which provide a pointer to the location where you saved the OBJ geometry file. After you add this code, your altered prop file will look as shown in Figure 12.15.

```
storageOffset 0 0.3487 0
objFileGeom 0 0 :Runtime:Geometries:PracticalPoser7:
Chap12:bench.obj
```

```
{
    version
        {
            number 7
        }
    prop bench
        {
        •••••••••••••••••••••••••••••••••••••••••••••••••••••••••
        }
            prop bench
            {
                    name bench
                    on
                    bend 1
                    dynamicsLock 1
                    hidden 0
                    addToMenu 1
                    castsShadow 1
                    includeInDepthCue 1
                    useZBuffer 1
                    parent UNIVERSE
                    creaseAngle 80
                    channels
                    {
```

FIGURE 12.14 The beginning of the prop file after all of the custom geometry has been removed.

```
{
    version
    {
        number 7
    }
    prop bench
    {
        storageOffset 0 0.3487 0
        objFileGeom 0 0 :Runtime:Geometries:PracticalPoser6:Chap16:bench.obj
    }
    prop bench
    {
        name bench
        on
        bend 1
        dynamicsLock 1
        hidden 0
        addToMenu 1
        castsShadow 1
        includeInDepthCue 1
        useZBuffer 1
        parent UNIVERSE
        creaseAngle 80
        channels
        {
```

FIGURE 12.15 The embedded geometry section is now replaced with a reference to the external geometry file.

7. Figure 12.15 also shows four lines that are highlighted with arrows. One of the lines contains the name of the object file (bench.obj). Make sure that the other three lines marked with the arrow name the prop the same as the object. For example, if your object is instead named benchseat.obj, the other three lines should read prop benchseat or name benchseat for the external call to the object to work correctly.

8. Save your edited prop file to the same location as previously saved, overwriting the version that contained the embedded geometry. The revision is now complete.

TUTORIAL 12.3   FIXING OBJ AND TEXTURE PATHS

When you save any type of content to the Poser libraries, Poser sometimes creates absolute path references to the geometry and texture map files. Absolute paths give a complete reference to a file. For example, if you loaded a texture from an external runtime file on your D drive, you might see a texture reference such as D:\Runtime\Textures\Jessi Clothing\dress.jpg.

The path works fine on your computer, and it will also work fine if someone else creates exactly the same path on their own computer. But if someone else chooses to install files to a different location, error messages will appear when the user tries to load the product from the library. This is why you should always use *relative* paths to geometry and image files in the items that you save to the library. The path to the OBJ file or texture map must always begin with *:Runtime*, and use colons (:) rather than backslashes (\) as separators to maintain compatibility with Macintosh file structures.

To edit file paths, follow these steps:

1. Open your library file in a text editor that can save ASCII-compatible text files. Files that can include references to OBJ or image files can include items in your Figures, Props, and Hair Libraries. Also make sure that you open an uncompressed version (CR2, PP2, or HR2) rather than a compressed version that cannot be edited (CRZ, PPZ, or HRZ).

2. Use the Search feature of your image editor to search for *OBJ* or *obj*. A reference to an OBJ file usually occurs only twice in a figure's CR2 file (see Figure 12.16), once in a prop's PP2 file (see Figure 12.17), and once in a hair set's HR2 file (see Figure 12.18). If your path contains forward slashes or back slashes and does not start with Runtime as shown in these figures, edit the file paths to use the proper syntax as shown in these examples. Try to keep paths as brief as possible, and do not exceed 60 characters so as to maintain Mac compatibility.

```
{
version
    {
    number 5
    }
figureResFile  :Runtime:Geometries:ArtyMotion:PetiteChou:PetiteChouDress.obj
actor BODY:1
    {
```

**Several sections that begin with the word actor appear
between the two OBJ references.**

```
actor skirt:1
    {
    storageOffset 0 0 0
    geomHandlerGeom 13 skirt
    }
    figureResFile
 :Runtime:Geometries:ArtyMotion:PetiteChou:PetiteChouDress.obj
actor BODY:1
    {
```

FIGURE 12.16   A figure file (CR2) includes two references to external
geometry that are separated by several *actor* sections. If the path is long,
it may wrap around to two lines, which has the same effect as chopping
the text at the place that the text wrapped to the new line.

```
{

version
    {
    number 4.01
    }
prop EgyptianThroneClassic
    {
    storageOffset 0 0.3487 0
    objFileGeom 0 0
 :Runtime:Geometries:Anton'sPeople:Treasures_Of_Egypt:EgyptianThroneClassic.obj
    }
```

FIGURE 12.17   A prop file (PP2) includes one reference to an external object.

```
{

version
    {
    number 4.0
    }
prop figureHair
    {
    storageOffset 0 0.34875 0
    objFileGeom 0 0 :Runtime:Geometries:3Dream:3DreamParadiseHair.obj
    }
```

FIGURE 12.18   A hair file (HR2) includes one reference to an external object.

3. In a similar manner, search for *JPG* or *jpg* in your library file. You'll
   see various types of references to JPG images in your library files that
   most often reference Diffuse, Bump, Displacement, or Specular maps.
   Figure 12.19 shows the correct syntax for an image map reference.

```
                          }
           node "image_map" "Image_Map"
                          {
                  name "Image_Map"
                  pos 473 23
                  nodeInput "Image_Source"
                          {
                          name "Image_Source"
                          value 29 29 29
                          parmR NO_PARM
                          parmG NO_PARM
                          parmB NO_PARM
                          node NO_NODE
                          file
  ":Runtime:Textures:ArtyMotion:Jessi:Immortals:JessiImDressTop.jpg"
                          }
```

FIGURE 12.19   Image map references should also begin with *:Runtime* and use colons rather than backslashes to denote the file path.

Verify that all paths to the images used as textures are correct, and use the correct syntax. Just as the paths to the OBJ files should be relative and not absolute, the same is true of the paths to image files. They should begin with *:Runtime* and use colons instead of backslashes to trace the path hierarchy. Also, keep in mind that there may be multiple images used in an object, and there can also be more than one material reference to a single image. For complete results, do a search through the entire file for the JPG or jpg file extension, until your text editor informs you that it cannot find any additional instances of the extension. You should also do a search for any of the other image file types that Poser can use as an image map source. These file types include TIF, PSD, and BMP.

TUTORIAL 12.4   **CREATING SMART PROPS**

There is only one difference between a regular prop and a smart prop. When you add a regular prop to a scene, it doesn't automatically attach itself to anything. On the other hand, when you add a *smart prop* to a scene, it automatically finds and attaches itself to the appropriate figure or body part.

To explain this a little bit further, let's say you are creating a scene in which a man is kneeling on the floor, looking up at a woman who is sitting on a couch. She is looking down at her hand. You find a nice diamond ring in your Props Library, and you add it to the scene. You quickly learn how difficult it is to move the ring into position on a figure that is already posed. When you try to grab the ring, you accidentally move other items in the scene. If you try to use the xTrans, yTrans, and zTrans dials in the Parameters window, it takes a lot of time to move the prop into place.

If you save the ring to your library as a smart prop, it automatically finds its way to the woman's left ring finger when you add it to the scene. To save the engagement ring to the library, select the ring, choose the body part that is supposed to be its parent (the body part to which the ring will attach itself), and then save the prop to the library. If the procedure is completed correctly, the ring will always attach itself to the figure's left ring finger whenever you add it to a scene, regardless of how that figure is posed. Table 12.2 includes prop information at a glance.

Table 12.2   Prop Information at a Glance

CONTENT TYPE	SMART PROPS
File Extensions	PP2 (not compressed); PPZ (compressed)
Path to Geometry Files	:Runtime :Geometries :(custom folder name)
Path to Texture Files	:Runtime :Texture :(custom folder name)
Path to Library Files	:Runtime :Libraries :Props :(custom folder name)

Before you save the smart prop to the library, use the Object > Change Figure Parent command to assign a parent to the prop.

To create a smart prop for the ring, follow these steps:

ON THE CD

1. Locate the ring.obj file in the Tutorials > Chap12 folder on the CD-ROM that accompanies this book.
2. Copy the ring.obj file to the Downloads > Runtime > Geometries > PracticalPoser7 folder that you created in Tutorial 12.1.

ON THE CD

3. Locate the ring.jpg texture file in the Tutorials > Chap12 folder on the CD-ROM that accompanies this book.
4. Copy the ring.jpg image to the Downloads > Runtime > Textures > PracticalPoser7 folder that you created in Tutorial 12.1.
5. Create a new scene in Poser, and add Jessi to the scene. Turn off Inverse Kinematics, and use the Joint Editor to zero her pose as shown in Figure 12.20. Also, open the Parameters window, and verify that the X, Y, and Z Trans dials on the hip and body are set at zero as well.
6. Choose File > Import > Wavefront OBJ. The Import Options dialog box appears. To import the ring in the same position in which it was modeled, leave all options unchecked as shown in Figure 12.21. Click OK to continue.
7. The Import: Wavefront OBJ dialog box appears. Navigate to the Downloads > Runtime > Geometries > PracticalPoser7 folder, and highlight ring.obj. Click Open to continue. The ring should be positioned on Jessi's left ring finger when it appears in the scene.

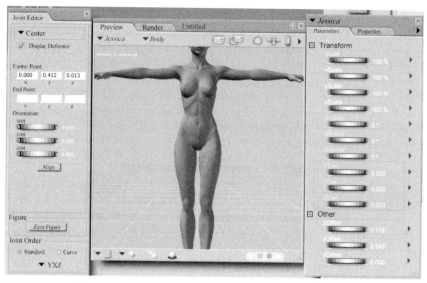

FIGURE 12.20 Add Jessi to an empty scene and zero her pose.

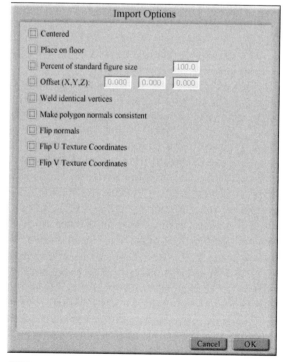

FIGURE 12.21 Leave all options in the Prop Import Options dialog box unchecked.

8. Choose Display > Document Style > Texture Shaded, or click the Texture Shaded (last) icon in the Document Display Style controls. The textures appear on the figures in the scene.

9. Choose Display > Camera View > Left Hand Camera, or click the Left Hand Cam icon in the Camera Controls. This focuses your current view on the left hand, where you can see the ring. Adjust the camera as necessary to get a good view of the ring on the hand. This prepares the camera view for the image that you will see in the library thumbnail. Figure 12.22 shows an example.

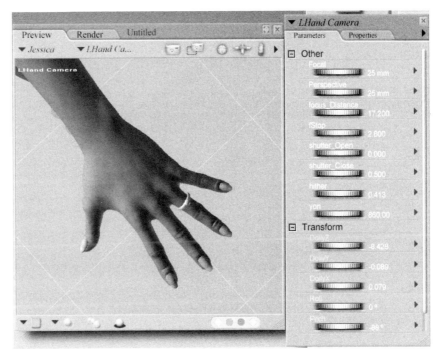

FIGURE 12.22   Adjust the Left Hand camera for a better view of the ring.

10. Adjust the lighting as necessary to get a good view of the ring. In addition, you may want to turn the display of shadows off before you save your ring to the library. Choose Display > Ground Shadows to uncheck the option if necessary.

11. You might notice that the diamond on the ring does not appear to be faceted. This is due to the Smoothing feature of Poser, which softens rough edges on low-resolution geometry to make it appear as though it is higher in resolution. However, in cases when you want faceted geometry, you can adjust the Crease Angle setting in the Properties

window. Any geometry that is below the setting will be smoothed. Any geometry that is above the crease angle setting will be faceted. For the ring, reduce the Crease Angle setting from 80 (the default) to 15 degrees, as shown in Figure 12.23. After you make this adjustment, you will see a faceted gemstone on the ring.

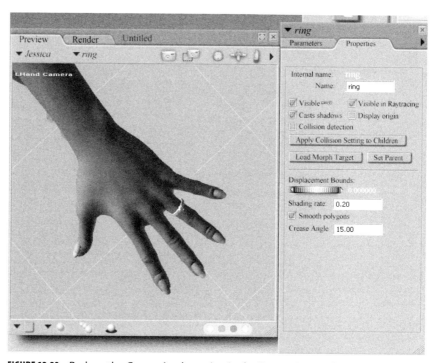

FIGURE 12.23 Reduce the Crease Angle setting in the Properties window so that the facets on the gemstone are not smoothed.

ON THE CD

12. Click the Material tab to go to the Material Room. Select the Simple view tab if necessary.
13. From the Object menu at the top of the Simple material view, select ring as the current object. The default material selection will be Gem.
14. Click the square that appears underneath the Diffuse Color rectangle. Locate the ring.jpg texture map in the Tutorials > Chap12 folder , and select it for the texture for the gem. The gem displays the texture and now should look more like a diamond.
15. Select Ring from the Material drop-down menu, and again select the ring.jpg texture map. The ring turns silver.

16. Click the Add Reflection wacro in the Material Room to add a raytrace reflection to the ring band. Your material settings should now look as shown in Figure 12.24.

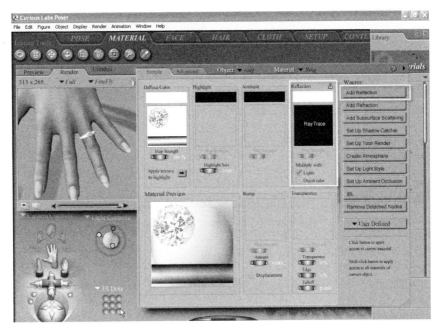

FIGURE 12.24   Click the Add Reflection wacro to add a raytrace reflection to the ring band.

17. Click the Pose tab to return to the Pose Room. To attach the ring to Jessi's finger, select the ring by clicking on it or by choosing it from the Current Actor menu in the Document window.
18. Click the Set Parent button in the Properties window. The Object Parent window opens.
19. Scroll down the list and choose lRing1 as the parent for the ring, as shown in Figure 12.25. The ring should now be attached to Jessi's finger.
20. Locate the Downloads > Props > PracticalPoser7 library that you created in the previous tutorial. Verify that the ring is selected as the current object, and click the Add to Library icon at the bottom of the Library window. The New Set dialog box opens.
21. Enter **Diamond Ring** as the name for the prop. *Do not* click the Select Subset button. Instead, click OK to continue.

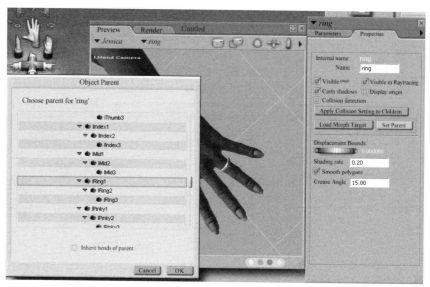

FIGURE 12.25 Choose the IRing1 body part as the parent for the ring.

22. The dialog box shown in Figure 12.26 informs you that the prop has a parent (the left ring finger, in this case). It asks if you want to save the prop as a smart prop. Click Yes to continue.

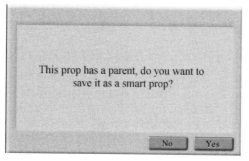

FIGURE 12.26 When a prop has a parent, Poser asks if you want to save it as a smart prop.

23. To test the figure, delete the existing ring from the left hand. Apply a pose to Jessi, and then add the engagement ring from the library. When you zoom in to the left hand with the Left Hand camera, you should see the ring on her left hand.

CREATING CONFORMING CLOTHING

One of the most common questions asked by people who are new to Poser is, "How do I make my own clothing?" The good news is that we are going to show you where to begin. The bad news is that we can't address *everything* that is involved.

You're about to embark on a long, technical journey that will take time and a lot of practice to master. To put it succinctly, the hardest and most tedious part of creating conforming clothing is getting it to work. If you take it one step at a time, you'll eventually find it easier and easier to create your own clothing.

Before we get into the steps that add a grouped model into the Poser library as a posable figure, we must stress one *very important* point. The steps that you are learning in this chapter are only the very beginning of a long road of learning. You must overcome many intricacies and technicalities to make conforming clothing work well. Many things can also go wrong, and it is hard to anticipate the difficulties that you will encounter along the way.

What we give you here is a starting point. For additional information beyond that which you will learn in this chapter, the following resources and solutions are recommended:

- A highly regarded member of the Poser community has prepared beginner-level tutorials that cover many features of Poser 4 and Poser 5. *Geep* (also known to the Poser community as *"Dr. Geep"*) has posted dozens and dozens of beginner-level tutorials that cover almost every aspect of Poser in an easy-natured and comical manner. In particular, you will probably want to seek out Geep's tutorials on the Group Editor, the Joint Editor, and Joint Parameters. You can find Dr. Geep's tutorials on his Web site at *http://www.drgeep.com/PoserTutorials.htm*.

- *No question is a bad question*. Don't be afraid to post messages in the community forums such as Renderosity, Poser Pros, RuntimeDNA, and DAZ3D. Many of the experts there assist in any way they can. In fact, chances are good that many folks in the community have encountered the very same problems, and you'll usually get an answer very quickly. Describe the problem that you're having, provide screen shots if possible, and above all, don't be embarrassed to ask questions.

MAKING A CR2 FILE

You've already learned that you must divide a clothing object into body part groups before you make it a posable figure. That isn't all that is necessary to make a figure posable, however. Poser doesn't know where the joints are in that clothing, and how to bend, twist, and rotate the joints, without specific information—information that is contained in a CR2 library file.

A CR2 file (which is the extension for files saved in the Figures Library) contains the information that turns your grouped clothing object into a piece of clothing that bends and moves. Basically, the CR2 tells Poser what body parts your clothing object has, where and how they bend, and what textures or materials each polygon in the object uses.

It's very difficult to create a CR2 for a totally original figure, such as a human character. Poser has the Group Editor to help you create groups, the Setup Room to help you create bones that move the groups, and the Joint Parameters window to help you specify how those joints move. However, when it comes to setting all of the parameters up for your model, it is a very tedious process.

When creating an original figure (such as a posable human or animal), there are two methods that you can use. In the older method, you begin by creating a text file that lists each body part in a hierarchical list. Each body part is preceded by a number that lists the level in the hierarchy where they belong. At the end of each line is a three-letter designation (such as xyz), which defines the order in which the joints bend, twist, and rotate. You save this text file with a PHI extension. After this process is done, you use the File > Convert Hierarchy File command to convert the file to a Poser figure. The final step is to use the Joint Editor to configure joint parameters that define how the joints bend, move, and twist. This is without a doubt the most difficult and time-consuming process of figure creation, and it is typically used when creating a totally original figure rather than clothing for an already existing figure.

For a complete description of creating a PHI file and turning it into a CR2 Character Library file, refer to "Tutorial: Poser Figure Creation" on pages 343 - 355 of the Poser Tutorial Manual, furnished in PDF format with Poser 7.

In the new method, you can use the Setup Room instead of the PHI file to design your bone structure. Then you follow in the Joint Editor with configuring the joint parameters.

Because it's difficult to create joints from scratch and because the clothing must bend almost identically with the original figure, most clothing modelers use the information from the original character when they create a CR2 for their clothing. That way, the clothing will bend and move exactly the same way that the original character does. It's much less tedious work. Reusing the information from the original figure is also the best option from a technical standpoint.

As you learned in the previous chapter, you divide conforming clothing models into the same body part groups that are used in the human figure. That is the first step of the process. After you add groups to a clothing model, you have to tell Poser how those groups are connected. There are basically two ways to accomplish this:

- Use a copy of the original character's CR2 file as a donor to create a CR2 for your clothing, as described in Tutorial 12.6.
- Use the Setup Room to apply bones from the original figure to your clothing. This effectively accomplishes the same thing as editing the CR2 file in a text editor, but it gives you a visual indication of the bone structure and also allows you to add additional bones. This process is described in Tutorial 12.7.

It is common practice for clothing creators to derive their own CR2 files from information contained in the original figure's CR2 file. Although you can *technically* use the CR2 from clothing made by others, that data is copyrighted by the original creator. It would be illegal for you to use the data without permission from the creator or creators of the clothing. Their clothing items contain custom variations of joint parameters that they worked very hard to create. If you want to use their work for your own projects, contact the original developer and ask their permission first.

REMOVING MORPHS FROM A CR2

When you use a donor CR2 or use the Setup Room to transfer bone and joint information to your own model, your clothing inherits the joint parameters from the donor object. That is exactly what you want to happen. What presents a bit of a problem, though, is that clothing *also* inherits the material and morph information from the donor object.

At first glance, you'll see the morph dials in the Parameters window, and you'll be delighted that the morph information appears in your clothing. However, when you try to adjust the morph dials you won't see anything happen. You see, for morphs to work, they must be copied between geometry objects that have exactly the same number of polygons, and the vertices that make up those polygons must be listed in exactly the same order. In other words, the geometry must be *identical* in its construction and in the order in which the OBJ file lists all of the vertices in the geometry.

The geometry of the donor object is guaranteed to be different from your clothing. As a result, the morph information from the original donor object does nothing but add extra and unnecessary overhead to your clothing object. It makes the file size much larger than it has to be due to thousands of extra lines of text. So the best thing to do is remove the morph information *before* you use the donor file for one or more articles of clothing. There are two ways that you can do this:

- Open the Parameters window in Poser 7. Start with the head, and locate the morphs in the selected body part. Poser does not allow you to delete the dials in the Transform category because they are necessary for posing and scaling the figure. Morphs usually appear beneath the category named Morphs. When you click the arrow at the right of a morph dial, choose Delete Morph from the menu that appears, as shown in Figure 12.27. After you delete all of the morphs, click the Add to Library icon at the bottom of your current Character Library. Enter a new name for the figure, and use this figure as your donor CR2 whenever you create clothing for this character. For example, if you remove the morphs from Jessi, save the new version to the Figures Library as **JessiBlank**. Use this clean version as a source CR2 each time you create clothing for Jessi.

You can also delete morphs in the Hierarchy Editor. Choose Window > Hierarchy Editor to open the Hierarchy window. Verify that the Show All Parameters option is checked. Morph parameter dials have a little dial icon displayed to the left of the dial name. Take care not to delete the standard dials that are required to pose or translate your figure or body parts (Taper, Scale, xScale, yScale, zScale, xRotate, yRotate, zRotate, xTrans, yTrans, zTrans, Twist, Side-Side, Bend, Up-Down, and so on). What you do want to delete are morphs that change the appearance of the figure.

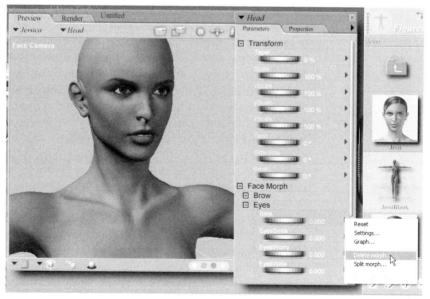

FIGURE 12.27   You can delete morphs from each body part using the Parameters window. Click the right arrow, and choose Delete Morph from the menu that appears.

- Open the figure's uncompressed CR2 (not the CRZ file) in Morph Manager 4.0, a free utility that you can download at *http://www.mor-phography.uk.vu/dlutility.html*. If a body part contains morphs, you will see a plus sign beside the body part. Expand the tree to reveal the morph names, which are preceded by the letter *M* as shown in Figure 12.28. *Do not remove the other joint parameters that are preceded with the letter C.* To delete a morph, click the morph name, and press the Delete key on your keyboard. Click OK when Morph Manager asks if you are sure you want to delete the morph. Complete this process until all morphs are removed, and then click the Save File button. Save the CR2 under a new filename, such as **JessiBlank**.

FIGURE 12.28   Morph Manager 4.0, a free utility that is widely used in the Poser community, allows you to delete morphs from your figures.

After you remove the morphs from your donor figure, be sure to save a copy to your Figures Library. Assign a different name so that you don't overwrite the original version that includes the morphs.

If you remove the morphs from Jessi.CR2 using the Remove Morph commands in the Parameters window, make sure that you have the Use File Compression option unchecked in the Misc tab of the General Preferences dialog box before you save the unmorphed version to the library. This will save the file as an editable CR2 instead of a compressed CRZ file.

TUTORIAL 12.5 USING A DONOR CR2

As mentioned earlier in this chapter, it is common practice to use joint parameter information from a posable figure's CR2 file when you design clothing for that figure. Those who design original figures (such as Jessi, James, Victoria 3, Apollo Maximus, LaRoo, and so on) realize that it is common practice for clothing designers to use the joint information from the original character. *In most cases*, you usually don't have to ask permission. When in doubt, it won't hurt to ask the individual or company if it's okay to use the CR2 from a character when you create clothing for it.

On the other hand, it is an entirely different story when you use information from a similar piece of clothing that someone else has created for the same character. It is entirely possible that the clothing has custom joint parameters, morphs, or other configurations that are copyrighted by the original creator and that you don't, by default, have the permission to duplicate. It's good, sound, professional practice to be respectful of the work of others from not only the moral perspective, but the legal one as well. If you don't have *written permission* to use joint parameters or morph information from clothing that has been created by others, *don't use it*. Use the information from the original character instead. Table 12.3 provides figure and character information at a glance.

Table 12.3 Figure and Character Information at a Glance

CONTENT TYPE	CHARACTERS, CONFORMING CLOTHING AND HAIR, POSABLE PROPS
File Extensions	CR2 (not compressed); CRZ (compressed)
Path to Geometry Files	:Runtime :Geometries :(custom folder name)
Path to Texture Files	:Runtime :Texture :(custom folder name)
Path to Library Files	:Runtime :Libraries :Character :(custom folder name)

Your content can be placed beneath any Runtime folder that you choose, as long as you begin the file paths in your CR2 with :Runtime as shown in Table 12.3. Your custom folder can be named as you choose. Most content creators include their Artist name or the Product name within their folder names.

That being said, it is relatively easy to convert a figure's CR2 to a clothing CR2. Simply follow these steps:

1. Save the geometry and texture files in the locations shown in Table 12.3. You can locate the files in any Runtime folder, as long as the folders beneath the Runtime folder are as shown in the table.

2. For purposes of this tutorial, you'll find three OBJ files in the Tutorials > Chap12 folder on the CD-ROM that accompanies this book. The files are named JessiConfSkirt.obj, JessiPants.obj, and JessiTShirt.obj. Copy them to the Downloads > Runtime > Geometries > Practical-Poser7 folder.

3. If you have not already done so, remove the morphs from the Jessi.CR2 object (located in the Poser 7 > Runtime > Libraries > Character > Jessi folder) using the Remove Morph commands in the Parameters window or by using Morph Manager.

4. Save the unmorphed version as **JessiBlank.CR2**. You can save it to the same folder as the original version as long as you assign a unique name. You might also want to make a copy of the Jessi.png thumbnail and save it as **JessiBlank.png** (the filename must be the same as the new CR2), so that the library item will have a thumbnail associated with it.

5. Open the JessiBlank.CR2 file in a text editor that can handle very large files (Microsoft Word, WordPad, or similar text editor capable of handling large files if necessary).

Some CR2 files can be hundreds or even over a thousand pages long, especially when morphs are included. Windows users will find this far too large for Notepad, but WordPad is capable of handling larger CR2 files.

6. We'll work on the T-shirt in this tutorial. The T-shirt is located in the Poser 7 > Downloads > Runtime > Geometries > PracticalPoser7 folder, and the object name is JessiTShirt.obj. The paths in the CR2 should look as shown in Figure 12.29. Notice that the edited path does not begin with the Downloads folder, and that it does begin with the Runtime folder. This ensures that the path will work in any Runtime in which the files are placed. Edit the paths to the OBJ file so that it points to the object you want to make posable, and remove the reference to the PMD file (the external binary morph file). Figure 12.29 shows both references in the CR2 file before and after they are edited.

7. Save your edited CR2 in the Figures Library in the same Runtime in which you saved your OBJ file. For example, we saved our OBJ files to the Downloads > Runtime > Geometries > PracticalPoser7 folder. You must also save the CR2 to the Downloads > Runtime Library. Create a folder in your Downloads > Runtime > Libraries > Character folder named PracticalPoser7, and save the edited CR2 as **JessiTShirt.CR2**. Figure 12.30 shows the correct location for the Geometry OBJ and the Figures CR2.

First Reference Before Editing:

```
|(
version
    (
    number 6
    )
morphBinaryFile :Runtime:Libraries:character:Jessi:Jessi.pmd
figureResFile :Runtime:Libraries:character:Jessi:Jessi.obj
actor BODY:1
```

First Reference After Editing:

```
    (
version
    (
    number 6
    )
figureResFile :Runtime:Geometries:PracticalPoser6:JessiTShirt.obj
actor BODY:1
        ,
```

Second Reference Before Editing:

```
    )
morphBinaryFile :Runtime:Libraries:character:Jessi:Jessi.pmd
figureResFile :Runtime:Libraries:character:Jessi:Jessi.obj
actor BODY:1
    (
```

Second Reference After Editing:

```
    )
figureResFile :Runtime:Geometries:PracticalPoser6:JessiTShirt.obj
actor BODY:1
    (
```

FIGURE 12.29   Edit both references to the OBJ file, and remove the references to the PMD file.

FIGURE 12.30   Make sure that you locate the Geometry file and the Figure Library file in the same Runtime folder. In this case, both are located in the Downloads Runtime Library.

Some text editors may enter a TXT extension after the filename when you save it. After you save your edited CR2, verify that the filename is JessiTShirt.CR2 and not JessiTShirt.CR2.TXT or JessiTShirt.TXT.

TUTORIAL 12.6   **USING THE SETUP ROOM**

 The Setup Room is likely the most confusing room for most users. In actuality, it's not that difficult to use. For a thorough discussion of the areas in the Setup Room, refer to Chapter 20 in the *Poser 7 Reference Manual*, which covers the purposes for all controls in the Setup Room, along with the process required to set up joints and other information.

This tutorial will give you the basic steps involved to convert a grouped clothing model into conforming clothing using the Setup Room. After you complete this tutorial you should have the basic knowledge required to make your clothing posable. However, you'll also need to remove some extraneous information from the CR2 file if you intend to share it with others.

One of three things can happen when you click the Setup tab to enter the Setup Room:

- If your scene is empty or if you select an item that is not a figure or prop when you enter the Setup Room, Poser informs you that you must have a prop or figure selected to enter the Setup Room. Choose OK to close the dialog box so that you can select the proper item.
- If you select a figure that is already grouped and boned (such as a posable figure or conforming clothing), when you click the Setup tab, you may receive a message that the figure contains morph targets and that changing groups in the Setup Room could make morphs unusable. Choose OK to continue if you simply want to modify the bones or joints for the figure. When you enter the Setup Room, you'll see the figure in its default position. You'll also see the underlying bone structure that makes the figure posable. An example is shown in Figure 12.31, where Jessi is shown in Outline display mode so that you can see the bones more easily.

 It is common practice to save geometry files to one of the Runtime: Geometries subfolders. If you use the Setup Room to make your geometry posable, Poser 7 automatically saves an OBJ file in the same location as the CR2 file and references that location in the CR2. You will have to edit the CR2 if you want to point to an OBJ file in the Geometries folder.

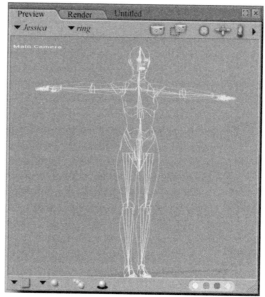

FIGURE 12.31   When you select a posable figure and enter the Pose Room, you see the bone structure for the figure.

- If you select a prop or an OBJ that you have recently imported into Poser, Poser informs you that your prop will be converted into a figure when you enter the Pose Room. The process to convert the figure is described in this tutorial.

In the tutorial that follows, we will apply the joint parameters from the JessiBlank.CR2 file that has had the morph information removed. We will apply the joint parameters to the JessiPants.obj file, which should be located in the Downloads > Runtime > Geometries > PracticalPoser7 folder.

To turn the JessiPants.obj file into conforming clothing using the Setup Room, follow these steps:

1. Use the File > Import > Wavefront OBJ command to import the Jes-siPants.obj file into an empty Poser scene. When the Import Options dialog box appears, do not check any options. After you locate and select the file, the pants should appear in the center of the stage as shown in Figure 12.32.
2. With the pants selected as the current object, click the Setup tab to enter the Setup Room. Poser displays a message that your currently selected prop will be turned into a figure if you continue. Click OK to enter the Setup Room.

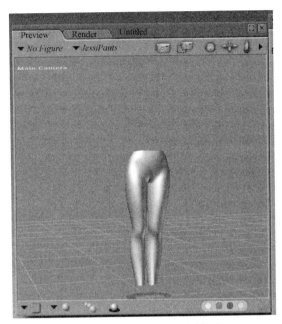

FIGURE 12.32   Import the JessiPants.obj file into an empty Poser scene.

 Newer figures that are coming out as this book goes to press are furnished with a DEV rig that you can use as a donor CR2 for clothing creation.

3. Double-click the JessiBlank CR2 library thumbnail. You will see bones appear on the figure as shown in Figure 12.33.

4. Return to the Pose Room. You'll notice that your pants are now posable, except the legs are bent a little bit. You should turn off IK, zero the pose, and then memorize that pose before you save the pants to the library. First, choose Figure > Use Inverse Kinematics, and make sure that no options are checked (on). Next, choose Window > Joint Editor to open the Joint Editor palette. Click any body part on the pants, and then click the Zero Figure button in the Joint Editor. The pants should go back to the default position.

5. To memorize the zero pose for the pants, choose Edit > Memorize > Figure. You won't notice any visible confirmation, but you can now save a preliminary copy of the pants to your library.

6. If you don't want shadows to appear in the library thumbnail, choose Display > Ground Shadows to uncheck the Shadow option if necessary. Position the camera to display the scene as you want your library thumbnail to appear.

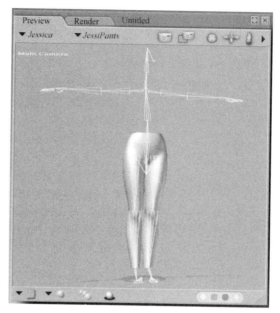

FIGURE 12.33 Apply the JessiBlank CR2 to the pants in the Setup Room. The bones appear on the figure.

7. Backtrack to the top level of the Poser Library, and then navigate to the Downloads > Figures > PracticalPoser7 Library. Click the Add to Library icon located at the bottom of the Library window. Your pants will appear in the library, and a miniaturized version of your Document window will appear as the thumbnail.

CLEANING UP THE CR2

Although the clothing is now posable you are not necessarily finished. There are some items that you will definitely have to clean up in the CR2 using either a text editor or a free CR2 editing program. Highly recommended is John Stalling's CR2 Editor, version 1.51, which displays the CR2 for JessiPants in Figure 12.34. You can download this file from *http://www.morphography.uk.vu/dlutility.html* (the same site that also provides Morph Manager 4.0, mentioned earlier in this chapter).

Common issues that you will have to clean up are the following:

• If the hip (on a male or female) and the chest (on a female) of your clothing disappear and display the hip and chest of the figure instead, your CR2 contains alternate geometry parts that must be removed.

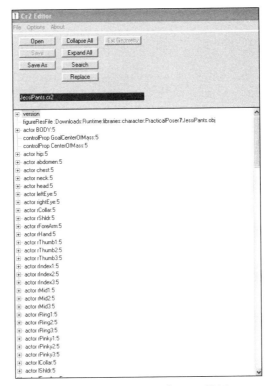

FIGURE 12.34 You will have to edit your CR2 in a text editor or a CR2 editing utility such as John Stalling's CR2 Editor.

Adult male and female Poser figures are often modeled with body parts that you can swap, depending on whether you want to show or hide the genitalia. There are lines in the CR2 that call other pieces of geometry when this is true. You have to remove those lines from the CR2. Use CR2 Editor to search for the string `alternateGeom`. You will probably find one or two sections that reference it, and you'll have to remove it from the CR2. Figure 12.35 shows one such reference.

- Each body part in the CR2 is followed by a colon (:), which is then followed by a number, depending on the number of figures that you opened in your scene before you created the figure. For example, you'll see lines that start with `actor hip:5` or `actor BODY:5`. It is common practice to have this last number be the number 1, so you'll want to search and replace all instances of `:5` with `:1`.
- Remove extra body parts that aren't needed. The general rule of thumb is "Start with the hip, and work your way through all parts you need, *plus one*." So, for example, your pair of pants has abdomen,

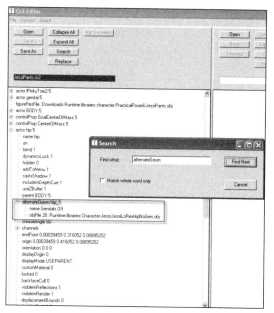

FIGURE 12.35   Remove alternate geometry references from the CR2.

hip, left and right thigh, and left and right shin sections. You want to keep all of those parts, plus chest (one higher than the abdomen) and the left- and right feet (one lower than the left- and right shins). Delete all other parts because they aren't necessary and will add extra weight to your file.

- Remove extra materials that aren't needed. You'll find the materials listed toward the end of the CR2 file. Notice, in Figure 12.36, that the pants inherited all of the materials from the donor CR2. The only materials that are needed are the Pants material and the Preview material. All of the other materials (Body, BottomEyelashes, TeethTop, and so on through Toenails) can be deleted because they are not a part of the Pants geometry. One easy way to clean up a CR2 is to start with the Blank.CR2, and remove all materials except for the preview material. All figures need a preview material, but make sure that it does not have any texture maps associated with it. Some Python scripts search for "Preview" as a placeholder to automatically add new materials to your figures and props. After you remove the materials, save the revised CR2 to your library under a different name, and use it as a donor CR2 for future projects.

- And now for the not-so-good news—you may have to tweak the joint parameters. You might have faces that fly away when you pose

```
allowsBending 1
figureType 1318
origFigureType 1318
canonType 8
conforming 0
material Body
material Preview
material BottomEyelashes
material TeethTop
material Gums
material TopEyelashes
material EyeCaruncle
material Head
material EyeSocket
material Tongue
material TeethBottom
material Eyeball
material Iris
material Pupil
material EyeTrans
material Fingernails
material Toenails
material Pants
displayMode USEPARENT
locked 0
attribute pmd_0
setGeomHandlerOffset 0 0.3487 0
```

FIGURE 12.36 Remove extra material references from the CR2.

the figure or parts that don't bend right when you conform the clothing to the figure. You may have to use the Joint Editor to tweak the joint parameters. Because there are so many different things that can happen with joint parameters, we advise that you seek out assistance from the experts in the Poser community. There are several forums online at Renderosity, DAZ3D, and PoserPros that are frequented by some of the best Poser content creators, who are more than happy to assist with questions and problems.

CONCLUSION

You've learned in this chapter, and in the previous few chapters, that it is a lot of work to model, UV-map, texture, group, and rig your Poser figures. However, in the long run, it is a very enjoyable and rewarding process. Along with learning something that is both artistic and technical, you are gaining the satisfaction of creating your own Poser content and enhancing your artwork with new skills and experience. The skills that you have learned in these past few chapters are only the beginning to a long road of learning and enjoyment, and we hope that we have inspired you to learn even more. Good luck with your Poser content creation efforts!

BASICS OF JOINT PARAMETERS

In This Chapter

- Boning a Figure: An Overview
- Tutorial 13.1 Adding Upper Bones
- The Joint Editor
- Adjusting Joint Parameters for Clothing

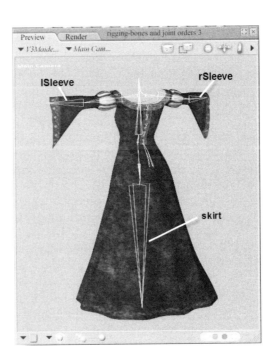

Boning a Figure: An Overview

Before we show you how to tweak joint parameters for clothing, you'll need a quick overview of how a figure is boned and rigged. In the following sections, you'll see how a model is brought into Poser and turned into a figure.

In reality, the process to bone and rig a figure is long and tedious and will result in a lot of pulled hairs. However, if you want to get the most out of Poser, you'll eventually learn how to model, rig, and clothe your own figures. There is a lot of satisfaction in reaching the finish line when you embark on this long road of learning.

Importing the Figure

Assuming that your figure is already modeled and has had the groups, materials, and UV coordinates assigned, the next step is to import the figure into Poser for rigging. You can do this in a number of different ways, but for the purposes of this book, you will get an overview of how to use the Setup Room to rig your figure.

The figure used in this example was created by Admir Hasanovic and is available for purchase at Turbo Squid (*http://www.turbosquid.com*) or at The 3D Studio (*http://www.the3dstudio.com*). To prepare the model for Poser, I grouped it similarly to the latest generation figures: the G2 versions of James, Jessi, Miki, Koji, Kelvin, and Olivia. These figures don't use a buttocks group between the hip and thighs (such as was used in DAZ's Millennium 3 figures). In addition, the chest now includes the female breasts instead of having them in each of the collar groups.

With that in mind, let's see how the bones for a figure are created from scratch. Use the File > Import > Wavefront OBJ command to import the grouped figure into Poser. The Import Options dialog box shown in Figure 13.1 displays several options to check. If you aren't sure that your figure is the proper size or in the proper location for Poser, it is best to choose the first three options: *Centered*, which places the figure in the center of the stage; *Place on floor*, which drops the figure's feet to ground level; and *Percent of Standard Figure Size*, which scales the model to a standard height of around 6 feet tall in the Poser universe. It's important to note here that Poser's scaling is miniscule in comparison to that used in other 3D software. Because our figure was correctly scaled and positioned for Poser, we left all options unchecked in the Prop Import Options dialog box.

After you import the figure, it should appear in the center of the stage. Now you can enter the Setup Room to create the bones for the figure. Make sure that your figure is selected, and then click the Setup tab. Poser informs you that your current prop will turn into a figure after you enter the Setup Room and asks if you want to continue. Choose OK to enter the Setup Room.

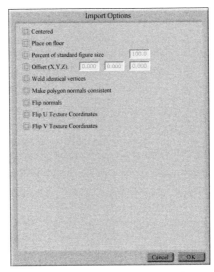

FIGURE 13.1 The Import Options dialog box appears when you import your OBJ file into Poser.

TUTORIAL 13.1   ADDING UPPER BONES

When you first enter the Setup Room, an HTML file appears and gives an overview of the process that we will show you here. After you read the Room Help, turn it off to give yourself some room as you work.

You'll also find it helpful to change to Outline display mode (Display > Document Style > Outline) and to view your figure through the Front camera (Display > Camera View > Front Camera) while you add bones to your figure. Figure 13.2 shows an example of what your screen might look like.

Once in the Setup Room, you'll need to add a bone for each group in your model. The groups in the model should follow the naming conventions outlined in the reference manual that comes with Poser, or as outlined in Chapter 10, "Groups and Materials for Models."

Each body part requires that you assign two names in the Properties window: the *internal name*, which is referenced by Poser to make the figure pose properly, and the external name, which is a more user-friendly name that appears to the user in menus. The internal name of the bone must match the group name in your model; otherwise, Poser won't know which polygons to assign to which bone. Although you can include extra bones in your model (more about that later), you can't leave any polygons that are not assigned to a bone.

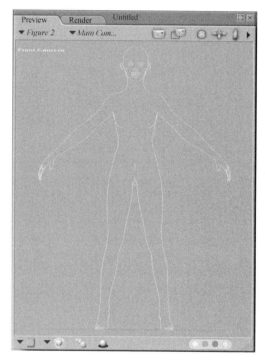

FIGURE 13.2 Use the Front camera and Outline display mode to create the bones in the upper part of the body.

To create a bone structure, or skeleton, follow these steps:

1. Choose the Bone tool from the Editing Tools. This is the icon that looks like a sailboat, between the Grouping tool and the Magnifier, as shown in Figure 13.3.

2. Start by clicking the pelvic region (for the hip), and click again at the start of the abdomen. This is the start and end of the hip bone. From this point on, you click at the end of the next body part in the chain, adding bones for the abdomen, chest, neck, and head. Extend the head bone up above the head just a little bit to ensure that all polygons are included in the range of the bone. Then, click toward the right eye to add a bone for the first eye.

3. The Setup Room always connects a new bone to the bone that is currently selected. To add the left eye, you have to click on the Head bone again. Then, add the bone for the left eye. You should now have a straight line of bones from the hip to the head and two branches that connect to the right- and left eyes.

4. Now you'll go back and name the bones that you've created. Click the hip bone, and open the Properties window. Enter **hip** in the Internal Name field. Click up the hierarchy chain, adding internal names for the abdomen, chest, neck, head, rightEye, and leftEye. Take care to use the correct names and capitalization, as Poser expects certain naming conventions to make the figure work properly. Refer to Chapter 10, "Groups and Materials for Models" for more information about group naming conventions.

5. Now go back and add the Name fields. You do it this way because of a little quirk in Poser. For some reason, Poser won't retain the Name field unless you leave a bone Property window and re-enter it. Add the same name in the Name field as you did in the Internal Name field, and press the Enter key to set the name.

6. Save your project. Poser will replace the external Name field with the default external names that it normally uses (such as *Hip* for *hip*, *Chest* for *chest*, and so on). Your project should look similar to Figure 13.3.

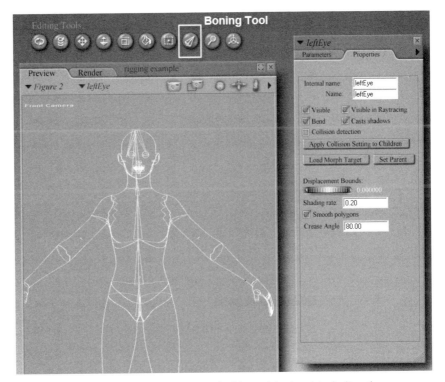

FIGURE 13.3   The chain of bones between the hip and the head, including the eyes, are added in the Front view in Outline display mode.

7. Return to the Setup Room after you save your file. To add the bones for the right arm, first click the Chest bone. Add four additional bones, and name them **rCollar**, **rShldr**, **rForeArm**, and **rHand,** respectively (watch the capitalization, these are standard group names).

8. Click the Chest bone again to add four bones for the left arm. Name them **lCollar**, **lShldr**, **lForeArm**, and **lHand,** respectively. Figure 13.4 shows the additional progress. You can save your file again to update you changes.

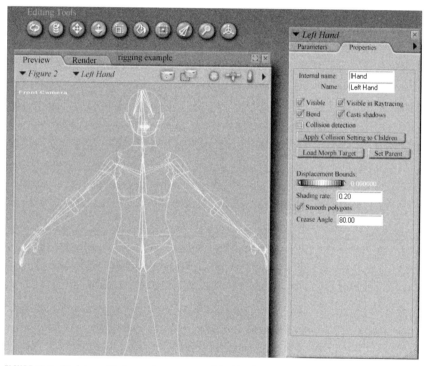

FIGURE 13.4 Right- and left arm bones are added in the Front view.

Adding Lower Bones

The lower bones are also added in the Front camera view. The process is the same as you have learned already, so we won't list them step by step. You click the hip and add four bones for one leg. For example, we'll take the right leg first, and assign internal names of rThigh, rShin, rFoot, and rToe in the Properties window. Go back and add the Name fields in the same order.

Again, starting from the hip, you add four bones to the left leg, assigning internal names of lThigh, lShin, lFoot, and lToe. Name fields are named the same in the second round of assignments. Now you have all bones except the fingers, as shown in Figure 13.5.

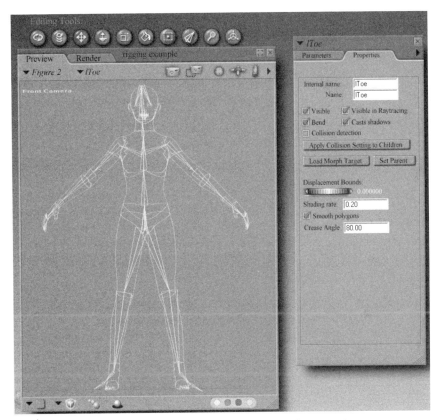

FIGURE 13.5   Bones for the right- and left legs are added in the Front view.

Adding Finger Bones

Depending on how your arms are positioned, you'll find it easier to use either the Top camera or the Right or Left camera to add your finger bones. In our case, because the arms are bent somewhat, it was easiest to use a Top camera to initially add the bones, and the Side camera to refine the positioning of the bones.

You add each finger one at a time, starting from the hand. Select the hand, and add the pinky segments, calling them **rPinky1** (closest to the hand), **rPinky2** (middle joint), and **rPinky3** (the tip of the finger). The third segment should extend beyond the fingertip just a bit.

Select the hand again, and add the rRing1, rRing2, and rRing3 segments. Continue in this manner until all finger bones are added. For the middle finger, name them **rMid1**, **rMid2**, and **rMid3**. The index finger segments are named rIndex1, rIndex2, and rIndex3. Finally, the thumb segments are named rThumb1, rThumb2, and rThumb3. Note that the finger names always begin with a lowercase *r* or *l*, and segment 1 is always the segment that is closest to the hand. When your groups are finished, they'll look something like the example shown in Figure 13.6, which shows the right hand bones as displayed through the Right Hand camera. Don't forget to repeat the entire process for the fingers on the left hand!

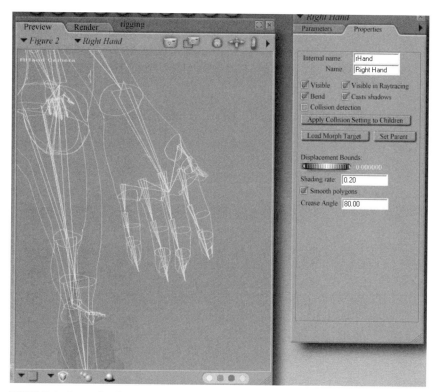

FIGURE 13.6 Bones for the right- and left fingers are added with the Top-, Left-, or Right cameras.

You will probably need to refine your bone placements while viewing the bones in other camera views. Use the Right-, Left-, or Top cameras as needed to align each end of each bone with the corresponding body parts. One way to approach this is to work on the right side of the model, and then use the Figure > Symmetry > Right Side to Left Side command to mirror the settings to the left side of the body.

After you add and tweak all of the bones, choose the Window > Hierarchy Editor command. Verify that all of your bones are connected in the right order. You will see all of the bones originating from the hip just as you created them. Figure 13.7 shows a portion of the bone structure in the Hierarchy Editor.

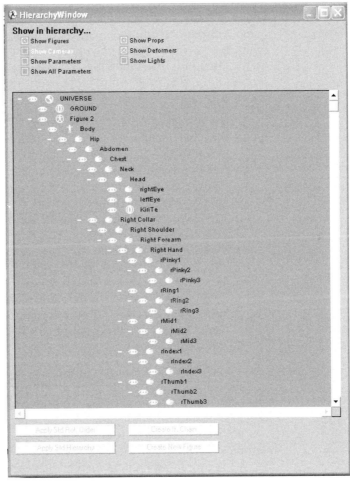

FIGURE 13.7   Use the Hierarchy Editor to verify that all of your bones are connected to each other in the correct order.

THE JOINT EDITOR

By this time, you're probably thrilled that you have a figure that has moving body parts. However, you've no doubt discovered that when you try to move the body parts, the figure doesn't pose extremely well. Body parts collapse on each other. Things fold where they shouldn't. Limbs crinkle like bent straws or fly away in mid air. The reason for this is because you have to work on the *joint parameters*. This long and tedious process can make or break a posable figure. With a lot of patience and determination, you can do it.

Joint parameters are not an easy topic to cover in a single chapter in a book. Nor are they an easy topic to cover generically because each body shape will require different joint parameters. To step you through the complete setup and rigging of a figure could take a whole book unto itself. And, to that end, the following resources can be of further assistance if you are interested in learning more about rigging your own figures and clothing:

> ***Secrets of Figure Creation with Poser 5:*** This book by B. L. Render, (known as bloodsong in the Poser community), published by Focal Press, August 2003 is without a doubt the most complete reference on the intricacies of modeling and rigging original Poser figures. Don't let the Poser version number hold you back . . . the process of rigging figures is basically the same in Poser 5, 6, and 7. This book is still a great resource for those who want to really get serious with Poser.
>
> ***3D Modeling for Poser Tutorial:*** This tutorial by Phil Cooke (known as PhilC in the Poser community) is another great reference for learning how to model and rig clothing. Formerly available on CD-ROM, this tutorial is now a downloadable product. For further information, as well as other products and content that can enhance your use of Poser, visit Phil's Web site at *http://www.philc.net/ tutorialsIndex.htm*.

To open the Joint Editor, choose Window > Joint Editor. The Joint Editor shown in Figure 13.8 opens, and the options that you see will vary depending on the body part that you have selected. Here, the hip is selected as the current body part.

Don't let all of these settings and controls intimidate you. We'll explain each of them in the order you'll probably need to use them. If you're making an original figure, you'll need to be familiar with all of the settings. After you complete the rigging for your original figure, save the completed figure to your Figures Library. Then, you can use those joint parameters as a starting point for your clothing and just tweak some settings here and there. We'll explain which settings you'll probably need to tweak so that your clothing works properly.

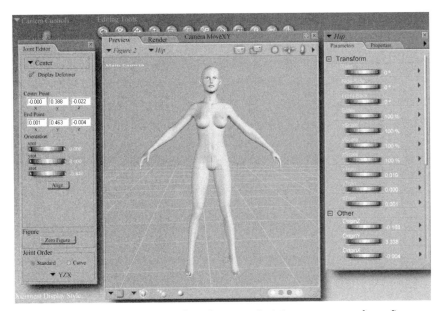

FIGURE 13.8   Use the Joint Editor (left) to fine-tune the joint parameters of your figure or clothing.

Setting Joint Orders

The first joint parameter that you'll have to set for an original figure is the Joint Order. It is good practice to set all of the joint orders before you leave the Setup Room. Doing so afterward may result in errors when you try to alter the rotation orders . . . while the rotation order does get altered in the selected body part, the changes may not occur in the corresponding lines in its parent.

Joint order settings apply to each body part in your figure. You'll find this setting at the bottom of the Joint Editor, as shown in Figure 13.9.

Basically, the joint order tells Poser which axis is responsible for twisting the body part, which axis is the most important rotation axis, and which is left over. The Joint Order setting should be set with the following points in mind:

- The first letter should always be the axis on which the joint twists. This should follow the main axis of the body part. In other words, it generally follows the axis on which the bone lies. For example, the forearm bone runs horizontally along the X axis, so you assign X as the first letter in the joint order. The shin bone runs vertically along the Y axis, so you place Y as the first letter in the joint order.

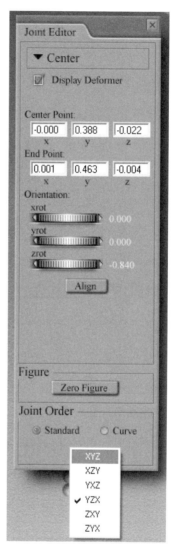

FIGURE 13.9 The Joint Order settings for each bone are the first settings you should complete.

- After you determine the first letter in the joint order, the last letter should be the most important rotation of the body part. The remaining of the three letters appears in the middle. For the forearm, the next most important rotation axis is the bend, which happens on the Y (or up and down) axis. So now we know that the first letter for the forearm is X, and the last letter is Y. So the proper joint order assignment for the forearm is XZY: it twists on the X axis, the least used axis is Z (side to side), and the Y axis is the most important rotation.

- There are two types of joint orders. Standard joint orders are used for most applications. Curve joint orders are used only for long, thin tails. They allow the tail to bend in a curve. To see the difference, you can create a long, thin multisegmented cylinder that has at least four segments. Configure one segment with Standard joint orders, and the remainder with the Curve joint orders. When you bend the Standard segment, you'll see a definite angle. When you bend the Curved segment you will see a more natural curve.

To keep it simple, here's a table that lists the correct joint orders for the parts that are most commonly used in human Poser figures when they are posed in the standard "T" position with the palms of the hands facing downward:

PART	JOINT ORDER
Head	YZX
Neck	YZX
Chest	YZX
Collars	XYZ
Shoulders	XYZ
Forearms	XZY
Hands	XYZ
Thumb Joints	XZY
All other finger joints	XYZ
Abdomen	YZX
Hip	YZX
Buttocks	YZX
Thighs	YZX
Shins	YZX
Feet	YZX
Toes	ZYX

After you set the Joint Rotation orders, it is a good idea to save your figure to the Figures Library. At this point, you can go to the Pose Room. Open the Runtime Library of your choice, and create a new folder in the Figures Library. Then, click the Add to Library button at the bottom of the Figures Library window. You'll be prompted to enter a name for your figure. Your figure should then appear in the Figures Library as shown in Figure 13.10.

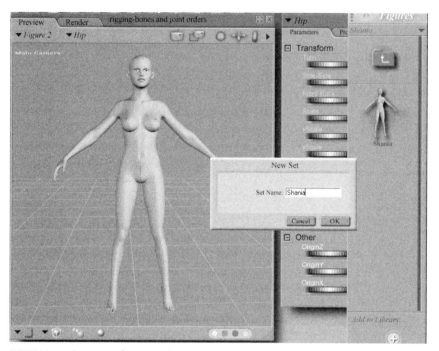

FIGURE 13.10   Save your figure to the Figures Library so you don't lose all your hard work.

You'll probably be thrilled that you now have a posable figure, but when you try to pose it there are some problems. The figure doesn't bend naturally. Parts squeeze together, or get squished, when other parts move around them. That is where joint parameters come in. You'll learn more about the Joint Editor in the sections that follow.

Renaming Joint Parameter Dials

By default, the dials of a joint are named xRotate, yRotate, and zRotate. It will make more sense to you (and others that use your figure) to rename these dials. Most often, the dials are renamed to *Twist, Bend, Side-Side, Up-Down*, or *Front-Back*, depending on the direction that each rotation moves. To change the name, double-click on the xRotate, yRotate, or zRotate Parameter dial in the Parameters window to open the dialog box shown in Figure 13.11. Then, enter the new dial name in the Name field.

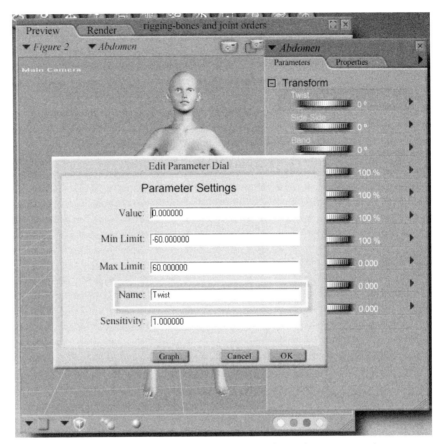

FIGURE 13.11   After you assign the correct joint orders for each joint, name the Parameter dials appropriately.

Setting Joint Centers

The next step in the process is to set the joint centers for each body part. Contrary to what you might think, the joint center is not in the center of the body part. Instead, the joint center is the point around which a joint pivots in any direction. The joint center is most often near the beginning of each body part, although it may not necessarily be in the exact center. The best way to learn how a joint works is to study how your own body moves.

It's fairly easy to move the joint center. When you select a joint and have Center showing in the Joint Editor, make sure that Display Deformer is checked (near the top of the Joint Editor). The center point is displayed as three green lines, arranged in a 3D crosshair. Figure 13.12 shows the three lines slightly enhanced so that you can see them better.

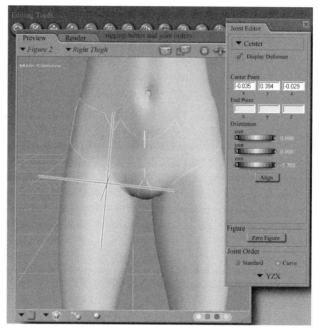

FIGURE 13.12   Three intersected lines represent the center point of the joint. This is a pivot point for all three axes of movement.

When you move the mouse cursor over the intersection of the three lines, the cursor turns into a bullet. At that point, you can drag the center point to visually place it at the best pivot point for the joint. Remember as you place the center point that it is common to all three axes for the joint, so try to place it accordingly.

After you place the center points for all body parts, the next step is to align all of the joints. Starting with the top of the hierarchy (usually the hip), work your way through each joint in order. Click the Align button to align the axes of the center point with the movement axes of the joint. This points the axis toward the center point of the child. Then, fine-tune the angle with the xrot, yrot, and zrot Orientation sliders as needed. If you find that you have to rotate the alignment more than 45 degrees in any axis, you may have the joint rotation order wrong. To test the rotations of the body part, click the part and use the rotation parameter dials (renamed from the default xRotate, yRotate, and zRotate as mentioned earlier) to verify that the joints pivot from an acceptable common position.

Many figure creators complete this process for all joints in the figure before they work on the additional joint parameters that follow in this chapter. For body parts that have right- and left counterparts, you can finish the adjustments on one side of the body and then use the Figure > Symmetry command to duplicate the centers on the opposite side. For example, you can set the joint centers for the right arms, hands, legs, and feet and then use the Figure > Symmetry > Right to Left command to copy them to the left side. When Poser asks if you want to copy the joint zone's setup also (as shown in Figure 13.14), answer Yes.

FIGURE 13.13 Click the Align button, and use the rotation dials to fine-tune the alignment of the center point.

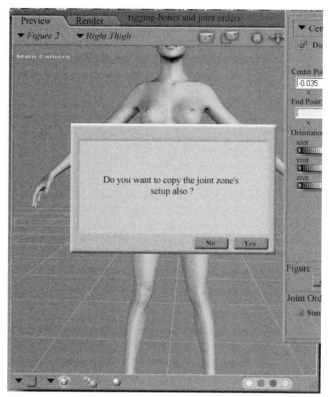

FIGURE 13.14 Use the Figure > Symmetry command to copy joint setups from one side of the body to the other.

Adjusting the Twist Axis

We mentioned earlier that the Twist axis was listed first in the joint orders. The configuration of the Twist axis differs slightly from the other two, which we will explain shortly. The Twist axis is represented by a handlebar that has a red bar on its parent end (its starting end) and a green bar on its child end (its finishing end). The Twist handlebar does not necessarily have to run the entire length of the body part. Instead, you place the handlebar *only* over the portions of the body part that you want to move when you use the Twist parameter dial.

Remember these key points when it comes to the Twist handlebar, which are illustrated in Figure 13.15:

- Any polygons above the red bar (the parent end of the Twist bar) will not move.
- Any polygons below the green bar (the child end of the Twist bar) will move completely.

- All polygons within the red and green bars will serve as the blending zone between the stationary and fully movable parts.

 You can also use spherical falloff zones (explained later in this chapter) to include or exclude polygons from the twisting motion.

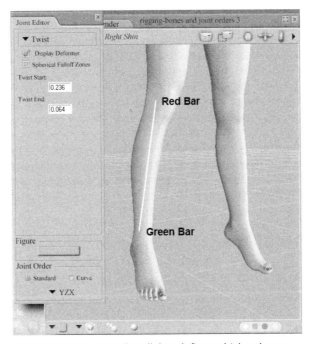

FIGURE 13.15   The Twist handlebar defines which polygons will twist when the Twist dial is turned. Polygons outside the Twist handlebar do not move.

Working with Inclusion and Exclusion Angles

So far, you've taken care of the first joint rotation: twist. Each joint has a total of three rotations. You learned that the first joint rotation is always the Twist parameter. The second joint is the least important rotation, and the third is the most important rotation. The names of the other two rotations are usually Bend, Up-Down, Side-Side, or Front-Back. An example of the settings used for these joints is shown in Figure 13.16. Notice that the settings for these joints are much different from the Twist settings. Four arms radiate from the center point of the right thigh in Figure 13.16. Once again, these arms are enhanced so that you can view them more easily.

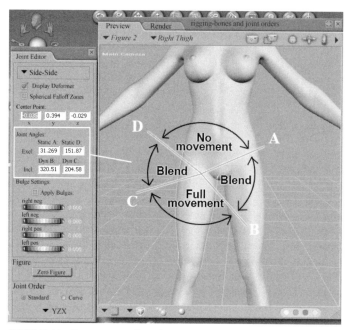

FIGURE 13.16 Four arms radiate from a center point for joints that are marked Bend, Up-Down, Side-Side, or Front-Back.

The center point in the middle of the four arms is the same center that was described in "Setting Joint Centers" earlier in this chapter. You may find that you might have to tweak its position as you refine the remaining two joint parameters. The basic rule of thumb here is tweak and test, tweak and test, and then tweak and test some more.

As you move each arm, you'll notice the numbers changing in the Joint Angles section of the Joint Editor. If you think of the center point of the four arms as the origin of the hands of a clock, zero degrees appears at roughly the 3:00 position. Now, move your eyes counter-clockwise around the circle from the zero point while you look at the four arms in the figure and compare them to the angles in the Joint Editor. You will first come to the Static A exclusion arm (red) at 31 degrees; next is the Static D arm (also red) at 151 degrees; third is the Dynamic C Inclusion (green) angle at 204 degrees; and last is the Dynamic B Inclusion angle (also green) at 320 degrees.

When setting joints that have inclusion and exclusion angles, the following rules apply:

- Any polygons that lie between the green Inclusion or Dynamic arms (marked B and C in Figure 13.15) will move completely. Their child parts will also move with them.

- Any polygons that lie between the red Exclusion or Static arms (marked A and D in Figure 13.15) will not move.
- Any polygons that lie between a red arm and a green arm (area A-C and area C-D in Figure 13.16) will blend and act as transition areas between the stationary zone and the moving parts.

Using Bulge Settings

When some joints bend, you need more control over how polygons react. The most common example is when you bend a figure's forearm and you want to keep the elbow pointed. The Joint Editor has a Bulge option that helps you control the shape of a joint when it bends.

For example, let's take a look at what happens to the knee of DAZ's Victoria 3 when we bend her right shin to 92 degrees. If we don't use the Bulge Settings options, her knee balloons out a bit too much. You can see this effect on the left side of Figure 13.17.

However, with the Apply Bulges setting turned on and some small adjustments to the Right Pos setting (−0.018) and the Left Pos setting (0.014), we see a very subtle but more believeable change in the shape of her knee when it is bent.

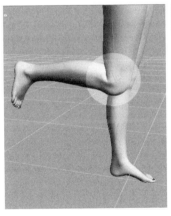
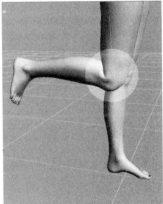

| Apply Bulges disabled | Apply Bulges enabled
Right Pos = -0.018
Left Pos = 0.014 |

FIGURE 13.17   When you enable the Apply Bulges option, you can control the shape of a joint when it bends.

The best way to apply bulges is to bend the limb using the Bend dial in the Parameters window. Then, check the Apply Bulges option. Adjust the Right Pos, Left Pos, Right Neg, or Left Neg dials in the Joint Editor as necessary to get the shape you want.

Adjusting Spherical Falloff Zones

Spherical falloff zones add additional control to joints that bend. They control the area and shape of the bend, and good use for spherical falloff zones is to control the shape of bends in the elbows, knees, or other joints when one side of the joint has to bend more than another.

Spherical falloff zones work similarly to the inclusion and exclusion angle bars. In the spherical falloff zones in Figure 13.18, note the following points:

- All polygons that lie only within a green zone will move totally.
- All polygons that lie only within a red zone will not move at all.
- All polygons that lie in the overlap of the green and red zones will become the blend zone that deforms between the stationary and moving parts.

Spherical falloff zones only affect the current body part and its parent. You may need to scale or rotate the spheres to get optimum results. Many find it easiest to reduce the scale of the zone, and set the x-, y-, and z rotation angles to zero and start from there.

Children of the current body part always move with the current body part.

The areas defined by the inclusion and exclusion angle bars take precedence over the spherical falloff zones. That is, if there are polygons that fall between the green and red spherical falloff zones but that also fall outside of a red exclusion angle, they will not move.

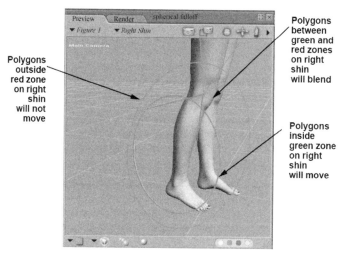

FIGURE 13.18 Spherical falloff zones allow you to further refine polygons that move and blend when a joint is bent.

After you get this far with an original figure, there are some additional tasks that you have to complete. For example, you still have to configure the eyes and the Inverse Kinematic (IK) chains for your figure. However, because our main focus is in learning about joint parameters for the purpose of making clothing, we recommend that you refer to the resources mentioned earlier for further information on figure creation. We will now turn to how the joint parameters that we have discussed in this chapter relate to the clothing that you create.

ADJUSTING JOINT PARAMETERS FOR CLOTHING

Now that you have a basic idea of the work that goes into making a posable character, you are probably thinking that it will be a chore to do the same for clothing. Fortunately, there is a solution . . . clothing makers typically start with the joint parameters of the figure for which the clothing is made. In fact, in the previous chapter, you learned how to use the Setup Room to apply the joint parameters of a figure to a clothing model to turn it into conforming clothing.

To make clothing work the best it possibly can, you'll need to become familiar with the Joint Editor and the parameters we have already discussed in this chapter. This is most evident when you create clothing that is not skin-tight. The looser clothing is, the higher the chances are that you'll have to modify the joint parameters in your clothing.

Adding Bones to Clothing

Sometimes, your clothing might require additional bones to pose parts of the clothing that don't fit into standard body part names. Now that you know how to build a skeleton from scratch, it should be easy to add extra bones to clothing!

In Chapter 12, "From Modeler to Poser Library," you learned the differences between conforming clothing and dynamic clothing. There is a third category of clothing that is becoming more popular in the Poser world: hybrid clothing.

Hybrid clothing combines the best of both worlds. It is very difficult, if not impossible, to create dynamic clothing that has a lot of modeled detail. On the other hand, it is very difficult to make conforming clothing that flows gracefully and naturally. Hybrid clothing allows you to conform the detailed parts and make the flowing parts dynamic.

The dress shown in Figure 13.19 is a great example of how hybrid clothing can be put to good use. Two of the hardest things to make conforming are bell sleeves and long skirts. In addition, the scooped neck and puffy sleeves, along with all of the modeled lacing on the back of the dress, would be very difficult if not impossible to put through the dynamic calculations required by the Cloth Room.

FIGURE 13.19 Some clothing is a challenge to make all conforming or all dynamic. The solution is to create hybrid clothing that uses both techniques.

Looking at the dress in the Setup Room, you are now able to see the bones in the dress. The first thing that you'll notice is that all of the extraneous bones have been removed. The only bones that remain from a "normal" figure skeleton are the hip, abdomen, chest, neck, and left- and right collars.

In addition to those standard bones, the model had three extra groups added to the geometry: rSleeve, lSleeve, and skirt. The polygons for the sleeves started after the sleeve puffs (which are part of the conforming collars). The skirt polygons start at about mid hip level.

In the Setup Room, three additional bones are added to the dress. The right collar part is assigned as the parent of the rSleeve group, the left collar is the parent of the lSleeve group, and the hip is the parent of the skirt group. Figure 13.20 shows the additional parts labeled.

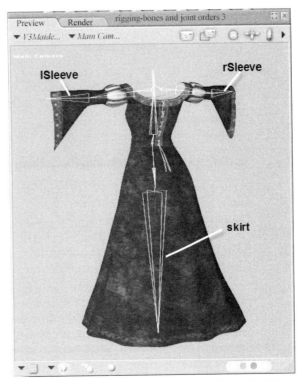

FIGURE 13.20 Three extra bones are added for each of the bell sleeves and for the skirt.

You can save hybrid clothing to the Figures Library, and you can conform the conforming parts to the figure before you enter the Cloth Room. The conforming parts will pose with the figure, but you'll need to create cloth simulations to pose the sleeves and skirt.

In the case of this dress, you have to create three cloth simulations:

- The first simulation is for the skirt, which should collide against the figure's legs, shoes, and any other body parts or props in your scene that will come into contact with the skirt.
- The second simulation is for the right sleeve (rSleeve), which should collide against the figure's right shoulder, forearm, and hand. You may also need to set it to collide with the skirt and any other props in the scene.
- The third simulation is for the left sleeve (lSleeve), which should collide against the figure's left shoulder, forearm, and hand, along with other items that it may come in contact with.

After you set up your cloth simulations, you can use the Animation > Recalculate Dynamics > All Cloth to calculate the simulations in the order in which you created them.

 Joint rotation orders and center points are usually inherited from the CR2 of the original figure. Both the figure and clothing should use the same center points and joint rotation orders.

Inclusion and Exclusion Angles for Clothing

When using the CR2 from a character, the chances are good that you'll need to make adjustments to the inclusion and exclusion angles of your clothing to prevent poke-through issues. This is especially true for clothing that is very loose or puffy. If you find that the puffy areas of clothing don't move as they should, move the green arms outward a bit until the puffy areas are included within the movable area.

Figure 13.21 shows an example of this. On the left side of the figure, you see the underarm poking through the sleeve puff. The reason this is happening is because the green arm that is closest to the figure's chest (shown thicker and in white for clarity) is too close to the puff of the sleeve. An adjustment has been made to the green arm on the right side of the figure to resolve the problem.

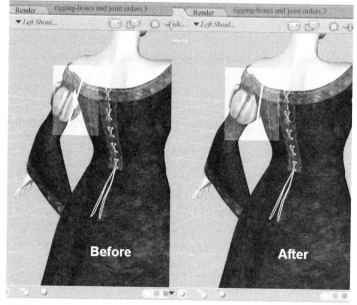

FIGURE 13.21 Adjust inclusion and exclusion angles to fix poke-through issues.

Inclusion and exclusion angles can also be adjusted when clothing crinkles and bunches up too much when a joint is bent. Just remember that you should test the changes in many different poses before you consider the change final or before you apply the change to the opposite limb with the Figure > Symmetry command.

Spherical Falloff Zones for Clothing

If you apply the joint parameters from a figure to conforming clothing that is made for that figure, you may see parts of the clothing spike outward when you move a body part on the figure. The usual reason for this is that the spherical falloff zones have to be increased in size in one or more directions to include the polygons that are not moving when you pose the part.

The way to remedy the spikes is to first zero the pose of your figure. Then, click the body part on the figure that you suspect is causing the problem. Move the offending body part in one direction only (Twist, Side-Side, Bend, Up-Down, or Front-Back) until you are able to reproduce the spike. Then increase the Scale settings of the Inner Mat Sphere (the green zone) or the Outer Mat Sphere (the red zone) until you eliminate the spike. The YScale and/or ZScale settings may need adjustments for sleeves, and the XScale and/or ZScale settings may need adjustment for pants. Test the other axes as well, just in case the spike was caused by a combination of more than one rotation. Use the Figure > Symmetry command to duplicate the settings on the opposite side of the body if necessary.

CONCLUSION

The Setup Room and the Joint Editor are perhaps two of the most difficult areas to master in Poser, but with determination and a lot of practice, you can master them. By doing so, you will enhance your enjoyment of Poser greatly because you'll be well on your way to making your own clothing and figures. Always remember to test, test, test, and test again. The more you work with these areas, the easier it will get!

ANIMATION OVERVIEW

By Phil Cooke

In This Chapter

- Arranging Your Workspace
- An Overview of the Animation Palette
- Keyframes and Interpolation the Easy Way
- Using Animation Layers
- Animation Sets
- General Animation Tips

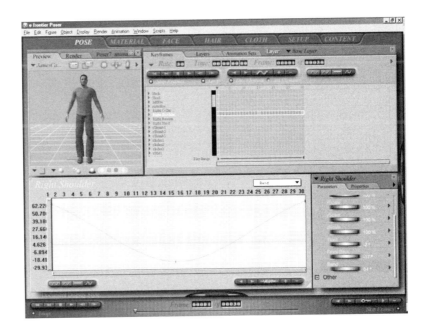

INTRODUCTION

Animation is one of the most rewarding aspects of 3D computer graphics; however, it is also one of the least understood. Poser 7 contains a comprehensive set of animation tools that will enable you to create sophisticated animations. The object of this chapter is to explain how to use those tools to create an animation. You may want to pause here and view the onscreen video tutorial contained on the CD-ROM accompanying this book, and then continue reading the rest of this chapter.

ON THE CD

ARRANGING YOUR WORKSPACE

Just as it can be frustrating to spend time finding the tools you need for a small home repair job, it can be the same with Poser animation. Getting the Poser tools organized is a good way to avoid that frustration from the start. Figure 14.1 shows one way to do this.

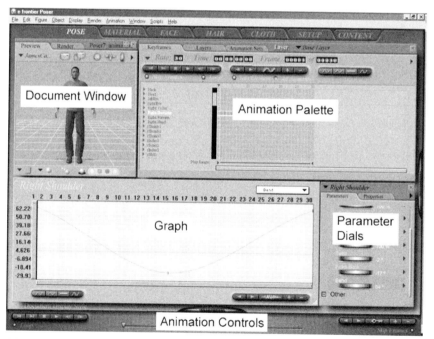

FIGURE 14.1 Lay out the most important animation tools neatly while you create and edit your animation.

Now let's take a look at these areas one by one to review how you use them while building your animations.

The Document Window

It's important to place the Document window in your work area because this is where you will view your animation. If you find that playback is slow, try the following to improve playback:

- Change the display style to one without textures such as Smooth Shaded (Display > Document style > Smooth Shaded).
- Change the display tracking to Box (Display > Tracking > Bounding Box only).
- Use a lower polygon figure. After the animation is completed, you can either swap to your higher polygon figure in the scene or save the animated pose that can then be applied to any figure later.

Animation Controls

Poser offers a number of different features that help you animate the objects in your scene. The first of these toolsets is the Animation Controls, which are shown in Figure 14.2. To display the Animation Controls, click the handle at the bottom of your screen to expand them. Click again to collapse the controls to make more room for your other Poser work.

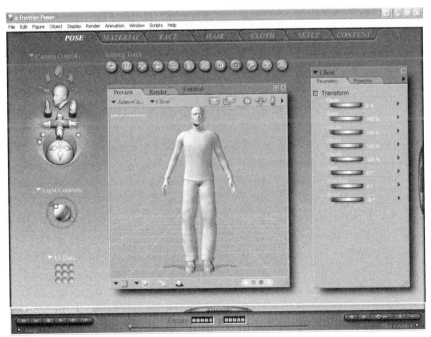

FIGURE 14.2   The Animation Controls are located at the bottom of the Poser interface.

The Animation Controls consist of three areas: the Timeline/Frame indicator, the Play controls, and the Keyframe controls. Each area is described in the following sections.

Timeline/Frame Indicator

The Timeline/Frame indicator, shown in Figure 14.3, is located in the center of the Animation Controls area. This set of controls helps you quickly move forward or backward to a specific frame in your animation. The first number in the frame indicator designates your current frame, and the second number in the frame indicator designates the total number of frames in your animation. Beneath the frame indicator is a scrubber that allows you to quickly scrub through the frames in your animation.

FIGURE 14.3   The Timeline/Frame indicator helps you quickly navigate through your animation.

To use the timeline and frame indicator:

- To navigate to a specific frame in your animation, enter the desired frame number in the first entry field.
- To add additional frames to your animation, enter the new total number of frames in the second entry field.
- To delete frames from the end of your animation, enter a lower number of frames in the second entry field. Poser will ask if you are sure you want to delete some frames. Click OK to delete them, or click Cancel to abort the operation.
- To scrub through the timeline, click the triangular scrubber handle shown in Figure 14.3, and drag left or right to scrub forward and backward in your animation. You will view your scene based on the display mode that you have selected with the Display > Tracking command.

Play Controls

The Play controls appear on the left side of the Animation Controls area. The Play controls, shown in Figure 14.4, are similar to those of a VCR. When you play back the animation, it will play back in the selected tracking mode.

FIGURE 14.4   The Play controls work similar
to those found on a VCR.

The Play controls consist of the following buttons:

First Frame: Click this button to move to the first frame in the animation sequence.
End Frame: Click this button to move to the last frame in the animation sequence.
Stop: Click this button to stop playback of the animation.
Play/Pause: Click to pause playback of the animation. If you click again, playback will continue from the paused location.
Step Backward: Click this button to move backward one frame.
Step Forward: Click this button to move forward one frame.
Loop: Click this button to play back your animation in a continuous loop. When this option is not selected, playback will only occur once.

Keyframe Controls

The third area of the Animation Controls displays the Keyframe controls. These controls help you add or remove keyframes, or quickly navigate from one to the next. The Keyframe controls are shown in Figure 14.5.

FIGURE 14.5   The Keyframe controls help you
add, remove, or navigate between keyframes.

The Keyframe controls consist of the following buttons:

Previous Keyframe: Click this button to move back to the previous keyframe for the selected object or body part.
Next Keyframe: Click this button to move forward to the next keyframe for the selected object or body part.
Edit Keyframes: Click this button to open the Animation Palette, which allows you to edit the keyframes in your animation. The

features in the Animation Palette will be described later in this chapter.

Add Keyframes: Click this button to add a keyframe at the current frame for the selected object or body part.

Delete Keyframes: Click this button to delete the keyframe for the selected body part, at the current frame.

Skip Frames: Click this option to allow Poser to skip some frames during playback so that your display can keep up with the speed of the animation.

The Parameter Dials

While you're working on your animation, it's a good idea to keep the Parameter dials open. You'll use them to control one or more aspects of the currently selected actor. The parameter dials can help you move, scale, position, translate, or apply morphs to the figures and props in your scene. Keep it close and handy because you'll use it a lot!

The Animation Palette

This is where most of the animation editing will take place. Full details are given later in this chapter. The Animation Palette may be accessed by clicking the "key" symbol on the right hand side of the Animation Controls window or by using the Window > Animation Palette command. It contains three tabs, Keyframes, Layers, and Animation Sets, all of which will be discussed in the following section.

The Graph Display

The Graph display provides a graphical view of the selected parameter value plotted against time. It is accessed by clicking the Show Graph Display button (red sine wave) in the Animation Palette, by using the Window > Graph command, or by clicking the small arrow to the right of any parameter dial and selecting Graph from the drop-down menu. More details about the Graph display are given later in this chapter.

An Overview of the Animation Palette

The Animation Palette can be considered as "control central" when it comes to editing or enhancing the features of your animations. There are three tabs in the Animation Palette: the Keyframes tab, the Layers tab, and the Animation Sets tab. The following sections will give you an overview of the features included in each of these tabs.

Common Controls

Several controls in the Animation Palette are common to all three tabs. In particular, you'll find controls to determine the playback speed, playback time indication, movie length and current position, and other helpful controls. These controls, shown in Figure 14.6, are divided into the following sections:

Rate: The Rate field (labeled number 1 in Figure 14.6) indicates the speed of your animation in frames per second (fps). Poser defaults to 30 fps, but you can also choose other common speeds from the Rate drop-down list. Speeds range from 12 fps (for computer multimedia or Flash animations) to 60 fps (for NTSC interlaced video).

Time: The Time indicator (numbered 2 in Figure 14.6) indicates the length of your movie at the point where the current frame indicator appears. The time is given in Hours: Minutes: Seconds: Frames format.

Frame: The Frame indicators (numbered 3 in Figure 14.6) display the current frame of your animation and the total length in frames. To navigate to a different frame in your animation, enter the desired frame number in the left field. To add additional frames to your animation, enter a higher value in the length field. You can also delete frames from the end of the animation by entering a lower value in the length field.

Frame controls: VCR-like controls appear in the left side of the Keyframes window (numbered 4 in Figure 14.6). These controls serve similar functions as the VCR controls described earlier in this chapter, under the Animation Controls section.

FIGURE 14.6   Several controls are common to all three tabs in the Animation Palette.

The Keyframes Tab

You can also see the Keyframes tab in Figure 14.6. This tab allows you to add, delete, or edit the keyframes in your animation. Keyframes are displayed in a grid, with the horizontal direction in the grid representing time, and the vertical direction in the grid listing all of the elements in your scene. Initially, all of the keyframes in your scene appear as solid green squares that mark the frame in which the keyframe occurs.

 The color of the keyframes varies, depending on the type of interpolation that is configured. For more information about keyframe colors and interpolation methods, see "Interpolation Controls" later in this section.

Frame Controls

In addition to the Frame controls previously mentioned as common to all tabs in the Animation Palette, the Keyframes tab has a couple of additional options shown in Figure 14.7:

Skip Frames: Drops some frames during playback so that your animation plays back more quickly. Use this option if your system resources don't allow playback in real time.

Loop: Plays the animation in a continuous loop until you stop playback and deselect the Loop option.

FIGURE 14.7 The Keyframes tab has two additional playback control options.

KEYFRAMES AND INTERPOLATION THE EASY WAY

The key to animation is keyframes. *Keyframes* mark a point at which a specific condition takes place in your animation. A keyframe can define a specific pose, a camera position, a lighting condition, a change in material, or any other property that is keyframeable. For example, you can pose your figure in a specific pose in the first frame of your animation, and then you can move to a later frame a few seconds later to modify the pose.

Let's explain this by getting you to act out a real world example. Imagine that you are standing up with your arms by your side. Now imagine yourself going through the following motions:

• Stand up with your arms by your sides. Hold that thought!
• Raise your right arm up in the air. Hold that thought!
• Lower your right arm so that you are standing as you were before. Hold that thought!

- Now sit down and imagine what you just did. You'll think of your first, second, and last thoughts in sequence and visualize the motions in between. This is exactly how Poser builds up an animation.

In fact, this is exactly how you can create your own animation:

1. At frame 1, have James standing with his arms by his sides.
2. Advance to frame 15, select his right shoulder, and set the Bend (zRotate) parameter dial to a value of -30 degrees.
3. Advance to frame 30, the final frame, and set his right shoulder back to its original value.

ON THE CD

Congratulations! You have just created a Poser animation! You'll find a completed version of this simple animation on the CD-ROM that accompanies this book. If you open the Tutorials > Chap14 folder, you'll find a project file named Poser7_animation_1.pz3. When you open the file, you'll see the project shown in Figure 14.8.

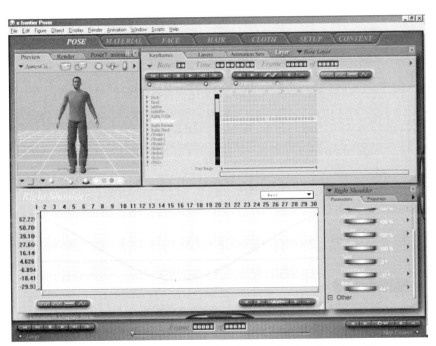

FIGURE 14.8   The Poser7_animation_1.pz3 file shows a simple animation of James raising and lowering his arms, like you just imagined!

Notice in the Animation Palette that there is now a horizontal green display indicating that values have been set for this actor for the frames indicated. You'll see that frames 1, 15, and 30 are highlighted. These are the keyframes. The values of the parameters in the in-between frames are calculated by Poser using *interpolation*. Poser knows the start- and end points and uses maths to come up with the intermediate values. The Graph Window now shows these values.

Poser has three ways of doing the calculations for the interpolation. Poser refers to these as *Sections* and they may be selected using the Animation Palette buttons shown in Figure 14.9. Left to right, they are Spline Section, Linear Section, and Constant Section. The fourth button is Break Spline, which will be detailed later.

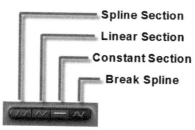

FIGURE 14.9   The interpolation controls allow you to select how keyframes will be blended.

The method is to select a keyframe in the Animation Palette and then click one of the Section buttons. The types of interpolation work as described in the following sections.

Spline Section

Spline Section keyframes are colored green and are the default method of interpolation. Generally, it's how the body moves. Remember when you imagined that you stood up and raised your arm? The motion was smooth, not jerky. This interpolation method creates smooth, graceful curves, or sine waves, between your keyframes. The movement from one keyframe to the next begins slowly, accelerates in the middle, and then slows again as it reaches the next keyframe.

Linear Section

ON THE CD

Linear Section keyframes are colored orange. This interpolation method creates straight, sawtooth-like transitions between keyframes that increase or decrease at a steady rate. A project file on the CD-ROM that accompanies this book shows how the arms respond with Linear Sections between the keyframes. Open the Tutorials > Chap14 > Poser7_animation_2.pz3 file to see the example shown in Figure 14.10. Here, the motion is set to a constant velocity. There is no gradual speeding up or slowing down of the motion. It starts at a run and keeps going at that speed until it stops. Although this is not quite so realistic for human motions, if you are just starting out with animations, it's a good method to adopt. This is because the motion before a keyframe does not affect the motion after.

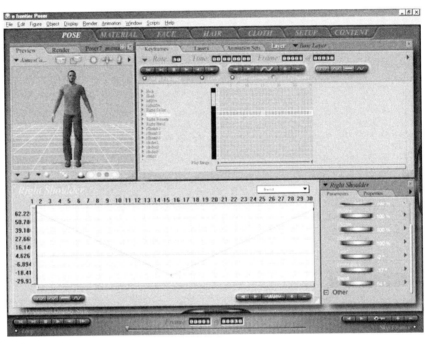

FIGURE 14.10   Linear Sections create straight transitions between keyframes.

Constant Section

Constant Section keyframes are colored gray. The pose at the first keyframe does not change until it reaches the second keyframe. The change is instantaneous and acts like a switch. The value only changes at the keyframe. If you open the Tutorials > Chap14 > Poser7_animation_3.pz3 file on the CD-ROM that accompanies this book, you'll see the project shown in Figure 14.11. James' arm is either up or down. There is no in-between.

ON THE CD

Breaking Splines

Now let's go back to Spline selection and consider what would happen if an extra keyframe were added at frame number 7. Our object here is to make James's arm relax slightly before it is raised.

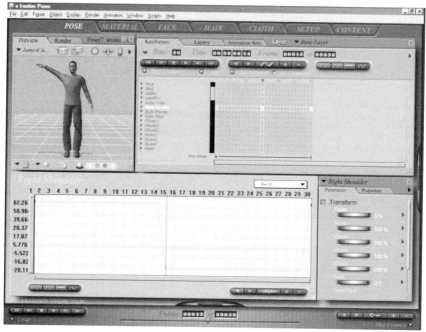

FIGURE 14.11 Constant Sections create no transitions between keyframes. The change is instantaneous from keyframe to keyframe.

ON THE CD

If you open the Tutorials > Chap14 > Poser7_animation_4.pz3 file on the CD-ROM that accompanies this book, you'll see the project shown in Figure 14.12. Here, you can see the extra keyframe in the Animation Palette.

But now look at the graph. Frames 1 to 15 look okay, but notice how frames 15 to 30 have been changed. Instead of the maximum amount of arm bending occurring at frame 15, it is now at frames 17 and 18. Plus, the bend is increased. In some cases, these differences may not matter. However, in many cases, it does matter and is the major cause of confusion for folks starting out in animation. To prevent the new keyframe from affecting later parts of an animation, you need to add a spline break.

ON THE CD

To break the spline, select frame 15, and then click on the Spline Break button. The result is shown in Figure 14.13 (which is also included in the Tutorials > Chap14 > Poser7_animation_5.pz3 file on the CD-ROM that accompanies this book). The spline (graph line if you will) has been broken at frame 15. Altering the bend value at frame 7 no longer has any effect on frames 15 to 30. To fine-tune this example even further if you require frames 15 to 30 to revert to sinusoidal, just add an extra keyframe at frame 16 with the same values as frame 15.

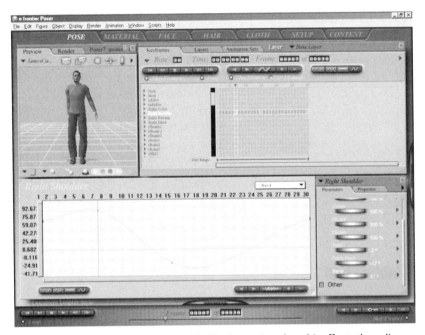

FIGURE 14.12   An extra keyframe is added in Frame 7 . . . but this affects the splines that occur later in the animation.

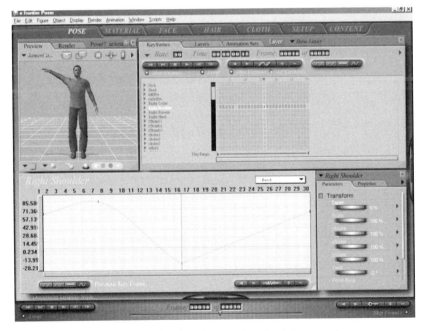

FIGURE 14.13   After adding a spline break, the animation is improved.

USING ANIMATION LAYERS

Poser 7 includes extra animation editing features with its addition of the Animation Palette's Layers tab, which is shown in Figure 14.14. You can use animation layers to build your animations in pieces. Later, you can move or hide layers without affecting content that appears in other layers. When you render a layered animation, all visible layers are composited together to create a single movie.

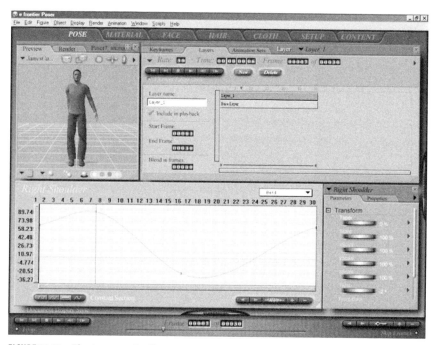

FIGURE 14.14 The Layers tab allows you to create multilayered animation that can be edited more freely and nonlinearly than single-layer animation.

The controls in the Layers tab assist you in creating layers in which to place additional scene elements. The Layers tab consists of the following controls:

New: Click this button to create a new layer in your animation.
Delete: After you select the layer you want to delete, click the Delete button.
Layer Name: Enter a name for the new layer in this field.
Include in Playback: When checked, this option will include playback of your layer when you preview your animation. When unchecked, the elements included in the layer will not animate.

Start Frame: Enter the frame number on which the layer will start.

End Frame: Enter the frame number on which the layer will end. This number cannot exceed the total number of frames in the base layer. If you need additional frames in your movie for the layer, you must add them to the base layer first.

Blend In Frames: Enter the number of frames at the beginning in which the current animation layer will blend in to the underlying animation layers.

Blend Out Frames: Enter the number of frames at the end in which the current animation layer will blend out to the underlying animation layers.

Composite Method: The Add composite method adds new layer data to the existing underlying data. The Replace composite method replaces underlying layers with the contents of the new layer data.

Move Up: Moves the animation layer up in the stack so that it takes higher precedence.

Move Down: Moves the animation layer lower in the stack so that it takes less precedence.

In the Layers tab, you can zero in to edit smaller sections of an animation and then blend them into the main animation. When you first view the Layers tab, it will contain just the base layer. To add a new layer, click the New button. The option to rename this layer is provided with the Layer Name edit box.

With the new layer selected, return to the Keyframes tab. There you will find . . . nothing! The green horizontal display line has disappeared, as shown in Figure 14.15, because we are now editing a new layer. The overall animation is still present as shown by the curve in the Graph window.

Let's continue editing by adding a bend to James's left shoulder. First, set up the layer start frame and end frame. This could be the full length of the animation; here the start frame is 14 and the end frame is 24. The number of frames over which this animation will blend in and out respective to the base layer is set at 3. Finally, the option was selected to add this animation to the base layer. The resulting Layer tab is shown in Figure 14.16.

The animation for James's left shoulder starts at frame 16, where the Bend value is set to +56 degrees. At frame 21, the Bend value is adjusted to -79 degrees. The graph will now look as shown in Figure 14.17, which is saved on the CD-ROM as Tutorials > Chap14 > Poser7_animation_ 6.pz3.

ON THE CD

If you return to the Layers palette, you will notice that it is possible to drag Layer 1 along the timeline, allowing you to freely control at which point in the animation the arm bends without destroying the other elements in your project.

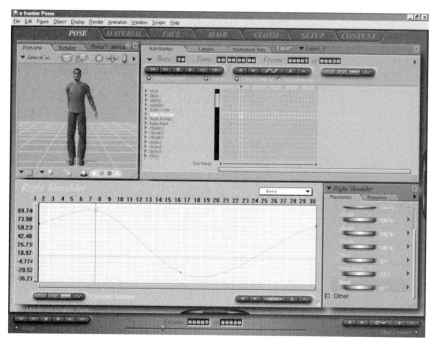

FIGURE 14.15 The addition of a new layer allows you to add keyframes in a new layer.

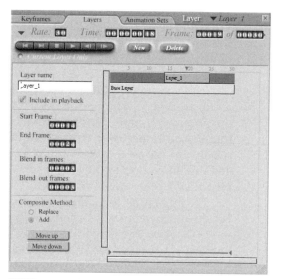

FIGURE 14.16 The new layer starts in frame 14 and ends in frame 24, with 3 blend in and blend out frames.

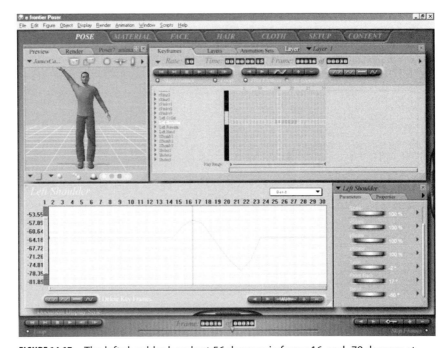

FIGURE 14.17   The left shoulder bends at 56 degrees in frame 16, and -79 degrees at frame 21.

It is important to understand the method by which the animation layers are composited together:

Add: Values of each parameter are added together for all layers. If James has a shoulder bend of 5 in the base layer and a value of 10 in Layer 1, then the resulting value is 5 + 10 = 15 degrees.

Replace: Parameter values of the upper layers will replace those of the lower layers. For the same example, because Layer 1 is above the base layer, the value used is 10. The 5 degrees of bend found in the base layer are ignored.

ANIMATION SETS

Python scripting or third-party applications (such as Viewpoint) use *animation sets*, as shown in Figure 14.18, to control animation properties. Extra attributes may be set using the Attributes button. For example, an attribute could be set to allow a script to automatically start an animation when the figure first appears in a scene.

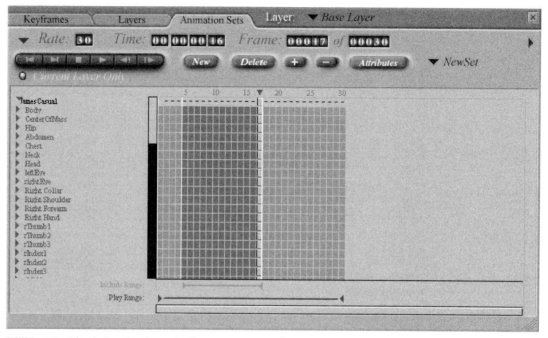

FIGURE 14.18 The Animation Sets tab allows you to control animation properties through Python scripts.

GENERAL ANIMATION TIPS

Cut, Copy, and Paste commands may be used throughout the suite of Animation Palettes. This may be facilitated by either using the Poser menu or keyboard shortcuts: [Command]/[Ctrl]+[X], [Command]/[Ctrl]+[C], and [Command]/[Ctrl]+[V].

You can highlight and then drag blocks of frames and keyframes. In the Graph window, you can highlight a selection of keyframes and drag left or right to reposition them within the timeline.

If the Ctrl (Command) key is held down, you can uniformly raise or lower all that parameter's keyframe values. An example where this is useful is when you have an animation of a figure that was made for flat shoes, but your selected figure is to wear high heels. Simply select the foot bend from the drop-down menu, and highlight all of the frame. Now, Ctrl+ drag all the values up or down by the required amount.

When creating animations, it's best to rough out the major movements first. Start with the hip, torso, and chest; then work down each leg; and follow this with the arms. Finally, fine-tune with animations to the hands, head, and expressions.

Consider using images as a background for reference. This method is called Rotoscoping and is still used by the major animation film companies. The Rotoscoper Python script by PhilC (*http://www.philc.net*) provides an aid in this method.

Animation Timing

Animation timing is also referred to as the *Frame Rate*, that is, how many frames will be shown per second. You should always consider where or how your animation is going to be used because media types vary:

- NTSC (US television): 30 fps
- PAL (European, Australian, and UK television): 25 fps
- Film: 24 fps
- Flash or other computer multimedia: 12 to 15 fps.

The frame rate may be set in any of the Animation Palette tabs. If you wanted to complete a 1-minute animation based on a frame rate of 30 fps, be prepared to create a total of 1,800 frames of animation. If each frame takes 5 minutes to render, this will take 150 hours to complete. Some forward planning regarding render optimization may be prudent.

Animations may be retimed using the Animation > Retime Animation command. The Retime Animation dialog box is shown in Figure 14.19.

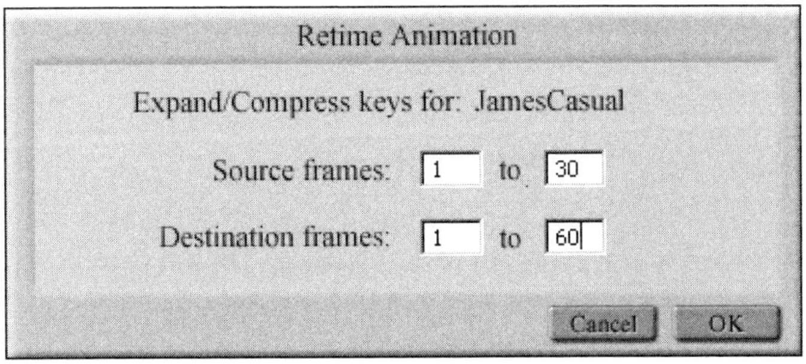

FIGURE 14.19   The Retime Animation dialog box allows you to adjust the timing of an animation to increase or decrease the frame rate.

On the other hand, when you resample keyframes, you increase or decrease the number of keyframes in the animation. To resample keyframes, use the Animation > Resample > Key Frames command. The Resample

Keys dialog box shown in Figure 14.20 appears. This enables you to in-crease or decrease the number of keyframes in the animation. We strongly suggest that you first save your scene prior to resampling. Poser 7 does have a much improved Undo/Redo system, but there is nothing like having a backup copy just in case!

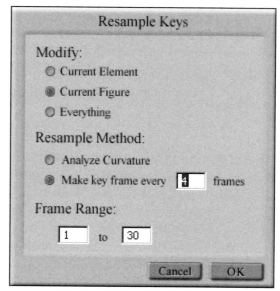

FIGURE 14.20   Use the Resample Keys dialog box to increase or decrease the number of keyframes.

Loop Interpolation

Many animations are cyclic in nature, for example, walking, running, waving an arm. Enabling Loop Interpolation from the Animation menu can help smooth out the jump from the final to the start frame and pro-vide a continuously smooth animation.

Quaternion Interpolation

This option was deliberately left until last because it should only used as a last resort. If your animation remains jerky even after every effort has been made to smooth it out, enable this option from the Animation menu. It will apply an algorithm to the animation in an attempt to rectify the situation.

CONCLUSION

In this chapter, you got a great basic overview of the principles of animating in Poser. The principles that you learned in this chapter go behind each animation that you will create in Poser, whether it be a few seconds or several minutes. Just break each motion and each scene down into its individual components, and work from there. With patience and study, you'll be creating interesting Poser stories in no time!

15

Walking, Talking, and More

In This Chapter

- Using the Walk Designer
- Tutorial 15.1 Changing the Figure Type
- Tutorial 15.2 Creating a Walk in Place
- Tutorial 15.3 Creating and Following a Walk Path
- Introducing the Talk Designer
- Tutorial 15.4 Using the Talk Designer

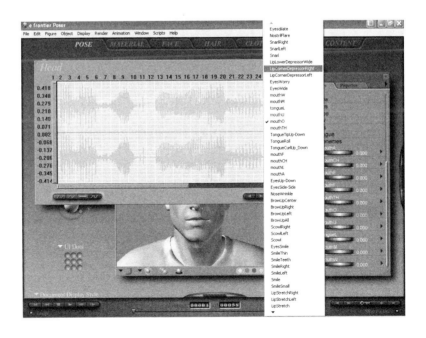

P oser provides a number of animation aids that help you achieve results quickly and easily. Among these aids are the Walk Designer and
the Talk Designer, which is new with the release of Poser 7. These two
features make it very easy to animate the characters in your movie projects.

In this chapter, you'll learn how to use the Walk Designer to create walk
cycles that walk in place or that follow a path. You'll also learn how easy it
is to use the Talk Designer to make your characters speak a few words.

USING THE WALK DESIGNER

The Walk Designer, shown in Figure 15.1, provides a quick and easy solution to making any two-legged character walk or run in a variety of different ways. You can create a walk cycle that stays in place, or you can create
a walk cycle that follows a path.

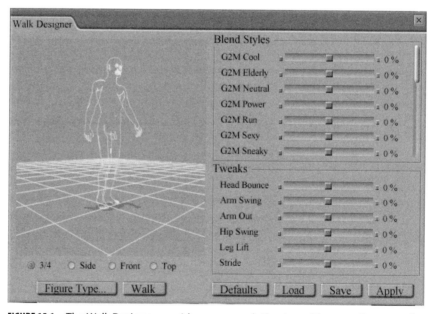

FIGURE 15.1   The Walk Designer provides an easy solution to making your figures walk
across your scene.

The Walk Designer contains the following controls and settings:

View Selection Options: By default, the Preview window displays
an outline of a figure in 3/4 view. Other options allow you to
view the walk from the Side, Front, or Top.

Figure Type: Click this button to preview your walk cycle with a different figure.

Walk: Click this button to animate the walk cycle in the Preview window.

Defaults: Click this button to return the Blend Styles and Tweaks options to their zero values.

Load: Click this button to load a walk cycle that you have previously saved to your hard drive.

Save: Click this button to save a walk cycle to your hard drive.

Apply: Click this button to apply the walk cycle to the figure that you have currently selected in your scene.

Blend Styles

The Poser 7 Walk Designer features some new blend styles that are specifically designed for the G2 figures (James G2, Koji G2, Kelvin G2, Simon G2, Jessi G2, Miki G2, Olivia G2, and Sydney G2). In addition, there are Blend Styles that work with older Poser figures as well.

The available Blend Styles, shown in Figure 15.2, are designed to work with both new and old Poser figures:

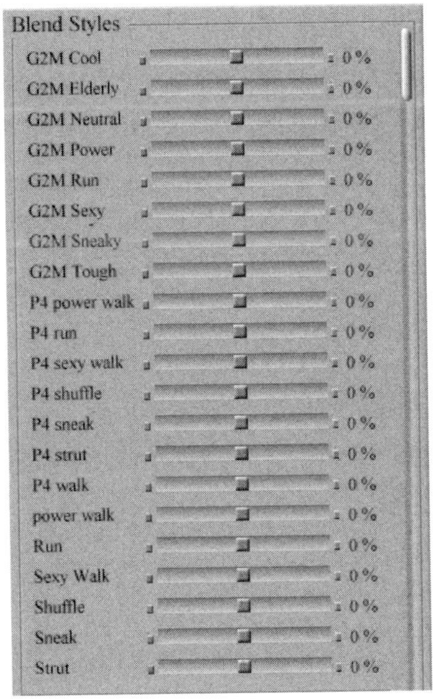

FIGURE 15.2 Blend Styles add a lot of variation to walks for new and old Poser figures.

For the G2 figures, use the following blend styles: G2M Cool, G2M Elderly, G2M Neutral, G2M Power, G2M Run, G2M Sexy, G2M Sneaky, and G2M Tough. The primary difference between the G2 figures and the older figures is that the G2 figures include a waist body part, whereas the older figures do not. This could affect the walk cycle and make the G2 figures walk a bit differently than the older figures.

For figures that are designed for Poser 4 and earlier versions (including Poser Pro Pack), use P4 Power Walk, P4 Run, P4 Sexy Walk, P4 Shuffle, P4 Sneak, P4 Strut, and P4 Walk.

For Poser 5 and Poser 6 figures, use Power Walk, Run, Sexy Walk, Shuffle, Sneak, and Strut.

Tweaks

Tweaks settings are shown in Figure 15.3. These settings add more variety to the way the head, arms, hips, and legs move during your walk cycle. *Head Bounce* bobs the head up and down. *Arm Swing* exaggerates the swing of the arms during the walk. *Arm Out* raises the arms out toward the side. *Hip Swing* exaggerates the side-to-side movement of the hips. *Leg Lift* bends the legs more at the knees during the walk. *Stride* increases the length of the stride with each step.

When using tweaks, a little goes a long way in making your walks appear more realistic and natural. For example, start with small settings, such as 5 to 15%, and preview the change by clicking the Walk button to view the effects in the Preview window.

Tweaks		
Head Bounce		0%
Arm Swing		0%
Arm Out		0%
Hip Swing		0%
Leg Lift		0%
Stride		0%

FIGURE 15.3 Use Tweaks to exaggerate head-, arm-, and leg movement.

TUTORIAL 15.1 **CHANGING THE FIGURE TYPE**

You don't have to use the default figure while you preview your walk cycle. In fact, in most cases, it's best to use the figure that you intend to animate. In the following tutorial, you'll import Simon G2 into the Walk

Designer so that you can create new walks for him in later tutorials in this chapter.

To change the figure in the Walk Designer, follow these steps:

1. Choose Window > Walk Designer to open the Walk Designer.
2. Click the Figure Type button at the bottom of the Walk Designer palette. The Open dialog box appears.
3. Locate the Poser 7 > Runtime > Libraries > Character > G2 > SimonG2 folder. Highlight Simon.crz, and click Open.
4. If Poser prompts you to locate the OBJ file for the figure that you are importing, locate the folder that contains the OBJ or OBZ file. In the case of SimonG2, the OBZ file is located in the same folder as the CRZ file. Highlight the OBZ file, and click Open.
5. Poser informs you that it is preparing the Walk Designer while it loads the various blend styles for the figure you are importing. Soon, your figure should appear in the Preview window in Outline display mode. Figure 15.4 shows Simon in the preview area of the Walk Designer.

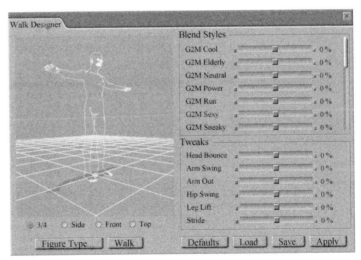

FIGURE 15.4   After choosing a new figure type, it appears in the Preview window.

TUTORIAL 15.2   CREATING A WALK IN PLACE

Poser allows you to use the Walk Designer in one of two ways. You can either create a walk cycle in which the character walks in place, or you can create a walk cycle in which the figure follows a path of movement. We'll look at the walk-in-place method first.

Walk-in-place walk cycles are excellent for use in game development, where animated sprites are used to make the figure move through the game. Animated sprites are typically rendered in several directions; that is, there are walk-in-place versions of the figure walking toward the left, right, front, back, and in the various diagonal directions. Walk-in-place animations are also good to use when you want to keep your figure centered in the scene and have the scenery scrolling behind the character.

To create a walk-in-place walk cycle for Simon, follow these steps:

1. With Simon loaded in the Walk Designer, click the Walk button. The figure in the preview area of the walk designer starts walking in a loop.
2. Adjust the G2M Blend Styles as desired until you like the walk that you see in the Preview window. You can also use the other Blend Styles if you desire, but remember that because the grouping and rigging of the G2 males are different from previous figures, the older Blend Styles may not work as well on Simon G2 as those marked as G2M.
3. Add some tweaks. For example, add about 5% each for Head Bounce, Arm Swing, and Leg Lift. Preview each change as you adjust the setting. Figure 15.5 shows some of the adjustments made to the G2M Blend Styles and some of the Tweaks settings.

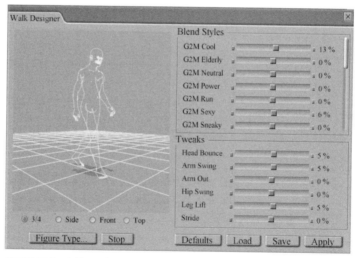

FIGURE 15.5 Adjust Blend Styles and Tweaks settings until you get a walk that you like.

4. After you arrive at a walk you like, click Stop to stop the preview.
5. To save the Poser Walk settings to your hard drive, click the Save button. Use the Save File As dialog box to locate the folder into which

you want to save the walk settings. Enter a name for your new walk, and click Save. Poser saves the file with a PWK extension. You then return to the Walk Designer.

6. To apply the walk to the figure in your scene, first use the Figure > Use Inverse Kinematics command to verify that Inverse Kinematics is turned off (unchecked) on the figure that you are applying your walk to.

7. Click the Apply button in the Walk Designer. The Apply Walk dialog box shown in Figure 15.6 appears.

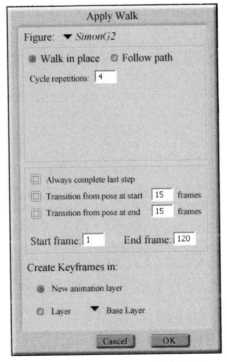

FIGURE 15.6   Use the Apply Walk dialog box to create a Walk in Place walk cycle.

8. All figures in your scene are listed in the Figure drop-down list at the top of the Apply Walk dialog box. Verify that the correct figure is selected. In this case, we select SimonG2.

9. Select the Walk in Place radio button. Enter the number of times you want the walk cycle to repeat in the Cycle Repetitions field. The default value is 4 repetitions.

10. Verify the start frame and end frame to apply your walk cycle. By default, Poser creates a 120-frame animation (4 repetitions at 30 frames per second) and starts the walk on the first frame. For this example, we will leave the settings at their defaults.

11. You can choose to put the keyframes of the walk cycle in a new animation layer or in the base layer. For this example, leave the setting at the default of New Animation Layer.

12. Click OK. Poser applies the walk cycle to the selected figure, which should now be posed in the first frame of the walk cycle. You can close the Walk Designer window at this point. Figure 15.7 shows an example of the walk applied to a figure.

FIGURE 15.7   After you apply the walk to your figure, he's ready to render!

TUTORIAL 15.3   **CREATING AND FOLLOWING A WALK PATH**

To make your character walk through a scene, you have to create a walk path. The process is very simple. In this tutorial, you'll apply a still pose to James Casual in the first frame, and then you'll create a walk path to make him walk across the screen. Finally, you'll add a different pose to the end of the animation.

1. Choose File > New to create a new Poser scene. The default figure appears in the scene. Replace him with James Casual (the Poser 6 male).
2. Open the Poser 7 > Pose > Poser 6 > James Pose > Standing > Standing Pose Library. Apply the Stand 02 pose to James in the first frame.
3. Choose Figure > Create Walk Path. If you zoom your camera out farther, you should see a spline curve with several points attached to it. This is the walk path. Figure 15.8 shows the path with James Casual at the beginning.

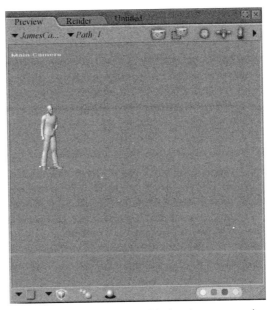

FIGURE 15.8   A walk path is added to the scene, and James Casual stands at the beginning.

4. If desired, you can change the shape of the walk path by moving the control points to different locations in your scene. You can also use the Parameters window to adjust the rotation, scaling, or translation of the path if desired. For example, in Figure 15.9, we have rotated the path by 10 degrees, scaled it up by 134%, and adjusted the X and Z translation dials to move the first point directly beneath James' feet.
5. Choose Window > Walk Designer to open the Walk Designer. If you saved your walk from the previous tutorials, click the Load button, and locate the walk that you saved. Otherwise, you can create a new walk for this example.
6. After you load or create your walk cycle, click Apply. The Apply Walk dialog box appears.

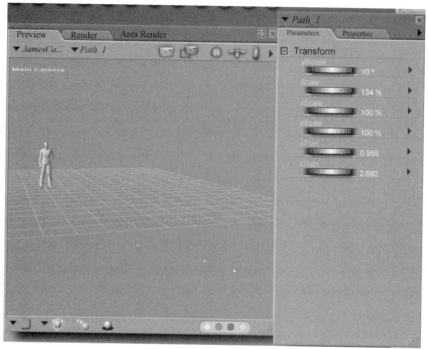

FIGURE 15.9   Parameters are adjusted to scale, rotate, and translate the walk path.

7. Choose JamesCasual from the Figure menu.
8. Select the Follow Path option. A menu will then prompt you to choose the path that you want to attach. There is currently only one path (Path 1) in the scene, which is selected by default.
9. You can optionally align the head to make it appear as though your figure is paying close attention to where he is going. The options are One Step Ahead, which makes the figure look closely toward the path; End of Path, which keeps the character's head focused on the final destination; or Next Sharp Turn, which focuses your figure's attention on the next turn he has to take. For this example, we will choose One Step Ahead.
10. The next set of options determines how the walk cycle starts and ends. If you check Always Complete Last Step, Poser adds enough frames so that the foot doesn't end up in mid air at the end of the animation.
11. Poser determines the number of frames to create based on the frame rate of your animation and the length of the path. In Figure 15.10, we see that Poser has calculated that the animation will take 271 frames for James to reach the end of the path. If you increase or decrease this value, it will affect the length of the steps he takes, and it may not look as natural.

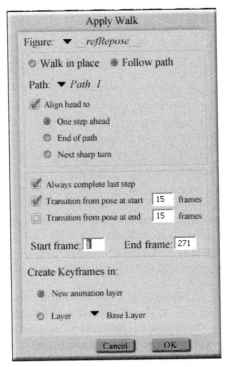

FIGURE 15.10   Poser automatically calculates the number of frames to complete your walk along the path.

12. Finally, you can choose to create the walk in a new animation layer or in any other layer that exists in your animation. For this example, we will create the walk in a new animation layer. This makes it easier to reposition or delete the layer should you not like the results.

13. Click OK to create the walk on the specified path. Then, preview the motion in the Pose Room and make adjustments as necessary in the Animation Palette.

You can save the pose and the associated walk path to the library. Open the Poses Library of your choice, and click the Add to Library button. Poser will first present a dialog box that allows you to choose the walk path along with other elements in your scene. After you select the items, Poser asks if you want to include morph channels or body transformations in with the pose. Then, Poser asks if you want to save the pose as a single-frame animation or multiframe animation. Choose the latter option, and then enter the frame numbers you want to save.

INTRODUCING THE TALK DESIGNER

One of the most exciting new features of Poser 7 is the addition of the Talk Designer, which will have your characters speaking in no time! The Talk Designer allows you to import a sound and automatically adds keyframes that move the character's mouth along with the spoken words. You can optionally type in the text of the audio file to assist Poser in determining how the words are formed.

The Talk Designer works in conjunction with a Viseme map, which is installed with Poser 7. This Viseme map, which is saved in XML format, tells Poser which morph parameters it should use when moving the mouth, face, and eyes on your figure while it speaks. In the case of James Casual, the Viseme map works with the following facial morphs to create his speech. Other characters should be similarly configured:

 In the following facial morph descriptions, uppercase letters are the hard pronunciation, and lowercase letters are the soft pronunciation of these letters).

MouthTH: This facial morph is used when speaking the letters s, S, z, Z, j, J, d, G, t, k, n, and N

MouthF: This morph is used when speaking the letters F and v.

TongueL: This morph is used for speaking the letters L, T, and D.

MouthM: This morph is used for speaking the letters m, p, and b.

MouthW: This morph is used for speaking the letters W, r, R, and u.

MouthE: This morph is used for speaking the letters e, i, E, and y.

MouthA: This morph is used for speaking the letters a, I, A, and H.

MouthCH: This morph is used for speaking the letters c and C.

MouthU: This morph is used for speaking the letters w, o, O, and U.

To open the Talk Designer, choose Window > Talk Designer. The Talk Designer window, shown in Figure 15.11, appears.

The controls in the Talk Designer serve the following purposes:

Input Files: Click the Sound File button to load an audio file. Click the plus sign next to the Supplemental Text field to expand a box and enter the text that corresponds to the audio file, or click the button to open a ready-made text file. If needed, you can also click the Viseme Map File button to open a custom-made Viseme map file.

Configuration: This section defines the character that will be used for the speech, the number of frames required for the animation, and which layer the speech animation should appear in. You can also adjust the amount of enunciation in the animation, with higher settings producing more animated results.

Head Motions: This section allows you to define the speed at which the eyes blink (in blinks per minute). The default of 12.5 bpm produces a blink every 4 to 5 seconds. You can also check or uncheck the options to create eye and head motion during speech.

Emotional Tweaks: Sliders allow you to add emotion to the speech. Various levels or combinations of Anger, Disgust, Fear, Joy, Sadness, or Surprise are added to the speech. Lower settings produce milder emotion, and higher values produce very animated and over-exaggerated results that are great for toon work.

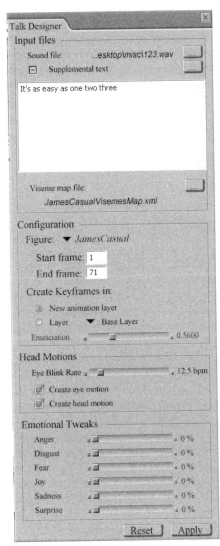

FIGURE 15.11   The Talk Designer helps you make your characters speak in sync with an audio file.

TUTORIAL 15.4   **USING THE TALK DESIGNER**

ON THE CD

Now you'll have a chance to play with the Talk Designer. Included on the CD-ROM that accompanies this book are two WAV files. You'll find them in the Tutorials > Chap15 folder. These files were specifically created for this book, so you are free to use one or both as you please.

To use the Talk Designer, follow these steps:

1. Choose File > New to create a new Poser scene. The default figure appears in the scene. Replace him with James Casual (the Poser 6 male).
2. Switch to the Face Camera by using the Camera Controls or by choosing Display > Camera View > Face Camera.
3. Choose Window > Talk Designer. The Talk Designer Palette appears.
4. Click the ellipsis button beside the Sound File category. Load one of the two audio files on the CD-ROM that accompanies this book. You'll find them in the Tutorials > Chap15 folder. Choose a file, and select Open to continue.

ON THE CD

5. Click the plus sign near the Supplemental Text area to expand the text window. Enter the text that applies to the audio file that you selected. EasyAs123.wav is a man's voice saying "It's as easy as one, two, three." EasyToMakeUsTalk.wav is a man's voice saying "It's easy to make us talk." A sample entry is shown in Figure 15.12.

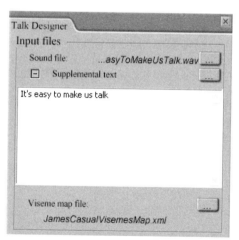

FIGURE 15.12   Enter text that corresponds with the audio file you are using.

6. In the Configuration section, verify that the correct figure is selected. The Start Frame and End Frame values are automatically determined by the length of the audio file and normally start at 1. If you change the start frame, make sure that you allow for the same number of

frames at the end. In other words, if you instead want the voice to start at frame 250, you will need to set the end frames at 307 to accomodate the 58 frames for the talk animation.

7. You can choose to create the talking keyframes in a new animation layer or in the base layer. If you create them in a new animation layer, it is much easier to move them to a new location if you have to later.

8. By default, the Enunciation is set to .56, which animates the facial morphs at a natural rate. If you need more enunciation (such as when someone is yelling or surprised), increase the values accordingly. A little goes a long way, so don't overdo it! The settings in the Configuration section should now look as shown in Figure 15.13.

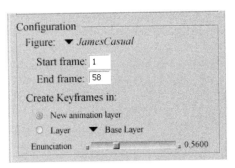

FIGURE 15.13   Configuration settings determine the length and position of the speech animation and how much enunciation will take place.

9. We'll leave the Head Motions section at their default settings. Instead, let's move on to the Emotional Tweaks. We'll add a little bit of Joy and a little bit of Surprise to the mix. Set each of these settings at 5% by dragging the slider to a new value.

10. Click Apply. After a brief wait, you should see the scene update in the Document window. When you play the scene, you should hear the audio file play. To see the animation, you may have to choose the Display > Tracking > Full Tracking command if your system resources allow.

If you find that you need to tweak the animation later on, click to select the head. Then open the Graph (Window > Graph), and select the morph that you want to adjust. It is extra work to do the tweaks, but it can improve the results dramatically.

CONCLUSION

Now that you've been introduced to some of the animation tools at your disposal, you are ready to make your characters walk and talk across the screen in many ways. This is only the beginning of a long journey into the intracacies of animation, but we hope we have inspired you to continue down this path!

RENDERING

In This Chapter

- Building Faster Scenes
- Poser 7 Rendering Environments
- Saving Time with Area Renders
- Comparing Renders
- Using the FireFly Renderer
- Tutorial 16.1 Setting Render Settings and Aspect Ratio

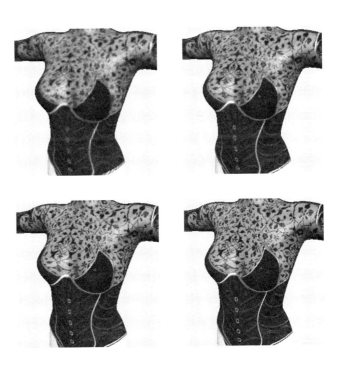

After you add content to your scene, pose your figures, or add keyframes for animations, the final step is to *render* your project. As you build your scene, you observe it through a Preview window, which gives an approximation of what your final image will look like. However, the Preview window doesn't display as much detail, nor does it represent lights, shadows, displacement, or other atmosphere effects as it would in your final version. When you render your image, Poser performs the final calculations to determine how lights, shadows, and other texturing and effects contribute to your scene.

Poser 7 provides several renders that you can use to complete your project. In this chapter, we will focus mostly on the FireFly renderer, which takes the most advantage of the complex materials you create in the Advanced Material Room view.

ON THE CD

You'll find information about the Poser 4 and Sketch Designer renderers on the CD-ROM that accompanies this book.

BUILDING FASTER SCENES

Regardless of what rendering engine you decide to use, the amount of time it takes to render is greatly affected by the elements that you use in your scene and the settings that you apply in the rendering engine. The following considerations can help reduce rendering time considerably:

Polygon counts: Use low poly-count models wherever possible. In particular, you can use low-polygon models for objects that are farther away from your camera. Many popular Poser figures come in low- and high-resolution versions.

Lighting considerations: Lighting affects rendering speeds. Scenes with fewer lights render much more quickly than scenes with many lights. Rather than use several lights in a scene, consider using a single IBL light or point light, with reduced intensity, to illuminate your entire scene with a minimum amount of ambient light. Then, enhance the lighting with additional spotlights where needed for drama or composition.

Shadow calculations: Lights that cast shadows take longer to render than those that don't. You can speed up renders by turning off shadows on lights that are not critical (usually only one or two lights need shadows).

Also, be aware that you will use more resources when you use Depth Map Shadows instead of Raytraced Shadows. Large shadow maps eat up resources and slow down renders. If your scene does use shadow maps, you can choose to reuse them after you place your objects where you want them. You speed up the final render time when you reuse shadow maps because you don't have to recalculate them.

Texture sizes: Image maps can use significant amounts of resources. Large image maps are a waste of computing power if you aren't doing close-ups. For objects that are close to the camera, such as full facial portraits, use maps that are at least equal to the size of your final render but no more than twice the size. You can use lower-resolution texture maps for objects that are farther away from the camera.

Using complex materials: Complex materials can also significantly increase your render times. Lights interact with materials; so if you are using complex materials that are transparent, are reflective, scatter light, or refract light, your renders will take longer. Use less complex materials on objects that are farther away from your camera to help keep your render times as short as possible.

POSER 7 RENDERING ENVIRONMENTS

Poser 7 gives you four distinct engines you can use to render your projects. You can choose from highly stylized rendered output, to cartoon-like renders, all the way to photorealistic renders, all without leaving Poser! You can access and configure each of these render engines with the Render > Render Settings command. The following sections briefly describe each of the tabs in the Render Settings dialog box.

Preview Renderer

The Preview Renderer allows you to render your Preview window using the current display mode settings and renders the Preview window to the size that you specify in the Render Dimensions dialog box (Render > Render Dimensions), up to 4096 by 4096. The Preview Renderer is an excellent source for flat-shaded illustrations for things like instruction manuals and cartoon-style renders.

The settings for the Preview renderer are shown in Figure 16.1 and include the following options:

Display Engine: Check the SreeD option if your graphics adapter does not support OpenGL display settings. If your graphics card does support OpenGL, check whether you want the OpenGL features to be supported by the hardware on the graphics adapter or through software.

Enable Hardware Shading: If you are using OpenGL hardware rendering, check this option to see the effects of certain advanced procedural shaders in your Preview window (bump maps, displacement maps, Ambient Occlusion, and other nodes will not display). This option may slow your preview performance if there are a lot of advanced procedural shaders in your scene and will not work for more than five lights. If your preview speed is affected, disable (uncheck) this option.

Optimize Simple Materials: Check this option if you do not want Poser to generate shaders for simple materials.

Style Options: These options relate to how lines, borders, and edges are displayed in the Preview window The Silhouette Outline Width setting controls the width of outlines used in Outline display style. The Wireframe Line Edge setting controls the width of the grid lines used in Wireframe display mode. The Toon Edge Line Width setting controls the width of the Toon Outline display option. Check the Antialias option to prevent a jagged appearance on diagonal lines.

Transparency Display: These options control how transparent textures are displayed in the Preview window. Choose Actual to display transparency maps exactly as they are configured by the Material Room. If you want to limit the amount of transparency, choose the Limit To option, and enter the maximum percentage that you want to display. By default, the limit is set to 90%.

Texture Display: The Preview Texture Resolution setting allows you to increase or decrease the maximum texture resolution that will display in the Preview window. Higher values mean that textures are more detailed but will also consume more resources.

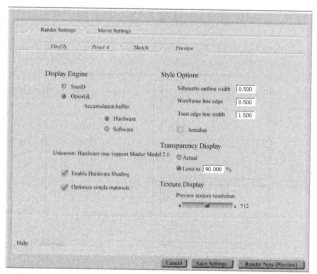

FIGURE 16.1   The Preview Renderer allows you to render your scene to any size up to 4096 by 4096, using the display mode that appears in the Document window.

After you configure your Preview Renderer settings, you can click the Save Settings button to store the settings and exit the Render Settings dialog box. After you use the Render > Render Dimensions dialog box to specify your render size, you can choose Render > Render or press F9 to render your document in the current display setting.

Sketch Renderer

The Sketch Renderer is shown in Figure 16.2. This renderer works in conjunction with the Sketch Designer, and provides an assortment of artistic drawing and painting effects that make your renders look hand drawn. It is a wonderful tool with the potential for some very creative results.

The Sketch Renderer settings window provides quick access to several sketch presets. To use one of the presets, click a thumbnail or select an option from the Sketch Preset menu. Click the Sketch Designer button to open the Sketch Designer window, where you can customize the appearance of the sketch render you want to create.

More information regarding the Sketch Renderer and the Sketch Designer is on the CD-ROM that accompanies this book.

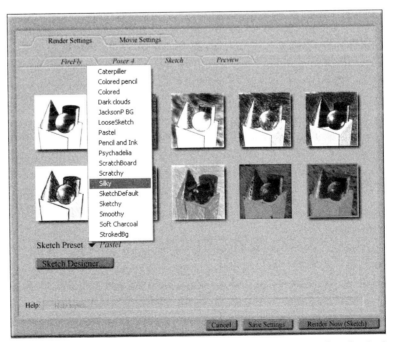

FIGURE 16.2   The Sketch Renderer allows you to create artistic renders that look as if they were drawn by hand.

Poser 4 Renderer

The Poser 4 Renderer is a scanline render engine that was used in versions earlier than Poser 5 (including Poser Pro Pack). It is included in Poser 7 to maintain compatibility with older content. Because of this, this renderer will not support advanced material shaders that use displacement, raytracing, or other advanced features that you create in the Advanced Material view. This render engine also supports bump maps with a BUM extension, which was a proprietary file format used in Poser 4 and earlier versions.

Figure 16.3 shows the settings you can configure for the Poser 4 render engine. These settings are as follows:

Antialias: Check this option to minimize jagged edges when light and dark areas meet in a diagonal line. Poser will smooth the transition between high contrasted areas to reduce the "stairstep" effect.

Use Bump Maps: Checked by default, this setting allows bump map effects to be included when you render. If bump maps are not producing the desired effect, verify that this option is turned on.

Use Texture Maps: Also checked by default, this setting uses texture maps when they appear in your materials. If left unchecked, each material in your scene will be rendered according to the color set as the Preview Color in the Material Room.

Cast Shadows: Check this option to render shadows in your scene. Uncheck the option to turn off shadows in your entire scene. You can also turn off shadow casting for any object in your scene. To do so, select an object and uncheck the Cast Shadows option in the Properties window.

Ignore Shader Trees: When checked, the Poser 4 render engine ignores advanced material shaders other than image maps. Check this option if you are using content developed for older versions of Poser, especially when they use bump maps saved in the BUM file format that was proprietary to earlier Poser versions. When you select this option, Poser disconnects all materials from the root node, and you will need to manually reconnect them.

Render Over: The options in the Render Over drop-down list allow you to choose the background over which your scene is rendered. Choose Background Color to render your scene over the current background color as set in the Material Room. Choose Black to render your scene over a black background, regardless of the background color that is set. Choose Background Picture to render your image over the background image that you imported with the File > Import > Background Picture command or as set in the Material Room. Choose Current BG Shader to render over the background as set in the background material of the Material

Room. To configure this material, choose Background from the Object menu in the Material Room, and connect the BG Color, Black, BG Picture, or BG Movie node to the Color input of the Background root node).

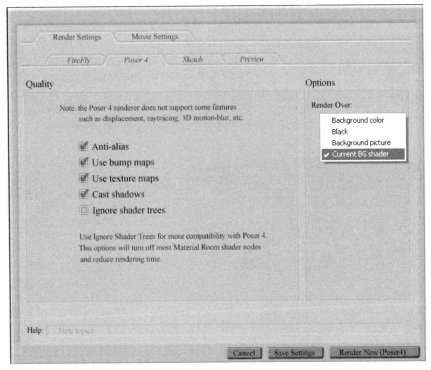

FIGURE 16.3   The Poser 4 renderer is a good choice to use when you need compatibility with older Poser content that does not use advanced material shaders.

SAVING TIME WITH AREA RENDERS

The Area Render feature allows you to select and render an area of your scene. It is particularly useful when you make changes in your scene, especially changes in lighting. With the Area Render feature, you can select a small portion of your screen for rendering instead of waiting for the entire screen to render again. This allows you to see the effects of your changes more quickly.

To render a specific area in your scene, click the Area Render symbol that appears at the top of the Preview window. Then, left-click and drag to select a rectangular area in the Preview window. Release the left mouse button to render the selected area. Figure 16.4 shows an area selected in the Preview window. The objects within the selected area are the only areas that will be rendered.

You can also use the Area Render to assist you in rendering large images that might task your resources. After you compose your scene and set the final render dimensions, start by selecting a rectangular area at the top of your Preview window. Save this first rendered image as Pass1, in an uncompressed file format such as TIF. Without making any changes to cameras, lights, or content in your scene, use the Area Render tool to select a second strip of your Preview window. Make sure that the new selection slightly overlaps the first area you rendered, as shown in Figure 16.5. Save the second render as Pass2.tif. Continue in this manner until you render every section of your scene. Then, you can use an image-editing program to composite and retouch the images where necessary.

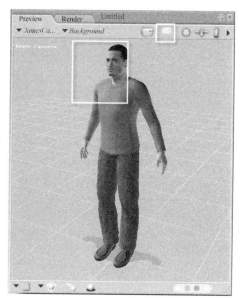

FIGURE 16.4 The Area Render renders a selected portion of an image, rather than the entire image.

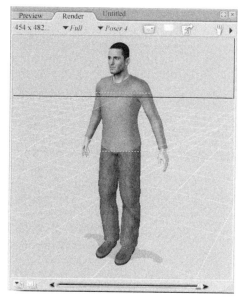

FIGURE 16.5 You can also use the Area Render feature to render sections of a large render one at a time. Later, you can use an image-editing program to composite the individual renders into a complete image.

COMPARING RENDERS

The Render Comparison feature allows you to compare two of your previously rendered images within the Preview window. Click the "stack of paper" icons on the bottom-left corner of the Render Document window.

This opens a list of your most recent renders. You can configure the number of renders held in the render cache in the Document tab of the Edit > General Preferences dialog box.

The Main Render, selected from the left list as shown in Figure 16.6, is placed beside the Compare Render that you select from the right list. After you select a render from each list, you can use the Render Wipe slider at the bottom of the window to reveal the renders side by side.

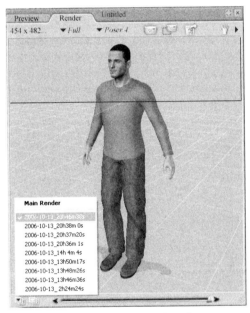

FIGURE 16.6   The Render Comparison feature allows you to compare two renders side by side to see which you like best. After you select two images, use the slider at the bottom of the Render window to compare the two renders.

USING THE FIREFLY RENDERER

For the remainder of this chapter, we're going to concentrate on helping you get the most out of the FireFly render engine. This renderer can produce a wide variety of results because it takes maximum advantage of the advanced material shaders available in Poser 7.

Considering that Poser 7 is very reasonably priced, it might surprise you to learn that the FireFly renderer is really a very sophisticated render engine. It takes advantage of displacement maps, enhanced reflections and shadows, atmosphere effects, depth of field, and raytraced material properties.

Within the FireFly section are the Auto Settings and Manual Settings. Each of the settings in these areas are described in the following sections.

FireFly Automatic Render Settings

The Automatic render settings in the FireFly renderer are shown in Figure 16.7. Several preconfigured settings, ranging from draft to final quality, can be easily accessed by moving the quality slider from left to right. The render presets on the left side are for preview or draft quality render. They render more quickly but are not as highly detailed. As you move closer toward Final quality, the renders take longer but become more realistic and detailed. As you move the quality slider toward the higher quality settings, you'll notice that the settings for the various rendering parameters will change as quality settings increase. The various settings and their functions are described next.

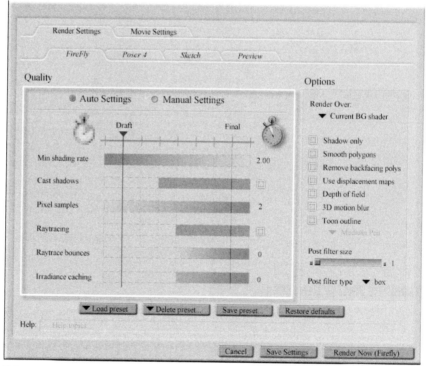

FIGURE 16.7   The Automatic Settings in the FireFly renderer provide several levels of preset rendering settings that range in render quality and speed.

Min Shading Rate: This value has to do with the micropolygon method of rendering scenes and determines how small the micropolygons will be. A shading rate of 1 means that the polygons in the object will be broken down into small pieces (micropolygons) that are equal to a single pixel of your rendered image. Draft quality renders use a Min Shading Rate of 2, whereas final quality renders use a Min Shading Rate of .5. Smaller values give crisper details, although your rendering time will increase. Figure 16.8 shows rendered examples of Min Shading Rates of 4, 2, 1, and .5.

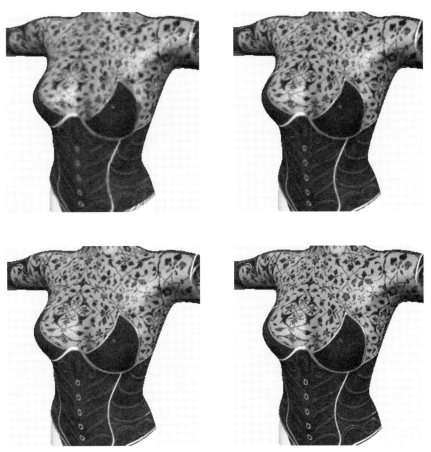

FIGURE 16.8   More detail is added as the Min Shading Rate decreases. Here you see examples of settings of 4 (top left), 2 (top right), 1 (bottom left) and .5 (bottom right).

Cast Shadows: This option enables or disables the calculation of shadows for the entire render. You can disable shadow casting on a case-by-case basis for any individual object in your scene. However, if shadows are turned off *here*, they won't get calculated *anywhere*.

Pixel Samples: This value is used to determine how many neighboring pixels are sampled during an antialiasing calculation. For each pixel that is being antialiased, the renderer samples a surrounding block of pixels and calculates the properties of the pixel based on the values of its neighbors. A value of 1 (which is used for draft renders) samples 1 pixel. A value of 3 (used for final renders) samples a 3 by 3-pixel area. Higher Pixel Samples values produce smoother images but take longer to render. Figure 16.9 shows the results achieved when the Pixel Samples setting is set to 1, 2, 4, and 6.

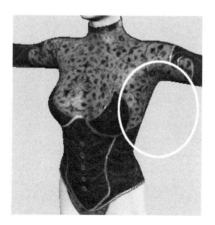 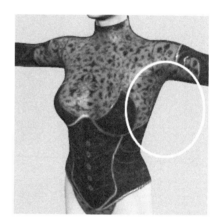

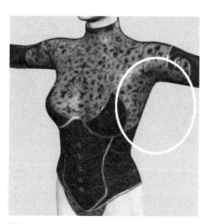 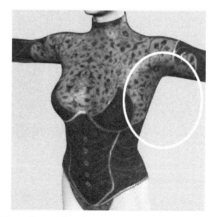

FIGURE 16.9   Antialising improves as the Pixel Samples setting increases. Here you see examples of settings of 1 (top left), 2 (top right), 4 (bottom left), and 6 (bottom right).

Raytracing: Check this option to enable or disable raytracing calculations. Some types of procedural shaders, such as the refraction and reflection nodes, require that raytracing be enabled in order to work. Raytracing is off for draft renders and on for final quality renders.

Raytrace Bounces: When raytracing is enabled, this parameter sets the limit on how many bounces each ray of light traces through. The number you set here should be proportional to the number of raytraced reflective or refractive surfaces that appear in your scene. Higher values give more realistic reflections and refractions; however, they also eat up more of your CPU and take longer to render. A medium-quality render might use one raytrace bounce, whereas a more realistic final quality render might use a setting of 4 or higher.

Irradiance Caching: This setting relates to the amount of lights and shadows that appear at any point in your scene and is most applicable to the various types of lighting nodes that you can use in your material shaders. This setting stores previous irradiance calculations that help speed up renders. Recommended settings are between 50 and 100. A higher value stores more information and helps reduce rendering time but produces less accurate irradiance.

FireFly Manual Render Settings

All of the settings that appear in the Auto Settings area also appear in the Manual Settings area. Here, you can override the automatic settings to fully customize how your renders are handled. The Manual Settings allows you to set each parameter individually. In addition to the Auto Settings we have already discussed, the following additional options appear in the Manual Settings area:

Acquire from Auto: Click this button to copy the values from the Auto Settings area to the Manual Settings area. From there, you can manually set each attribute that was discussed in the Automatic Rendering section.

Max Bucket Size: If you observe the progress of a FireFly renderer, you will notice that the renderer displays one block at a time as your scene goes through the rendering process. This block of information is called a *bucket* and represents the number of pixels that are rendered at the same time. Larger bucket sizes use more of your system's resources but can also speed up your renders if you have the computing power to support them. If your bucket size is too large for the amount of resources you have available, you may run out of system resources. If Poser freezes during rendering, use a lower bucket size setting the next time you try to render the scene.

Min Displacement Bounds: By default, FireFly looks in all directions from your geometry to determine the amount of displacement that may need to occur. The displacement bounds setting sets a limit on how far FireFly looks in each direction. When you use displacement maps, you must tell the FireFly renderer to displace the surface of an object by a value at least as high as the setting used in the displacement value set in the root node for the material. If you set the FireFly setting too high, the result will go out of the bounds of the current bucket calculation. This will cause your object to look like it has black holes or polka dots sprinkled all over it. A high value also eats up resources quickly and requires longer rendering times.

Additional Rendering Options

Common to both Auto Settings and Manual Settings are additional rendering options that appear in the right section of the Render Settings window. These settings are shown in Figure 16.10.

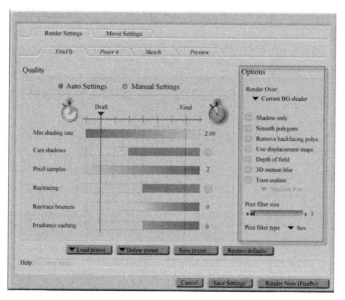

FIGURE 16.10   Additional rendering options determine other features used at rendering time.

The additional rendering options are as follows:

Render Over: The Render Over options in the FireFly renderer are similar to those previously discussed for the Poser 4 renderer. The drop-down list allows you to choose one of several options to use as the background when rendering. The Background Color, Black, and Background Picture options render objects in your scene over a color of your choice, black, or the background picture you have loaded, respectively. The Current Background Shader option gives you the opportunity to specify a complex procedural shader as the background.

Shadow Only: This option renders only the shadows that are cast by the objects in your scene. When you choose to render shadows only, all other render settings are overridden. This feature allows you to combine the shadow-only render with a render that has no shadows enabled in a graphic program. You can later use a graphic program to independently manipulate the shadows, providing very fine control without having to continually adjust and re-render different lighting settings.

Smooth Polygons: The FireFly rendering engine uses polygon subdivision to smooth the polygon joints on objects. When polygon smoothing is turned on, you can improve the appearance of a low-polygon model so that it looks smoother and softer rather than faceted. The amount of smoothing is controlled with smoothing groups or by setting a crease angle threshold in the Properties window. The *Poser 7 Reference Manual* discusses this subject in Chapter 15, "Smooth Shading."

Remove Backfacing Polys: This setting tells the FireFly renderer to ignore polygons that are on the backside of the object and not directly visible from the current camera position. By ignoring polygons not seen by the camera, your renders complete much more quickly. However, if your scene uses raytraced reflective materials, make sure that the backs of your objects do not show up in any reflection. Otherwise, you may get weird-looking reflections that show your objects with holes in them.

Use Displacement Maps: When using displacement in your renders, check this option and set your Min Displacement Bounds setting slightly higher than the highest material displacement setting used in your scene.

Depth of Field: Check this setting to calculate depth-of-field effects in your render. The depth of field is set in properties for the camera that is being used as the render view.

More information about depth of field can be found in Chapter 2, "Using Cameras."

3D Motion Blur: A great way to give the impression of fast-moving objects is to blur them. This parameter enables blurring based on the rate of position change of an object from one animation frame to the next. Blurring is affected by shutter open and close times, with longer exposures (shutter open time) producing more pronounced blurring effects.

Toon Outline: This is a post-render operation that draws an outline around the objects in your scene. There are nine outline styles: Thin Pen, Thin Pencil, Thin Marker, Medium Pen, Medium Pencil, Medium Marker, Thick Pen, Thick Pencil, and Thick Marker.

Post Filter Size: A post-render filter smooths, or antialiases, your render. The filter samples a group of pixels surrounding the current pixel and calculates a weighted average of the entire group to determine what that center pixel's characteristics are. Increasing the filter size increases the area used for group calculation, which in turn increases render times. Using too large a sample may cause undesirable blurring. The effect that this filter has is also dependant on the final size of your rendered output, so you may need to change this as you change the size of your final output.

Post Filter Type: This defines the type of calculation the post filter uses to antialias your render. The types of post filters that FireFly supports are the following:

Box: This gives each pixel in the sample equal weight.
Gaussian: This filter varies the weight of a sample based on the distance from the center of the sample area. The Gaussian curve is sometimes called the "standard distribution curve" or the "Bell curve."
Sinc: A Sinc filter applies a declining sine-wave weight to the samples based on the distance of the sample from the center. Imagine a rock falling into the water and the ripples in the surface that are created as a result. These ripples are the sine wave that will be produced—one large rise in the center with crests that decrease in amplitude the farther from the center you go.

Saving Render Settings

If you create custom rendering configurations in the Manual Settings area, you can save and later recall them. To save a render setting, click on the Save Preset button located at the bottom of the Render Presets window. Poser will prompt you to enter a name for your render preset, as shown in Figure 16.11.

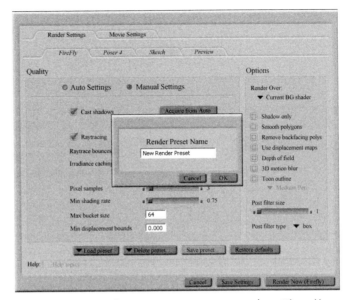

FIGURE 16.11   Poser allows you to save custom render settings. You can recall them any time by clicking the Load Preset button.

After you save your preset, you will be able to access it any time by clicking the Load Preset button at the bottom of the Render Settings window.

To restore your settings to the default settings, use the Restore Defaults button.

TUTORIAL 16.1   SETTING RENDER SETTINGS AND ASPECT RATIO

The aspect ratio of an image is simply the ratio of its width to its height. If an image is 11 inches wide by 14 inches tall, its aspect ratio is 1:1.27. (The 1.27 is derived by dividing the height by the width, which in our case is 14 divided by 11.)

Poser 6 makes it super easy to get the right dimensions and aspect ratio for your renders. You typically don't even have to do any calculations to set up renders for specific output dimensions. For example, let's say you need a 5 × 7-inch final image, and the printer requires 300 dots per inch (DPI) of image to create optimal output. It is very easy to set this up in Poser:

1. Choose Render > Render Dimensions to open the Render Dimensions dialog box shown in Figure 16.12.

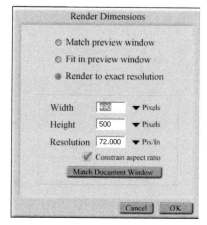

FIGURE 16.12 The Render Dimensions dialog box allows you to specify the dimensions and DPI for your final renders.

2. Temporarily uncheck the Constrain Aspect Ratio option until you enter the final width, height, and resolution of the image.
3. Select Render to Exact Resolution from the upper section of the Render Dimensions dialog box.
4. Enter **300** into the Resolution field, and select Pix/In from the units pull down. This sets the resolution at 300 DPI.
5. Now enter **5** into the Width field, and select Inches from the units pull down.
6. Enter 7 into the Height field, and select Inches from the units pull down. You will now have a render that is exactly 5 inches wide by 7 inches tall, which is 300 DPI.
7. Now, check the Constrain Aspect Ratio again. By doing so, you can change the Width or the Height value, and the other value will change automatically to keep the same relative proportions. Let's say that you have another frame that has the same aspect ratio as your 5 χ 7-inch frame, but it is 8 inches wide instead of 5. As long as the Constrain Aspect Ratio option is selected, you can easily get a perfect fit by simply going back into the Render Dimensions dialog box and changing the 5-inch Width entry to 8. Your Height value will be calculated automatically for you when you change the Width value. Alternately, if you change the Height value, the Width value will be recalculated to maintain the same aspect ratio.

Production Frame

The Display > Production Frame > Image Output Size selection displays a production frame indicator inside your Preview window. If your Preview window's aspect ratio is not the same as your rendered output settings, you will see the production frame in your Preview window to let you see what objects in your scene will appear in the render. The area that falls within the rendered area appears lighter than the area that will not be rendered. Figure 16.13 shows the production frame in your Preview window. The aspect ratio of the production frame in this figure is different than that of the Preview window. With this useful option, you can see exactly what objects will appear in your render.

FIGURE 16.13   The production frame is indicated by the lighter gray rectangle (outlined in white) within the Preview window.

CONCLUSION

We thought it was important that you know about the power of the Poser rendering engines because we hope this knowledge will inspire you to try new things and go farther with your renders than you might have otherwise. The more you know and understand about *how* Poser's render engines work, the easier it will be for you to get the types of results you imagine.

A

ABOUT THE CD-ROM

The CD-ROM included with *Practical Poser* 7 includes all of files necessary to complete the tutorials in the book. It also includes the images from the book and demos for you to use while working through the tutorials and exercises.

Denise wishes to extend her humble gratitude and appreciation to those individuals and companies mentioned below, who have graciously and generously allowed us to share some exciting content with you on this CD-ROM. All of these individuals continue to demonstrate over and over that the Poser community is filled with passionate and generous individuals who come together to promote the phenomenon that is Poser.

CD FOLDERS

Content

Includes quality content from some of the leading content providers in the Poser community, including the following wonderful goodies for you to add to your Poser scenes:

- **Aset Arts,** a group of seasoned and talented artists that have created Poser content for eFrontier, DAZ, Renderosity, and other popular Poser sites, share several articles of clothing and textures. Arien (whose texturing skills are featured in several chapters of this book) includes textures for both the Djinni outfit and the Crafted Swordsman. Deecey shares her Booties for Jessi, Terai Yuki 2, Miki 1 and Kate, with their

base textures. Luthbel contributes The Crafted Swordsman, a wonderful fantasy outfit for Aiko 3. I'd like to thank the other members of my
talented team for their generosity!

- **DAZ3D** (*http://www.daz3d.com*) shares PC and Macintosh-compatible
versions of several Poser figures, including the Toon Bot Chomper,
Aiko 3.0 Base (including textures, Mimic phoneme morphs, hair
style, poses, and so on); Civil Servant for Aiko 3; and the Toonimal
Vulture, Bat, and Lemur. Special thanks to Steve Kondris and Dan
Farr for their generosity and contributions to this project.

- **e frontier** (*http://www.e-frontier.com*), makers of Poser 7 and Shade 8
have been a tremendous source of encouragement and content for
this project. We thank them for their wonderful selection of poseable
figures: the Dino Pack Version 1 and Koji Version 1. Many thanks to
Steve Yatson and Tori Porter for these great gifts, and to Uli Klumpp
for his prompt attention to questions and comments during the
progress of this book.

- **Fredrik,** a favorite of many who frequent the Poser communities,
shares a wonderful outfit for Aiko 3: His Djinni belly dancing outfit is
sure to please users of the DAZ Aiko 3 figure. Thank you, Fredrik, for
allowing us to include your file on our CD!

- **Linda White** includes original photographs for the tutorials in the
lighting chapter. Thanks again, Linda, for allowing us to use your
wonderful photos!

- **PhilC (Phil Cooke)** shares a copy of his unique and practical female
figure, KISS. You can find out more about this figure at Phil's web
site, *http://www.philc.net* <*http://www.philc.net/*>. Thank you, Phil, not
only for sharing your figure with us, but for your expert technical
help and suggestions throughout the development of this book. This
folder also includes a web page with a great animation tutorial video
prepared by Phil (see animation1.htm).

Demos

- **UV Mapper** (*http://www.uvmapper.com*) Perhaps the most widely
used UV mapping program in the Poser community, Steve Cox has
shared with us the free "classic" version of UV Mapper in both Windows and Mac format. But to fully appreciate the UV Mapping tutorials presented in this book, a demo version of UV Mapper Professional
is also provided in both formats. Thank you, Steve, for sharing these
files with us!

HTML

- This folder includes HTML pages of additional basic material that was included in Practical Poser 6, but which was removed to make room for new and additional material in this current edition of the book. Open index.htm to begin your exploration of this content.

Images

- All of the images from within the book. These files are set up by chapter and Appendix B.

HTML

- This section includes basic material that was previously included in Practical Poser 6, the previous edition of this book. To view the material, open the index.htm page in your browser.

Tutorials

- All of the files necessary to complete the tutorials in the book including necessary Poser content, textures, and images. These files are all in common formats that can be read by most 3D applications, and they are set up in the applicable chapter folders.

SYSTEM REQUIREMENTS

Minimum system requirements are the same as those for the Poser 7 application, which are:

Windows

- Windows 2000 or XP
- 700 MHz Pentium class or compatible (1 GHz or faster recommended)
- 512 MB system RAM (768 or more recommended)
- OpenGL-enabled graphics card or chipset recommended (recent NVIDIA GeForce or ATI Radeon preferred)
- 24-bit color display, 1024 × 768 resolution
- 1 GB free hard disk space (4 GB recommended)
- Internet connection required for Content Paradise
- DVD-ROM drive

Macintosh

- Mac OS X 10.3.9 or 10.4
- 700 MHz G4 processor (Intel Core Duo or 1 GHz G4 or faster recommended)
- 512 MB system RAM (768 MB or more recommended)
- 1 GB free hard drive space (4 GB recommended)
- 24-bit color display, 1024 × 768 resolution
- OpenGL-enabled graphics card or chipset recommended (recent NVIDIA GeForce and ATI Radeon preferred)
- Internet connection required for Content Paradise
- DVD-ROM drive

In addition, you will need Poser 7, with the latest service releases and the latest video drivers that are available for your video card.

INSTALLATION

To use this CD-ROM, you just need to make sure that your system matches at least the minimum system requirements. Each demo has its own installation instructions and you should contact the developer directly if you have any problems installing the demo. The images and tutorial files are in jpeg and obj file formats and should be usable with any 3D application.

FREQUENTLY ASKED QUESTIONS

GENERAL INTERFACE QUESTIONS

Q: I set my General Preferences to customize my startup settings, but now my Document window is stuck near the top of the screen when I open Poser. How do I get it back?

A: Go back to the General Preferences dialog box (Edit > General Preferences), and reconfigure Poser to start up in factory state in both the Document and Interface tabs. Restart Poser again to get your Document window back. Then, you can reconfigure your startup preferences again. If you previously saved a copy of your preferences, you can copy them back to the Poser 7 > Runtime > Prefs folder.

Q: I know I can change the background color of the Poser interface. Can I change the color of the fonts or the font that is used?

A: Neither the font or the font color can be changed at the present time.

Q: I have two monitors. If I put some items on the second monitor, can I save my interface settings that way?

A: Yes. For example, if the Document and Render windows are on your second monitor when you close Poser, they will open up in the same position when you next open Poser, providing that you selected the Launch To Previous State option in the General Preferences dialog box.

BUILDING SCENES

Q: What are the Editing tools at the top of the screen used for?

A: The Editing tools, from left to right, are used as follows. To show or hide them, choose Window > Editing Tools. Note that the Editing tools vary slightly from room to room.

> **Rotate:** Rotates a figure, body part, or prop.
> **Twist:** Twists a figure, body part, or prop. The same as using the Twist dial in the Parameters window.
> **Translate/Pull:** Moves a figure up, down, left, or right.
> **Translate In/Out:** Moves a figure forward or backward.
> **Scale:** Increases or decreases the size of a figure or body part.
> **Taper:** Tapers a body part. Select the Taper tool, and then drag over a body part to taper it. Drag left to increase the size of the outermost end of the chain, or drag right to decrease the size.
> **Chain Break:** The Chain Break tool allows you to prevent parts from moving when you pose other parts. For example, if you don't want the shoulders to move when you pose the forearm

and hands, you can apply a chain break to the shoulders. Click the Chain Break tool to select it, and then click the figure where you want to break the chain. Click the Chain Break icon again with the Chain Break tool to remove it.

Color: Allows you to change the color of an item in your Document window or the background color of the Poser interface. Click the Color tool, and then click the object you want to change. A color palette then allows you to choose a color. Continue in this manner until you change the colors that you want to change, and then click the Color tool again to turn it off.

Grouping Tool: Allows you to create groups in your objects and assign polygons to them. The Grouping tool is covered in Chapter 10, "Groups and Materials for Models."

View Magnifier: Allows you to zoom in to an area in the Document window. Select the View Magnifier, and then draw a rectangle around the area you want to view more closely.

Morphing Tool: Allows you to visually adjust morph settings of a figure by sculpting changes.

Direct Manipulation: Allows you to rotate, twist, or bend body parts using one tool. Three circles represent the axes that will be affected by the tool. Drag the yellow square along the axes that you want to change to rotate, twist, or bend the part.

Q: How about the Parameter dials? What do they do?

A: The Parameter dials can also help you pose a character, but they also contain several other dials that help you personalize your figures.

Q: What are Memory Dots used for?

A: There are actually three kinds of dots: UI Dots, Camera Dots, and Pose Dots. Click the down arrow near the label to choose between them. Choose Window > Memory Dots to show or hide the dots.

Memory dots allow you to store settings for poses, user interface, and cameras so that you can go back to them later. For example, if you create a pose that you like but want to experiment a little further in case you can make improvements, click one of the Pose Dots to store the pose in one of nine dots. When a dot contains information, it will change color; a gray dot is empty. Experiment a bit, and then click the same dot again to return to the saved pose for more experimentation.

You can also store interface settings or camera positions in a similar manner. Pose Dots and Camera Dots are saved until you begin a new project or close Poser. Interface Dots are saved between projects, but you lose them when you close Poser.

Q: How are Pose Memory Dots different from using the Edit > Memorize and Edit > Restore menu commands?

A: You can use the Pose Dots to memorize up to nine poses that are specific to your current scene. A good use for pose dots is to save incremental poses while you experiment on additional versions. This way you can experiment with slight changes to a pose as you perfect it and decide which version you like best.

The Edit > Memorize and Edit > Restore commands allow you to save more than just a pose. It also stores Morph Dial settings in addition to pose information. You can memorize and restore position, scale, morphs, parameters, materials, parent/child relationships, and so on for the entire scene (All), an entire figure, or an element (body part, prop, single camera, or single light).

Q: When I create a new scene, my figure appears all gray. How do I change that?

A: To change the way items are displayed, you use the Display > Document Style, Display > Figure Style, or Display > Element Style commands. Alternatively, you can use the Document Style, Figure Style, or Element Style controls in your Poser interface.

The Document Display Style controls are shown in Figure B.1. If you do not see the controls on your screen, choose Window> Preview Styles to display them.

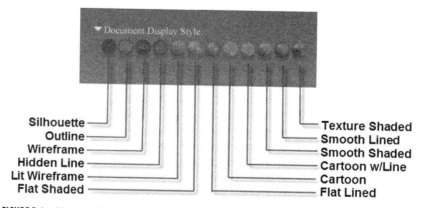

FIGURE B.1 You can choose a display style from the Display Style controls.

You can actually display the contents of the entire document window, a single figure, or a part of a figure in one of 12 different styles, as follows:

- To display everything in your Document window in the same style, choose Display > Document Style, and then select the display mode you want to use.
- To display one figure in your Document window in a selected style, click the figure you want to change, and choose Display > Figure Style. Select the display mode you want to use. You can also choose Use Document Style to use the same display mode that you selected for the entire document.
- To display part of a figure in a selected style, click the part you want to change. Choose Display > Element Style, and select the display mode you want to use. You can also choose Use Figure Style to use the same display mode as the figure that contains the selected part.

The various display modes are shown in Figure B.2.

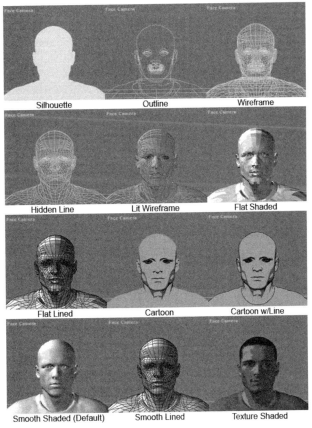

FIGURE B.2   Poser offers 12 different display style options.

Q: When I add a second figure to the scene, it merges into the first one. How do I prevent that?

A: You can move the character with the Translate tools. You might find it easier, however, to select the figure's body or hip, and use the xTrans, yTrans, or zTrans dials in the Parameters window to move the figure.

Q: How do I remove a figure or prop from a scene?

A: Select the figure or object that you want to delete (either by clicking or by using the Select Figure menu in the Document window), and press the Delete key.

Q: I changed a lot of morph dials on my figure, and I'm not happy with the results. Is there a quick way to remove all of the body morphs and start all over?

A: If you don't want to lose your pose, save the pose to the library first. Select the figure, and choose Edit > Restore > Figure. All morphs will be reset, and the figure returns to its default pose. After that, you can reapply the pose that you saved in the library.

Q: Is there a quick way to remove all of the face morph settings and start all over?

A: You can actually select any morphed part on a figure and return it to its default state. Click to select the face (or any other body part), and choose Edit > Restore > Element. The selected body part returns to its default state.

Q: Some adult figures are anatomically correct. Sometimes it shows through the clothing. How do I fix that?

A: You can hide the offending parts with the Figure > Genitalia command.

Q: Can I make figures of different ages in Poser?

A: The Figure > Figure Height command changes body proportions, but this method of altering a figure's proportions was created for earlier versions of Poser. Nowadays, it is more compatible with the older Poser 2 figures that come with Poser 6. Poser 2 didn't have the morphing capabilities that were introduced in later versions, and the figures weren't as detailed.

Although the Figure > Figure Height command will work on more recent figures, you will probably find that the results it produces aren't quite as realistic as you would think. Because modern Poser figures are more detailed than earlier versions, applying this command to an adult figure will create a muscular toddler that isn't very realistic. You would then have to adjust the clothing as well.

You can alter more modern Poser characters through the use of morphs. Recent Poser figures are often furnished with face and body morphs that allow you to create figures of any age or shape. You also have younger versions of Poser characters, such as Ben and Kate (the Poser 6 children), and the DAZ Young Teens, Preschool Kids, and baby.

Q: Is there a way to copy one side of my figure's pose to the other side so that the left and right sides are symmetric?

A: Yes, indeed there is! You can pose all or part of a figure the same as the other side, or even swap sides, with the options in the Figure > Symmetry command:

> **Left to Right:** Applies the poses on the figure's left side to the right side to make the sides mirror each other.
>
> **Right to Left:** Applies the poses on the figure's right side to the left side to make the sides mirror each other.
>
> **Swap Right and Left:** Simultaneously applies the pose from the left side to the right, and from the right side to the left.
>
> **Left Arm to Right Arm:** Applies the poses on the figure's left arm to the right arm to make the arms mirror each other.
>
> **Right Arm to Left Arm:** Applies the poses on the figure's right arm to the left arm to make the arms mirror each other.
>
> **Swap Right and Left Arms:** Simultaneously applies the pose from the left arm to the right, and from the right arm to the left.
>
> **Left Leg to Right Leg:** Applies the poses on the figure's left leg to the right leg to make the legs mirror each other.
>
> **Right Leg to Left Leg:** Applies the poses on the figure's right leg to the left leg to make the legs mirror each other.
>
> **Swap Right and Left Legs:** Simultaneously applies the pose from the left leg to the right, and from the right leg to the left.
>
> **Straighten Torso:** Straightens the torso as it relates to the position of the body.

Q: If I try to pose a body part with the Editing tools, the pose gets way out of whack and the figure looks like a pretzel. How can I prevent that?

A: There are actually a couple of different commands in Poser that can help you with that problem:

> **Turn Limits On:** The main figures that you use in Poser have limits on the joints. That is, there are predetermined settings that specify how far a joint is allowed to bend, move sideways, or twist. By default, Poser doesn't use these limits, and what happens is that joints very often get posed far beyond the limits that are humanly

possible. However, when you enable the Figure > Use Limits option, Poser does not pose joints any farther than the set limits. This option helps you create poses that are more realistic.

Use Auto Balancing: The Auto Balance feature helps you achieve realistic poses. Basically, this feature adjusts poses to keep the figure as close as possible to the center of its weight distribution, which Poser calculates based on the shape of the body. Therefore, with auto balancing, a figure should automatically balance itself to respond to poses that are unnatural for a figure. To enable or disable auto balancing, choose the Figure > Auto Balance command. When there is a check beside the command, it is enabled.

Q: When I load a figure from the library, its feet don't always line up with the default ground of my scene. How do I get my figure to drop to the default ground level of my scene?

A: The Figure > Drop to Floor command drops your figure to ground level, which is at the 0 coordinate of the Y (up and down) axis.

However, sometimes you might have props or scenery in your document window that places "ground level" above or below the 0 coordinate. In that case, you will need to select the Hip or Body of your figure, and move the yTrans parameter dial up or down until your figure is placed correctly.

One of the most common mistakes made by new users of Poser is that figures hover over the ground. This is because in some cases, you need to make adjustments to the pose. The point closest to the ground makes contact with the ground when you use the Drop to Floor command. If, for example, the foot is bent, you may need to adjust the position of the feet so that they do not appear as though your figure is floating above the ground.

The best way to make these adjustments is to put your document display style to Outline mode (Display > Document Style > Outline) and to use one of the orthogonal cameras (Left, Right, Top, Bottom, Front, or Back) so that you are not viewing your scene at an angle while you fix the feet.

Q: I have several objects in a scene. Sometimes when I want to pose or move a figure or object, I accidentally move another one by mistake. Is there any way to prevent that?

A: There are several ways that you can control this. After you get a figure or other item posed the way you like, you can prevent further changes using any of the following methods:

Hide the figure: You can hide the figure from view by using the Figure > Hide Figure command. Click the figure you want to hide, and then choose the command. Continue in this manner until you hide all the figures that interfere with the parts you want to edit. To unhide all hidden figures, choose Figure > Show All Figures. You can also use the Hierarchy Editor (Window > Hierarchy Editor) to unhide selected figures. Simply click on the eye icon of a figure or part name to unhide it.

Lock the figure: Choose the figure that you want to protect. Then choose the Figure > Lock Figure command. This will lock the figure in place and prevent you from moving the figure or changing its pose.

Lock a body part or prop: If you want to prevent changes to a single body part or a prop, choose Object > Lock Actor. This will cause a body part to stay in place in relation to its parent. In other words, you can lock the position of a forearm in relation to the upper arm, but if you move the upper arm, the forearm will move accordingly.

Lock the hands: Hands are the most time-consuming to pose, especially if you've posed them around an object. You can use the Figure > Lock Hand Parts command to lock a hand into position. This will prevent changes in hand and finger positions while you work with other areas in your Poser scene.

Use the Chain Break tool: The Chain Break tool, which displays a link on its icon, allows you to prevent movements of body parts below a specified level in the hierarchy. For example, if you want to pose the lower portions of an arm but leave the shoulder in place, you can put a chain break at the shoulder before you move the lower portions. For the Chain Break tool to work, you have to turn Inverse Kinematics off with the Figure > Use Inverse Kinematics command. Further information about the Chain Break tool can be found in the Poser 7 Reference Manual.

Q: Can I raise or lower the level of the ground plane of my scene?

A: No, you can only move the ground left, right, forward, or back. As an alternative, you can use the Square, Square Hi-Res, or One Sided Square props that are found in the Props > Primitives Library. Scale the square prop to the desired size, and then adjust the yTrans setting to raise or lower the prop.

Q: If I can't use Python scripts, how do I get a figure into its default pose?

A: Although it's not as quick as running the ZeroAll python script that is mentioned in Chapter 3, you can use the following procedure:

1. Click the figure you want to zero.
2. Choose Edit > Restore > Figure. This removes morphs and scaling from the figure but may not return the figure to its proper default pose.
3. Choose Window > Joint Editor. The Joint Editor window opens.
4. If the Joint Editor informs you that no body part is selected, click any body part on the figure that you want to zero. Click the Zero Figure button in the Joint Editor.
5. If the Parameters window is not open, choose Window > Parameters to open it.
6. Select the Hip body part for the character, and verify that the xTrans, yTrans, and zTrans values are all set to 0.
7. Select the Body part of the character, and verify that its xTrans-, yTrans-, and zTrans values are also set to zero.
8. For complete thoroughness, verify that each body part has Scale, and xScale, yScale, and zScale values set at 100%. If you have to change any values to get the scaling back to 100%, save the figure to the library so that you won't have to change them again the next time you have to zero the figure.

Q: Can I make a figure hold something (like a ball), so that when I move the hand, the ball moves with it?

A: Yes. Using the ball as an example, here are the steps:

1. Use the Editing tools or the xTrans, yTrans, and zTrans dials in the Parameters window to position the ball in your figure's hand.
2. Pose the fingers around the ball. You will probably get better results by using the dials in the Parameters window rather than trying to pose them with the Editing tools.
3. Select the ball as the current figure.
4. Choose Object > Change Parent. Select the appropriate hand (right or left, depending on which hand is holding the ball) as the parent to the ball. Now whenever you move the hand, the ball follows. You can still move the ball, but its relation as a child to the hand will remain until you "unparent" it. To "unparent" the ball, select it, choose Object > Change Parent, and choose UNIVERSE (the first object in the hierarchy) as the parent.

CAMERAS

Q: How do I use the camera controls?

A: The Camera Controls allow you to select cameras for various purposes or to move them so that you can get a better view of the items in your Poser document. Figure B.3 shows the Camera Controls:

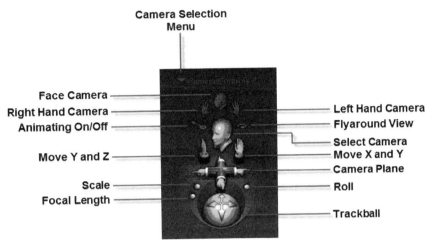

Camera Selection
Menu

Face Camera

Right Hand Camera

Animating On/Off

Move Y and Z

Scale

Focal Length

Left Hand Camera

Flyaround View

Select Camera

Move X and Y

Camera Plane

Roll

Trackball

FIGURE B.3   Camera Controls allow you to select and manipulate Poser's cameras.

The controls serve the following functions:

Camera Selection Menu: Click the Camera Selection menu to display a list of cameras to choose from.

Face Camera: The Face Camera is good to use when you are creating a face expression or using Face Morph dials to create a unique character. The camera remains fixed on the character's face, even as you zoom in, out, or rotate the camera view.

Right Hand and Left Hand Cameras: These cameras keep the designated hand in view, even while zooming in or out or rotating the camera. Their purpose is to keep the camera centered around the hand while you pose it—most especially while posing a hand to hold another object.

Animating On/Off: When you are posing body parts or props for the purposes of animation, you sometimes have a need to adjust cameras so that you can get a better view of things. However, each time you move a camera in a frame of an animation, it adds a keyframe that keeps track of the position change. As a result, you may accidentally add animation keyframes without intending to do so. One way to prevent this from happening is to turn camera animating off. To turn camera animation off, click the key icon to turn it red. Click it again to resume camera animation.

Flyaround View: Click this icon to get a 360-degree flyaround view of your scene. Click again to turn the flyaround view off.

Select Camera: Click to cycle through the various camera views. Starting from the Main camera, the icons appear in the order shown in Figure B.4.

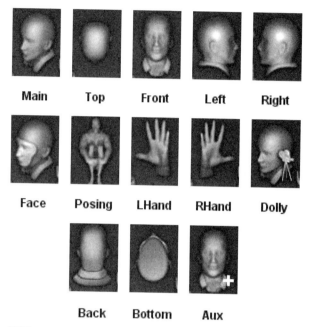

FIGURE B.4 Use the icons in the Select Camera area to select a camera view.

The mouse displays a double-arrow cursor when you are able to select a camera. To advance forward in the list, click the icon at its right side, or drag the mouse to the right to advance quickly. To move backward in the list, click the left side of the icon, or drag your mouse toward the left.

Move Y and Z: Your mouse cursor displays arrows when you position it over this control. Click and drag left or right to move the camera along the Z (forward/backward) plane. Drag up or down to move the camera along the Y (up/down) plane.

Move X and Y: Your mouse cursor displays arrows when you position it over this control. Click and drag left or right to move the camera along the X (left/right) plane. Click and drag up or down to move the camera along the Y (up/down) plane.

Camera Plane: Click and drag left or right to move the camera along the X (left/right) axis, or up or down to move the camera along the Z (forward or back) axis.

Scale: Click and drag left to increase the scale of the camera. This "zooms in" to the scene without affecting focal or perspective settings. Click and drag right to decrease the scale of the camera, which "zooms out" without affecting focal or perspective settings.

Roll: Click and drag toward the left to roll the camera clockwise. Click and drag toward the right to roll the camera counterclockwise.

Focal Length: Click and drag toward the left to decrease the camera's focal length; click and drag toward the right to increase the focal length.

Trackball: Click the trackball to give the current camera focus. You can move the trackball at any incremental angle to change the view. Drag the trackball up to look above a scene, down to look below a scene, and left or right to view the scene from either side.

Q: Can I make cameras always look at an object, even when I move the object?

A: If you want to make a camera follow an object, first select the camera, and then choose Object > Point At. When the Hierarchy window comes up, choose the item or body part that you want the camera to follow.

You can also make objects follow the camera. For example, you can make eyes always look toward a camera as you position it. To do so, select the object (such as the left eye or right eye), choose Object > Point At, and then choose the camera that you want the object to follow.

Note, however, that if you try to make the head follow a camera, the top of the head points to the camera rather than the front of the head.

LIGHTS AND SHADOWS

Q: How does a light probe work?

A: The purpose of a light probe is to simulate the lighting conditions in a photograph or movie. Imagine the light probe as an invisible hemisphere that surrounds your scene.

The area in the center of the light probe is the area of the hemisphere that is directly overhead at the highest part of the hemisphere. The outer edges of the light probe are the lowest parts of the hemisphere, which encircle the scene at floor height. The top of the light probe determines the lighting conditions at the back of your scene. The bottom of the light probe determines the lighting conditions at the front of your scene.

Q: Can I use an AVI or MOV file for an image-based light probe?

A: Yes. One way to accomplish this is to set up your IBL light in the Material Room first, using the IBL wacro. During this process, the wacro will prompt you to select an image. After this process is complete, your IBL light will be configured properly. All you have to do afterward is disconnect the Image Map node and replace it with a Movie node (New Node > 2D Textures > Movie).

Q: Can I make a light that looks something like a movie being projected onto a screen?

A: Yes. After you create a spotlight, go to the Material Room, and change the color of the light to white. Then, attach an Image Map node (New Node > 2D Textures > Image Map) or a Movie node (New Node > 2D Textures > Movie) to the Diffuse channel. Check the Auto Fit option in the Image Map node to fit the image in the spotlight.

FACE ROOM

Q: If I apply the Face Room head to the figure so that the original head gets replaced, how do I get the old head back?

A: The Edit > Restore > Element command won't work if you apply a Face Room head to your figure. To restore the original head, return to the Face Room. Click the Reset Face Room button that appears below the Face Sculpting area. Click the Apply to Figure button in the Actions area. When you return to the Pose Room, the default head should appear on your figure.

Q: I used the Face Room to create a face morph. But when I go back to the Pose Room and dial the Face Room morph to 1, the eyes look funny. What happened?

A: When you use the Face Room to spawn morph targets for a face, it also spawns morph targets for the Left Eye and Right Eye. They also have to be set to 1 to restore the entire face to the shape you created in the Face Room.

Q: Are there other programs available that work like the Face Room so that I can use them on other figures?

A: The code used in the Face Room module was licensed by e-Frontier from Singular Inversions, the makers of FaceGen Modeler and FaceGen Customizer. You can learn more about these packages at *http://www. facegen.com*.

HAIR ROOM

Q: When I save my hair projects to the library, you can't see the hair in the thumbnails. How do I get the hair to show up?

A: The thumbnails in the Poser library are saved in PNG format and measure 91 × 91 pixels. Some people render a scene and save it as a PNG file with a transparent background. The transparent background is important for the thumbnail to display properly. After rendering, resize the PNG file to 91 ? 91 pixels, and assign the same prefix as the library item. For example, if you have a hair file named Joni'sHair.HR2, name the PNG file Joni'sHair.PNG.

Q: How do I get rid of bald spots in dynamic hair?

A: "Bald spots" are less prominent if you use the proper lighting in conjunction with the Opaque in Shadows option in the hair material. Go to the Material Room, and select one of the hair sections. Verify that the Opaque in Shadow option is checked in the hair material. If that does not resolve the problem, adjust the lighting so that some lighting comes from above the head so that shadows are generated. Finally, if you still see bald spots, you can increase the hair density a little bit at a time until the baldness is less obvious.

UV MAPPING

Q: You've shown how to map skirts, pants, and shirts. What about dresses?

A: For the most part, you've learned the basic techniques for dresses already. Think of a dress as nothing more than a shirt and a skirt combined. If desired, you can then stitch the shirt and dress together at the waist, and relax it.

Q: What about organic models, such as humans or animals? How do you map those?

A: Break it down into pieces. For example, you can detach the head from the body and map it in cylindrical mode. The eyes, of course, are spherical. The teeth are arranged in the mouth in a shape of a "C," which is basically half of a cylinder. The tongue can either be two planes (top and bottom) or cylindrical with a seam along the bottom of the tongue.

Now, what about the body? Take the hands and feet away from the remainder of the body for a moment. What basically remains is something similar to the shirt and pants that you learned how to map in this book! Go one step farther than the pants, however, and join the vertices in the center, near where the groin is. Then, relax the two sides until the vertices that you joined are blended together.

As for the hands and feet, all you have to do is divide the hands in half as if you're slicing the top away from the bottom—one side of the hand shows the palm and underside of the fingers, whereas the other side of the hand shows the tops of the hands. Split the feet in half so that one view shows the top, and the other half shows the sole of the foot. After you break it into individual sections like this, UV-mapping a human becomes predictable and methodical.

Q: Sometimes after I relax things in UV Mapper, there is still a little bit of distortion. Can I eliminate it entirely?

A: It depends on the software you use and how skilled you are in using it. One thing that was not covered in this book was the Interactive Mapping mode in UV Mapper Professional. When you choose Interactive mode, you can move or rotate a spherical, planar, or cylindrical indicator to align the UV map more accurately with your models. The texture map updates in real time while you make the adjustments.

There are also additional UV-mapping programs that have more advanced mapping and relaxing features in addition to features that allow you to paint directly on the 3D models. However, they are also much more expensive than UV Mapper Professional. If you are interested in researching them further, go to *http://www.righthemisphere.com* for information about Deep Paint 3D and Deep UV; or *http://www.maxon.net* for information about Maxon Body Paint.

MATERIALS

Q: What is a gather node?

A: A gather node is a very powerful and complex procedural shader that allows you to create materials that actually accumulate light from their surroundings. This works well for simulating the reflected light interacting between two objects that are close to each other (think "radiosity-effects") or even simulating a glowing object. The effect is perfect for creating a lightsabre or bioluminescent sea creature.

In Figure B.5, you can see where the ground material has "gathered" the light from the bumpy-torus object. The material on the torus uses a high ambiance value to enable the gather node of the ground plane material to "collect" the light coming from the torus. In our example, we did not use any lights, rather, we made the torus self-illuminating.

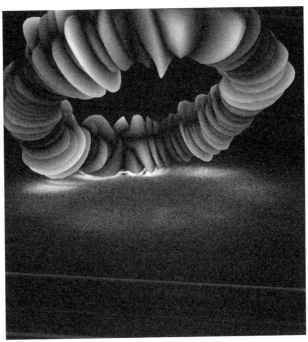

FIGURE B.5   The gather material node creates a material that collects and emits its own light.

You will need to use the FireFly rendering engine to take advantage of the gather node. You will also need to make sure you have raytracing enabled. Using the gather node will increase your rendering times significantly.

Q: What is up with my displacement? Why does it have black spots? Something very wrong happened here!

A: When your Displacement Bounds are too small, you may find that your materials develop black "specks," or even what appear to be large black "holes" in unexpected places. This happens because the displacement on the material is too large to be contained within the current boundary.

Here's what happens: The render engine begins by assuming that every pixel in the image is black, or zero (R=0, G=0, B=0), until calculated otherwise by the interaction of light with the various material properties of objects visible at that pixel. When the displacement calculation overflows the current Displacement Boundary, the tips of the displaced mesh move outside the current render bucket. Once outside the current bucket, the color at that point remains unknown, or uncalculated, and therefore stays zero, its default value.

Whenever you use displacement, make sure that you set the Min Displacement Bounds settings for the FireFly render engine. The Min Displacement Bounds should be large enough to handle the largest displacement of all the materials in your current scene. Also, keep in mind that using displacement in your materials will take longer to render. Setting the Min Displacement Bounds too high may have a negative impact on rendering performance. As a rule, set the Min Displacement Bounds to be roughly twice the largest displacement of any of your material.

Q: Can I create water that actually looks like water?

A: We found a really nice tutorial online that does a wonderful job explaining the aspects you should consider when creating a realistic water material. Stuart Runham's Water Tutorial can be found here: *http://www. stu-runham.co.uk/water.htm.*

Q: I want to make a mirrored surface; what do I need to do?

A: The quickest way to create a true reflective material is to use the Material Room wacro Add Reflection. After the reflection node has been added, you can tweak parameters to accommodate your lighting conditions.

Remember to enable raytracing, and pay attention to the number of ray bounces you have configured. More bounces will yield a more realistic mirror but will also slow down the render considerably. A Ray Bounce setting as low as 2 may be sufficient to create a convincing mirror material.

Q: What's the quickest way to create a displacement map?

A: If you are using a simple image-based texture, the quickest way to create a displacement map is to tie the texture map that you use for your Diffuse channel into the Displacement channel as well.

If you want a bit more control, you can create a grayscale copy of the same map you are using for your Diffusion channel and use that instead. For the purposes of creating a displacement map, you are only interested in the brightness component of the texture, so the color data is extraneous. After you have your grayscale image, you can edit it using your favorite image-editing program to maximize the range of brightness to give you the widest possible range of displacement at render time.

If you are using a procedural shader to drive the Diffusion channel of your root material node, you can tie that node into the Displacement channel of the root node as well.

Don't forget that you can always include additional shader nodes to create more interesting and natural displacement effects, regardless of if you are using a procedural shader or image-based texture map to drive your Displacement channel. For example, you can add a Noise node to create some random bumps to bias the value of your existing Displacement output—essentially creating bumps within bumps.

The white values of your displacement map or procedural shader will create a larger displacement than black areas, with absolute black areas not being displaced at all and absolute white areas being displaced the maximum amount.

Q: Can I create glowing objects?

A: Yes! See the Gather Node answer.

Additionally, if you are not adverse to some post-work, there is a nice tutorial available online written by Jim Harnock, which shows how you can create a halo around your glowing objects. The tutorial can be found here: *http://www.students.yorku.ca/~harnock/tutorials/sabre.htm.*

Q: How can I make fur without using Poser Hair?

A: A quick technique to simulate the look of fur is to use displacement at render time.

With Poser 7, all you need to do is add a Noise node and attach its output into the displacement parameter's input on the root node. After you have your Noise node attached, make sure you also set your Min Displacement Bounds and enable the use of displacement maps in the FireFly render engine's parameter palette.

Q: What the heck is a Node Mask and why should I use one?

A: A Node Mask is simply a template that defines where, on your object, a certain node will have its effect. It's rather like using a stencil to control where paint goes on. Instead of paint, however, the Node Mask determines where a particular node will apply its effects to the object.

Once again, we'll point you to Jim Harnock's Web page to show you not only how you can create your own node masks but also give you an idea of what you can do with them. The Jim's Node Mask tutorial can be found here: *http://www.students.yorku.ca/~harnock/tutorials/nodemask.htm*.

RENDERING

Q: How can I speed up my renders?

A: There are a few things you can do to help speed up your renders:

- Use smaller texture map images.
- Use low poly figures whenever possible.
- Use less complex procedural shaders and materials for objects that are not critical to your design.
- If you aren't using a true reflective material, try enabling the Remove Back Facing Polygons option.
- Decrease the Pixel Samples.
- Increase the Minimum Shading Rate.
- Don't use Texture Filtering.
- Use reflection maps rather than raytraced reflections.
- Disable Raytracing.
- Don't use Ambient Occlusion.
- Disable shadows on lights that are not the primary light sources for your scene.
- Reduce the complexity of as many textures in your scene that you can.
- Reuse texture and shadow maps whenever possible.
- Keep your hard drives defragmented.
- Don't run other applications.

Q: FireFly looks like it has stopped rendering and/or stops responding while rendering.

A: If you find that your Poser "goes out to lunch" when you try to render, you can do a few immediate things to help speed things up:

- Reduce shadow map sizes.
- Reduce the Render Bucket size.
- Reduce the number of Pixel Samples.
- Increase the Shading Rate.
- Disable shadows on noncritical lights.

Q: My objects have black holes where I don't expect them. Why?

A: If you are using displacement, you may need to increase your Min Displacement Bounds. If you aren't using displacement but have overlapping or closely positioned object surfaces, you may need to enable displacement on the material that is having problems to lift the surface of the object a bit. If you need to do this, remember to enable displacement mapping in the Render Palette.

If you don't have overlapping object surfaces increasing the Shadow Min Bias on your light(s) might fix the problem.

If the holes are all facing away from the camera, you may have enabled the Remove Backfacing Polygons option.

Q: Everything gets puffy when I render it! Help!

A: If you have enabled smooth polygons in the object's properties, you may find that your object bloats at render time. This happens because the object's polygons are not specifically optimized for Poser or polygon smoothing algorithms. For an object to accommodate smoothing on selective polygon intersections, the object must be created with very small polygons right at the joints where smoothing is not desired.

The preceding figure illustrates why objects sometimes "bloat" when polygon smoothing is enabled. The top-left image represents two polygons that form a corner, polygon 1 (yellow) and polygon 2 (orange). The top-right image shows the surface that is created when polygons are smoothed. The bottom-left image shows an object that "looks" like it has the same corner; however, it is constructed with an additional, very small row, of polygons: 3 (blue) and 4 (green). The image on the bottom right shows the resulting smoothing that will occur.

You can see that in the two right side images that the corners will appear very different when the polygons are smoothed. This is because smoothing works relative to the scales of the affected polygons. Smaller polygons in the corners, or joints, will make the smoothed corner appear crisper and less bloated.

In other cases, not all the joints on an object are actually "welded" together. This will keep the edges of the object crisp; however, unwelded edges may also affect how seamless and procedural textures appear. Welding or not welding edges of objects when they are created should be evaluated on a case-by-case basis depending on the type of object, the morphs that are typically applied to the object and the complexity and types of materials that object is usually mapped with.

Q: What's the quickest way to set up a material that uses refraction?

A: The quickest way to set up a material that uses refraction is to use the Wacro, "Add Refraction." This will create a new Refraction node, which plugs into the Refraction Color channel of the root node. Make sure you set the Transparency, Transparency Edge, and Translucence_Value values, and enable Raytracing. You'll have to use the FireFly rending engine, too.

Q: Can Poser 7 load texture files larger than 4096 pixels?

A: Yes! Unlike previous versions of Poser, Poser 7 now allows you to load image maps that are larger than 4096 pixels.

INDEX